RELIGION, POLITICS AND SOCIETY IN MODERN TURKEY

Edinburgh Studies on Modern Turkey

Series Editors: Alpaslan Özerdem and **Ahmet Erdi Öztürk**

International Advisory Board
- Sinem Akgül Açıkmeşe
- Samim Akgönül
- Rebecca Bryant
- Mehmet Gurses
- Gareth Jenkins
- Ayşe Kadıoğlu
- Stephen Karam
- Paul Kubicek
- Peter Mandaville
- Nukhet Ahu Sandal
- M. Hakan Yavuz

Books in the series (published and forthcoming)

Gezi: The Making of a New Political Community in Turkey Kaan Ağartan

One Hundred Years of Greek–Turkish Relations: The Human Dimension of an Ongoing Conflict Samim Akgönül and contributions by Tiphaine Delenda

Guardianship and Democracy in Iran and Turkey: Tutelary Consolidation, Popular Contestation Karabekir Akkoyunlu

Turkish–Greek Relations: Foreign Policy in a Securitisation Framework Cihan Dizdaroğlu

Policing Slums in Turkey: Crime, Resistance and the Republic on the Margin Çağlar Dölek

Spatial Politics in Istanbul: Turning Points in Contemporary Turkey Courtney Dorroll and Philip Dorroll

Islamic Theology in the Turkish Republic Philip Dorroll

The Kurds in Erdoğan's Turkey: Balancing Identity, Resistance and Citizenship William Gourlay

Religion, Politics and Society in Modern Turkey: 1808–2023 İştar Gözaydın

Turkey's Political Leaders: Authoritarian Tendencies in a Democratic State Tezcan Gümüş

The Politics of Culture in Contemporary Turkey Edited by Pierre Hecker, Ivo Furman and Kaya Akyıldız

Peace Processes in Northern Ireland and Turkey: Rethinking Conflict Resolution İ. Aytaç Kadioğlu

The British and the Turks: A History of Animosity, 1893–1923 Justin McCarthy

A Companion to Modern Turkey Edited by Alpaslan Özerdem and Ahmet Erdi Öztürk

The Alevis in Modern Turkey and the Diaspora: Recognition, Mobilisation and Transformation Edited by Derya Ozkul and Hege Markussen

The Decline of the Ottoman Empire and the Rise of the Turkish Republic: Observations of an American Diplomat, 1919–1927 Hakan Özoğlu

Religion, Identity and Power: Turkey and the Balkans in the Twenty-first Century Ahmet Erdi Öztürk

Turkish-German Belonging: Ethnonational and Transnational Homelands, 2000–2020 Özgür Özvatan

Contesting Gender and Sexuality through Performance: Sacrifice, Modernity and Islam in Contemporary Turkey Eser Selen

Turkish Politics and 'The People': Mass Mobilisation and Populism Spyros A. Sofos

Industrial Policy in Turkey: Rise, Retreat and Return Mina Toksoz, Mustafa Kutlay and William Hale

Electoral Integrity in Turkey Emre Toros

Memory, Patriarchy and Economy in Turkey: Narratives of Political Power Meral Uğur-Çınar

Erdoğan: The Making of an Autocrat M. Hakan Yavuz

edinburghuniversitypress.com/series/esmt

RELIGION, POLITICS AND SOCIETY IN MODERN TURKEY

1808–2023

İştar Gözaydın

EDINBURGH
University Press

Edinburgh University Press is one of the leading university presses in the UK. We publish academic books and journals in our selected subject areas across the humanities and social sciences, combining cutting-edge scholarship with high editorial and production values to produce academic works of lasting importance. For more information visit our website: edinburghuniversitypress.com

© İştar Gözaydın, 2024, 2026

Edinburgh University Press Ltd
13 Infirmary Street
Edinburgh EH1 1LT

First published in hardback by Edinburgh University Press 2024

Typeset in 11/15 EB Garamond by
IDSUK (DataConnection) Ltd, and
printed and bound by CPI Group (UK) Ltd,
Croydon, CR0 4YY

A CIP record for this book is available from the British Library

ISBN 978 1 3995 2666 1 (hardback)
ISBN 978 1 3995 2667 8 (paperback)
ISBN 978 1 3995 2668 5 (webready PDF)
ISBN 978 1 3995 2669 2 (epub)

The right of İştar Gözaydın to be identified as author of this work has been asserted in accordance with the Copyright, Designs and Patents Act 1988 and the Copyright and Related Rights Regulations 2003 (SI No. 2498).

CONTENTS

Acknowledgements	viii
Note on Transliteration	xii
List of Abbreviations	xiii
Introduction: Navigating the Tapestry of Modernity, Islam and Diversity in Turkey	1
1 Ottoman Modernisation	22
Differing Historiographies	23
A Brief Overview of the Era	25
The Role of the *Ulema*	34
*Tarikat*s (Dervish Orders) and *Tekke*s (Dervish Lodges)	35
Alevi Population	36
The Non-Muslim Population	38
Women, Religion and Modernisation	39
2 A Single-party Regime	48
Struggle for Independence (1919–23)	48
Establishing a Republic (1923–38)	51
İsmet İnönü as the '*Milli Şef*' (National Leader) (1938–46)	65
The Alevi Population: Dersim Massacre	68

	The Non-Muslim Population	69
	Women in Nation-building	72
3	Transition to the Multi-party Regime	82
	Cumhuriyet Halk Partisi in Power	83
	Demokrat Parti in Power	86
	Bediüzzaman Said-i Nursi and *Nur* (Light) Movement (*Nurculuk*)	90
	The Diyanet	92
	The Non-Muslim Population	94
	Women in the 1950s	99
4	After the Military Coup of 1960 (1960–80)	105
	The 1961 Constitution	106
	A Brief Overview of the Era	109
	Political Parties and their Leaders	116
	Religious Circles	123
	The Alevi Population	130
	The Non-Muslim Population	133
	Women in the 1960s and 1970s	133
5	After the Military Coup of 1980 (1980–2002)	141
	1982 Constitution	142
	A Brief Overview of the Era	147
	Political Parties and their Leaders	157
	Religious Circles	164
	Alevi Population, Identity Formation and Political Structuring	168
	The Non-Muslim Population	170
	Women in the 1980s and 1990s	171
6	Under AKP Rule (2002–23)	180
	A Brief Overview of the Era	181
	Political Parties and their Leaders	190
	Religious Circles	197
	The Alevi Population: Legal Struggles	201

The Non-Muslim Population	205
Gender Issues in Turkey in the First Quarter of the Twenty-first Century	207
Conclusion: What Next for Turkey?	219
References	228
Index	273

ACKNOWLEDGEMENTS

I grew up in a non-practising Muslim family in İstanbul. Being an only child, I have always loved books and music, and my dear late parents, Nuran Birand Gözaydın and Orhan Gözaydın, helped me dive deep into the Western classics and Western classical music. Religion was not part of our habitus in any sense; it was only in my teens that the notion of faith began to fascinate me. Having never been a practising member of an institutionalised religion myself, I have spent my life trying to understand what religion means. My academic life has been shaped by this quest, as well. I was a PhD candidate in the 1980s as well as a research assistant in the Administrative Law Department at Istanbul University. My pained efforts to find a meaningful academic topic were relieved one day when Prof. Bülent Tanör, whom I have always been proud to call my mentor and a friend, suggested that I work on the Diyanet. While my initial research had a very technical legal focus, my academic journey down the years led me to take an interdisciplinary approach to religion and politics.

Turkey has always been a rewarding laboratory for social scientists interested in observing religion. It has also provided me with several opportunities to actively defend human rights. The late 1980s was a very dark period for Turkey, but one that also witnessed voices in civil society making themselves heard and the founding of numerous human rights NGOs. I am very proud to have been a member of three since the very beginning: the (Helsinki) Citizens' Assembly, *Sokak* weekly and Açık Radyo.

In 2009, I rewrote my *Müslüman Toplum Laik Devlet* [Muslim Society Laic State] from 1993 (AFA), which was subsequently published as *Diyanet: Türkiye Cumhuriyet'nde Dinin Tanzimi* [Regulating Religion in Turkey] by İletişim. I am grateful to Kerem Ünüvar for all his efforts and support through the processes required to publish each new edition of the book, including the updated 2020 version which contains a near-hundred-page-long overview of 2009–19.

Working on the update was a healing process of sorts for the injustice of losing my freedom for over a hundred days, for the months of judicial struggles, and for being deprived of my passport for three full years. I am deeply indebted to my dear lawyer friends who stood by me through the judicial process out of friendship alone: Murat Dinçer, Erdal Doğan, Betül Sümer, Ergin Cinmen and Hürrem Sönmez. How can I forget Murat and Sinem (Azbazdar Dinçer) picking me up from Şakran/Aliağa prison outside Izmir, taking me to Foça for wonderful fish and *rakı*, then driving me all the way to İstanbul on the night of 30 March 2017?

Justice was eventually served, but those absurd trials caused irreparable damage. I lost İskender Savaşır, the apple of my eye, just four and a half months after his diagnosis which coincided with my acquittal in the court of first instance: who is to say his condition was not triggered by his anxiety over my situation? Words are insufficient to express my gratitude to Zeynep Gürerk Atbaşoğlu, Cem Atbaşoğlu, Elvan Şafak, Cemal Bulut, Kayra Bulut, Cengiz İpek, Şamil Sarıbaş, the whole Adapazarı group, Buğda Savaşır Uluğ and Artin Göncü for being there in every sense during his treatment. I thank each and every one of them for their incredible generosity; I have no words to express my debt to them.

I have lived through a good deal over the last seven years. I prefer to accept these experiences as having enriched, not diminished, me. I owe a debt of gratitude to all the friends who stood by me, and to everyone who supported me without knowing me personally. When you are imprisoned, receiving letters and parcels is a source of joy, a break from the greyness of your days inside. How can I ever forget the first two letters I received in jail, from Beril Sözmen and Ceren Göker, and all the many others that would follow, and the parcels my dear *Sib*(el Demirtaş) sent me each and every week? Nor will I ever forget the support and dozens of books I received from my New York University Master of Comparative Jurisprudence (MCJ) group during my imprisonment, or the international lobbying they engaged in on my behalf. Umut Özkırımlı, how could I possibly forget everything you wrote on my behalf during that difficult period? And I am grateful to Eric Palmer, Winfred (Wini) Schmitz, Ayşe Tütüncü, Ahmet İnsel, the late Aydın Engin, Ceren Kenar, Karabekir Akkoyunlu, and all the others who, though I may not know you personally, made calls out of the goodness of your hearts to argue for the release of myself and others. I am also very thankful to Ferhat and Çiğdem Kelamet Kentel, Nilüfer and Beytur Borovalı, and others that supported us through those hard times.

I am grateful to the entire Gergedan Bookstore team and to our seminar group there (Rüyam Yılmaz, Eylem Rakıcı, Hatice Kara Savacı, Arzu Babaç, Gülyüz Yolga, Meltem Kora, Semra Örmeci, Sema Germen, Ece Ejder, Deniz Eskier, Evren Gönlüm, Kevser Üstündağ, Özlem Özcan Günhoş, Mehmet Emin Atılgan, Gözen Niron, Ayşegül Sunar) for their invaluable support not only during these events, but also for reawakening in me an academic enthusiasm for my work over the last five years. Receiving the University of Oslo's Human Rights Award, the Lisl and Leo Eitinger Prize, was an honour. I am deeply thankful to my friends Martin Toft and Ola Gamst Saether for all their support. To be awarded the University of Leipzig's Leibniz Professorship was yet another great honour, even though I have been prevented from being there in the flesh. Markus Dressler was there for me at every step in the process, and I would like to thank him most cordially for all his efforts.

While writing the book, I had a wonderful circle of friends who gave me invaluable feedback: Ayhan Aktar, Ahmet Balcıoğlu, Doğan Bermek, Selim Deringil, Markus Dressler, Oğuz Gürerk, Huricihan İslamoğlu, Ayşe Kadıoğlu, Abdülhamit Kırmızı, Dorian Lesley-Jones, Christoph Neumann, Nazlı Ökten and Amy Singer, and thank you so much for your time and points of view. If I did not have Dorian nagging me on and on, it would have taken me much longer to finish the book. Nu, my mom, used to call our friendship 'siblinghood of the single children' and she was very right; I had Dorian (and Sib) by me for over thirty years at every occasion: weddings, funerals, trials . . . I feel extremely lucky to have friends who supported me no matter what throughout the writing of this book: Candan Uca, Nazlı Uca, Ayşe Öncü, Gürcan Koçan, Berke Baş, Mir Baş-Jones, Aline Pennisi, Ezgi Keskinsoy, Bülent Somay, Yasemin Aydın, Fatih Ceran, Taptuk Emre Erkoç, Ayşe Erçetin Erkoç, Betül Durmaz, Salih Doğan, Ayça İnce Önkal, Aslı Vatansever, Nil Mutluer, Aslı Öğüt Erbil, Emine Beler, Nur Altun, Selmin Özken, Yasemin Sicimoğlu, Betül Akpınar,

Lale Özer, Jeffrey Haynes, Ioannis Grigoriadis, Guy Ben-Porrat, Luca Ozzano, Chiara Maritato, Mustafa Arslantunalı, Nurcan Gündoğan, Banu Güven, Ayşe Gülsevin Tamer, Zeynep Günal, Ferial Tuncer, Aylin Denker, Serkant Ali Çetin, Köken Ergun, Nilgün Arısan Eralp, Soli Özel, Erdağ Aksel, Fuat Keyman, Zeynep Sayın, Zeynep Birand, Bizden Zeren Titiz, Gürhan Ertür, Ahmet Uluğ, Victoria Holbrook and Bente Nikolaisen – I thank you all. Whoever finds a friend truly finds a treasure!

An academic's legacy consists of the work they produce, but there are their students, too. I met Ahmet Erdi Öztürk in 2011 by chance at a conference whose advisory committee I was on. Since then, he has been my student, my colleague, my friend, my son, my confidant . . . I can never thank him enough for everything he has done for me.

I would especially like to thank the 'Studies on Modern Turkey' team at Edinburgh University Press – Alpaslan Özerdem, Emma House, Isobel Birks, Louise Hutton and Eddie Clark – for their support and guidance, along with Sue Dalgleish and Sarah Sturzel. I am also grateful for the valuable comments from the anonymous reviewers of my proposal for this book, and for Michael Eleftheriou's efforts in helping to make the book much more readable.

When I started following Emre Mantaş's photographs on Instagram a couple of years ago, I fell in love with them. I knew I wanted one of them to be the cover of this book, and though I found one after the other that I loved, when the right one came along one day, I was in no doubt: 'Yes yes yes. That's it!' Thank you very much Emre, and Naz Öke for making the cover exactly how I wanted it.

And last but not the least, I owe Ayten Karabaş so much for her daily support, care and love over the last twenty years and more. My life would not be the same if she were not part of it.

The untimely loss of my beloved husband, İskender Savaşır, has not been easy for me to digest, and I don't suppose I ever will, not fully. This book, and hopefully others to follow in the future, would not have been possible without him: he may no longer be physically present in my life, but *İsk* is with me always. Let this be another contribution to the oeuvre I dedicate to him. Of course, all the errors are my own.

Gümüşsuyu, İstanbul
September 2023

NOTE ON TRANSLITERATION

I have mostly used the Turkish spelling for terms, names and titles in Ottoman-Turkish throughout the text, rather than strict transliteration. Transliteration of Turkish and Arabic words have been eclectic. I used terms that are commonly used in English such as the Koran, Sunna, mufti, hadith. Apart from such Anglified terms, for terms like *şeyhülislam*, *hutbe*, *hatip*, *ezan*, *minber*, *medrese* and *müderris* I used the Turkish versions. Muslim Ottomans and Turks did not have family names until the Surname Law of 21 June 1934. This ruling required all citizens of the Turkish Republic to adopt a family name by 1 January 1935. I used the last names taken later in parentheses in narrating events before 1935.

ABBREVIATIONS

AKP	Justice and Development Party (*Adalet ve Kalkınma Partisi*)
ANAP	Motherland Party (*Anavatan Partisi*)
AP	Justice Party (*Adalet Partisi*)
ASALA	Armenian Secret Army for the Liberation of Armenia
BBP	Great Unity Party (*Büyük Birlik Partisi*)
BP	Union Party (*Birlik Partisi*)
CHP	Republican People's Party (*Cumhuriyet Halk Partisi*)
CIA	Central Intelligence Agency
CKMP	Republican Peasants' Nation Party (*Cumhuriyetçi Köylü Millet Partisi*)
DBH	Democratic Peace Movement (*Demokratik Barış Hareketi*)
DEP	Democracy Party (*Demokrasi Partisi*)
DEVA	Democracy and Progress Party (*Demokrasi ve Atılım Partisi*)
DGM	State Security Courts (*Devlet Güvenlik Mahkemesi*)
DİTİP	Diyanet Turkish-Islamic Union (*Diyanet İşleri Türk İslam Birliği*)
DP	Democrat Party (*Demokrat Parti*)
DSP	Democratic Left Party (*Demokratik Sol Parti*)
DYP	True Path Party (*Doğru Yol Partisi*)
ECHR	European Convention on Human Rights
ECtHR	European Court for Human Rights

EU	European Union
FP	Virtue Party (*Fazilet Partisi*)
HADEP	People's Democracy Party (*Halkın Demokrasi Partisi*)
HAK-İŞ	HAK-IS Confederation (*Hak İşçi Sendikaları Konfederasyonu*)
HDP	Peoples' Democracy Party (*Halkların Demokratik Partisi*)
HEP	People's Labour Party (*Halkın Emek Partisi*)
HP	Populist Party (*Halkçı Parti*)
Hüda-Par	Free Cause Party (*Hür Dava Partisi*)
HYD	Helsinki Citizens' Assembly Turkey (*Helsinki Yurttaşlar Derneği*)
İBDA-C	Great Eastern Islamic Raiders Front (*İslami Büyük Doğu Akıncıları Cephesi*)
İHD	Human Rights Association (*İnsan Hakları Derneği*)
İKD	Progressive Women's Association (*İlerici Kadınlar Derneği*)
JİTEM	Gendarmerie Intelligence Counter Terrorism (*Jandarma İstihbarat Terörle Mücadele*)
KAGEM	Women, Family and Youth Centre (*Kadın, Aile ve Gençlik Merkezi*)
LGBTI+	Lesbian, Gay, Bisexual, Transgender, Intersex+
MAZLUM-DER	Association for Human Rights and Solidarity for the Oppressed (*İnsan Hakları ve Mazlumlar için Dayanışma Derneği*)
MÇP	Nationalist Labour Party (*Milliyetçi Çalışma Partisi*)
MDP	Nationalist Democracy Party (*Milliyetçi Demokrasi Partisi*)
MGK	National Security Council (*Milli Güvenlik Konseyi*)
MHP	Nationalist Action Party (*Milliyetçi Hareket Partisi*)
MİT	(Turkey's) National Intelligence Organization (*Milli İstihbarat Teşkilatı*)
MNP	National Order Party (*Milli Nizam Partisi*)
MP	member of the parliament
MSP	National Salvation Party (*Milli Selamet Partisi*)
MÜSİAD	Independent Industrialists and Businessmen's Association (*Müstakil Sanayici ve İş Adamları Derneği*)

NATO	North Atlantic Treaty Organization
NGO	Non-governmental Organisation
ÖDP	Freedom and Solidarity Party (*Özgürlük ve Demokrasi Partisi*)
OHAL	State of Emergency (*Olağanüstü Hal*)
PKK	The Kurdistan Workers' Party (*Partiya Karkeren Kurdistane*)
RP	Welfare Party (*Refah Partisi*)
SHP	Social Democratic Populist Party (*Sosyal Demokrat Halkçı Parti*)
SODEP	Social Democracy Party (*Sosyal Demokrasi Partisi*)
TBMM	Turkish Grand National Assembly (*Türkiye Büyük Millet Meclisi*)
TBP	Union Party of Turkey (*Türkiye Birlik Partisi*)
TDV	Turkish Diyanet Foundation (*Türkiye Diyanet Vakfı*)
THKO	People's Liberation Army of Turkey (*Türk Halk Kurtuluş Ordusu*)
THKP-C	People's Liberation Front of Turkey (*Türkiye Halk Kurtuluş Partisi-Cephesi*)
TİHV	Human Rights Foundation of Turkey (*Türkiye İnsan Hakları Vakfı*)
TİP	The Workers' Party of Turkey (*Türkiye İşçi Partisi*)
TÖB-DER	Turkish Teachers' Union (*Tüm Öğretmenler Birleşme ve Dayanışma Derneği*)
TRT	Turkish Radio and Television (*Türkiye Radyo ve Televizyonu*)
US/USA	United States (of America)
VP	Homeland Party (*Vatan Partisi*)
YÖK	Council of Higher Education (*Yüksek Öğretim Kurumu*)
YTB	Presidency for Turks Abroad and Related Communities (*Yurtdışı Türkler ve Akraba Topluluklar Başkanlığı*)
YTP	New Turkey Party (*Yeni Türkiye Partisi*)

Dedicated to the memory of
İskender Savaşır
with love, joy, gratitude
and an ever-lasting feeling of absence
since his loss...

Perhaps the happiest tale is the one about the lovers who grow to respect each other, and experience – or try to experience –the miracle of genuine equality in love, even if they have to die and buried in order to come together ... The cardinal virtue worth learning is perhaps equality.
        Bilge Karasu ([1980] 2003), 'Where the Tale Also Rips Suddenly',
        The Garden of Departed Cats (translated by Aron Aji), 245.

There is a gaping chasm between those who say 'this is what I know to be true' and those who say 'what I know to be true should be the truth for everyone', and one of the most important duties of the intellectual is to challenge this 'command mode', regardless of the understanding that gave rise to it.
        Enis Batur (1985), *Alternatif: Aydın*, 16.

INTRODUCTION: NAVIGATING THE TAPESTRY OF MODERNITY, ISLAM AND DIVERSITY IN TURKEY

> Then gradually my logic changed. Even my view of the world, my view of things, my understanding of people changed. Actually, this did not happen in a day. In fact, it happened with great difficulty and step by step. It even happened despite me many times. But it happened.
>
> Ahmet Hamdi Tanpınar, *Saatleri Ayarlama Enstitüsü* (1961)

This book is a reading of Turkey's entanglement and struggle with modernity, Islam, diversity, democracy and human rights/liberties over slightly less than the last two centuries. Its major argument is that the relationship between religion and state forms an important dimension not only of official state ideology, but also in interrelations between different groups in society and in those groups' relations with the state. And not only any religion as a faith system; laicism, too, served as a crucial marker in republican Turkey's political identity in the context of interactions between state and society. Which is to say that, even in early republican times when the pendulum swung towards a strict *laïcité*, religion was there in very many senses. Consequently, one of the questions that arises regarding the more common understanding of religion is: 'What happens if there is no space left for religion in the public sphere?' The sacralisation of the state and its leader(s) has been a path followed in the political modernisation processes. This in turn raises the question: 'Is secularism a kind of religion that passes itself off as "rational"?' Since the political pendulum swung towards a less strict understanding of secularism after the transition into a multi-party regime in Turkey, the question has been: 'Is there a way of retaining secularity without secularism?'[1]

Turkey is currently part of a broader trend towards authoritarianism and the erosion of political institutions and the rule of law by leaders around the globe who initially came to power through the ballot box (Gözaydın 2017: 259). The increasingly authoritarian and overtly Sunni Islam-based political discourse in Turkey under AKP (*Adalet ve Kalkınma Partisi*) rule makes use of religious language and imagery as a systematic attempt to infuse nominally secular notions – nation/people, democracy, state, national interest – with sacred, Islamic and moral meanings. In other words, a sacralisation of the political realm reminiscent of trends from the 1930s appears to have come to the fore once again. Accepting the fact that interactions between religion, politics and society form an important dimension of national ideology, throughout this book I ask the question 'What conditions are required to establish a political regime that meets the demands of diverse communities within a country?' My critical scrutiny of the history of modern Turkey provides no answer other than a constant need for Hannah Arendt's definition of politics as a polyphonic musical performance: different voices, all of them heard individually and collectively, forming a harmony.

Modernity is one of those concepts that people hardly ever agree upon. Essentially, we are talking about a process whereby the basic value in the economy shifts from land to money, the primary economic activity moves from agriculture to commerce, rationality takes precedence over religious references, the ideology of nationalism emerges and grows, and nation states become the prevalent political structures; in short, 'Everything that is solid melts into air'.[2] I am one of those who define modernity as a process and a paradigm shift in the economy, politics, social structures and culture that emerged in Western Europe, gradually escalated from the 1500s on, and eventually brought the entire globe under its influence. In this approach, enlightenment – that is, modernity's intellectual dimension – -shines a light on rationality and the human mind, casting belief systems referencing the divine into shadow.

The institution of religion has always been in an ambivalent position, irrespective of geography. The common denominator in the process of modernity happens to be those political powers which perceive the institution of 'religion'[3] as a rival, and often find a solution in a control mechanism of sorts.

Structurally, the United States can be regarded as the first modern nation state: its structure is that of a modern republic. Thus, the founding fathers of this political body were tired of the religious wars in the lands they had left behind. Aware of the inconveniences of preferring a single belief, they sought to introduce the concept of secularity, defined roughly as 'the principle of distancing political power from religious institutions and belief groups', into their legal and political systems. In parallel, France, which had a history of severe religious wars and was also in the process of transforming itself into a nation state at this time, adapted an understanding coined as *laicité*; here, religious authority is taken under the control of the political power. At this point, one should bear in mind that the experiences, worries and fears of each political formation, as these are produced by its own particular history and culture, lead to different practices, and that there is no single application of these principles. One should also be aware how difficult and problematic it is to define and use concepts such as laic, secular, and even religion in any common sense. In *Formations of the Secular* (Asad 2003), Talal Asad discusses the formation of the concept of 'secular' in history, employing a very sophisticated and stimulating perspective inspired by Wittgenstein to reveal that such concepts, along with religion and ritual, are themselves products of their histories and local processes. The work of Andrew Davison (1998; 2003), who discusses the concepts of secular and laic in the context of Turkey, and of Ahmet T. Kuru (2009), who coins a set of crucial terms in the field, go some way towards overcoming the challenge of defining these terms.[4]

It is clear that, in the foundation of the Republic of Turkey, which has been a project of modernity, a structure such as Islam, in which religion and the state were intertwined,[5] would be a great competitor for the Kemalist cadres who were trying to construct the ideology of modernity and indoctrinate the country with it. At that time, the dominant Sunni Islamic understanding,[6] which included accepting that sovereignty in politics was manifested in the Caliph-sultan, contradicted the republican view, which argued that sovereignty belonged to the nation. The founding cadres, who wanted to rid themselves of this powerful rival, adopted a 'reformist approach'. Meanwhile, the first important legal steps towards a modern Republic were taken in three consecutive laws ratified in the parliament of Turkey on 3 March 1924: the Law on the Annulment of the Ministry of *Şeriat* and Religious Foundations and the Ministry of the General Staff (Law 429); the Law on the Unification of Education (Law 430); and the Law on the Annulment of the Caliphate[7] and the Exile of the Ottoman Dynasty from the Frontiers of the Turkish Republic (Law 431). Another law, namely the Law on the Annulment of the Religious Courts and Modification of the Judgement of the Organization of Judiciary, dated April 1924, comprised a complementary step. In addition to these regulations, a policy of consigning religion to the private sphere was forcefully implemented: the law on banning the *tekke* (lodge), *zaviye*[8] and shrines (1925) was another means of erasing religion from the public sphere. As Ayşe Kadıoğlu puts it:

> While the logic of the Ottoman Empire had made it possible to embrace and synthesize national, religious, and westernist currents, after the proclamation of the Turkish Republic in 1923, republican laicism evolved at the expense of the autonomous development of religious identities and by making religion subservient to the nation-state. (Kadıoğlu 2010: 491)

Significance of Preferring the Principle of Laicism

It is evident from the relevant legal and political literature of the period that the founding decision-making elite of the Republic of Turkey used the term '*laic*' rather than 'secular'. I do not think this was purely a linguistic choice. When we look at those political structures in which *laïcité* is applied, the common denominator is the state's dominance over religious affairs. Furthermore, the Republic of Turkey has flourished in a region where political power has dominated religious authority throughout history. The religion–state relations of the Ottoman political structure which eventually took the place of Byzantium in history exhibited a continuity with what had come before.[9] In both structures, political power had significant control over the religious authority. That the *şeyhülislam*, the highest religious authority after the sultan, was appointed, dismissed and in some rare cases executed by the Caliph-sultan is indicative of this power structure.[10]

I use the term *laicists* for those who prefer the state to control religion, in contradistinction to secularism, which implies the separation of state and religion. As Rex Ahdar and Ian Leigh point out:

> The longstanding French policy of *laïcité* exemplifies ... desire to restrict, if not eliminate, clerical and religious influence, over the state ... The modern Islamic society of Turkey is similarly an example of a state founded on strongly secular principles where restrictions on individual religious liberty have been

introduced to prevent pressure being exerted by the predominant religious group. (Ahdar and Leigh 2005: 73)

The initial drive for *laicist* policies and legislation on the part of Turkey's republican decision-making elite would alter not only the supra-structure of the country in the direction of a modern/Western body, as the Ottoman modernisers had sought to do, but also modernise Turkish society as a whole. I should underline that 'Turkish *laicité* (hereinafter *laiklik*) is not a separation of religion and state; it points to a particular lifestyle (Kadıoğlu 1998b: 63).[11] Traditional belief systems appeared as a threat to this lifestyle. In other words, religion was perceived as a rival to modernity, as it was in almost every other state introducing similar processes.[12] The founding elite of the Republic of Turkey therefore implemented policies to remove religion from the public realm and reduce it to a matter of individual faith and practice, so that the principle of freedom of religion protected privatised religion[13] only. Thus Sunni-Islam, the predominant faith system of the land since the thirteenth century,[14] was relegated to the private sphere.

Mustafa Kemal Atatürk's policy on religion and state affairs was to remove religion from the social realm and 'confine it to the conscience of people', making it a set of beliefs that would not extend beyond the personal lives of Turkey's citizens. Thus, the aim was to reduce religion to a matter of faith and prayer, and the principle of freedom of religion and conscience was to protect only individualised religion and prayers. Religion was to remain in the personal domain and necessitate state intervention to the extent that it concerned and objectified the social order.[15] In Ayşe Kadıoğlu's words: 'Republican laicism did not accompany modernization; rather, it became a project to realize the goal of becoming western' (Kadıoğlu 2010: 490). The Turkish Republic was designed to be a strictly temporal state. Mustafa Kemal stated this clearly in his speech inaugurating Turkey's parliament on 1 November 1937: 'We get our inspirations not from the heavens or invisible things but directly from life' (Atatürk 1997: 423). These were clearly the words of a typical Enlightenment secularist, separating religion and state to ensure that dangerous religious passions and 'superstitions' would be confined to the private sphere. The purpose of the new leadership in this period was to secularise and modernise not only the state and the 'political', but also to transform society into a modern body.

The 1924 Constitution was amended to include the principle of laicism for the first time in 1937. Şükrü Kaya (1883–1959), Minister of Internal Affairs at the time, expresses his views on behalf of the government:

> Friends, this country has suffered a lot from the influence of soothsayers on consciences and in the affairs of the state and the nation . . . If we are determinists in history, if we are pragmatic materialists in our actions, then we must make our own laws . . . We do not interfere in the slightest with the freedom of conscience of individuals and their adherence to the religions of their choice. Everyone's conscience is free. The freedom we want, the purpose of *laiklik* is to ensure that religion does not influence the affairs of the country. This is the framework and limits of *laiklik* in our country . . . We say that religions should remain in consciences and temples, and not interfere in material life and world affairs. We do not and will not interfere (Bravo, applause). Another mean legacy of the Turks is their adherence to a number of *tarikats*. We know that the only correct path and *tarikat* for the Turk is nationalism based on positive sciences. Following this path is the greatest strength for the material and spiritual life of the Turk (Bravo, applause).[16]

The constitutional amendment was unanimously accepted by parliament and *laiklik* became a constitutional 'requirement' as of 5 February 1937.

Why Was the Diyanet Established?

In 1924, the founders of the Republic of Turkey established a body called the Diyanet İşleri Reisliği (Presidency of Religious Affairs/hereinafter the Diyanet) to manage religious affairs regarding Islam within the administration. An answer for the above question may be found primarily in the system of checks and balances built into the legal order to protect the political structure. Paradoxically, the state used the Diyanet against religion and its undesirable impact in the socio-political field (Gözaydın 2014 and 2020). It appears that in this context, laic simply means a 'state governed by norms that have non-religious references'. It is interesting to observe that the state's understanding of *laiklik* has changed over time from a rigid Kemalist version of militant secularism which stresses 'freedom from religion' to the conservative Turkish-Muslim understanding of the word as 'the control of religion' (Yavuz 2009: 163). The liberal conception of secularism, which stresses the separation of politics from religion (freedom of religion), never dominated the political realm in Turkey's history.

The absence of an independent religious institution in Islam – unlike Christianity, which has its church system – is one of the most important factors legitimising the state's intervention in religion, which it categorises as a public service. Given that a public service can be defined as any activity managed by public legal entities or private entities supervised by the state for the purpose of meeting a shared and general need which has acquired a degree of importance for the people, the state's involvement in religious affairs in this context is generally accepted as not conflicting with secularist principles. An assessment of the duties of the Diyanet in this context reveals that duties such as 'the management of places of prayer' and 'providing correct publications of the Koran' are indeed public services fulfilling a collective need. However, the state also makes use of the Diyanet as an administrative tool to propagate its official ideology regarding Islam in parallel with its fulfilling duties such as 'enlightening society about religion' and providing 'religious education'. That the functionaries of the Diyanet are civil servants, no matter if they are scholars as well, makes the institution an instrument of the state.[17] Producing an official understanding of Sunni Islam and disseminating it through several channels has been the main objective of the Diyanet.[18] Thus, every understanding of Islam other than the Sunni-referenced ones the state prefers, as its predecessor the Ottoman Empire did, has been de facto officially excluded throughout the Republican era, despite the provisions for equality and freedom in constitutions and related legal texts. Thus, different interpretations such as Alevi Islam are not officially recognised as a part of the Muslim belief system.

Nationalism is the Requirement of the Modern State ...

Empires contained ethnic diversity, religious groups, different languages and various cultures which would come to be perceived as a weakness in the modern state as imagined communities.[19] When the requisite cohesion between different groups in society could not be achieved in Turkey's nation-building process, the resulting identity polarisation made it easier for political parties in power to attempt to engineer the society of their own imagination (Şar 2019); the means they used to implement these policies in the 1930s and after the 2010s are strikingly similar in this sense. As the ideology on which the modern nation state was built, nationalism was envisioned by the founders of the Republic of Turkey as the cement in a secular and modern political structure. In the framework of this project, the function of nationalism was to create a secular social identity reference that would replace traditional/religious loyalty references. The constructed 'Turkishness' was not all-embracing at all: treatment of non-Muslim minorities in the new Turkey of the time contained population exchanges; 'citizen, speak Turkish!' campaigns; economic policies that can be described as harassing at the very least ... Kurds had their share in this constructed nationalism as well.

Although the nationalist vision of the founding elites was not fully adopted by the majority of society, the trend towards nationalism that began during the1940s gradually became the mainstream of centre-right politics. However, it should also be noted that the discursive use of nationalism has not been confined to the right wing of the political spectrum in Turkey; it has always been employed in so-called left narratives, especially along *ulusalcı* lines.[20]

But the Social Cement Has Always Been Islam!

As Ioannis Grigoriadis puts it (2013: 117–22), very few groups that immigrated to the Ottoman state and the Turkish Republic in the nineteenth and twentieth centuries could compete with the Turkishness of the Gagauz in terms of their ethnicity and language. However, not granting the Christian Gagauz people the right to migrate to Turkey to become Turkish citizens during the early republican period shows how important a role religion played in defining Turkish national identity.[21]

By the late 1960s, right-wing nationalism had moved from the fringes to the centre in Turkish politics. The religious policies of the right-wing parties have always been dominated by conservatism and nationalism in Turkish Islamism. Since the transition to multi-party politics, Islam has come to be seen as a source of social solidarity and an important element in Turkish national identity. It is necessary to stress this rupture, since Islam was seen by the founding Kemalist decision-making elite as the reason for the decline of the Ottoman state and the Turkish nation falling behind the West politically, economically, militarily and intellectually.

Founded in 1970, *Aydınlar Ocağı* (Hearth of Literati)[22] provided the ideological infrastructure for the Turkish–Islamic synthesis that emerged politically in the 1980s.²³ Grigoriadis argues that the importance of this association is its audacity in synthesising two previously incompatible concepts: Kemalism and Sunni Islam (2013: 105). On 31 March 1975, Süleyman Demirel, head of the centre-right *Adalet Partisi* (Justice Party/AP) and prime minister at the time, formed a right-wing coalition known as the 'Nationalist Front' with the pro-religious *Milli Nizam Partisi* (MNP) and ultranationalist *Milliyetçi Hareket Partisi* (MHP). Thus, 'right-wing militants now saw themselves as part of the state machinery, as their leaders ruled the coalition, which gave them protection and the opportunity to terrorize their political opponents' (Ahmad 2003: 142). In 1978, more than a hundred people died and hundreds were injured in the seven-day attacks on the Alevis in Kahramanmaraş. In all, 210 homes and seventy offices were destroyed.²⁴ 'Neo-Ottomanist'²⁵ seeds and policies were sown at this time: the expression 'By the will of Allah and the wishes of 800 million Muslims, the age of "being a master" is opening up for us again' used by Ahmet Kabaklı, one of the founders of the *Aydınlar Ocağı*, in his newspaper column can be considered one of the first steps in this direction.²⁶ This ideological infrastructure, which was in line with the United States' green belt policy, which sought to counterbalance the Soviet influence by supporting Islamisation, was carried into politics with the 1980 military regime.

The article in the 1982 Constitution regarding the Diyanet requires the institution to support national solidarity and integration in line with the principle of *laiklik*. In other words, the Diyanet was constitutionally charged with protecting the Turkish national identity.

The current administration, the *Adalet ve Kalkınma Partisi* (AKP), was voted into office in the 2002 elections. The distribution of economic capital was the key to the AKP's rise to power, while the creation of a large pious middle class that was no longer excluded from political power helped to consolidate the AKP's political success over the years. Although the AKP was the main recipient of right-wing support, due to the collapse of other right-wing parties, the party also won the support of different groups, including liberal and leftist circles, with the democratising policies it implemented in its first years in power. However, since 2007, Turkey has been the scene of a reckoning with various politically different or differentiated groups which have been assailed by a number of executive and judicial processes. What is publicly known as the 'Ergenekon case' was the first of these reckonings. The

Ergenekon trials took place between 2008 and 2016: 275 people, including military officers and journalists alleged to be members of Ergenekon, a clandestine secularist organisation, were accused of organising a coup against the AKP government. The trials resulted in lengthy prison sentences for the majority of the accused, though these were overturned in April 2016 by the Supreme Court of Appeals due to lack of evidence that such an organisation actually exists, along with breaches in due process during the collection of evidence (Mecellem 2016: 134–6).

On 7 February 2012, Hakan Fidan, the undersecretary of the *Milli İstihbarat Teşkilatı* (MİT, Turkey's National Intelligence Organization) was subpoenaed by the specially authorised Istanbul Chief Public Prosecutor Sadrettin Sarıkaya to testify as a suspect in a political operation. That marked the start of the war between the Fethullah Gülen community and the AKP government. The animosity between the two parties became more public with the large-scale bribery/corruption operation of 17 December 2013. The tension between the two parties, which has been rising since 2014, resulted in the coup attempt of 15 July 2016, which was attributed to the Gülen community – the so-called 'Fethullahist Terrorist Organization' (FETÖ) – by the AKP government. Since then, a large number of institutions, including education and training institutions at every level, health institutions and companies allegedly to be connected with the Gülen community, have been seized by decree; their properties were transferred to the Treasury, security and judicial proceedings were initiated against their officers and other persons alleged to be involved.[27] It is interesting to observe that, although the social cement is supposed to be the Sunni understanding of Islam throughout the history of Turkey, the political powers still need at some point to rid themselves of similar rivals. This decision not to share political authority also involved a re-distribution of economic capital. It should also be underlined that having different praxis of Sunni Islam also played a significant role in the Gülen–AKP dispute: belonging to Nurcu and Nakşibendi *tarikats*.

'New Turkey', an accelerating AKP discourse, expanded the powers and activities in which the Diyanet was involved.[28] Social engineering efforts observed during the founding period of the Republic in Turkey were brought back into use to ensure the transformation to the society envisioned by the AKP cadres; but while the legal and administrative tools were similar, the objectives were, needless to say, completely different. Over the years, Turkey has created an enormous transnational religious network in Europe, Asia and most of Africa via the Diyanet and other transnational apparatuses; this allows it to play a prominent role as an actor internationally, with an increasingly authoritarian and overtly Islam-based policy domestically and abroad (Öztürk 2021).

What Happens to Those who Interpret Islam Differently?

Since Ottoman times, the interpretation of Islam by political powers in Turkey has always been in a Sunni mould; different interpretations of Islam, especially Alevi Islam,[29] have been excluded. The state oppression and mass killings that began in the sixteenth century were severe enough to force the Alevi population to start concealing their identities to avoid discrimination. In a 2008 study, Elizabeth Özdalga states that: 'When asked about their complaints, Alevis often mention compulsory religious education, difficulties in establishing and running a *cemevi*, and a lack of representation in the state.' It can be seen that Alevi demands remain the same today, despite a number of crucial judicial gains made before international courts. One cannot, therefore, disagree with Elise Massicard's analysis of this issue: 'Although there is no doubt that social debates on identity and pluralism have increased after the 1980s, it is clear that distinctions have become sharper and differences are still illegitimate and cause for stigmatization' (2006: 82).

The last two decades have seen Alevi demands for fundamental rights and equal citizenship taken before the courts, initially in Turkey and then internationally. The legal rights gained through the five cases referenced below in international courts over the past decade have been significant. Thus, the European Court of Human Rights (ECtHR) decided in 2010 in *Sinan Işık* v. *Turkey* that Turkey was in breach of the European Convention on Human Rights. The case was filed by an Alevi citizen who did not want to have 'Islam' written in the 'religion' section of his identity card. Recognition of Cem Houses (*cemevi*) as Alevi places of worship was brought before the court in *Cem Vakfı* v. *Turkey*, with the ECtHR resolving in 2015 that Turkey was once again in breach of the European Convention on Human Rights. The other two cases in which Turkey was found to be in the wrong by the ECtHR concerned compulsory religious instruction (*Hasan and Eylem Zengin* v. *Turkey*, 2007;

Mansur Yalçın and others v. *Turkey*, 2014). In both cases, the Court concluded that the Turkish educational system did not meet the requirements of objectivity and pluralism, and that insufficient content was provided to respect Alevi parents' beliefs. On 26 April 2016, the Grand Chamber of the European Court of Human Rights, in *İzzettin Doğan and Others* v. *Turkey,* concluded that Turkey had violated the European Convention on Human Rights, calling the inability of adherents to the Alevi faith to benefit from religious public services as 'religious discrimination'.

On 9 November 2022, the Presidency of Alevi-Bektaşi Culture and Cemevi was established as an administrative unit under the Ministry of Culture and Tourism. This constitutes another instance of the state acknowledging Alevism as a cultural entity rather than a confessional group.

And, What if You Are a 'Non-Muslim'?

As Talal Asad states in his *Secular Translations: Nation-state, Modern Self and Calculative Reason*: 'Even if, unavoidably, there *is* a degree of religious or ethnic heterogeneity in society, there must be a clear and permeant demographic majority of those who know that the state belongs principally to them; minorities must be small enough to be easily controllable' (2018: 143). During the respective modernisation processes of the Ottoman Empire and the modern Republic of Turkey, non-Muslim minorities suffered more than their fair share of persecution at the hands of those who believed the state belonged principally to them; this persecution amounts to serious crimes against humanity.

The Treaty of Lausanne, which regulates the status of minorities in Turkey, was signed on 24 July 1923. The treaty provided non-Muslim minorities in Turkey with some rights, but some of its provisions were potentially problematic. Thus, it was interpreted that Turkey's non-Muslim population consisted of only three large Greek Orthodox, Armenian Orthodox and Jewish communities.[30] Consequently, Turkey did not consider the rights of Syriac Orthodox and Syriac Chaldean, Latin Catholic and other non-Muslim groups with Baha'i faiths to be subject to the Lausanne protection plan.[31] Moreover, even in relation to the three major communities, implementation remained inadequate, particularly in matters relating to property and religious/educational institutions.[32] Defining Turkishness was a priority for modern Turkey in the 1920s.[33] The intense debates in parliament over the eighty-eighth article of the 1924 Constitution, which defined Turkishness, contained many discriminatory expressions, some of which could now be described as hate speech.[34] Attempts to Turkify and marginalise the non-Muslim population grew more brutal in the 1920s.[35] In the 1930s, state-orchestrated pogrom against the Jews took place in Thrace.[36] As these accumulated,

> the negative legacy of the past would resurface later in the atmosphere of the Second World War, recreating the trauma of the Armistice and the War of Independence. As a result, the Wealth Tax, enacted in 1942 with the aim of rightly taxing profits from speculation and black-market transactions, would be applied in a completely discriminatory manner only against citizens of Jewish and Christian faith and apostate[37] citizens. (Bali 2006: 49)

Another state-orchestrated pogrom, this time against the *Rum* population of Istanbul, took place in 1955. Looters attacked property belonging to non-Muslims (predominantly Greeks, but also other religious minorities), but also churches and cemeteries, destroying sacred paintings, crosses, icons and other sacred objects. All seventy-three Orthodox churches in Istanbul were set on fire (Güven 2011). The Turkish state's policy of harassing and expelling all minorities from Anatolia proved largely successful in the 1950s. In this context, the pogrom of 6/7 September 1955 would prove to be a particularly 'successful' continuation of the efforts to eradicate Istanbul's Christian communities.

In my analysis of the non-Muslim population, the rest of society and the state, I would like to underline two aspects. Initially, the pogroms and the wealth tax were incidents in which non-Muslim wealth was looted or transferred to Muslim ownership. It should not be forgotten that the man in the street, along with Muslim merchants and industrialists, benefitted from these events, the responsibility for which lies not only with the government but also with the people. Secondly, it should not be overlooked that non-Muslims are engraved in collective memory as 'unreliable elements' due to the events that took place in Istanbul especially during the Armistice era and the occupation of Izmir. Islam constitutes a very important reference in society and divides society into two ranks: Muslims and non-Muslims.

The Current State of Affairs

Zafer Yılmaz, in his in-depth and thought-provoking article entitled 'The AKP and the spirit of the "new" Turkey: imagined victim, reactionary mood and resentful sovereign', examines the 'state of mind' of the 'new Turkey'. He underlines a reactive mood that has been built in Turkey over the last decade by AKP cadres, manipulators of Turkish-Islamic opinion, and right-wing intellectuals (Yılmaz 2017). This emotional environment reveals a wounded polity full of fear, anger and resentment. This subject perceives itself as being surrounded by a threatening and dangerous world, so the reactive mood produced both a longing and desire for the golden age of the Ottoman Empire,[38] and growing resentment towards the republican elite. This mood includes unlimited political paranoia, crude imaginings of conspiracy, a common discourse of social suffering/victimisation, and an enthusiastic desire for power, which powered the AKP's ideological shift away from the Gezi events towards the July 15 coup attempt, and replaced a sterile conservative-democratic discourse with a narrative that has a much more Turkish-Islamic emphasis. Pro-AKP media circles played a major role in this transformation. With these steps, the current authoritarian structure was built legally and politically; but there is no indication that the mood has changed to one of satisfaction and peace. The extensive use of the Diyanet by the AKP governments and the religious policies they have implemented, feeding into the anxieties and fears of a large part of the population, are deepening the polarisation in Turkey.

The Scope, Structure and Methodology of the Book

Having worked academically for over three decades on politics with a focus on religion, state identity and the interaction of both with society, I seek in this book to scrutinise Turkey's history from the modernisation processes at work in the Ottoman era through to the current era. Rejecting linear and state-centric models of history, the book seeks to trace the complex relations between society, religion, secularism, state identity and their reflections in state power and daily life. In order to analyse how these notions have been utilised politically and as a means of social engineering in varying contexts, the book compares six eras in Turkey's history: 1808–1923 (Ottoman modernisation); 1923–46 (single-party regime); 1946–60 (transition to the multi-party regime);

1960–80 (after the military *coup d'état* of 1960); 1980–2002 (after the military *coup d'état* of 1980); 2002–22 (under the rule of the AKP). I admire Eric J. Zürcher's well-accepted periodisation, which reads Turkey's history between 1908 and 1950 as a period of continuity with common human resources and hence with similar policies and objectives. This said, I preferred to have chapters titled the way they are, since I am tracing changes and continuities in state ideology and institutions. The book is therefore divided into six chapters, with each one scrutinising one of the aforementioned periods.

Chapter 1 focuses on the Ottoman era. The book takes the Ottoman era to be the past where the roots of several issues that remain contentious in the relationships between religion, state and society can thus be found. Consequently, the topics covered in the book go beyond political and legal developments to include non-Muslims; the Alevi issue is first discussed in this chapter. I am not a historian, and assuredly not an Ottomanist, but I am aware that nineteenth-century issues I focus on in this book, such as the reign of Mahmud II, the end of the Janissary corps and the Tanzimat, reveal continuities with previous centuries. Nevertheless, I had to choose a starting point, and mine is 1808 and the crowning of Mahmud II.

Chapter 2 deals with the era before the multi-party regime. This is a time in which attempts were made – some futile, some successful – to construct a fundamentalist project of modernity. The establishment of the Republic of Turkey, policies enacted by the decision-making elite to manage religion (Islam), the Lausanne Treaty and its regulation of the status of 'minorities', Turkification policies, legislation to construct a laic state, and attempts at socially engineering a 'modern/Western' society are some of the topics discussed in this chapter.

Chapter 3 is about the transition to the multi-party regime. After the transition to a multi-party regime in Turkey, the *Demokrat Parti* (Democrat Party/DP) wins the elections of 1950 and rules until the military coup of 27 May 1960. This is a period in which the opposition organises itself in the system of political representation against rigid *laicist* policies. Changing politics as well as continuities regarding religion are evaluated in this chapter.

Chapter 4 focuses on the years after the military coup of 1960. The 1961 Constitution emerges as a means to overcome obstacles to rights and liberties that had been in place in the Republic thus far. The acceleration of diversity in political representation, the establishment of the Constitutional Court, the military intervention (memorandum) of 12 March 1971 and its impact, further legislation to regulate religion as a public service, and political struggle are some of the topics covered in this chapter.

Chapter 5 looks at the years after the military coup of 1980. In contrast with the 1960 Constitution, which prioritised individual rights and freedoms, the 1982 Constitution sought to secure the state against citizens and other forces. Quests to forge new paths in politics and society, the effects of neo-liberalism, the emergence of a Turkish–Islamic synthesis in governmental policies, the (re)organisation of the Alevi identity, the acceleration of the Kurdish issue and its impact on the relationship between religion and state are some of the key topics in this chapter.

Chapter 6 concentrates on the AKP era. The stunning victory of the AKP in the parliamentary elections of 2002 marked a profound change in Turkish politics. With this, a new political elite arose from a social base that had been largely neglected since the founding of the Republic in 1923. The AKP eliminated military tutelage and proposed significant initiatives to empower the citizenry and sustain civil liberties, both of which were important steps towards democratisation. Positive steps were taken towards solving the Kurdish issue and the democratisation efforts taken in pursuit of European Union membership were remarkable. However, signs of yet another fundamental transition began to emerge after 2007, as the emphasis on democracy seemed to fall away, the AKP's conservative Islamist discourse intensified, and attempts were made to construct a hegemonic authoritarian regime. The Gezi Park protests of 2013, the coup attempt of 15 July 2016, the transition to the so-called presidential regime, Turkey's new claims in the international arena, the ruling party's attempts at social engineering, and the changing objectives of the Diyanet are some of the topics discussed in this chapter.

Finally, the Conclusion provides a general evaluation of religious, political and societal relations in Turkey along with an attempt at making forecasts for the short, medium and long-term.

In other words, this book is a critical reading of Turkey's history with a focus on religion, politics and society and how these interact, and thus challenges the 'master narrative' of modern Turkish history. Earlier academics in particular working on the Ottoman nineteenth century seem to have had a tendency to minimise the importance of religion for both the state and the society. The modernisation process has been mostly read as an aspiration for westernisation and secularisation. This dominant narrative of these earlier academics was formulated by Bernard Lewis (*The Emergence of Modern Turkey*, 1961) and Roderic Davison (*Reform in the Ottoman Empire 1856–1876*, 1963) in the 1960s, the decade in which modernisation/secularisation theories were at their most influential. However, a similar account of the history of modern Turkey prevails through the works of academics like Enver Ziya Karal, which set the master narrative. Niyazi Berkes's seminal book on secularism (*The Development of Secularism in Turkey*, 1964) reflects the spirit of the Republic as a modern secularised state with a past in the nineteenth century. The influence of this narrative can also be seen in eminent later works, such as Erik J. Zürcher's *Turkey: A Modern History* ([1993] revised edn 2017) and Donald Quataert's *The Ottoman Empire, 1700–1922* (2005). Another overview of the era, M. Şükrü Hanioğlu's *A Brief History of the Late Ottoman Empire* (2008), and Carter Vaughn Findley's *Turkey, Islam, Nationalism and Modernity* (2010) provide new perspectives, but do not fundamentally change the narrative's content. İlber Ortaylı's *The Empire's Longest Century* (1983, in English 2021) updates views on these issues, but remains within the parameters of the narrative. *Religion, Politics and Society in Modern Turkey: 1808–2023* aims to read the history of modern Turkey with a focus on how religion, politics and society interact by considering religion to have not been purely a matter of faith in Turkey's Muslim society, but also a vital element of personal identity.

The qualitative nature of my research is due to the comparative historical methods I employ. By comparing certain periods in the history of modern Turkey, I undertake a thematic analysis of modern Turkey.[39] One method I use on occasions is 'process tracing' which 'attempts to identify the intervening causal process – the causal chain and causal mechanism – between an independent variable (or variables) and the outcome of the dependent variable' (George and Bennett 2005: 165). I also use the methodological tool of 'path dependence',[40] whereby past events or decisions constrain later events or decisions, to examine the relevant institutions and socio-political conditions in particular historical periods. 'Critical junctures'[41] in particular shape subsequent conditions by creating a path dependence. My theoretical approach focuses not only on the relations between religious, political, social and economic groups, it also emphasises the connections between ideas, policies and material conditions. Religion, thereof as an intrinsic part of identity, has the capacity to shape politics and power relations; whereas identity is a frame of reference within which the socio-political environment is discernible (Öztürk 2021: 34).

It may be argued that religion is a form of power resource and an instrument with distinct effects within various fields in the socio-political arena, and this study seeks to explain how religion, the instrumentalisation of religion, and the management of religion have always been present in the history of modern Turkey.[42]

Notes

1. For a brief but rewarding set of arguments on these concepts, see Torpey 2010: 277–86.
2. The quote in full: 'All that is solid melts into air, all that is holy is profaned, and man is at last compelled to face with sober senses, his real conditions of life, and his relations with his kind.' Karl Marx and Friedric Engels (1848) *The Communist Manifesto*.
3. On the question 'What is religion?', see Smith 1998; Torpey 2010: 271–7.
4. For an intellectually stimulating work challenging the understandings of 'religion' and 'secularity' by underlying the border shifting between the two concepts and their evolving thereof, see Dalacoura 2019.
5. Islam claims authority over all spheres of life, and the interconnectedness of religious obligation and political rule is classically expressed as *islam din wa dawla* (Islam is religion and state). However, for a convincing advocacy of the concept of 'Islamic secular' as a field of action and thought outside of the sharia but still inherent in the Islamic tradition, see Sherman Jackson (2017: 1–31) and the works of Talal Asad (1993, 2003, 2006, 2018). Shahab Ahmed's *What is Islam? The Importance of Being Islamic* (2016) provides some very profound and sophisticated views on the issue. Also, for discussions on the concepts of Islam/religion/state/secular in line with challenging readings, see Dressler, Salvatore and Wohlrab Sahr 2019. Although it is not in a political context and does not relate to Islam, for an insightful discussion of the relationship between religion and the secular which compares and contrasts the views of Bernard Williams, Alasdair MacIntyre and Charles Taylor, see McPherson 2018.
6. In this respect, see the Religious Authority Symposium organised by the Theology Faculty of Karadeniz Technical University in Rize on 12–13 September 2003: 'Obeying the rulers (*al-amr*) after Allah and the prophet is one of the

things that believers are ordered to do' (Yusuf Şevki Yavuz, 'Kur'an-ı Kerim'de Dini Otorite', 31); '... political and legal sovereignty as an authority is only and only peculiar to God' (Vecihi Sönmez, 'Hakimiyet veya Dini Otoritenin Meşruiyeti', 221; both quotes from Karadeniz Teknik Üniversitesi Rize İlahiyat Fakültesi 2006).

7. The abolition of the Caliphate in 1924 was perhaps the most significant step towards providing legitimacy to the new Turkish state on the basis of a national identity above religion (Berkes [1964] 1998: 463).
8. A *zaviye* is a building associated with Sufis in the Islamic world. It can serve a variety of functions including those of a place of worship, school, monastery, dormitory and/or mausoleum.
9. In a lengthy article first published in 1931, Fuat Köprülü came to the conclusion that few immediate links between the two socio-political systems can ever have existed. However, the Byzantine–Ottoman transition and thus linkages between the two societies, have recently become a fruitful field of study. See Matschke 2002. Furthermore, a close reading of Köprülü's last chapter is interesting: in it, he explains that many Islamic institutions have Roman roots, indicating a very substantial indirect Byzantine impact.
10. The Sultan appointed the patriarchs and, later, the chief rabbi, as well.
11. For a summary of the discussion on *laiklik*, see Öztürk and Sözeri 2018: 7. On the terms '*laic(ité)*', the secular, secularisations, secularisms and post-secular, see Gözaydın 2014: 1215.
12. For a scrutiny of religion in modern times and secularism as one of the pillars of modernity, see Cady and Hurd 2010.
13. For the understanding of 'religion is a private affair' and its consequences for modernisation processes, see Casanova 1994: 40–66.
14. It should also be noted that the religious picture of Anatolia in the thirteenth and fourteenth centuries appears complex. For a conceptualisation of 'metadoxy' in this period, see Kafadar 1995: 74–7.
15. Actually, this was a political/legal enforcement of the 'secularization thesis' (see Casanova 1994: 17–39) and of the privatisation of religion through adoption of the right to individual belief, 'a product of the only legitimate space (that was) allowed to Christianity by post-Enlightenment society' (Asad 1993: 45).
16. *TBMM Zabıt Ceridesi* (proceedings), V, 16 (1937), 60–1.
17. For a thought-provoking comparative analysis of the power structuring between scholars, merchants and the state (military elite) in Western Europe and the Muslim World throughout history, with the consequences of the decline or rise of any one group, see Kuru 2019.

18. Prof. Ali Bardakoğlu, a former president of the institution, states that: 'The Diyanet, as a public institution, has a special role in the production and transmission of religious knowledge ... [it] produces sound religious knowledge' (2004: 367 and 369). Adjectives such as 'sound', 'authentic', 'real', 'healthy', 'objective' and 'sensitive', frequently used by the authorities for the information produced by the Diyanet reveal an essentialist approach that distinguishes 'legitimate' and 'illegitimate' religious approaches.
19. On coining the term 'imagined communities' and its sophisticated contextualisation, see Anderson [1983] 1991.
20. The Turkish concepts of '*milliyetçi*' and '*ulusalcı*' both mean 'nationalists', deriving respectively from '*millet*' and '*ulus*' meaning nation in current Turkish. However, the older word '*milliyetçi*' has been connoted with the right wing, whereas the newer version '*ulusalcı*' is associated with the secularist left wing. For a detailed treatment of these concepts, see Özkırımlı 2011: 89.
21. 'The hidden face of the Republican imagined Turkish identity has always been Islam' (Yavuz 2000: 25).
22. '*Aydın*' in Turkish is a difficult concept to translate into English. Instead of 'intellectual' I deliberately used the word 'literati' as in Şerif Mardin's definition in his article '"Aydınlar" Konusunda Ülgener ve bir İzah Denemesi', 1984: 10.
23. Gökhan Çetinsaya bases his claim that I agree with that there is no fundamental contradiction between religion (Islam) and nationalism (Turkism) on a historical perspective, and argues that the emergence of the Turkish–Islamic synthesis is understandable on three grounds: (1) Turkism and Islam were closely linked from the beginning in the development of Turkish nationalism and modernist Islam; (2) among Turkists, those who rejected Islam were in the minority, as were the Islamists who rejected nationalism; (3) these groups were fed in their entirety by the same intellectual sources: that is, the works and ideas produced in 1950–70. Çetinsaya argues that Islam and nationalism had developed in tandem since Ottoman times (1999: 350–75).
24. http://bianet.org/english/english/103813-remembering-the-maras-massacre-in-1978; http://bianet.org/english/politics/170324-37-years-after-maras-massacre.
25. On neo-Ottoman policies, see M. Hakan Yavuz 2020.
26. Ahmet Kabaklı, 'Değerlerimizin İdrakine Doğru', *Tercüman*, 23 April 1983.
27. According to the Amnesty International report, over 50,000 people were detained in the first year. *Amnesty International Report 2017/18 – The State of the World's Human Rights*. Available at: https://www.amnesty.org/download/Documents/POL1067002018ENGLISH.PDF.

28. For developments regarding the Diyanet after 2009, see Gözaydın 2020: 311–75.
29. For a sofisticated reading of Alevism as Islam rethinking Shahab Ahmed's conceptualisation of Islam, see Oktay-Uslu 2020.
30. For rights under the Treaty of Lausanne, see Yıldırım 2015: 167–73.
31. Today, newer non-Muslim groups such as the Jehovah's Witnesses and Turkish Protestants are also not recognised as non-Muslim minorities protected under the Treaty of Lausanne.
32. Government policies and politics also affect perceptions and attitudes in society: 'At the popular culture level, there is a strong tendency to view non-Muslim Turkish citizens not as equal citizens but as foreigners whose allegiance to the Turkish state is questionable' (Özbudun 2012: 68).
33. For the shortcomings in the implementation of the rights granted by the Treaty of Lausanne, see Senem Aydın-Düzgit 2014: 319.
34. *TBMM Zabıt Ceridesi* (proceedings), II, e 8/1 (1923), 908–11.
35. On 'Speak Turkish' campaigns and other discriminatory acts against the non-Muslim population in the 1920s and 1930s, see Cagaptay 2006.
36. For an insightful account of policies to Turkify diverse non-Muslim population in Turkey's history, see Ayhan Aktar 2021b.
37. The author is referring here to *dönme*, a group of Jews who converted to Islam in the nineteenth century.
38. Reinvention of the Ottoman past has existed all through republican Turkey, even though the essence was altered. For a brilliant comparison of this phenomena in republican times, see Danforth 2016.
39. For comparative historical analysis in the social sciences, see Mahoney and Rueschemeyer 2003.
40. For two articles that conceptualise 'path dependence' as a social process, see Pierson 2000 and Thelen 2000.
41. On 'critical junctures', see Capoccia and Kelemen 2007; for an article that aims at 'advancing our understanding of critical junctures in the evolution of religious/secular regulations, referring to those moments in history when one particular arrangement is adopted among several alternatives, establishing an institutional trajectory that is resistant to change in the following years', see Lerner 2014.
42. On the link between religion, identity and politics, see Fox and Sandler 2005; King 2003; Kratochvíl 2019; Modood 2010; Oppong 2013; Philpott 2007.

1

OTTOMAN MODERNISATION

> For us, modernization means being able to build and use automobiles and airplanes like Europeans, not to resemble Europeans in form and livelihood.
> Ziya Gökalp, *Türkleşmek, İslamlaşmak, Muassırlaşmak* (1918)

Ottoman modernisation emerged as an attempt to survive in an era in which nineteenth-century empires were collapsing. Modernisation processes can be traced back to the late eighteenth century in terms of updates to military technology; however, legal and political actions aimed at capturing the changing spirit of the times began in the nineteenth century.[1] Even though I perceive Ottoman times as the past of the modern Republic of Turkey, there are as many ruptures as there are continuities between the two. While the latter is nationalistic in character, in the Ottoman nineteenth century, religious affiliation was still the most influential shaper of communal identity.[2] As Albert Hourani puts it: 'The Muslim element (was) the strongest pillar of the Ottoman *ummah*, and the Turks have always been its defenders and possessors of power in it' (Hourani 1991: 185).[3] Several issues that are still contested in Turkey, like the relationships among religion, state and society, are deeply rooted in Ottoman times. As Şerif Mardin puts it: 'It is these conflicts that made up the latent social infrastructure of Turkish politics. It is, therefore, not entirely surprising that it is these conflicts which have kept recurring in the politics of the Turkish Republic' (Mardin 2006: 22).

Differing Historiographies

'Looking from the present day to the past, we may be able to reconstruct a series of plausible causalities and deterministic developments. Indeed, the construction of plausible narratives about the past is very much what one calls "writing history"' (Somel, Neumann and Singer 2011: 2). The Ottoman historiography of the Ottoman modernisation process generally attributes the 'reforms' of the time to external pressures exerted by a European-dominated world. According to this dominant narrative, the Gülhane Rescript of 1839 was the birth certificate of westernisation and secularisation.[4] It was drafted by Mustafa Reşid Paşa, a statesman and bureaucrat with a wide-ranging knowledge of Europe and foreign languages.[5]

However, alternative historiographies exist in late Ottoman studies. Cem Emrence states that the imperial experience has been approached in three 'episodes' in late Ottoman studies (2011: 15–34). He places the modernisation approach mentioned below in 1950–70; macro models that produce dependency and world-systems perspectives in 1970–90; and the bargaining view that promotes a negotiation model to explain the Ottoman past to the years after 1990. It should also be noted that syncretic works have combined these waves of late Ottoman history writing (Ahmad 2003; Quataert 2005; Zürcher 2017)

I would like to add a fourth, which underlines the significance of religion (Islam) among late Ottoman decision-making elites. In his ground-breaking article from 1994 entitled 'The Islamic roots of the Gülhane Rescript', Butrus Abu-Manneh asserts that the edict was drafted with Islamic sensibilities in order to win over Muslims who had been alienated by Mahmud II, 'the Infidel Sultan'.

Modernisation Approaches

Modernisation approaches put the impact of the West, and thus secularisation, at the centre of the analysis. According to Bernard Lewis and others who take the 'modernization' perspective, the story of the Middle East, late Ottoman times and Turkey should be told in terms of the Western impact and the domestic response to it (Davison 1963; Lewis 2002, 2004), which is to say with modernisers/reformers on one side and conservative/traditionalist reactionaries on the other.[6] In this view, the West is a civilisational asset of a universal nature. Modernisation was a state-led discourse perceived as being synonymous with westernisation focused on supra-structural activities in education, the legal system and the state bureaucracy.[7]

Şerif Mardin reads the westernisation agenda and efforts at modernisation as a loss of legitimacy in the eyes of some parts of society, and this loss leading to a deep alienation and divide between the political elite (centre) and the masses (periphery) which would accelerate later in republican Turkey (Mardin 1973 and 1997).

Macro Models

Macro models focus on the socio-economic aspects of the narrative with reference to global processes. The dependency school, social history research and world-systems perspective introduce alternative readings to modernisation approaches. Çağlar Keyder's *State and Class in Turkey: A Study in Capitalist Development* (1987) proposes an interpretation of the history of modern Turkey based on the country's incorporation into the capitalist world system (dependency school approach). This perspective attaches imperial processes to global structures of power and inequality (1987: 25–48). The world economy plays an establishing role in class formation and social resistance in late Ottoman times.[8] Capitalism was the dynamic that drove the transformation of the late Ottoman body. Loans from European markets at high rates of interest led to foreign control over Ottoman finances (Pamuk 1987) and consequently of Ottoman politics.

A prominent outcome of Turkey's economic integration into the world system was modern class formation (Kasaba 1988).[9] Drastic changes in land ownership through the Ottoman Land Code of 1858 shaping hierarchies, especially at the local level, and the political outcomes of this change in the region became a focus for agrarian studies from the 1980s (Gerber 1987; Keyder and Tabak 1991; Macauley 2009).[10]

Bargaining Perspectives

Bargaining perspectives shifted the focus to state–society relations via historical narratives that give them agency in the forming of the region in modern times (Kayalı 1997). Scholarship from the bargaining perspective not only provides a reading of the multi-layered character of the late Ottoman state-building process, it also highlights imperial ideologies of legitimacy and survival.[11]

Underlining the cooperation between the political elite at the centre with local intermediaries, bargaining perspectives differ from modernisation approaches and macro models which centre on the constitutive impact of the West and the world economy, respectively. Works written from bargaining perspectives read late Ottoman times through political bargains struck between the state and social actors (Barkey 2008: 1).

Significance of Islam

The works of Butrus Abu-Manneh (1994, 2001, 2015) led the way to an alternative narrative built on themes of state, faith and nation following the line of argument he pursued in his doctoral dissertation: 'Some Aspects of Ottoman Rule in Syria in the Second Half of the Nineteenth Century: Reforms, Islam and Caliphate', supervised by Albert Hourani, completed in 1971. Abu-Manneh focuses on the Müceddidiyye branch of the Nakşibendi, an order which originated in India. According to Abu-Manneh, this branch's Halidi suborder in particular had a significant impact on politics and society in modern Turkey from the early nineteenth century on.[12] He therefore discusses throughout his oeuvre the role played by Sunni-orthodox Islam in the transformation of the Ottoman Empire in the nineteenth century.

Unlike proponents of the modernisation approaches, Carter Findley (2010) perceives the tension between secular nationalists and Islamists as the leitmotif of modern Turkey, and recognises the significance of Islamic currents in the Ottoman Empire and Turkey.

By challenging existing teleological accounts, recent scholarship in late Ottoman studies by inter alia, Yakoob Ahmed,[13] Jun Akiba (2018), Frederick Anscombe (2014), Adrian Brisku (2017), Benjamin Fortna (2002: specifically, 1–42), Abdülhamit Kırmızı (2019a), Aylin Koçunyan (2018), Christine Philliou (2011), Stefano Taglia (2015, 2016), Alp Eren Topal (2021) and Ali Yaycıoğlu (2018) have increasingly followed the road opened by the late Butrus Abu-Manneh.

A Brief Overview of the Era

Mahmud II

Janissaries, the professional Ottoman military force established in the 1370s, was abolished by Mahmud II (1808–39), who also launched a series of social and administrative reforms he deemed necessary for the survival of the empire.

On 15 June 1826, when the Janissaries staged an armed revolt in protest at a series of military reforms he had introduced, the Sultan ruthlessly crushed the uprising, killing some 6,000 Janissaries. Two days later, he declared the Janissary corps disbanded,[14] an event that came to be known as the 'Auspicious Occasion' (*Vaka-ı Hayriye*).[15] This was followed by his suppression of the Bektaşi Order, the Janissaries' traditional ally.[16] The state seized assets belonging to the Bektaşi orders and would later transfer them to the Nakşibendi order.[17] The estates of the empire's three richest Jewish bankers were also confiscated, and the bankers executed as associates of the Janissaries (Finkel 2005: 438–9). Thenceforth, control over all religious foundations/endowed property (*evkaf/vakıfs*) passed to the state, which instituted a ministry for the purpose (*Evkaf-It Humayun Nezareti*, 1826).

The Mahmud II era witnessed the birth of a number of state reflexes that have reappeared numerous times in the history of modern Turkey, when deemed necessary. Newly invented concepts like 'enemy of the state' (for the Janissaries) and 'enemy of the faith' (for the Bektaşi order)[18] were followed by others like the confiscation of opponent's financial assets, the imposition of dress codes, and using religious authorities for legitimation.

In 1826, Mahmud established a new army called the *Muallem Asakir-i Mansure-i Muhammediye* (Trained Victorious Muhammadan Soldiers). He also decreed that each new regiment should have a *mekteb* (school) to instruct the recruits in Islam (Aksan 2007: 328–329).

The dress codes that would later become a tool for the political powers to impose the lifestyles they themselves espoused on the whole of society were first imposed by Mahmud II. His introduction of Western-style uniforms for the military and requirement that the civil bureaucracy wear Western suits was one of the reasons he was called 'the Infidel Sultan'.

Mahmud stressed that his subjects would receive equal treatment, with no regard paid to their religious affiliations.[19] He tried to secure the loyalty of his non-Muslim subjects through appeasing policies such as allowing new churches to be opened (Beydilli 2000) and officially recognising new religious groups like the Catholic Armenians (Beydilli 1995). In addition, he sought to secure the cooperation of the *ulema*[20] in his reforms by reconciling Islamic principles of law and justice with the Western principles of the ideal state and society.

Rebellions of the time sought to make Mahmud II charge the *şeyhülislam* Yasincizade Abdülvahhâb Efendi (1758–1833) with elaborating an Islamic theory of total obedience to the sultan (Erşahin 1999). The result was the argument that sharia norms could be set aside in times of 'evil and corruption', so the ruler could re-establish 'civilization'.[21]

In Frederick F. Anscombe's words: 'Mahmud himself remains something of an enigma' (Anscombe 2010: 168).[22] Mahmud's actions can be read as being motivating by hopes of regaining the upper hand over his ideological rival,[23] Mehmed Ali Paşa (1769–1849), Governor of Egypt, and by a desire to deactivate the nationalism that was exhilarating Christian subjects such as the Greeks. There is an apparent paradox between his use of elements designed to please the religious authorities and the sort of authoritarian conduct that earned him the sobriquet 'the Infidel Sultan'. Nevertheless, his efforts helped him to remain on the throne until his death in 1839.

Tanzimat

Shortly after succeeding Mahmud II, on 3 November 1839, Sultan Abdülmecid (1839–61) issued the Gülhane Rescript that set in motion the process known as the Tanzimat (reorganisation/giving order), an era of fundamental change in Ottoman government. Many scholars divide this era into the first Tanzimat period (1839–56) and the second Tanzimat period (1856–76).

'Who drafted the 1839 Edict' is still an issue of debate among scholars of the late Ottoman period. Though it is now generally attributed to Mustafa Reşit Paşa, a significant group of scholars favour Butrus Abu-Manneh's (1994) account of affairs. According to Abu-Manneh, while growing up, Sultan Abdülmecid had been exposed to Nakşibendi-Mücahidi beliefs through his tutors and his mother, Bezmiâlem.[24]

Arguing the matter thoroughly, Abu-Manneh concludes that, while Mustafa Reşid Paşa may have had a hand in the text, the higher *ulema* of the time, led by *Şeyhülislam* Mekkizade Mustafa Asım Efendi (1762–1846), also played a significant role in its composition.[25] The specifically Islamic jurisprudential character of the Rescript supports this assumption. The Gülhane text makes three promises:

- all subjects are given the right to be treated in accordance with the law (*şeriat* and regulations in accordance with Islamic legal principles); no one is to be above the law. This provision stems from an acknowledgement that Ottoman decline was due to arbitrary and despotic government;

- tax collection is to be reorganised to make it orderly;
- military recruitment is to be reorganised to make it orderly and 'extended to non-Turkish populations'; this provision was not implemented until the Balkan Wars.

Selim Deringil discusses the Tanzimat at length as the arrival of the concept of the 'rule of law'. According to Deringil, what made the Tanzimat special, and the Gülhane Rescript in particular, was the fact that the sultan swore an oath in the chamber of the holy relics in Topkapı Palace to uphold the promises he had made in the edict (Deringil 2012: 30–8).

The 1850s, a period of political turbulence in Istanbul, witnessed the rise of two statesmen at the Sublime Porte: Mehmed Emin Âli (1815–71) and Keçecizade Mehmed Fuad Paşa (1815–68).[26] In Fuad Paşa's words: 'Islam was, for centuries, in its environment, a wonderful instrument of progress. Today it is a clock that is behind time and must be set' (Davison 1963: 90). Thus, a second reform decree, the Imperial Rescript of Reforms (*Islahat Fermanı*), was issued in 1856, granting legal and civic equality to the empire's non-Muslim subjects, who had been denied it in the Gülhane text of 1839.[27]

The 1860s saw a group of young bureaucrats and intellectuals who were dissatisfied with Tanzimat initiatives – İbrahim Şinasi (1826–71), Namık Kemal (1840–88), Ziya Bey (later Paşa) (1825–80), Ali Suavi (1839–78) and others – join forces into a group of young Ottomans who defended liberal values with Islamic arguments.[28] Even though they were never tightly organised and their organised activities were limited to a period of no more than five years, they would have a disproportionate influence in Turkey and beyond (Zürcher 2017: 64).[29]

Succeeding Abdülmecid, his brother Sultan Abdülaziz (1861–76) issued a *ferman* a few days after his accession to relieve concerns about the sustainability of the Tanzimat.

The Nizamiye Courts and the Mecelle

Criminal law was the first legal realm regulated after the 1839 Edict.[30] The Criminal Code of 1840 (*Ceza Kanunname-i Hümayun*)[31] was followed by additional regulations in 1851 and 1858.[32] These were followed by regulations impacting on commercial and procedural law.[33] Councils established throughout the Ottoman lands to implement the newly adopted criminal codes evolved into a new court system in the 1860s. The Nizamiye (regular) courts, which were largely inspired by French law and set up to address criminal cases as well as civil and commercial disputes, signified the end of the *şeriat* courts (Rubin 2011: 1–2).[34] However, the human resourses necessitated to run this judicial system were supplied by the *ulema*. Abdülhamit Kırmızı underlines the significance of the *ulema* in the Nizamiye court system (Kırmızı 2019a: 10–12). For their part, Avi Rubin and Jun Akiba suggest that the judicial reforms of the Tanzimat period were heuristic in nature (Rubin 2011: 23; Akiba 2018), challenging the narrative of a policy of decisive modernisation/westernisation in the Tanzimat era.

The *Mecelle-i Ahkam-ı Adliyye* (the Civil Code, commonly referred to as the Mecelle) was produced to be administered by the Nizamiye courts to fulfil the need for a law that could be applied to non-Muslims as well as Muslims, The Mecelle was applied in all Ottoman courts, apart from those in Egypt and the Arabian Peninsula. A comprehensive compilation of *şeriat* norms, it covered the areas of debt, property, personal status and juridical law in accordance with the Hanafi *fiqh*. The Mecelle was promulgated between 1869 and 1876. Even though it served as the civil code and resembled such codes in the West in its format, it did not contain all the sections found in Western civil codes, such as family and inheritance laws. Nevertheless, it did institute a standardisation that conformed with modern requirements. As Christoph Neumann puts it:

> This constituted, on the one side, an 'act of reform', since it contributed to the centralization of state institutions and the unification of the empire's system of law. On the other hand, it was a 'reactionary' act, since it countered a proposal to adopt a version of the French civil code. The codification of the Hanafi sharia meant the victory of the holy over the secular law. (Neumann 2002: 58)

Ahmed Cevdet Paşa (1822–95) was primarily responsible for the compilation of the *şeriat* in the Mecelle in his position as president of the council of judicial ordinances from 1868.[35]

Thomas Bauer's sophisticated reading of Islamic intellectual history may comprise a retort to the fact that 'the greatest opposition to the codification of Hanafi law came from the office of the *Şeyhülislam*' (Neumann 2002: 58):

> Intellectuals of the Ottoman era were confronted with the accusation that their sophisticated play with words addressed only a small elite. It may be correct to say that the stylistic devise of ambiguity found great interest within the learned

elite, which consisted largely of legal scholars. This is not astonishing, since legal scholars, as interpreters of normative texts, were charged with the task of domesticating the ambiguity of these texts. Their awareness of ambiguity kindled a delight in playfully creating ambiguity in texts of all sorts. Ambiguity is regarded here not as a defect, but as artistry. (Bauer 2021: 177)[36]

The Mecelle was abolished in 1926 and replaced by the Turkish Civil Code, which was adopted with slight changes from the Swiss Civil Code, three years after the founding of the new Turkish Republic.

Abdülhamid II

(Ahmet Şefik) Mithat Paşa (1822–4) was one of the initiators of the coup of 30 May 1876 that ended the Abdülaziz era. He received support not only from the agrarian middle class, but also from the *softas*, the students in the religious schools, many of whom came from villages and towns in Anatolia and the Balkans (Karpat 2001: 104). Abdülhamid II (1876–1909) succeeded his older brother, Murad V (1876), who reigned briefly after their uncle Abdülaziz. Mithat Paşa became Abdülhamid's grand vizier.

As he had promised, Abdülhamid promulgated a constitution, the *Kanun-i Esasi*.[37] The first Ottoman parliament convened on 19 March 1877 (Devereux 1963: 138–41). It survived less than a year; Abdülhamid 'temporarily prorogued' the parliament on 13 February 1878 (Us 1954: 407). He also exiled Mithat Paşa to Taif, and had him killed there in 1884 (Uzunçarşılı 1985).

Under the Hamidian regime, Islam was used as a mobilising force in a specific context: determined to portray himself as a caliph in the role of 'renewer of the faith' Abdülhamid II tried to restore the moral strength of the community.[38] Selim Deringil, in his thought-provoking work on the ideological underpinnings of the Hamidian regime, looks at Abdülhamid's efforts at image management and damage control (Deringil 1998).

Abdülhamid's attachment to Islam was a reflection of his own beliefs as well as the necessities of the times. The 1877–88 war with Russia forced hundreds of thousands of Muslim refugees from lost territories in the Balkans and the Caucasus to resettle within the empire (Anscombe 2014: 113).[39] Pan-Islamic policies such as stressing the title of 'caliph' were a means of legitimation as well as a defence (Deringil 2007: 48, 251–2).[40] It is interesting that even as an endorser of pan-Islamic thinking, Abdülhamid did not respond to the petition made by Ismail Gaspıralı, a prominent Crimean Muslim journalist, for a pan-Islamic congress that later took place in Cairo in November 1907. He appears to have been concerned that such a gathering would provoke 'racialized Islamophobia'[41] – the so-called Muslim peril – in Europe (Aydın 2017: 67).

Over the years, Abdülhamid's personal insecurities and fears led to a growing domestic espionage network, 'with people of all ranks being encouraged to report on the activities of the others' (Zürcher 2017: 75). Nevertheless, paradoxically but as might be expected, his escalating authoritarianism brought an opposition into being. As a result, the Young Ottoman movement of the 1860s entered the stage once again, albeit with a new set of actors. The initial organised group appears to have been established in the Military Medical College in 1889, and this gathering ignited others in the years that followed. Internally, the society was renamed the *İttihat ve Terakki Cemiyeti* (Committee of Union and Progress/CUP), however they were still known internationally as Young Turks/*Jeune Turcs*. While dedicating itself entirely to overthrowing Hamidian rule, the Young Turks movement was itself divided, with two principal groups emerging from the many: the Liberals led by Prince Sabahaddin (1877–1948) and the Unionists led by Ahmet Rıza Bey (1859–1930).[42]

As Yusuf Akçura (1876–1935) noted in his article *Üç Tarz-ı Siyaset* (Three Types of Politics) in *Türk*, a Cairo-based newspaper, in 1904: Ottomanism,[43] Islamism and Turkism were the policy choices on the table by the start of the twentieth century Ottoman realm. Mümtaz'er Türköne answers the question, 'When, where, by whom and why Islam has been transformed into a mass ideology' thus: 'Islam was transformed into an ideology in Istanbul from 1867 to 1873 by a group of Ottoman intellectuals in order to resist the challenges of the modern world' (Türköne 1991: 13).[44] 'Islamism . . . became a political current once *Sırat-ı Müstakim* ("Straight Path", and also the name of the bridge leading to paradise) began to be published in Istanbul on 14 August 1908' (Köroğlu 2007: 27; Somel 1987). Meanwhile, Abdülhamid II was supporting Nakşibendi/Halidi structures as well as the Kadiri and Rıfai orders (Vural 2019).

In 1907, the *İttihat ve Terakki Cemiyeti* merged with a secret association of Ottoman officers and bureaucrats called the Ottoman Freedom Society in Salonica to expand its membership. This was a significant step towards the

Young Turk Revolution of 1908.⁴⁵ Elections for a new parliament went ahead, and *İttihat ve Terakki Partisi* candidates won a majority of the seats. A bicameral parliament was opened by Sultan Abdülhamid on 17 December 1908 (Finkel 2005: 513).

In February and March 1909, opposition escalated against the *İttihat ve Terakki* administration, which was accused of authoritarianism.⁴⁶ Eventually, an uprising known as the 'March 31 (in the Rumi calendar) Incident' began on 13 April 1909, led by Islamist extremists, but joined by several disenchanted groups. In three days, the counter-coup was crushed by the Action Army (*Hareket Ordusu*), which marched to Istanbul from Salonica. On 27 April 1909, the parliament deposed Sultan Abdülhamid II (Zürcher 2017: 91–6).⁴⁷ The new grand vizier was Sait Halim Paşa (1863–1921).⁴⁸

Life Under the İttihat ve Terakki *Administration and the End of the Empire*

Abdülhamid's brother Reşad ascended the throne as Sultan Mehmed V (1909–18). A revised version of the Constitution was produced in 1909: henceforth, the Sultan would only have the power to appoint the grand vizier and the *şeyhülislam*. Constitutional changes were followed by several legislative measures, including a new law on military service: all male Ottoman subjects, Muslim and non-Muslim, now had a duty to serve in the military.

The inner circle of the *İttihat ve Terakki* party at the time consisted of Enver Paşa (1881–1922),⁴⁹ (Mehmet) Talat Paşa (1874–1921),⁵⁰ (Ahmet) Cemal Paşa (1872–1922),⁵¹ Halil Menteşe (1874–1948),⁵² Bahaettin Şakir (1877–1922)⁵³ and Dr (Selanikli) Nazım (1870–1926).⁵⁴ There was political competition among different parties in the political arena from 1909 to 1913 (Zürcher 2017: 97–101). In January 1913, during the First Balkan War, the Unionists (*İttihatçılar*) succeeded in staging a 'fully-fledged military coup' (Aktar 2021c) against the (Kıbrıslı) Kamil Paşa (1833–1913) Cabinet, and took full control over domestic politics. Even though Sait Halim Paşa served as the new grand vizier, the regime developed into a so-called 'triumvirate' of Enver, Talat and Cemal Paşa.⁵⁵

In the late Young Turk period, concepts such as *şeriat*, *din* and the Islamic state were understood in the context of a social and political order in which religious norms and modern institutions complemented each other harmoniously. Ziya Gökalp (1876–1924), a prominent sociologist and political activist, was the preeminent exponent of this idea.⁵⁶ *İttihat ve Terakki* adopted a more Islamist policy at its congress in September 1913, and *Islam Mecmuası* (Islam Review) was first published in February 1914 with their sponsorship. *The Review* became a rival of the more conservative *Sebilürreşad* (Path of Guidance). It is not surprising that Mehmet Akif Ersoy (1873–1936),⁵⁷ one of the most discussed names in modern Turkish literature, whose approach Erol Köroğlu describes as 'Islamic patriotism' (Köroğlu 2007: 137–46), publishes in *Sebilürreşad*. Mehmet Akif, as a pan-Islamist and an opponent of Turkish nationalism, was also brave enough to criticise it explicitly. Nevertheless, in the service of *Teşkilat-ı Mahsusa*,⁵⁸ he went to Germany to make speeches in the mosques to Muslim prisoners of war and prepared propaganda bulletins for them in December 1914 (Köroğlu 2007: 140–1).

Ottoman participation in World War I was actively sought by leaders of the *İttihat ve Terakki*. Sultan Mehmed Reşad officially declared Holy War (*cihad*) on the powers of the Entente⁵⁹ after consulting the *şeyhülislam* Hayri Efendi (Ürgüplü) (1867–1921) on 14 November 1914.⁶⁰ 'The First World War altered Ottoman society in ways no political or ideological programme had succeeded in doing – and in the long run brought the empire's dissolution' (Finkel 2005: 533). One of the most controversial issues in modern Turkish history took place during this war, in 1915: the Armenian relocations, deportations and massacres.⁶¹

The Mondros (Mudros) Armistice ended World War I for the Ottoman state, but actually amounted to an Ottoman capitulation. The triumphant powers occupied Istanbul initially on 13 November 1918 and more extensively on 16 March 1920. The victors imposed the Treaty of Sèvres (August 1920) on the government of Mehmed VI Vahdettin (1918–22), who was destined to be the last sultan of the Ottoman Empire, which included provisions for the partition of Anatolia. In Erik J. Zürcher's words:

> The sultan, like his predecessors, thought along dynastic and religious lines. What mattered was the preservation of the dynasty, of Istanbul as the seat of the Caliphate and his own authority over the Muslim population of the Middle East, for which he felt a strong responsibility. He was not a nationalist . . . and he cared little for the complete independence of Anatolia or any other region. (Zürcher 2017: 136–7)

Meanwhile, struggles were ongoing in Anatolia from November 1918 into the spring of 1921. The War of Independence was fought in 1921–2 by a national resistance movement. Eventually, on 2 November 1922, the Turkish Grand Assembly in Ankara declared the abolition of the Ottoman sultanate.[62]

The Role of the *Ulema*

'*Ulema*' is the plural of the Arabic word '*alim*' ('man of knowledge'). It was used in the Ottoman Empire to refer to those who were trained in the Islamic religious sciences (which included the Koran, the teachings of the Prophet Muhammad, and Islamic jurisprudence), and were members of the Ottoman religious intelligentsia: the *ilmiye* hierarchy. The head of the Ottoman *ulema* was the *şeyhülislam* or chief mufti of the capital, appointed by the sultan from among the most distinguished scholars of the religious sciences.[63] Contrary to the narratives in the official Turkish historiography regarding their diminishing position, the *ulema* did play an important role in the life of the late Ottoman state and society. The nineteenth-century reforms organised various institutions associated with the *ulema* into departments in the office of the *Şeyhülislam* (*Meşihat-ı İslamiye*). In Tanzimat institutions, the *ulema* began to play a role in all the newly established structures. In other words, their position was not limited to the traditional posts teaching and preaching Islam, or performing religious duties in the mosques (Kırmızı 2021: 32–8).[64]

The *İttihat ve Terakki* authorities reorganised the powers of the *Meşihat-ı İslamiye* from 1912 to 1917. Initially, they managed to remove competences regarding the judiciary and education from the jurisdiction of that institution. Some scholars have interpreted this move as a step towards secularisation (Akşin 1997: 127), but the narratives and documents of the *İttihat ve Terakki* administration itself reveal the opposite to have been the case (Aslanmirza 2021: 26–30).[65] For decades, the historiography of Ottoman modernisation and reform viewed the *ulema* as a reactionary force opposed to reform, but 'the ulema's aspiration to ensure the long-term viability of the religious establishment was interlaced with concerns about the future of the empire and its Islamic character' (Bein 2011: 30). İsmail Kara, in his paper 'Turban and fez: Ulema as opposition' concentrates on the *ulema*'s growing support for the opposition to Abdülhamid II and their participation in the *İttihad ve Terakki* movement (Kara 2005). Presenting a selection of oppositional pamphlets and other publications from the period written by members of the *ulema*, he uses numerous illustrative examples to analyse the transformations in their general worldview, arguing that the changing times eventually led to an intellectualisation, in the modern sense of the word, of the *ulema*.

*Tarikat*s (Dervish Orders) and *Tekke*s (Dervish Lodges)

Tarikat means 'path' in Arabic. Western scholars refer to the mystical traditions in Islam, known in Arabic as *tasawwuf*, as Sufism. Both the Arabic and English terms are derived from the Arabic *sufi*, meaning 'mystic'. In Ottoman Turkish, the more commonly used word for a mystic was dervish (Agoston and Masters 2009: 539). Until the nineteenth century, there was no central institution to administer the *tarikat*s and *tekke*s. After some initial moves in the Selim III (1789–1808) and Mahmud II (1808–39) eras, the *Meclis-i Meşayih*, a regulatory body for the Sufi orders, was eventually established in 1866 under the *Meşihat-ı İslamiye*.[66] In 1868, the *Meclis-i Meşayih* was composed of five members, each from a different *tarikat*, headed by Osman Selahaddin Dede, the *şeyh* of the *Yenikapı Mevlevihanesi* (M. Kara 1977: 248–69; Aydın 1998; Kara 2002).[67]

In Kemal H. Karpat's words: 'The Nakşbandia was probably the single most powerful social, political and ideological force shaping the cultural history of Asian Islam in general, and the Ottoman Empire in particular, during the nineteenth century' (Karpat 2001: 107). The Nakşibendi tradition received a major boost from the teaching and writings of Ziyaeddin Halid, commonly known as Mevlana or Şeyh Halid (1776–1827),[68] a Kurdish scholar from Shahizur in Iraqi Kurdistan. Şeyh Halid had a marked concern for the *şeriat* and the preservation of the Ottoman state as its protector (Algar 1990: 37). The Nakşibendi order treated the state as a necessary instrument for the achieving of Islamic ideals. According to the Halidi understanding, the implementation of Islamic law is a *sine qua non* for a just society. The state-centrism of the Nakşibendi was promoted by Şeyh Halid: he asked his followers to 'pray for the survival of the exalted Ottoman state, upon which Islam, too, depends for its victory over the enemies of religion' (Hourani 1981: 76). Thus, since he had devoted himself to promoting the moral and spiritual rebirth of the Muslim community gathered around the Ottoman Caliphate, Mevlana Halid pursued a careful and deliberate policy of state penetration through the recruiting of *ulema* and high-ranking bureaucrats (Yavuz 1999: 131). Stressing direct engagement with politics and society, Şeyh Halid's post was in time handed over to Ahmed Ziyaüddin Gümüşhanevi (1813–94)[69] (Abu-Manneh 1992), and eventually to Mehmed Zahid Kotku (1897–1980) of the İskenderpaşa circle, which would in later years have numerous politicians and bureaucrats among its members.

Hakan Özoğlu, in his exploration of the nature of Kurdish nationalism in its formative period, underlines the significance of religious affiliations. The Şemdian family of Nehri, which emerged as political and military leaders of the Kurds in the second half of the nineteenth century, claimed a connection to the *silsile* (spiritual genealogy) of the Nakşibendi's Halidi suborder (Özoğlu 2001: 387–8). Such a pedigree obviously generated the cultural, social and economic capital the family needed to acquire influence and vast land holdings.

Michael E. Meeker, in *A Nation of Empire: The Ottoman Legacy of Turkish Modernity*, his highly original study that investigates the transition from empire to nation state in the eastern Black Sea Coast from an anthropological perspective, states that: 'After Sultan Abdülhamit II ascended the throne, an imperial policy of pan-Islamism further served to stimulate religious teaching and learning in the district of Of' (Meeker 2002: 273). It is interesting that, despite this, *tekke* numbers were relatively low in the coastal region at the time. Meeker interprets this data 'as a sign of the preference for "official" as opposed to "charismatic" Islam by all the population of the coastal region' (Meeker 2002: 273 n. 42).

İsmail Kara asserts that, after 1909, it can be commonly observed both in periodicals published by *tarikat* circles and in other writings by *tarikat* members that, while the *İttihat ve Terakki* and the new constitutional regime was praised, the despotic Hamidian times were condemned unreservedly (Kara 2014: 74).

Alevi Population

The connection between the Ottoman ruling house and Sunni Islam intensified in the sixteenth century after the Kızılbaş (Redhead) revolt.[70] This group supported Shah İsmail I (1501–24 of Iran) in his struggle against the Ottomans.[71] In time, the Ottoman religious establishment preferred to become an exclusively Sunni institution dominated by practitioners of the Hanafi school of law. Shia in general, and Kızılbaş in particular, were not recognised or formally represented within it, and were viewed as deviators from the straight path of Islam and a politically unreliable element. 'This pejorative connotation remained largely in place when the term "Alevi" began to appear more frequently in the final decades of the Ottoman Empire' (Dressler 2013: 2).

Markus Dressler argues in *Writing Religion: The Making of Turkish Alevi Islam* that the primary motivation for the reconceptualisation of the Kızılbaş as Alevis was political, in the context of Turkish nationalism in the last decades of the Ottoman Empire.[72] The aim was 'reducing – though, crucially, not totally eliminating – their socio-religious and political otherness in order to assimilate them into the nation-in-formation' (Dressler 2013: 5).

During Abdülhamid II's reign, the emphasis on orthodoxy was pronounced, with all other interpretations of Islam attracting attention of the state. No wonder, then, that the Ministry of Education was instructed in 1890 to send preachers to the Kızılbaş of the vilayet of Sivas. Or that the *mutasarrıf* (administrator) of Tokat was ordered to make a census of the Kızılbaş population in his area in 1891; he was also instructed to take measures so these people could be 'rescued from their ignorance and shown the high path of enlightenment' (Deringil 1998: 82).

In 1891, the Ottomans formed irregular militia called the *Hamidiye Hafif Süvari Alayları* (Hamidiye Light Cavalry Regiments),[73] which were mostly recruited from Sunni Kurdish tribes. Enver Behnan Şapolyo reports that these units, which were already notorious for their involvement in the massacres of Armenians in 1894–6, also attacked Kızılbaş tribes (Şapolyo 1964: 286), especially in Dersim; those attacks would also be extended to Varto, Adıyaman, Karakocan and Harput where there were large Alevi communities. Hamidiye troops were also involved in acts of aggression against the Assyrian Christian populations of Malatya, Maraş, Antep and Mardin.[74]

In the late *İttihat ve Terakki* period, Baha Said (1882–1939), a member of the Central Committee, began to write about the Kızılbaş-Alevis in nationalist journals and dailies in 1918.[75] On the surface, these were ethnographic studies with sociological and historical elaborations. Dressler asserts that the writings of Baha Said and others in *İttihat ve Terakki* circles suggest a number of intertwined motives, all within the framework of Turkish nationalism (Dressler 2013: 128–33). Ironically, these articles came to the attention of

Sultan Mehmed Reşad and the *Şeyhülislam* and were censored, as they were perceived as 'Kızılbaş propaganda' (Hür 2013: 18). Eventually these articles were published unexpurgated in *Türk Yurdu*, a nationalist review, in 1926–7.

The Non-Muslim Population

Religious pluralism, including both the spectrum within Islam and non-Muslim communities, was a characteristic of the Ottoman Empire (Bauer 2021: 271–2). In the Ottoman Empire *millet* meant a religious community, specifically non-Muslim religious minorities represented within the empire by an official political leader. In the early nineteenth century, documents consistently affirmed that non-Muslims were organised into three officially sanctioned *millet*s: the Greek Orthodox, headed by the ecumenical patriarch; the Armenians, headed by the Armenian patriarch of Istanbul; and the Jews, headed after 1835 by the *hahambaşı* in Istanbul. However, there were many more congregations in Ottoman lands.

Catholic and Protestant missionary activity in Ottoman lands was targeted at non-Muslim groups, since converting Muslims to other faiths was a capital crime.[76] The Ottoman government never outlawed missionary activity. During the reign of Sultan Abdülhamid II, the concern was that Protestant missionaries would proselytise among groups that were either heterodox Muslim, like the Druze and Alevi (Arab/Kurd/Turk), or not Muslim at all, as in the case of the Ezidis. Catholic missionaries from the West concentrated their efforts on bringing the hierarchy of the various churches into communion with Rome. In some Eastern churches in the Ottoman Empire, the missionaries succeeded in creating schisms in the eighteenth century. For example, a group of Nestorian Christians broke away from their traditional leadership with the support of Roman Catholic missionaries active in the region and were acknowledged as a Uniate Church by Rome. The pro-Catholic party took the name *Keldani* (Chaldean*)*, by which the Church had been known in both Arabic and Turkish, while the traditionalists continued to call themselves *Süryani* (Syrians). This created confusion for those outside the community, since the larger Jacobite (Syrian Orthodox) Church also used that name. In the nineteenth century, the traditionalists began to call themselves Assyrians, the name by which the community is known today.[77] Protestant missionary activities influenced the Armenian populations, resulting in a substantial number of conversions.

In the Tanzimat era, new regulations were adopted among the long-established communities (Findley 2010: 100).[78] The Armenian Apostolic patriarchs had problems imposing their authority when lay members of the community took advantage of the Edict of 1856 and promulgated a national constitution for the Armenian *millet* in 1863.[79] In a similar move, Bulgarian Orthodox leaders submitted demands including church services in Bulgarian, Bulgarian-speaking prelates, the establishment of a national church, and a form of political autonomy to both the Sublime Porte and the Ecumenical Patriarchate.[80] The ecumenical patriarch of the Greek Orthodox Church was the head of the Orthodox *millet* in the Ottoman Empire. The reforms instituted in the Tanzimat era strengthened the control the churches could exercise over the lives of the faithful by granting governmental recognition to their local councils and school systems.[81] In this period, the Ottoman government recognised the patriarch in Dar-ul Zafaran as the head of the 'Ancient Syrians' and the Catholic patriarch in Aleppo as head of the Syrian Catholic community, thereby creating two separate *millet*s for the *Yakubiler* (Jacobites).[82]

Copts, Christians indigenous to Egypt, were influenced by the Tanzimat reforms as well. The Coptic laity pushed their clergy into accepting the supervision of a religious council (*majlis al-milli*) over the financial and civil affairs of the Coptic community.[83] Melkite Catholics[84] received recognition as an independent *millet* in 1848.

As Christian minorities began to articulate nationalist alternatives to the Ottoman Empire, most Jews feared that any new states formed would be less liberal and tolerant than Ottoman imperial rule; as a result, the ties between the various Jewish communities and the Ottoman sultans grew stronger in the nineteenth century.[85]

Under Abdülhamid II, from 1895 to 1897, Armenians converted *en masse* in Anatolia to escape death in the massacres of 1894–6. These were actions to escape the Hamidian massacres; some later converted back to their former faith, some did not.[86]

Women, Religion and Modernisation

In gender studies of modern Turkey, a new historiography began to be produced in the late 1980s. Since then, Turkish feminist historians and academics have begun to challenge the Kemalist legacy. Fatmagül Berktay argued for continuities between the Ottoman Empire and the new Republic in terms of the existence of patriarchy (Berktay 2003: 88–111). Madeline C. Zilfi edited a book on Ottoman women's historiography with contributions from fourteen scholars; covering a spectrum from court cases and tax registers to music and dance, the papers focus on non-elite Ottoman women from the sixteenth to the nineteenth century (Zilfi 1997). The work revealed that there were women in business who also sought their legal rights in regional courts. In addition, a number of works have focused on publications targeting women readers in the late Ottoman period as a means to analyse the era from a gender perspective.[87] Duygu Köksal and Anastasia Falierou's *A Social History of Ottoman Women: New Perspectives* contained fifteen valuable contributions to the field (Köksal and Falierou 2013).

In Tuğba Karaman's words:

> Ottoman women who contributed to the press from the mid-nineteenth century increasingly identified themselves as Muslim as well, and used an Islamic filter to decide what to adapt from the West, as well as reinterpreting Islamic sources and Islamic history to make their case. One of the three characteristics of the ideal woman was being a good Muslim, in addition to a good mother and wife . . . It serves to explain their attempts to prove the superiority of Islam and Islamic values over Western culture and mores, as well as their patriotism. (Karaman 2016: 127–8)

This conduct may be read as a 'bargaining with patriarchy', a concept developed by Deniz Kandiyoti which refers to strategies and negotiations engaged in within culturally constructed constraints and from a position of weakness (Kandiyoti 1988a). No rupture appears between the Ottoman times and the new Republic in terms of the weight of patriarchy.

Notes

1. On the argument that would have Ottoman modernisation beginning almost in parallel with the formation of modern kingdoms in seventeenth-century Europe, well before the reforms of the nineteenth century, see Abou-El-Haj 2005 and Tezcan 2010.
2. '. . . the Ottoman state remained an Islamic political identity from its beginning to its end, . . . the populations under its control similarly identified themselves

primarily by religious criteria in affairs transcending the purely local …' (Anscombe 2014: 4). '… the latent ideal of an "Islamicly" organized society no doubt also played a role as a vector in the totality of forces at play in the Ottoman social dynamic, within the administration as well as among the folk' (Mardin 1991: 117). 'The Ottoman Empire distinguished itself by creating a strong Islamic religious identity, yet taming it through state-dominated and state-guided administrative structures' (Barkey 2012: 19).

3. Ahmet Yaşar Ocak categorises Islamic perceptions among the Ottomans into four groups: state Islam, ulema Islam, Sufi Islam and popular/folk Islam (2021). On religious sentiment in Muslim Ottoman society, see Arpaguş 2014.
4. Berkes 1998: 144–7.
5. Kaynar 1954; Lewis 1961: 105–6. Shaw and Shaw (1977: 60) state that: 'The text itself (was) prepared under Mustafa Reşid's guidance at the Porte by its Consultative Council' without providing any evidence. For a differing view, see Abu-Manneh 1994; Finkel 2005: 449; Kırmızı 2019b; Silverstein 2010: 34–5).
6. For a brilliant challenge of this assumption and its basis in a binary between westernisation reforms versus Islamic conservatism, see Yaycıoğlu (2018). Focusing on Sultan Selim III's (1789–1808) military reform programme, known as the *Nizam-ı Cedit* (New Order), the author elucidates a discursive alliance between military enlightenment and Muslim activism (a part of the trans-Islamic Nakşibendi-Mücahidi network) against a Janissary-led popular resistance that sought to protect local conventions and traditions.
7. For an institutional history of the changing bureaucracy, see Findley 1980; for a social history of the members of the bureaucracy, see Findley 1989.
8. *The Ottoman Empire and the World-Economy* (1987), edited by Huri İslamoğlu-İnan, provides seventeen thought-provoking articles that discuss late Ottoman times through case studies and from the perspective of Immanuel Wallerstein's modern world-system theory.
9. Reşat Kasaba redefines the role of the local Christian bourgeoisie. For a comprehensive understanding of the critical role of the emerging Ottoman bourgeoise in social change, see Göçek 1996.
10. Huricihan İslamoğlu suggests a comparative historiography focused on law, ownership and legitimacy (İslamoğlu 2021: 185–202).
11. For a discussion of several imperial legitimation mechanisms, see Deringil 1998.
12. For an account of Abu-Manneh's works, see Kırmızı (2019b).
13. See the podcast 'Why Should Ottoman History be Taught as Islamic History?', 14 August 2020. Available at: https://podcast.isar.org.tr/12-why-should-ottoman-history-be-taught-as-islamic-history-yakoob-ahmed-history-society/.

14. In İlber Ortaylı's words: 'The Janissaries were abolished with great tumult, bloody slaughter, betrayals and murders. These events, which were described with great horror by Adolphus Slade Pasha (the British Naval Adviser), make it necessary to view the title "the just" (*adli*) bestowed on Sultan Mahmud II' (Ortaylı 1999: 67) with suspicion.
15. Ahmet Vefik, in his *Fezleke* (1869), treats 1789–1869 'as an age of transition to a better state', using the term *Vaka-ı Hayriye* and linking it to the Gülhane Rescript as the result of this event. See Neumann 2002: 73 and n. 44.
16. On the Bektaşi order, see Birge [1937] 1994; on the later Tanzimat and Abdülhamid II periods, see Abu-Manneh 2001: 135–7.
17. On the Bektaşi, and especially the Nakşibendi-Mücahidi orders in 1826, see Abu Manneh 2001: 59–71.
18. See Yıldız 2009: 31–130.
19. For a work on a network of Christian elites known as Phanariotes, institutionally affiliated with Ottoman governance, see Philliou 2011.
20. *Ulema* is the plural of the Arabic word *alim* ('man of knowledge'); in the Ottoman Empire, the term *ulema* referred to those who were trained in the Islamic religious sciences (such as the Koran, the teachings of the Prophet Muhammad, and Islamic jurisprudence), and were members of the Ottoman religious establishment: the *ilmiye* hierarchy (Agoston and Masters 2009: 577–8). On the role of *ulema* in the reform era, see Cihan 2004 and Yurdakul 2008.
21. Şerif Mardin comments that 'this constitutes Mahmud's contribution to political philosophy' (1962: 149 and n. 49).
22. For an analysis of Mahmud II, his deeds and Muhammad Ali, see Anscombe 2010: 167–83.
23. On Ottoman narratives of Muhammad Ali as an alternative model for political development, see Neumann 2002: 71–8.
24. On Abdülmecid's religiosity, see also Finkel 2005: 449; Kırmızı 2019a: 8.
25. For an article challenging Abu-Manneh's claims, specifically about the 1839 text, see Eldem 2022.
26. On Ali Paşa, see İnal 1969: 4–58; on Fuad Paşa, see İnal 1969: 161–95. On the roots of their power, see Abu-Manneh 2001: 115–24.
27. On reactions against the 1856 Edict, see Abu-Manneh 2015, especially 135–6. 'According to an anecdote recounted about Fuad Pasha, one of the key figures of the Tanzimat Era, when a member of the opposition commented that the government had done a great job in laying cobblestones on a street in the Sublime Porte quarter and widening that street, the pasha replied: "We used the stones that people have being throwing at us"' (Ortaylı 2021: 293).

28. As 'the Muslim interpreters of the new order', see Karpat 1972: 262–70.
29. See also Mardin 1962.
30. On judicial reforms in the criminal domain of the law, see Miller 2005.
31. For an analysis of this Code, see Candan 2015.
32. For an analysis of this Code, see Akgündüz 1987.
33. On the refashioning of the legal system in the late nineteenth century, see Gözaydın 2002.
34. On the Ottoman judicial structure after Tanzimat, see Ekinci 2004; Demirel 2007.
35. Christoph Neumann's (1999) *Araç Tarih Amaç Tanzimat: Tarih-i Cevdet'in Siyasi Anlamı* (original, in German, *Das indirekte Argument: Ein Plädoyer für die Tanzimat vermittels der Historie. Die geschichtliche Bedeutung von Ahmed Cevdet Paşas Ta'rih*) is a very interesting analysis of the thinking of a reformer with a strong Islamic identity. See also Birand [1957] 1998: 28–32.
36. Yet another view is that: 'the Islamic legal system, although in the main unsystematically linked with Qur'an and the Sunna, was not founded on a systematic intellectual working out of the sociomoral values of the Qur'an . . . Nevertheless, as the nineteenth-century Ottoman effort in the work *Majalla* clearly shows, a system of law can very well be built on it' (Rahman 1982: 29).
37. On the Islamic character of the text, see Hanioğlu 2008: 113.
38. For a review of Abdülhamid II's reign through an account of the *şeyhülislams* of the times, see, Sırma 2022: 83–148.
39. The total number of Muslim immigrants from the Crimea, Caucasus and Balkans who had settled in Anatolia (and, to a lesser extent, Syria and Iraq) by 1908 was in the region of 5 million. An Ottoman official estimate gives the total number of immigrants in the Ottoman territories in the nineteen years between 1877 and 1896 as 1,015,015 (Karpat 1985: 55).
40. On Abdülhamid's fears and concerns on the issue of the Sultan's political-legal role as caliph, see Finkel 2005: 493–9.
41. On Islamophobic sentiment in Europe and Ottoman responses in defence of Muslim rights in international law, see Aydın 2017: 94–8.
42. For a thorough class-based analysis of the disagreements within the Movement, see Ahmad 1993: 33–51.
43. See Topal 2021.
44. İsmail Kara asserts that the term *İslamcılık* (Islamism) was used by Ziya Gökalp (İ. Kara [1986] 2020: 33). For an article on the definition of Islamism, see Çiğdem 2004: 26–33.
45. On the path to the 1908 Revolution, see Hanioğlu 2001.

46. On Masis Kürkçügil's assessment, with a reference to Rakovski's prediction in an article published in *Socialisme* in 1908 that 'The autocratic sultan will be replaced by a less autocratic oligarchy', see Kürkçügil 2023: 20, 128–9.
47. Nahid Sırrı Örik's (1895–1960) historical novel *Sultan Hamid Düşerken* (1947) is a fiction that narrates the events of 1908–9 using fictitious as well as real characters who reflect the political, but also the social and psychological, climate of the times.
48. Sait Halim Paşa was a prolific writer on social and Islamic matters, who advocated that social regeneration was to be found in a return to Islamic values, though this should be done in accordance with the times and needs of society (Tunaya 1991: 50–7).
49. A leading member after 1906. After the coup of 1913, he became a general and Minister for War. Enver fled to Germany after the defeat of the empire in 1918. There, he tried to organise a worldwide Muslim revolutionary movement that failed in 1921. He died in a battle against the Red Army.
50. The most prominent civilian member of the party, especially after the 1908 revolution. Fled to Germany in 1918. Assassinated by an Armenian in Berlin because of his involvement in the Armenian genocide.
51. One of the earliest and most prominent members. Prefect of Istanbul after the 1913 coup. Minister of public works and the navy. Governor of Syria during World War I. Fled to Germany in 1918. Assassinated by an Armenian in Tblisi.
52. President of the Council of State in Said Halim Paşa's cabinet after the 1913 coup. Minister of Foreign Affairs and Justice in Talat Paşa's cabinet. Exiled to Malta in 1919, released in 1921. Tried for his role in the İzmir conspiracy in 1926, but was not charged. Between 1931 and 1946, he served as an independent MP for İzmir. He retired to his estate in Milas in 1946 and died in 1948.
53. Although Bahaettin Şakir never held an official political post after the 1908 revolution, he was one of the most influential people in the *Ittihat ve Terakki* party, both as a member of its central committee in 1912–18 and the chief of the political bureau of the Special Organizations in 1914–18.
54. One of the earliest members. A member of the central committee after the 1908 revolution. Minister of education in 1918. Fled the country before the Mondros armistice. Executed in 1926 for his alleged role in the İzmir conspiracy.
55. Especially after 1914, some scholars name Halil Menteşe as the third party in the triumvirate, rather than Cemal Paşa. See Ayhan Aktar, 'Paşam, biz bu harbe niçin girdik? Osmanlı Devleti'nin Savaşa Giriş Kararı (Şubat-Ekim 1914)', https://www.youtube.com/watch?v=WsbYxR3Oa8M.

56. For a fresh and thought-provoking article on Ziya Gökalp, see Dressler 2015. See also Ziya Gökalp's *Turkish Nationalism and Western Civilization*, translated and edited with an introduction by Niyazi Berkes (2022, Columbia University Press). For an excellent analysis on Gökalp's approach, see Parla 1985.
57. Mehmet Akif Ersoy was an Islamist activist and scholar of Albanian descent, who authored the Turkish National Anthem during the Turkish War of Independence and was the initial author of an official Turkish translation of the Koran.
58. *Teşkilat-ı Mahsusa* (Special Organization) was a secret organisation established under Enver Paşa within the *İttihat ve Terakki*. It was an intelligence and propaganda organisation that was active between 1913 and 1918. *Teşkilat* was officially established on 17 November 1913, and was later transformed, on 5 August 1914, into an official organisation under the Ministry of War. The *Teşkilât-ı Mahsusa* was officially dissolved on 9 October 1918, when the *İttihat ve Terakki* government was no longer in power.
59. Triple Entente describes the informal understanding between the Russian Empire, the French Third Republic and the United Kingdom of Great Britain and Ireland as well as Romania, which joined later.
60. On this declaration and its text, see Zürcher (2016) *Jihad and Islam in World War I* and Meriç (2014) 'Siyaset Fetva İlişkisi: Birinci Dünya Savaşında Cihat Fetvası'.
61. On this issue, see Göçek 2006. Also see Mann 2005, specifically 111–79; Suny 2015; and Morris and Zeevi 2019.
62. An excellent historical fiction that narrates the final years of the Ottoman Empire is Mithat Cemal Kuntay's (1885–1956) *Üç İstanbul*, which deals with the late Hamidian, *İttihat ve Terakki* and armistice periods in Istanbul. Life in Istanbul between 1918 and 1922 is very interestingly narrated in two other novels: Yakup Kadri Karaosmanoğlu's (1889–1974) *Sodom ve Gomorra* and Ahmet Hamdi Tanpınar's (1901–1963) *Sahnenin Dışındakiler*. On *Sahnenin Dışındakiler* (Those outside the scene), see Göknar 2003.
63. For a substantial study on *şeyhülislam* from 1789 to 1922, see Yakut 2005.
64. David Kushner was one of the first scholars to question the then prevalent narrative that asserted a 'weakening significance of the ulema in the Ottoman system' (Kushner 1987). İlber Ortaylı claims that 'the more the Empire modernised, the more the influence of the *İlmiye* class declined'; however, he adds: 'It should be acknowledged that it was precisely in this period that madrasah officials carried out the most important internal restructuring in the entire history of the Empire', underlining the importance of the *Medtesetü'l Kuzat* (madrasah of kadıs) (Ortaylı 2021: 179).

65. Masami Arai claims that the ethos of the *İttihat ve Terakki* administration sought to Islamise the state, not to secularise it (Arai 1992).
66. For relations between the *Meclis-i Meşayih*, *ulema* and *tarikat*, see Kara 2003: 325–57.
67. For *tarikat*s in the Ottoman Empire, see Gölpınarlı 1969: 187–230, 257–92.
68. For the rise and expansion of the Nakşibendi-Halidi suborder in Ottoman lands during the nineteenth century, see Abu-Manneh 2001: 13–57.
69. When Ziyaüddin Gümüşhanevi died, Abdülhamid II ordered him entombed at the entrance to Süleyman the Magnificient's *türbe* (grave/mausoleum) (Karpat 2012: 215).
70. The group was named thus after their red headgear. See Yar 2016: 27–30.
71. For the historical transformation of the Safavid sufi order into a Shia state in the course of the fifteenth century, see Baltacıoğlu-Brammer 2021. When the Safavid state was founded in 1501, the Ottoman territories had not yet expanded eastwards from Sivas, so the region was not under Ottoman control. Instead of fighting the Ottomans, Shah Ismail, a member of the Erdebil Hearth, fought for independence and headed east. On the Ottoman Sunni state versus Safavid Shia propaganda, see Ocak 1999: 82–5.
72. In nineteenth-century Ottoman censuses, the Kızılbaş were counted as Şii Muslims. See the census records in Karpat 1985: 57. 'It is interesting to note that up until as late as 1912 the Armenian Patriarchate listed the Kizilbas, the Zazas, and the Tchareklis as groups belonging to "other religions", although they all were Muslim' (Karpat 1985: 53 n. 29). For the formation of Islam-Turk heterodoxy in Anatolia as a historical background to the Alevis, see Ocak [1980] 2000.
73. On these regiments, see Klein 2011.
74. For *İttihat ve Terakki* policies regarding the Kızılbaş Kurds of Dersim and others, see Dressler 2013: 115–22. Also, for Armenians who converted to Alevism, see Gündoğan 2022.
75. According to Enver Behnan Şapolyo, Talat Pasha, in his first days as grand vizier, said in the general assembly of the *İttihat ve Terakki*: 'We have taken over this nation. But Anatolia is a closed box for us, we must first get to know the inside of it, and then I believe that we may serve this nation in a worthy manner.' Ziya Gökalp then said: 'We made a political revolution. In other words, we changed the political form by establishing a constitutional administration. However, the greatest revolution is the social revolution. The revolutions we can make in our social structure, in the field of culture, will be the biggest and most productive. This can only be achieved by getting to know the social morphology and social physiology of Turkish society. These are also social institutions. The

most important of these are the various religious beliefs of Anatolia, the sects, Turkmen tribes . . . Let's send friends who are deemed scientifically qualified to examine these institutions to open this box.' Thus, Baha Said was sent to examine the Kızılbaş and Bektashis, Bursalı Mehmet Tahir and Hasan Fehmi Hoca were sent to examine the Ahis, and Esat Uras was sent to examine the Armenians, and these people submitted their reports to the Ministry of Interior as a result of their surveys. See Şapolyo 1964: 2–3.

76. 'The issue of apostasy from Islam (*irtidad*) is a particularly thorny one. The commonly accepted belief among Muslims is that the apostate (*mürtedi*) is liable to execution according to the *sharia*' (Deringil 2000: 550). See also Deringil 2012: 20–3.
77. For an interesting account of these communities through the eyes of a British traveller (a major and intelligence agent) in the late nineteenth–early twentieth century, see Soane 1912.
78. See also Kamouzis 2012. In his chapter, Dimitris Kamouzis not only highlights the role played by the different elites within the *Rum milleti* after Tanzimat, but also surveys similar experiences in other *millet*s.
79. For further information on the subject, see Artanian 1988.
80. For a development of the issue, see Markova 1983.
81. For detailed information on the Greek Orthodox Church, see Gondicas and Issawi (eds) 1999. However, it should also be noted that the Greek reaction to the reform edict was: 'the state has made us equal with the Jews. We were satisfied with Muslim superiority' (Hanioğlu 2008: 75).
82. Jacobites are known as the Syriac/Syrian (*Süryani*) Orthodox. For more information, see Joseph 1983.
83. On the Copts, see Meinardus 1999.
84. Melkite Catholics, or Greek Catholics as they are sometimes known, were the Orthodox Christians of Syria who chose to accept the spiritual authority of the Roman Catholic Pope in the eighteenth century.
85. For further reading, see Levy 1994.
86. For these conversions as survival, see Deringil 2009 and Deringil 2012: 197–239.
87. For two relatively early but descriptive works, see Çakır 1994 and Demirdirek 1998; for press and gender in the Hamidian era, see Frierson 2005; for a PhD thesis that analyses the gendered representations of Ottoman-Turkish modernisation focusing on the debates in Ottoman women's periodicals, see Karaman 2016.

2

A SINGLE-PARTY REGIME

> Governments are our enemies; nations are our friends and our righteous rebellion is the force in our hearts
> Halide Edip Adıvar, 'Sultanahmet Protest on 6 June 1919' ([1962] 2007: 39)

The Armistice of Mondros (Mudros/30 October 1918)[1] gave the Entente powers the right to occupy any part of the Ottoman lands they might deem necessary for security reasons. Soon after the immediate occupation of most parts of the Empire in accordance with the terms of the Armistice, a resistance movement began to be organised in Anatolia.

Struggle for Independence (1919–23)

The occupation of Izmir by Greek forces on 15 May 1919 was an important stage in the start of the national struggle in Anatolia. Local *Müdafa-i Hukuk Cemiyetleri* (Defence of National Rights Societies)[2] had held twenty-eight separate congresses in Anatolia by 1920 (Findley 2010: 221). As an outcome of these meetings, a steering committee was elected and Mustafa Kemal (1881–1938) made its president.[3] In December 1919, the Representative Committee moved to Ankara (Zürcher 2017: 151). The leadership rallied the Anatolian-Turkish Muslims by emphasising their common religion, shared history and joint territory (Yıldız 2001: 89–101). Mustafa Kemal also managed to win the support of the Kurdish notables and religious leaders (Ünlü 2018: 148–9).[4]

Meanwhile, the Ottoman capital was occupied twice, first on 13 November 1918 and then on 16 March 1920. In the first occupation, important and strategic points within Istanbul were taken under control, but the Ottoman administration was left intact; with the second occupation, the bureaucratic apparatus was created anew by the occupation forces. The landing of troops in Istanbul by the Allied Powers led to heated and angry debates in the Ottoman Parliamentary Assembly. These debates led to the end of the Assembly, and the Ottoman parliament was dissolved on 21 December 1918 by order of the Sultan.

In Istanbul, *Şeyhülislam* Dürrizâde Abdullah Efendi (1867–1923) issued a *fetva* (fatwa) on 11 April 1920 declaring that the resistance forces in Anatolia were infidels, and that it was incumbent on believers to kill them. Five days later, another *fetva* was issued, this one by the Mehmet Rifat Efendi (1861–1941/later Börekçi), the mufti of the Ankara government, declaring that that the caliph was the prisoner of the infidels, and it was the duty of the faithful to save him and the Ottoman state (Mango 1999: 275). Subsequently, a circular which Mustafa Kemal sent out on 21 April 1920 about the inauguration of the Assembly provided for ceremonies that would touch religious sentiments (Erdem 2021: 1060–2). Thus, while the date initially chosen for the opening of the Assembly was 22 April, a Thursday, Friday was later preferred, as the Muslim holy day,[5] and it was decided that the inauguration ceremony should take place on 23 April 1920.

When the name of the Assembly was discussed at a private meeting held on the evening of 22 April, Hamdullah Suphi Bey proposed '*kurultay*' (convention), a word of Turkish/Turanian origin, while Celalettin Arif Bey, the president of the last Ottoman Parliamentary Assembly, suggested '*Meclis-i Kebir-i Milli*' (Grand National Assembly). However, following a proposal made by Mustafa Kemal Paşa, the Assembly was ultimately named the '*Türkiye Büyük Millet Meclisi*' (Turkish Grand National Assembly/TBMM) (Adıvar [1962] 2007: 135).[6]

As planned, sheep were sacrificed, the Koran was recited by Mehmet Rifat Efendi (Kutay 2022: 182)[7] and relics of the Prophet were carried in a procession accompanied by a crowd shouting '*Allahuekber*' (God is great). The procession stopped in front of the building, where more prayers were recited and more sheep were sacrificed (Mango 1999: 277).[8] A long speech by Mustafa Kemal then transferred leadership of the national resistance movement to the

Türkiye Büyük Millet Meclisi (Atatürk 1997: 12–14). A declaration was prepared and announced on 25 April 1920; it stated that the aim of the TBMM was to save the Caliph-sultan from enemy tutelage, to liberate Istanbul from enemy troops, and to not let the nation be inflamed by enemy provocations. It was repeatedly stated at the meeting on 28 April 1920 that the Sultanate and the Caliphate were to be saved (Sarıçoban 2019: 1577).[9]

An act dated 2 May 1920 introduced the *İcra Vekilleri Heyeti* (Committee of Executive Commissioners), a government composed of eleven ministers. The first line provides for a *Şer'iyye ve Evkaf Vekaleti* (Ministry of Religious Affairs and Pious Foundations) to be competent for religious services, religious education, religious publishing, the issuing of *fetva*, and religious foundations.[10] The *Şer'iyye ve Evkaf Vekaleti* was later abolished, on 3 March 1924 (Kaplan 2011: 117–27).

The special commission that was charged with drafting a constitution finalised its draft on 20 January 1921, and the document was approved by the Assembly. The 1921 Constitution (*Teşkilat-ı Esasiye Kanunu*), which was written to cater for the needs of an extraordinary era and to fill in for the lack of a government, consisted of twenty-four articles. The first nine articles concerned the basic principles underlying the state. It stated that sovereignty belonged unconditionally to the nation (Article 1), and that the executive and legislative powers belonged to the Assembly (Article 2).[11]

The first National Assembly was quite a heterogeneous body, and differences in ethos were quick to emerge. In March 1921, a group called the *Muhafaza-i Mukaddesat Cemiyeti* (Association for the Preservation of Sacred Institutions) was formed, led by Hoca Raif (Dinç), a cleric and one of the organisers of the Congress of Erzurum in 1919. Mustafa Kemal organised his more dependable followers into the *Müdafa-i Hukuk Grubu* (Defence of Rights Group) in May 1921. The opposition founded the *İkinci Grup* (Second Group)[12] in the Assembly early in 1922 (Zürcher 2017: 159).

After the victory at Sakarya,[13] the Grand National Assembly granted Mustafa Kemal the title *Halâskar Gazi*[14] (Liberator and Warrior for Islam) (Mango 1999: 322). When the Council of Ministers decided to organise a final attack on 14 August 1922, the Turkish corps marched on the offensive. The attack started on 26 August 1922, the Turkish Army entered İzmir on 9 September 1922, and the war ended on 18 September 1922, when the Greek

Army quit Anatolia completely. Eventually, the glorious victory won by the resistance movement was sealed by an Armistice signed on 11 October 1922, in Mudanya, a coastal town in the south of the Sea of Marmara. On 1 November 1922, the Grand National Assembly voted to abolish the sultanate, and Sultan Mehmed VI Vahdeddin was succeeded as caliph by his cousin Abdülmecid, who was elected to the office by the Assembly.

Establishing a Republic (1923–38)

The negotiations in Lausanne came to an end, and the treaty was signed on 24 July 1923, nullifying the Treaty of Sèvres.[15] The treaty provided for a compulsory population exchange; one in which religion was equated with nationality. On 30 January 1923, a protocol had already been signed between Turkey and Greece on the exchange of the Greek and Turkish peoples. According to this protocol, beginning on 1 May 1923, a compulsory exchange was to be undertaken between Turkish nationals of the Greek Orthodox religion settled in Turkish territory and Greek nationals of the Muslim religion settled in Greek territory. None of these persons was to be permitted to return to Turkey without the permission of the Turkish Government or to Greece without the permission of the Greek Government. The protocol also provided for some exceptions: namely, Greeks residing in Constantinople, and Muslims residing in Western Thrace. Article 2 of the protocol stated that: 'As restricted by the 1912 Law, all Greeks residing in the City of Constantinople before 30 October 1918, shall be deemed to be Greek inhabitants of Constantinople (*İstanbul'un Rum ahalisi*). Muslims settled in the territory east of the demarcation line established by the Treaty of Bucharest of 1913 shall be considered as Muslims residing in Western Thrace (Muslim inhabitants of Western Thrace).' The 1.2 million Christian Orthodox population of Turkey was considered Greek and resettled to Greece (many spoke only Turkish). Similarly, nearly 400,000 Muslim inhabitants of Greece were deemed to be Turks and resettled in Turkey (Mavrogordatos 2003: 129; Findley 2010: 226), as citizens respectively of those countries.[16]

The Assembly voted to proclaim Turkey a republic on 29 October 1923; Mustafa Kemal was elected its President. On 9 September 1923, the *Halk Fırkası* (later *Cumhuriyet Halk Partisi*: CHP) was officially established.

The Sunni character of the new regime may be surmised from several legal regulations of the time. For instance, the *Köy Kanunu* (Village Law) of

18 March 1924 includes building a mosque (*mescid*) among the actions required of all villagers. And although the 1927 official population figures reveal that 80 per cent of the population was resident in rural areas including non-Muslims and Alevis, no exception was provided for non-Muslims and Alevis in the Village Law (Aslan 2021).

On 20 April 1924, a new constitution, the *Teşkilat-ı Esasiye Kanunu*, was ratified in the TBMM. In the context of state and religion relations, the 1924 Constitution initially stated that the official religion of the Republic of Turkey was Islam, and that the Grand Assembly was to issue legislation and apply *şeriat* norms. The oaths to be sworn by the President and members of the parliament were formulated in religious terms. However, these religious regulations were abolished in 1928, resulting in the secularisation of the 1924 Constitution.

On 1 June 1924, a list of 150 people whom the decision-making elite of the time considered traitors to the new regime was issued by a decree (no. 544) of the Council of Ministers on the grounds that they had committed high treason under the Law on High Treason (*Hıyanet-i Vataniye Kanunu*) enacted on 29 April 1920. Three years into the exile of the 150, the Assembly resolved additionally that they should be stripped of their citizenship, property and right to inherit by a law dated 28 May 1927. In 1938, the Turkish government granted the 150 a limited amnesty (Özoğlu 2011: 15–78).

Nineteen twenty-three was also a year in which the founding political elite of Turkey were still using Islamic jargon to emphasise the significance of religion and religious unity for the emerging nation.[17] On 7 February 1923, Mustafa Kemal addressed the public from the pulpit in the Balıkesir Zağnos Paşa Mosque. The significance of the venue apart, the context of the speech was significant for its Islamic framing:

> Allah birdir, şanı büyüktür . . . Arkadaşlar! Cenab-ı Peygamber mesâisinde iki dârai iki haneye mâlik bulunuyordu. Biri kendi hanesi, diğeri Allah'ın evi idi. Millet işlerini, Allah'ın evinde hallederdi . . . Efendiler! Camiler, birbirimizin yüzüne bakmaksızın yatıp kalkmak için yapılmamıştır. Camiler itaat ve ibadet ile beraber din ve dünya için neler yapılmak lazım geldiğini düşünmek, yani meşveret için yapılmıştır . . . İşte biz de burada din ve dünya için, istikbal ve istiklâlimiz için, bilhassa hakimiyetimiz için neler düşündüğümüzü meydana koyalım . . . Minberler halkın dimağları, vicdanları için bir menba-ı feyz, bir menba-ı nur olmuştur.

(Allah is one, Allah is glorified . . . Friends! His Excellency the Prophet had two homes. One was his own, one was the house of Allah. He used to do his public work in the house of Allah. Sirs! Mosques are not built for us to prostrate ourselves and then stand up again without looking at each other. Mosques are built for debates, that is for consultation on what has to be done in religious and worldly affairs, as well as for obedience to God and prayer. Let us here divulge what we have thought about the sacred and the profane, about the future and our independence, and especially about our sovereignty.)

(Atatürk 1997: 98–100)[18]

However, 3 March 1924 was a very significant date in the history of modern Turkey. This is due to three consequent legislative actions in terms of state–religion relations: Law on the Annulment of the Ministry of Şeriat and Religious Foundations and the Ministry of the General Staff; Law on the Unification of Education; and Law on the Annulment of the Caliphate and the Exile of the Ottoman Dynasty from the Frontiers of the Turkish Republic. Third March 1924 is the date on which the pillars of the *laik* regime were erected through law. The religious realm was redefined by legislation (Kara 2004: 180–1).

The Diyanet

Law 429 (on the Annulment of the Ministry of *Şeriat* and Religious Foundations and the Ministry of the General Staff) abolished the *Şeriye ve Evkaf Vekaleti* (Ministry of Religious Affairs), and instituted a new administrative unit called the *Diyanet İşleri Reisliği* (Presidency of Religious Affairs). In other words, the new regulation placed the management of religious affairs in the hands of an administrative unit, not a Cabinet ministry. In terms of administrative law, a ministry is hierarchically the apex of the central administration, and it is a political unit. Thus, the decision not to place the institution of 'religion' within a political body was a key element of the overall policy adopted by Turkey's founding political decision-making elite, who wished to establish a secular state and to modernise society. They did not want to have a ministry within the Cabinet dealing with religious affairs. Instead, by assigning religious affairs to an administrative unit, the ruling elite both took religion under their control and sought to detract from the potentially sacred significance of the Diyanet.

The first article of Law 429 stated that the Diyanet had been formed as a part of the Republic to administer all provisions concerning faith, rituals and the institutions of Islam. The article also explicitly pronounced that all other affairs were to be legislated on by the parliament, namely the Grand National Assembly of Turkey, and implemented by the Cabinet formed by that body. This was an attempt by the decision-making elite of early republican Turkey to secularise the sources and references of the legal system, and their attempt has proved successful to date.

The goal of the new leadership in this period was to secularise and modernise not only the state and the 'political', but also society, which it would transform into a modern body. In fact, the radical programme of reform and westernisation that the republican cadres pursued in the 1920s and 1930s had begun earlier, in Ottoman times in the mid nineteenth century, with – in particular – the adoption of Western codes and political principles. In this context, the major difference between Ottoman and republican westernisation/secularisation was the spectrum of their *telos*; also, *laiklik* was the pillar for the republican founding elite, which designed the Diyanet as an administrative tool for the regulation of Islam. As Levent Köker puts it: 'it is not at all clear that Kemalist nationalism was anti-religious. Rather, it was trying to articulate religion with the new *raison d'état*, and this is illustrated, I believe, by institutionalized state control over religious institutions and practices' (Köker 1997: 70). Nevertheless, the absence of a clergy in Islam has been a means to legitimise state intervention in religion, and the categorisation of the latter as a public service. Also, it is worth underlining that:

> the term *Diyanet* was carefully chosen in legislative discussions to express religious affairs in the sense of 'matters of personal piety' over its potential alternative *diniye*, which could have implied the new institution's religious responsibilities in the fields of the economy, society, policing and education, which are intentionally distributed to other branches of government. (Hassan 2011: 454)

Therefore, as Bryan S. Turner and Berna Zengin Arslan note, the foundation of the Diyanet not only defined 'religion' more narrowly as a set of worshipping activities (*ibadet*) and beliefs (*itikat*), it also opened up a space within the state for the representation of a 'true' Islam (Turner with Zengin Arslan 2013: 214). However, it should be noted that a preference for using adjectives like 'sound' (Bardakoğlu 2004: 369), 'authentic' (Bardakoğlu 2004: 371), 'true',[19] 'healthy',[20] 'objective' and 'accurate'[21] indicates an essentialist approach that produces categories of legitimate and illegitimate religions. This may be read in line with the legal and political construction of religion in early republican Turkey. İsmail Kara reads the Diyanet throughout the history of the Republic as an institution that 'fulfils the demands of the governments on religious issues; paves the way for new religious interpretations in the direction of modernization; legitimizes the new interpretations; dims, changes and transforms the way the masses perceive and live their religion' (Kara [2008] 2017: 115). In Markus Dressler's words, it is the role of the Diyanet to define, represent, organise and regulate public forms of Islam (Dressler 2010: 125).

Börekçizade Mehmet Rifat Efendi, one of the most prominent figures in the struggle for independence, was appointed the first president of the Diyanet on 1 April 1924. He would serve in this post for seventeen years, until his death on 5 March 1941.

Unification of Education

The Law on the Unification of Education (*Tevhid-i Tedrisat Kanunu*/Law 430) abolished all religious instruction in state schools and placed education under state control through the Ministry of National Education (Kaplan 1999: 159–60). This constituent regulation aimed to put an end to the dual structure of education as an amalgam of secular and religious educational institutions. The Law was another means by which the republican founding elite could keep Islamic teachings under control. Being very much aware of the importance of Islam for the Muslim nation of Turkey, the answer to the question 'Who is a Turk?' given by Hamdullah Suphi Tanrıöver (1885–1966), the Republic of Turkey's second minister of education, is significant: 'He who speaks Turkish, is a Muslim, and bears a love of Turkishness is a Turk. In him, we seek a unity of language, unity of religion, and unity of will' (Salmoni 2000: 26). İsmail Hakkı Baltacıoğlu, one of the best-known pedagogues in late Ottoman and modern Turkey, is reported to have responded thus when asked, in the presence of Mustafa Kemal, whether religion was a necessary component of the national curriculum: 'Religion is a social institution. It exists in reality. But the state is not obliged to teach it in its schools. State education must be laicized' (Ergin 1977: 1648). As a result of the Law on the Unification of Education, a total of 479 medreses and Koranic courses were closed, and compulsory schools which followed a national curriculum devoid of religious instruction were established (Agai 2007: 150).

Abolishing the Caliphate

The Caliphate had emerged as a significant political issue in the late Ottoman period, because this symbol of the spiritual leadership of the Muslims served the interests of the Ottoman government, even as its power over territory inhabited by Muslims in Eastern Europe waned (Binder 1988: 129).[22] By a similar logic, the Caliphate was retained even after the abolition of the Sultanate. The Caliphate in Istanbul claimed spiritual authority over several hundred million Muslims, an overwhelming majority of them under colonial rule. In time, strategic reasons would lead the republican founding elite to consider abolishing the institution. In his speech preceding the abolition of the Caliphate, Mustafa Kemal declared that:

> For salvation in the next world and the happiness of the nation in this world, it became imperative to move decisively and without delay to free our consciences and religious beliefs, which are sacred and sublime, from politics and from all accretions which have proved to be an instrument for all kinds of shady and unstable games of interests and ambitions. (İnalcık 2017: 123)

Upon the enactment of the Law on the Annulment of the Caliphate[23] and the Exile of the Ottoman Dynasty from the Frontiers of the Turkish Republic (Law 431, 3 March 1924), the last caliph, Abdülmecid Efendi, was exiled to France.[24] The abolition of the Caliphate was the most visible sign of the increasingly autocratic hold Mustafa Kemal and his most trusted colleagues exercised over the Assembly (Finkel 2005: 546).[25]

Further Steps Towards Secularisation[26]

The three enactments of 3 March 1924 were followed by another statute, the Law on the Annulment of the Religious Courts and Modification of the Judgement of the Organization of Judiciary, on 8 April 1924. This legislation secularised the judicial system completely. In addition to these regulations, a policy of privatising religion was forcefully implemented: the law banning religious shrines – which is to say the *tekke* (dervish convents), *zaviye*[27] and mausoleums (*Tekke ve Zaviyelerle Türbelerin Seddine ve Türbedarlıklar ile Bir Takım Unvanların Men ve İlgasına Dair Kanun*, 30 November 1925) – was an additional means for erasing religion from the public sphere.[28] Konya's Mevlana Dervish Lodge, a very rich complex with Seljuk and Ottoman architecture and artifacts, was reopened to visitors as a museum by a Council of Ministers decision dated 6 April 1926 (Kara 1977: 274 fn75). Then, on 26 December 1925, the Assembly adopted the international Christian calendar and twenty-four-hour clock.[29]

On 17 February 1926 the Assembly enacted a Civil Code (*Türk Kanun-ı Medenisi*) modelled on Swiss legislation. It regulated the relationships experienced at every stage in an individual's social life from birth to death, including personal rights, family law and inheritance. The Code was thus yet another significant piece of social engineering aimed at westernisation and secularisation. Women also gained a set of new rights: marriage agreements were henceforth to be made in the presence of a civil servant rather than a clergyman; divorce at the husband's discretion was ended; and women acquired equal inheritance rights. 'But, as in many European countries at the time, men retained a privileged position as heads of the household: women could not take outside work or travel abroad without the permission of the *chef de famille*' (Mango 1999: 437). The preamble to the *Türk Kanun-ı Medenisi*, written by Mahmut Esat Bozkurt, Minister of Justice at the time, included the following:

> States that have a legal body with religious references cannot meet the needs of the nation and the people, in short because religions have dogmatic norms. Life goes on, necessities change rapidly, religious norms become little more than dead words in the presence of life, which never stops moving. Not changing is a must for religions. Consequently, religions should remain a matter of individual conscience. This is the most significant difference between modern and ancient civilizations. Laws that have religious references link the societies that enforce them to the primitive eras in which those religions emerged, thus impeding their progress.[30]

On 20 May 1928, the law adopting the numerals used internationally was enacted by parliament (*Beynelmilel Erkamın Kabulü Hakkında Kanun*). The republican decision-making elite took one of its most radical steps on 1 November 1928, replacing the Arabic alphabet with a new Turkish alphabet based on the Latin script (*Türk Harflerinin Kabul ve Tatbiki Hakkında Kanun*). This had been a highly contentious issue since the 1910s. At the Izmir Economic Congress in February–March 1923, three workers' delegates proposed a motion in favour of adopting the Latin alphabet. However, the chairman, Kazım (Karabekir), overruled the motion out of order, since it would be damaging to the unity of Islam. He went on to make a speech in which he noted:

> At once, we shall be placing a splendid weapon in the hands of all Europe; they will declare to the Islamic world that the Turks have accepted the foreign writing and turned Christian. The diabolical idea towards which our enemies are working is precisely this. (Lewis 1999: 32)[31]

Nevertheless, Mustafa Kemal was determined to change not only the alphabet, but the language as well. Completing the legislation, courses were run in 1929 to teach reading and writing all over Turkey.[32] Ayasofya (Hagia Sophia) was converted into a museum by a decree of the Council of Ministers on 24 November 1934; when it opened on 2 February 1935, it was the world's first mosque-turned-museum (Öztığ and Adısönmez 2023).[33]

Reactionary Developments

On 17 November 1924, the *Terakkiperver Cumhuriyet Fırkası* (Progressive Republican Party), the first opposition party in republican Turkey, was established by thirty-two deputies from the People's Party including Kazım (Karabekir), Rauf (Orbay), Ali Fuat (Cebesoy), Refet (Bele) and Adnan (Adıvar). This was preceded by friction throughout the winter and spring of 1924 between the wing of the People's Party led by Mustafa Kemal and İsmet (İnönü) and the opposing group led by Hüseyin Rauf. 'The actual split took place in the context of a debate over the government's handling of the resettlement of Muslims from Greece, especially with respect to the possessions of the Greeks who had had to leave, which was that had given rise to widespread corruption' (Zürcher 2017: 169). The New Party's programme revealed its liberal character by advocating decentralisation, the separation of powers, and evolutionary rather than revolutionary change. The party was closed down on 3 June 1925, for allegedly supporting the Şeyh Said rebellion and seeking to exploit religion for political considerations.[34]

The so-called Şeyh Said revolt began on 13 February 1925 in Diyarbakır; it was to be the first of many Kurdish uprisings in the 1920s. Şeyh Said (1865/66–1925) was a Nakşibendi sheik from Palu, Elazığ. The abolition of the Caliphate, on top of the violent oppression of the Kurdish peoples and language sparked a series of rebellions in the region. The uprising, which was overtly Kurdish and Islamist in character, had been put down by the end of May 1925 with much blood shed (Finkel 2005: 550). On 4 March 1925, Prime Minister İsmet (İnönü) introduced a bill in the Assembly which passed into law as the *Takrir-i Sükun Kanunu* (Law on the Maintenance of Order); it empowered the government to suppress actions that caused 'disturbance of the order' over the next two years, and to hand the perpetrators over to courts named Independence Tribunals (*İstiklal Mahkemeleri*).[35] This regulation was used to suppress the Kurds, but also to silence all opposition (Öngider 2009: 312–18).

Independence Tribunals[36] were initially established on 18 September 1920 to try illegalities committed during the Independence War. Later, they were used, especially between 1923 and 1927, to sanction opponents both actual and potential of the new regime. For instance, the Ankara Independence Tribunal condemned İskilipli Atıf Hoca to death for opposing the Hat Law[37] (*Şapka İhdası Hakkında Kanun*, 25 November 1925), and he was hanged on 4 February 1926. The plot to assassinate Mustafa Kemal in İzmir in 1926 was also used to silence the political opposition; even though the plot was genuine, the measures taken afterwards were excessive and helped make Mustafa Kemal and his close circle the unrivalled rulers of Turkey.[38]

Mustafa Kemal, growing aware of the growing resentment and discontent against the new regime, asked Fethi (Okyar) to establish a new party. Consequently, Fethi Bey founded the *Serbest Cumhuriyet Fırkası* (Liberal Republican Party) on 12 August 1930, with a programme that advocated 'a liberal economic policy and encouragement of foreign investment, as well as freedom of speech and direct elections'[39] (Zürcher 2017: 180). In October 1930 local elections, the

Serbest Cumhuriyet Fırkası managed to win twenty-four of the 502 municipalities. Even though that was a relatively low ratio, the election outcomes caused unease among *Halk Partisi* members. On 16 November 1930, Fethi felt he had little choice but to close down the *Serbest Cumhuriyet Fırkası*.[40]

On 23 December 1930, in Menemen, a small town close to İzmir, a group of dervishes led by a certain Derviş Mehmed demonstrated for the restoration of the *şeriat* and the Caliphate. They were met by a group of soldiers under Lieutenant Mustafa Fehmi Kubilay, who demanded that the mob surrender. Instead, the soldiers were attacked by the demonstrators, who also cut off Kubilay's head and paraded with it on a stick. Even though the ringleaders, including Mehmed, were killed on the spot, the incident provoked a major response from the government: martial law was declared, over 2000 arrests were made, and twenty-eight people were executed.[41]

Nutuk *(the Speech)*

Mustafa Kemal gave a long speech at the Second Congress of *Cumhuriyet Halk Fırkası* in Ankara on 15–20 October 1927; on stage for roughly six hours a day, the speech was some 36.5 hours long.[42] In Andrew Mango's words, it was 'an apologia and a polemic' (Mango 1999: 462). In *Nutuk*, he gives his account of the years between the Independence War and the first years of the Republic. The text not only refers to military, political and diplomatic history, it also provides critical portraits of various persons, with Mustafa Kemal explicitly expressing his views and judgements on many of his opponents, including Rauf (Orbay).

Toni Alaranta asserts that Mustafa Kemal began to establish himself as the new 'Father of the Nation' with this speech:

> Although Mustafa Kemal was not given the honorary name of 'Atatürk' (the Father Turk) officially until 24 November 1934, in the *Nutuk* Mustafa Kemal is already Atatürk: the narrator of the *Nutuk* already possesses signs of the 'Father' . . . The assertion that the image of the Father Turk was born in the *Nutuk* and has been at the centre of the symbolic universe of Turkish political culture ever since is, with the idea of the enlightenment as a telos of history, the most important argument for claiming that the basic legitimation tools employed by the Kemalist state elite were constructed in the *Nutuk*. (Alaranta 2011: 103)

In 1928, a year after Mustafa Kemal's seminal speech, an autobiography written in response by Halide Edip (Adıvar), who had escaped to Europe in 1926 with her husband Adnan Adıvar (1882–1955) after they had been accused of treason, was published.[43] Her *My Share in the Turkish Ordeal* was followed up with several other accounts of the events of the Independence War in Turkish, but none would be allowed to be published in Mustafa Kemal's lifetime.[44]

In 1963, Tarık Buğra published *Küçük Ağa* (The Little Aga), a novel on the Independence War, which takes a critical look at the transition from the Ottoman Empire to the Republic. In his preface, the author states that:

> At that time, as always, this nation felt the love of homeland and the well-being of the state intertwined with religion. As always, all wars had been a holy war. The symbols of homeland and nation were united with the symbol of religion on one flag which were three sacred sensitivities. The destiny of this nation, and this nation itself, had always been this flag throughout the centuries. And this flag was conveyed by the representative of the God in the world (*halife-yi rû-yi zemin*), the ruler of the universe (*şah-ı cihan*). It was displayed in order to topple crowns and thrones, to conquer new lands so they could be added to our own. Our lives were regulated by this tradition. One day, this nation which had always believed it existed with this tradition, was called under a different flag. The flag was another flag, the hand that unfurled the flag was another hand. This new flag was a different one, the hand that displayed this flag was a different hand. But this new flag, too, was calling for action for habitus and for fatherland. The hope for liberation was counterposed against the six centuries of traditions of livelihood. The history of no nation has ever seen such a tragic contradiction. Taking the right side in this conflict was no longer a virtue; it required a superiority of vision that could not be expected of everyone. On the other hand, you could not blame those who were wrong, for as guilty as the violet is for its purple colour, so guilty were these people for being wrong. The great contradiction between this hope of salvation and six centuries of tradition led to a tragedy even darker than defeat and foreign occupation.

This is a very insightful analysis of the dilemmas and hesitations involved in taking or changing sides in the early 1920s.[45]

Reform in Religion

The reform of the religion process, which had been accelerated by the enactment of the three consecutive laws on 3 March 1924[46] continued with the *Dini Islah Beyannamesi* (Declaration on the Improvement of Religion) in 1928. The document was prepared by the Faculty of Divinity at *Dârülfünun* (İstanbul University). That the language of the rituals would henceforth be Turkish is one of its highlights. However, the declaration did not receive the expected official support. In Bernard Lewis's words:

> It was possible to turn the Ottoman sultanate into a national republic, with a president, ministries and parliament. It was not possible to turn the mosque into a Muslim church, with pews, organ, and an imam-precentor. In all but one respect, the recommendations of the committee were a dead letter, and even the Faculty of Divinity itself proved to be premature. The teachers, themselves of the *medrese* tradition, did not take kindly to the task assigned to them, and the atmosphere of the time was not conductive to its realization. (Lewis 1961: 415)[47]

Even though the attempt at improving religion was abandoned, it was accepted that Turkish was to be used in religious rituals. In fact, such tendencies had been notable for quite some time.[48] Ziya Gökalp wrote *Vatan* (Homeland) in 1918:

> A country where the call to prayer is in Turkish sung
> So that the peasant would know what the prayers command
> A country where the Koran at school is recited in the Turkish tongue
> So that what God orders will be manifested to all, old or young
> O, the son of Turk, that is your homeland[49]

The project for Turkification of Islamic rituals accelerated in 1932 by direct order of Mustafa Kemal. Hafız Yaşar (Okur) recited the Koran in Turkish for the first time at Istanbul's Yerebatan Mosque on 22 January 1932.[50] On 18 July 1932, Diyanet Regulation 636 announced that the *ezan* (call to prayer) would soon be recited in Turkish. On 2 July 1941, an amendment to the Turkish Penal Law provided for three months' imprisonment and a fine of

10 to 200 liras for reciting the *ezan* in Arabic, thereby making Turkish compulsory for the *ezan* (Gözaydın 2020: 28).⁵¹ Resistance to the Turkish *ezan* during the 1930s would result in several arrests. The memoirs of a village preacher in Güneyce in the Black Sea region, Hafız Mehmet Kara, reveals antipathy to the compulsory Turkish *ezan*: as a child he was asked by the older villagers to recite the Turkish *ezan*, so they would not have to recite it in Turkish themselves (Kara 2000: 92).

From 1932 to 1947, religious education was given only in Koran courses run under the auspices of the Diyanet. The Ministry of Education tried to have these courses brought under its regulation, but Mehmet Rıfat Efendi (Börekçi), the Diyanet chair, resisted, labelling the courses vocational and increasing their number to thirty-six (Kaplan 2011: 15). In 1933, when *İstanbul Dârülfünun* was reconstituted as Istanbul University, the Faculty of Divinity was closed. The Islam Studies Institute was established in its place within Istanbul University's Faculty of Letters. However, this Institute, which was a research-only institution with no teaching capacity, was itself closed down in 1936 (Tunçay and Özen 1984: 5–28).⁵²

The transformation of values targeted by *laiklik* through education is quite revealing of the positivist understanding espoused by Mustafa Kemal and his circle and labelled as 'positive and empirical science'. If we accept that positivism was reflected in Young Turk thinking, and moved from there to Kemalism in its Comtean form, then we must accept that the Kemalist understanding and practice of secularism sought to replace Islamic belief with a new religion, a scientific faith (Köker 1990: 168).

As an ideology, Kemalism appears to be moving step by step in early republican Turkey towards becoming a 'civic religion'.⁵³ Mete Tunçay writes that Mustafa Kemal looked coldly upon the growing sanctification of his person, but he did not object to these efforts to fill the urban population's spiritual void (Tunçay 2005: 338).

Unification of Cumhuriyet Halk Fırkası *and the State Apparatus*

On 10 November 1924, the name *Halk Fırkası* (People's Party) was extended to *Cumhuriyet Halk Fırkası* (Republican People's Party). At the Party's Fourth Congress in 1935, it would be renamed once again, this time to *Cumhuriyet Halk Partisi*, and İsmet (İnönü) would declare that congruency between the state apparatus and the Party organisation would henceforth be official policy (Zürcher 2017: 178). On 18 June 1936, the Ministry of the Interior was annexed to the General Secretariat of the *Cumhuriyet Halk Partisi*: as a result, the provincial governors would automatically head their local Party branches. On 5 February 1937, the six objectives of *Cumhuriyet Halk Fırkası* – nationalism, populism, statism, *laiklik* and revolutionism – would be enshrined in the Constitution as the guiding principles of the Republic of Turkey.

From 1923 to 1946, 1037 individuals would be elected as members of parliament. Of them, 1032 were either Party candidates or independent candidates supported by the Party. Only in the 1923 general election did two candidates succeed in being elected to parliament without the Party's support: Zeki (Kadirbeyoğlu) from Gümüşhane and Emin (Sazak) from Eskişehir. In the by-elections at the end of 1924 and start of 1925, three others would win more votes than the *Halk Fırkası* candidates: Şevket (Ödül) from Kırklareli, Zeki (Karakimseli) from Kayseri, and (Sakallı) Nurettin Paşa from Bursa. After that, until 1946, the membership of the Assembly would be drawn exclusively from the Party's candidate lists (Demirel 2014: 9).

Atatürk's Death

Mustafa Kemal was given the honorary name of 'Atatürk' (the Father Turk) officially on 24 November 1934. Having implemented a substantial portion of his programme, Mustafa Kemal Atatürk died on 10 November 1938, at the age of fifty-seven. In Şükrü Hanioğlu's words: 'The radicalism of Atatürk's program led to the authoritarian character of his politics. Like many other transformative state builders, he harboured little tolerance for dissent or criticism' (Hanioğlu 2011: 318). 'All (his) efforts at social engineering, many of which appear quixotic in hindsight, stemmed from a strong ideological commitment to forcing Turkey to absorb "civilization" and in the process become an integral part of the "civilized world"' (Hanioğlu 2011: 370). As Andrew Mango puts it, 'Atatürk was a competent commander, a shrewd politician, a statesman of supreme realism. But above all he was a man of the Enlightenment. And the Enlightenment was not made by saints' (Mango 1999: 528).[54]

In Esra Özyürek's conceptualisation as 'the commodification of state iconography', Atatürk constitutes the central focus of the political sphere in Turkey, from the perspective of both the political elite and the masses

(Özyürek 2006: 93–124). Nazlı Ökten argues that Atatürk is 'a common point of reference that guarantees identification for the masses' and that for others 'who are deprived of the means of efficient participation in the public sphere, he is an intermediary medium' (Ökten 2006: 112). Some of Recep Tayyip Erdoğan's supporters have equated him with Atatürk, a practice made particularly apparent when they use re-formulated Kemalist slogans, such as *'Adam İzindeyiz'* (Man, we follow in your footsteps), in place of *'Atam İzindeyiz'* (Father, we follow in your footsteps). That Erdoğan has encouraged such comparisons reveal the Atatürk's continued relevance at all fronts in Turkey (Yanarocak 2017).

İsmet İnönü as the *'Milli Şef'* (National Leader) (1938–46)

On 11 November 1938, İsmet İnönü (1884–1973) was elected President of Turkey by the Assembly. On 26 December 1938, the *Cumhuriyet Halk Partisi* decided at an extraordinary convention to endow on Atatürk the title of Eternal Leader (*Ebedi Şef*). İsmet İnönü was named the Party's leader for life and accorded the title of 'National Leader' (*Milli Şef*) (Mango 1999: 529).

During World War II, which began immediately after his election as President, İnönü tried to keep the country out of the conflict.[55] Immediately after World War II, both developments in international politics and new formations within the country brought about significant changes in the general character of the regime. Josef Stalin, the leader of the Soviet Union, one of the victors of the war, demanded Kars, Ardahan, Artvin and Sarıkamış from Turkey (Gürün 2010: 276–86). These demands forced Turkey to establish closer relations with the other victors, the United States and the United Kingdom. Stating that it was ready to provide military and economic support, the US demanded the establishment of a democratic system based on free elections in Turkey in return for the aid envisaged by the Truman Doctrine (Satterthwaite 1972: 74–84).

In religion and state relations, İsmet İnönü broadly followed Atatürk's policy. Although, by temperament, İnönü might have seemed more well-disposed to religion than his predecessor (Geyikdağı 1984: 65), the following correspondence makes it evident that religion had now been brought under strict state control: on 20 October 1939, Rıfat Börekçi, the Chair of the Diyanet, wrote to the Prime Minister to complain about the police banning a public prayer meeting at Atıf Bey (Altındağ) in Ankara during Ramadan. He argued that a ritual of this sort did not require prior permission, but added that 'If permission is needed, the Diyanet is the only institution that can allocate space for religious rituals.' The Prime Minister passed the matter to Governor Nevzat Tandoğan of Ankara, who replied personally with a detailed account of the situation. The point that needs to be underscored is his statement that: 'The Mosque is the proper place of prayer. If needed, nobody else but the highest civilian authority within the administration shall be the unit to make new allocations for rituals.'[56]

Hasan Ali Yücel as Minister of Education

Hasan Âli Yücel (1897–1961) was appointed Minister of National Education on 28 December 1938. *Köy Enstitüleri* (Village Institutes) were established during his tenure in 1940 by İsmail Hakkı Tonguç (1893–1960). Until they were closed down, these institutes trained 20,000 students to serve as village teachers. The Higher Village Institute department, which trained teachers for the Village Institutes, was closed on 27 November 1947; the instructor courses ended on 28 June 1948.[57]

A report dated 30 April 1942 sent from the British Embassy in Ankara to the British Foreign Office contains the minutes of a private meeting between the British Council representative in Ankara and Hasan Âli Yücel. The memo is interesting in so far as it reflects Yücel's views on religion: he informs Grant, the British Council representative, that the first priority of state policy was the Turkification of Islam for local consumption. The translation of the Koran into Turkish was part of this process, Yücel notes, saying that this was the only way to save Islam from Arab influence. Yücel said that Şerefeddin Yaltkaya (1880–1947), the Chair of the Diyanet at the time,[58] was also in favour of this idea. The intention was to Turkify Islam, but not to make it the state religion. Grant claims in his memorandum that Yücel confessed that he hoped he would see the end of the Diyanet within a decade. The interview becomes even more interesting at this point:

> The Minister's real desire was, by Turcising Islam to reduce it from magic to literature, and so rationalize it out of existence as religion. The Minister's chief collaborator in this movement is his Director-General of Primary Education, Hakkı Tonguç, who is working on strictly laicist lines in the schools and calculates that after ten years more these will have done their work. The minister

estimated that at present less than 5,000,000 Turks were on the side of 'progress', adding that when he had 5,000,000, he would be content. This appeared to indicate that he considered the remaining 70 per cent. of the population as a hopeless task, and I asked him his opinion about these weaker spirits, including, presumably, most of the women. I expressed the view that no country in the world had ever succeeded in persuading, e.g. elderly women to be irreligious, and that he too would be unable to. But he maintained that when the present lot die off, the new ones will have been properly educated and will be duly laic. I suggested that human nature in most cases needs religion, and that this laicism would leave a vacuum; did Turkey intend to fill this with a state mysticism? The Minister denied this with sincerity, stigmatizing such things as an evil product of Nazism, and pointed out that the people on whom he was working were (outside the towns) fundamentally nature-worshippers and he considered that they would be quite happy without their Islamic veneer.

A comment on this memorandum forwarded by the British Embassy in Ankara is also interesting:

A great many Turks – perhaps 70 per cent – are practising Moslems, who, while perhaps not very devout, still go to the Mosque, say their prayers etc. (e.g. the Minister of Education himself has been observed at Mosque during Ramadhan). The remaining 30 per cent are, for the most part, '*croyants mais pas pratiquants*' (believing but not practising), though there are doubtless many members of the younger generation who have no definite religious opinions whatever. Very few Turks, however, are actively atheistic or anti-Moslem. After the death of Atatürk, and given the personal preferences of his successor, religious observances and pious gestures naturally came a little more into the picture, but we do not consider that there has been any religious revival in the proper sense of the word. One thing, however, has been constant both during and after the rule of Atatürk, namely that the practical test of a true Turk is to be a Moslem. The State may be as laic as possible and religion not mentioned, but no non-Moslem could or can become an official, an officer or a judge, or bear arms for the country.[59]

Religious Education

Even though, back in 1925, the decision-making elite of the new Republic seemingly deemed it necessary to provide soldiers with religious education, with Ahmet Hamdi (Akseki)[60] (1887–1951) asked to write a book of religious instruction for them (*Askere Din Dersleri*), religious lessons were gradually removed from all education programmes in later years. While they were initially included in primary schools for two hours a week, they were removed from the secondary school curricula in 1927, and from primary schools and teachers' colleges between 1929 and 1931. This also included minority schools: a circular sent to these schools banned 'education based on religious principles' as well as 'religious propaganda'. Accordingly, pictures of saints were to be removed from textbooks and crosses were to be taken down from buildings. The only exception were village primary schools, where religion classes were offered for one hour a week until 1940 (Toprak 2019: 110–11).

On 24 December 1946, the Assembly debated religious education. Many of the members of parliament expressed their views in favour of providing religious courses in schools. Muhittin Baha Pars from Bursa (1884–1954) and Hamdullah Suphi Tanrıöver from İstanbul (1885–1966) demanded that religious education be introduced into schools to 'provide moral resistance against the danger of communism'. However, Prime Minister Recep Peker (1889–1950) opposed these ideas, arguing that 'to consider fundamentalism, that has the capacity to grow sneakily, as a precautionary measure to protect the body from a social poison called communism is more or less like assuming that a lethal poison can be cured with another poison that is at least as lethal'.[61]

However, at the Seventh Congress of the *Cumhuriyet Halk Partisi* convened on 17 November 1947, some measures were agreed that would liberalise several Party principles on religion. In February 1949, optional religious education was added to the curricula of primary school grades 4 and 5. In addition, on 4 June 1949, the Faculty of Theology was established at Ankara University to train high-level clergymen. The task of establishing accelerated *imam-hatip* (imam and preacher) courses assigned to the Ministry of National Education in 1948 was implemented, and the first two ten-month courses opened in Ankara and Istanbul on 15 January 1949; they would be followed by other courses in other provinces.[62]

The Alevi Population: Dersim Massacre[63]

The Dersim region, where Turkey's Alevi Kurds are concentrated (van Bruinessen 1992b: 29–33),[64] was one of the settlements where the state was unable to establish authority in the early years of the Republic, as it had been in the final years of the Ottoman Empire. As a result of various reports prepared between 1926 and 1935, and of decisions taken by the highest echelons of the state, the Law on the Administration of Tunceli Province was passed by the Assembly on 25 December 1935 and entered into force on 2 January 1936. This legislation assigned a status different to that of all other provinces to the region.[65]

An intensive programme of construction activity was begun in Tunceli province in 1936 and police stations were established and roads and bridges built. Some tribes and leaders in the region reacted to these developments, and when tensions in the region escalated, Tunceli was placed under military siege in the winter of 1936–7; people could neither enter nor exit the province.

After Nowruz (21 March) 1937, when the tribes burned various buildings, ambushed security forces and raided police stations, public order measures were introduced at a meeting of the Council of Ministers chaired by Atatürk and attended by the Chief of the General Staff, Fevzi Çakmak (1876–1950) on 4 May 1937. Within this framework, it was envisaged that a powerful and effective assault would be launched in the region, the rebellious populace would be gathered together and transferred to another place, villages would be raided to collect weapons and people, and villages would be 'completely destroyed'.

In the first months of the rebellion, the rebels inflicted casualties on the military units, while the air force, whose pilots included Sabiha Gökçen,[66] Atatürk's adopted daughter, was effective in its attacks. During the military operations, people in many places abandoned their villages and took refuge in caves, but many died when the caves were attacked with flame-throwers.

In all, fifty-eight rebels were captured. Their trials were held in Elazığ. The capital sentences handed down by the court were executed on 15 November 1937. In June 1938, the military operation started again and the death toll rose into the thousands. It is estimated that 46,000–63,000 people were killed, with a further 1,500 people, mostly children, missing.

Military measures continued for a long time. The Law on the Administration of Tunceli was repealed on 1 January 1947.[67]

The Non-Muslim Population

Turkey's official state policy on its minorities was established by the Lausanne Peace Treaty of 24 July 1923. The treaty defines non-Muslim citizens of Turkey as minorities.⁶⁸ Although they were not explicitly named, the Lausanne Treaty has generally been assumed to cover the three largest non-Muslim communities in Turkey at the time: the Armenian, Greek Orthodox and Jewish communities. The mass migration of the Rum population both before and after the Treaty of Lausanne marked the beginning of the process of nation-building and the politics of homogenisation that stigmatised and marginalised the Greek, Armenian and Jewish populations in Turkey as the Other. 'As the 1920s progressed, firms, shopkeepers, companies and even professionals such as doctors and lawyers were told to dismiss their non-Muslim employees and hire Muslim Turks instead' (Aktar 2021a: 104). These were de facto demands and pressures made and applied without legal justification by the Ankara government to create a national bourgeoisie through slogans like 'Turkey for the Turks!' (*Türkiye Türklerindir*).⁶⁹

Law on Goods Abandoned by the Armenians (Emval-i Metruke/Tasfiye Kanunları)

On 22 September 1922, the Ankara government reinstated the decree of 26 September 1915 which confiscated the so-called 'abandoned goods of the Armenians'. The 1915 decree had been repealed by the Istanbul government on 8 January 1920 (Akçam 2004: 239). The property of Armenians who had not been exiled were not confiscated. On 15 April 1923, another law was enacted to liquidate the so-called abandoned goods.⁷⁰ Two laws issued on 28 May 1928 provided for (1) the transfer of the property of individuals who had been deported or exchanged, or had escaped or were absent, to be registered with the Land Registry and titled to the Treasury (Law 1331);⁷¹ and (2) for this property to be included as assets in the Budget (Law 1349).⁷²

A Set of Campaigns: Citizen Speak Turkish!

During the late 1920s, a public campaign entitled *Vatandaş Türkçe konuş* (Citizen, speak Turkish) was begun when İsmet İnönü gave a speech emphasising the need for everybody in Turkey to speak Turkish. The Istanbul Law Faculty Students' Association took a decision at its annual congress on 13 January 1928 to enforce the campaign. Particularly in Istanbul, minorities were forced to speak Turkish, especially by university students. Extending into the 1940s, one of the main targets of this campaign, perhaps the only target,

y's Sefardi Jews, who continued to speak an older version of Span-
) as their primary language (Gökberk 2020: 109). Nevertheless,
eks, Armenians, Circassians, Bosniaks, Arabs and others were
 public for speaking their own languages' (Cagaptay 2006: 25–6).
nicipalities began to implement fines for those who were caught
nguages other than Turkish. Some provincial governors began
ose who were heard using another language, with the endorse-
e government.[73] The campaign slowed down in 1928, though it
ally end.

ogrom in Thrace

me anti-Semitic publications appeared in Turkey, namely two jour-
 and *İnkılâp* (later *Milli İnkılâp*) (Cagaptay 2006: 142–3). It is dif-
imate the impact of these journals on society, however some studies
acian incidents of July 1934 assert that international affairs, espe-
azi influence at the time, increased the impact of such publications
 1996; Levi 1996; Toprak 1996). Ayhan Aktar, on the other hand,
 due to limited communication networks, the lack of a nationwide
lcast, and low levels of literacy, Nazi sentiments did not have much
urkey (Aktar 2021b: 279–311). In July 1934, the situation got out
owever, and Jewish homes and businesses were attacked and looted
li. Many people were beaten and harassed. Incidents occurred in
.[74] Ayhan Aktar underlines the responsibility borne by the govern-
he *Cumhuriyet Halk Partisi* for these events, referring to diplomatic
ence from both the British and US embassies (Aktar 2021b: 307–9).

h Tax

came with wartime economic stresses topped by a highly discre-
cy choice of the government, the so-called Wealth Tax. The Wealth
as approved following only trivial debate in the Assembly on 11
 1942. For the purpose of administering the tax, Faik Ökte, the
rector for the province of Istanbul, divided society into four cat-
uslims, non-Muslims, foreigners and *Dönme* (Ökte 1951: 81–5).
category was reserved for descendants of Jews who had converted

70 per cent of the proceeds from the tax came from Istanbul. Article 12 of the Wealth Tax Law provided for payment of the tax within 15 days. Those taxpayers who were unable to pay their tax began to be sent to work camps to perform physical labour. The first party of thirty-two, which consisted entirely of Istanbul non-Muslims, set off for Aşkale in the province of Erzurum on 27 January 1943. Others followed, and twenty-one people died 'in-debt' in Aşkale (Aktar 2021a: 145–83). Clearly, the 'Turkification' policies included the forced transfer of non-Muslim capital.[75] The Wealth Tax was withdrawn in March 1944.[76]

Papa Eftim and the Turkish Orthodox Patriarchate

During the 1919–22 Turkish–Greek war, Papa Eftim (born Pavlos Karahisaridis, 1884–1968), a local Orthodox priest from Akdağmağdeni (Yozgat), initiated the establishment of a Turkish Orthodox Church. His aim was to separate Turkophone Orthodox Christians from the Fener Ecumenical Patriarchate (Benlisoy and Benlisoy 2022: 15). Papa Eftim's demands were discussed in the TBMM (Baş 2005: 48–52). Eventually, in October 1922, the foundation of the Turkish Orthodox Church was announced in Kayseri (Benlisoy and Benlisoy 2022: 130; Baş 2005: 53–7). When the compulsory exchange of populations of 1924 deprived Papa Eftim of his potential congregation, he tried to take the Patriarchate and İstanbul Rum community under his control between 1923 and 1930 (Benlisoy and Benlisoy 2022: 163). On 2 October 1933, Papa Eftim besieged the Holy Synod and appointed his own replacement. In 1924, he began conducting the Christian liturgy in Turkish. However, despite all his efforts, the immigration and citizenship policies of the 1930s made it clear that the glue holding Turkish society together was the Turks' Muslim faith. The agreement between Turkey and Romania in 1936, which included the Muslim population while excluding the Christian Gagavuz Turks, makes it clear that religion was a *sine qua non* in Turkish national identity (Benlisoy and Benlisoy: 289–314).[77]

Women in Nation-building

As Carter Vaughn Findley puts it: '(Mustafa Kemal) resembled nationalist leaders of his generation in other developing countries in combining patriarchal authoritarianism in private life with strategic motivation to mobilize women for nation building' (2010: 278–9). One of the most important components of the 'ideal' society envisioned by the founding cadres in the early years of the Republic was the image of the 'modern Republican woman', who is depicted posing in Western clothes in her modern home, or in an exemplary uniform at official ceremonies, working in public institutions or pacing the wide boulevards of the capital.[78] Although some areas of emancipation have partially opened up, especially for upper-middle-class urban women, the majority of women remain on the margins of or outside modernisation (Kandiyoti 1988b; Tekeli 1991). Furthermore, women will only become part of the nation through their roles as mothers and housewives within the family. Given this, Serpil Sancar suggests that the Turkish experience should be read as 'family-oriented modernization' (Sancar 2012). 'State feminism', which was part of the nation state project, did not bring about a questioning of the patriarchal order or sexual freedom (White 2003: 145). Nezihe Muhiddin's futile struggle for women's political and social rights in the early years of the Republic, between 1924 and 1927, under the umbrella of the Turkish Women's Union (*Türk Kadınlar Birliği*), and the strategies introduced in response by the republican regime to suppress and direct women's activities, are indicative of the approach taken by the early republican decision-making elite.[79]

Turkish women were given the right on 5 December 1934 to participate in general elections and to elect and be elected as deputies.[80] General elections in which women participated for the first time with these rights were on 8 February 1935. A total of eighteen women candidates nominated by the Party won seats and entered parliament.

Notes

1. 'Those who read the Armistice of Mudros understood the catastrophe that had befallen the Turkish nation, and they also saw that the occupation of Istanbul rendered the catastrophe inconceivable' (Karabekir 1933–51: 18).
2. The *Müdafa-i Hukuk Cemiyeti* in Ankara was established by Mehmet Rıfat Efendi, who was to be the first president of the Diyanet in 1924 (Kaplan 2011: 12, 52–60).
3. Even though Mustafa Kemal Paşa had joined *İttihat ve Terakki* in 1908 and been one of the inner circle of activist officers, he was not associated with the wartime policies of Enver and Talat. In Eric Jan Zürcher's words, 'Mustafa Kemal's combination of high standing within the army and, politically speaking, clean hands made him an

ideal candidate for the leadership of the resistance' (Zürcher 2017: 141). Halide Edip (Adıvar) describes him, in line with the impression he made on her back in 1919, as 'The hero of Anafartalar in Çanakkale, the aide-de-camp to the Sultan and a man of great intelligence and ambition' (Adıvar [1962] 2007: 25).

4. Mustafa Kemal's conduct at this juncture was significant for his cause, because his later policies differed. In his work *Türklük Sözlemesi* (The Contract of Turkishness), Barış Ünlü argues that in addition to being Turkish and (Sunni) Muslim, being blind to the treatment of non-Muslims and Muslim groups resisting Turkification, especially Kurds, are the three basic conditions of the contract of Turkishness (Ünlü 2018).

5. For the considerations regarding such a change of day, see Nadi 1957: 55–7.

6. Halide Edip Adıvar (1884–1964), author and political activist, had attended the war of independence personally and was granted the title corporal.

7. Mehmet Rifat Efendi, who was sentenced to capital punishment by Istanbul Government on 6 June 1920, had been elected as a member of the parliament representing Menteşe (Muğla) on 1 April 2020 (Kaplan 2011: 13–14, 100–16). He resigned from being an MP to become the Mufti of Ankara on 17 October 2020.

8. 'When they arrived at the gate of the Assembly, Mustafa Kemal asked Mustafa Fehmi Gerçeker, a clergyman from Bursa, to read the opening prayer in Turkish' (Özteke 2019: 270). This is quite significant for language of religious rituals debates.

9. The language, content and main concepts of the *İstiklal Marşı* (national anthem), which was written in February–March 1921 during the national struggle for independence and adopted by the assembly, forms part of the religious discourse of the period. On the *İstiklal Marşı*, see Kara 2021. 'While there was not a single word about Turks, Turkey, or Turkishness in the national anthem, which consists of ten long stanzas, there were repeated references to Islam and God. Similarly, Mehmet Akif's imagination of *vatan* in the national anthem was more religious than national. He elevated *vatan* to a sacred territory that should be defended by the "God-worshipping nation"' (Özkan 2014: 93–4).

10. *Düstur*, III/I, 6 [*Düstur* is the publication in which all the legislations of the parliaments in Turkey made since the late nineteenth century have been published. Republican times start in part III, 23 April 1920–27 May 1960, with 41 volumes published each year. It includes laws and by-laws, international agreements, some high court decisions, etc. Part IV: 27 May 1960–1 November 1961. Part V: 1961 onwards]. On continuity between *Şeyhülislamlık* and *Şer'iyye ve Evkaf Vekaleti*, see Kara [2008] 2017: 62.

11. On this so-called 'assembly government system', in which the parliament is invested with executive as well as legislative power, see Soysal and Sağlam 1983: 22–3.
12. On this group, see Demirel 1994.
13. 'I know that this is a turning point in a Turk's life. After Sakarya, our life will move on to another phase' (Adıvar [1922] 2007: 158). For a fictional account of the occupation of İstanbul in 1918 and the war of independence, see Halide Edib (Adıvar)'s novel *Ateşten Gömlek* (A Shirt of Fire), serialised in a daily newspaper in 1922. Another novel that narrates the independence struggle sincerely is Kemal Tahir's *Yorgun Savaşçı* (Exhausted Warrior).
14. The term *gazi* used for Muslim frontier fighters became a title of honour bestowed on Muslim rulers who won distinction in the fight against the infidels (Lewis 1988: 74).
15. For discussions and decisions regarding minorities at the Lausanne Conference, see Kılınç 2013: 277–94 and Oran 2004: 61–80.
16. For a heartbreaking compilation of oral histories relating to the compulsory exodus of the *Rum* population of Anatolia, see Millas (ed.) 2001. On the reciprocal compulsory exodus from Greece to Turkey, see Arı 1995. On the effect of the exchange on Turkey's economy, see Aktar 2021a: 73–94.
17. 'The incorporation of religious vocabulary helped to nationalize Islamic identity' (Yavuz 2000: 23).
18. In his memoirs, Kazım Karabekir, who was with Mustafa Kemal at the time of the speech, states that Mustafa Kemal sought his opinion after he had spoken. Karabekir asked Mustafa Kemal: 'Isn't it enough that we have suffered for bringing world affairs into mosques, my pasha? Why do we bring our national affairs into the mosques again? And why do you, as the commander-in-chief, engage with religion and the caliphate like a man of religion, even going further?' (Mumcu [1977] 2006: 66–7). For an analysis of Mustafa Kemal's speech in the mosque, see Özdalga 2022: 6, 231–2.
19. TV interview, Channel 7: *Ters Köşe* hosted by Akif Beki and Fehmi Koru on 21 December 2003.
20. TV interview, Channel 7: *İskele Sancak* hosted by Ahmet Hakan Coşkun on 16 January 2004.
21. News item entitled 'Head of Religious Affairs Görmez receives members of US Religious Freedoms Commission' on the *Diyanet* official website, 7 February 2014. Available at: http://www.diyanet.gov.tr/tr/icerik/news (accessed 17 February 2014).

22. Dale F. Eickelman and James Piscatori read this politics as reinventing the caliphal tradition (Eickelman and Piscatori 1996: 30).
23. The abolition of the Caliphate in 1924 was perhaps the most significant step in giving legitimacy to the new Turkish state on the basis of a national identity that is above religion (Berkes 1998: 463). For an inspiring analysis of the power struggle as reaction, see Özoğlu 2011.
24. On later conferences aimed at instituting a caliphate by seeking to establish a new lineage distinct from the Ottoman caliphate, see Aydın 2017: 136–49; Binder 1988: 129–58; Finkel 2005: 546.
25. For an inspiring analysis of the power struggle among prominent political actors of 1922–3 through a document dated 15 October 1923 and penned by Maynard B. Barnes, the US consul and delegate of the US High Commissioner in Turkey, see Özoğlu 2011: 155–66. The report, entitled 'Political Situation in Turkey', was prepared in Ankara for the US Secretary of State in Washington. Also, for a critical analysis of the abolition of the Sultanate and the Caliphate, see Deringil 1993: 176–81.
26. For the actions and reactions of the clergy to the republican reforms, see Hicret K. Toprak's *Mihrap, Minber ve Devlet: Tek Parti Döneminde Diyanet İşleri Başkanlığı* (2019); especially 227–68.
27. A *zaviye* is a building associated with Sufis in the Islamic world. It can serve a variety of functions as a place of worship, a school, monastery and/or mausoleum.
28. Şerif Mardin reads Mustafa Kemal's attitude towards the *tarikats* as 'related to his attack against stifling gemeinschaft . . . it is clear that what Atatürk had in mind was to disallow the influence of local charismatic leaders who were either notables with local political power or appeared as ignorant and cunning figures exploiting the lower classes' (Mardin 1981: 216). Considering the prominence of religious notables in the Independence War, this reading would appear highly questionable.
29. For a detailed account of the transition from the Muslim solar to the new calendar, see Mango 1999: 437.
30. For the whole text, see https://hukukbook.com/743-sayili-turk-kanun-u-medenisi-gerekcesi/.
31. On the debates since the 1910s, see Lewis 1999: 29–37.
32. On the alphabet reform, see Şimşir 1992.
33. Atatürk declared that Ayasofya 'should be (a) monument for all civilizations' (quoted in Bordewich 2008). With the conversion of Ayasofya into a museum, its imam Hakkı Aydoğan was considered to be on permanent leave; after his death,

the appointments continued as they did at every other mosque. In other words, the position of imam at Ayasofya was never abolished after 1934, even though it was converted into a museum.

34. For an excellent study on *Terakkiperver Cumhuriyet Fırkası*, see *Political Opposition in the Early Turkish Republic: The Progressive Republican Party 1924–1925* by Erik Jan Zürcher (1991).
35. For some observations on the Şeyh Said revolt and its aftermath, see Özoğlu 2011: 89–112.
36. On Independence Tribunals, see Aybars 1975.
37. For a psychoanalytical reading of the hat reform, see Somay 2014: 131–8.
38. For a critical evaluation of the İzmir assassination plot and the conspiracy trials, see Özoğlu 2011: 125–54. Also see Mango 1999: 444–53.
39. Turkey still had a system of two-tier elections at the time.
40. For an inspiring study on the *Serbest Cumhuriyet Fırkası* and the severe opposition that surfaced at the time in the Ege region, see Öz 2019. Also see Emrence 2006. For Fethi Okyar's account of the *Serbest Cumhuriyet Fırkası* and the times in question, see Okyar 1980 and 1987.
41. For a thorough analysis of the Menemen/Kublay incident, see Azak 2010: 21–43.
42. For a psychoanalytical reading of the *Nutuk*, see Somay 2014: 139–44. For an analysis of the *Nutuk* and other of Atatürk's speeches and statements, see Parla 1991a and 1991b.
43. She returned to Turkey in 1939, becoming first a professor of English literature at Istanbul University, then a member of the parliament in 1950. For a comparison of the two texts, see Adak 2003: 509–27.
44. On Mustafa Kemal's reaction to Karabekir's memoirs, see Mango 1999: 462–3.
45. İsmail Kara narrates a similar story by quoting a dream: a group of religious notables meet at a town in Anatolia in the 1930s to perform a prayer to curse Mustafa Kemal. A couple of hours before the planned ritual, Şeyh Rahmi Baba (Sezgin), the host, dreams that the Prophet Muhammed handed Turkey over to Mustafa Kemal. Interpreting the dream, the group decide to abandon the ritual (Kara 1998: 15–16).
46. It should be added, too, that on 5 March 1924, a Council of Ministers decree stipulated that no names were to be mentioned in the *hutbe*s, only the salvation and bliss of the nation and the Republic were to be prayed for (Kara 2023: 4). The *hutbe* is the sermonising part of a longer ritual, the Friday noon service, also known as *cuma*, the name for Friday in the Turkish language.
47. For a detailed account of this process, see Kara 2016: 130–49)

48. For the pre-republican background of worship in Turkish, see Azak 2010: 46–9.
49. I would like to thank Dr Bülent Somay for translating the poem.
50. On rituals in Turkish, see Toprak 2019: 122–50.
51. On the birth of the Turkish *ezan*, see Azak 2010: 54–8.
52. For an excellent account of the resistance in society against reforms in early republican Turkey, especially in the context of religion and religious education, see Özdemirci 2022.
53. For Kemalism as a secular religion conceptualised in three pillars, namely civilisation/West, science and nationalism, see Atalay 2018. Especially, adaptation of Süleyman Çelebi's (1351–1422) *Mevlid* (epic poem honouring the birth of prophet Muhammed) into Atatürk by Behçet Kemal Çağlar (1908–69) is remarkable: Turkishness and nation replaces Allah and Atatürk replaces the Prophet Muhammed (Atalay 2018: 327).
54. For another well-written biography of Mustafa Kemal Atatürk, see Kreiser [2010] 2018. The original is in German and entitled *Atatürk: Eine Biographie* published in 2008. For a very interesting account of the Atatürk and his times, see Gingeras 2019.
55. A day-by-day account of the war era and İnönü's stance on entering the war can be found in the memoires of Faik Ahmet Barutçu, who served as a member of parliament for Trabzon from April 1939 to November 1943. See Barutçu 2001: 257–639. Another memoire which reflects İsmet İnönü's success in keeping Turkey out of the war is that of Haldun Derin, who served first as Atatürk's and later İnünü's chief of staff; see Derin 1995: 184–5. Also, for the foreign policy conducted by İsmet İnönü and Turkish diplomats in the Ministry of Foreign Affairs during World War II, see Deringil 1989, specifically 48–57.
56. Republic of Turkey, State Archives, Office of Prime Ministry, 30-10-0-0; box no. 26; file 151; no.14.
57. For a biography of Hasan Âli Yücel, see Bora 2021.
58. Mehmet Şerafettin Yaltkaya was the second president of the Diyanet, serving from 14 January 1942 to 23 April 1947. The funeral ritual for Mustafa Kemal Atatürk was by Yaltkaya, when he was the director of the Institute of Islamic Studies. He was not a member of the Diyanet before he was appointed to its Chair. Yaltkaya took a soft and harmonious stance to religious rituals in the Turkish debates in 1932, translating forty-six suras into Turkish and writing a text stating that the Turkish translation of the Koran could be read in prayer. Upon the death of Rıfat Börekçi, he was appointed Chair, probably under the auspices of Hasan Ali Yücel, a close friend (Kara and Gündoğdu 2019: 256–7). Also, see Kara [2008] 2017: 81.

59. Report dated 30 April 1942 sent from the British Embassy in Ankara to the British Foreign Office, see *British National Archives*, FO 371/33375, R3203/810/44. I would like to thank Prof. Ayhan Aktar for bringing this document to my attention.
60. Akseki was initially appointed vice-director of the Diyanet in 1939 under Şerafettin Yaltkaya; upon his death, he became its third president. In Kemal Karpat's words: 'Clearly, Akseki played a crucial role in shaping the structure and philosophy of the *Diyanet* and the government's policy towards Islam in Turkey' (Karpat 2012: 220–1).
61. *TBMM Zabıt Ceridesi* (minutes of the Assembly), V, VIII, 3 (1947), 444–6; specifically, 445.
62. For a set of personal stories conveyed through interviews on religious education and religious life in the early republican era, in three volumes, see Öcal 2008. Also, see Gökaçtı 2005.
63. 'The Dersim region was oppressed not primarily because of its Alevism, but primarily because of its Kurdishness and its tribal character, which was considered rebellious against the state. This oppression, however, also soured relations between the prospective government and a section of the Alevi population. After an initial phase in which the majority of Alevis supported the Republic, with the death of Mustafa Kemal in 1938 and the hardening of the regime, the deterioration of the economic situation, the imposition of heavier taxes and the suppression of the Dersim rebellion, perhaps Alevis became more distant' (Massicard 2013: 149). See also Gezik 2012.
64. Martin van Bruinessen states that the 1937–8 uprising was by Alevi Kurds alone; it was not supported by Sunni Kurds at all (van Bruinessen 1992b: 31). See also Aksoy 2016.
65. By the above-mentioned legislation the province was renamed Tunceli. On changing the name Dersim to Tunceli and some of the reports on the region from the early republican period, see Bora 2013: 77–96. Also, on the comment made by Abdullah Alpdoğan (1878–1972), the Governor of Dersim/Tunceli, in 1936, that 'Kurds are mountain Turks', see Kirişçi and Winrow 1997: 108. Alpdoğan was the commanding officer of the military forces in Tunceli, and general inspector of the province, between 1936 and 1938.
66. Sabiha Gökçen (1913–2001) was adopted in her teens by Mustafa Kemal. It is generally held that he took her into his confidence more than he did his other children. She was trained in the Soviet Union as a combat pilot.
67. For a detailed account of the Dersim uprising of 1936–8, see Deniz 2020.
68. On the Lausanne Conference negotiations vis-à-vis minorities, see Aktar 2021a: 119–20.

69. Ayhan Aktar elaborates on actual practices in the early years of the Republic, describing discriminatory policies directed against non-Muslim minorities and using Taha Parla's characterisation of corporatism. Parla argues that: 'Corporatism as a model and philosophy of society, then, may be expressed in the form of a well-formulated, programmatic political ideology, or it may remain as a loose worldview. At another level, or dimension, corporatism is a system of actual practices and policies that are the result of, or in conformity with, such a world-view or ideology. At a third level or dimension, corporatism, beyond the de facto manifestations of the second level, unfolds in a de jure manner as tangible political institutions and legal structures' (Parla 1985, 46). For Aktar, the most effective way of understanding the creation of a national state, the resulting power structure, and the dominant conception of nationalism, was to follow the shadow of the state over its minorities (Aktar 2009).
70. For detailed information and an analysis of the legal regulations on the 'abandoned goods of the Armenians', see Akçam 2012. For a compilation of related legal regulations, see Kardeş 2008.
71. *Mübadil, Gayrimübadil, Muhacir ve Saireye Kanunlarına Tevfikan Tevzi veya Adiyen Tahsis Olunan Gayrimenkul Emvalin Tapuya Raptına Dair Kanun.*
72. *Emval-i Metrûke Hesab-ı Cariyelerinin Bütçeye İrat Kaydına Dair Kanun.*
73. Özkırımlı and Sofos 2008: 167.
74. For a chronology of these incidents, see Aktar 2021b: 282–4.
75. The memoires of Prof. Sabahattin Zaim (1926–2007), an economist, clearly reveal 'Turkish' contentment with this unlawful and inhuman legislation: 'The development of the Turkish private sector has a lot to do with the wealth tax law. Before that, the entrepreneurial power of the Turks in Istanbul was very weak. The private sector was almost entirely owned by Jews, Greeks and Armenians. Since the state directed public-sector investments to Anatolia, the share of Turks in Istanbul's industry was very small . . . As for the Wealth Tax, yes, although it cannot be said that this tax was fair, in terms of economic policy it was a law that enabled the establishment of the Turkish Private Sector in big cities such as Istanbul, Ankara and Izmir. It had the effect of breaking the trade monopoly established by non-Muslims with the privileges from the Tanzimat period. In this respect, Şükrü Saraçoğlu and the administrators of the time should be remembered with mercy' (Zaim 2008: 127). For an excellent set of articles on non-Muslim minorities in Turkey and Turkification policies in the early republican era, see Aktar 2021a. For a discussion of the wealth tax, see also Bali 1999.
76. For a novel that deals with the wealth tax, see *Salkım Hanımın Taneleri* (Salkım Hanım's Beads) by Yılmaz Karakoyunlu.

77. Sema Erder, in her book *Zorla Yerleştirmeden Yerinden Etmeye* (From Forced Relocation to Displacement), states that many provisions of the 1934 Settlement Law relating to the settlement of Turks repatriated from abroad and resettled internally support claims that Turkish nationalism was Turkic, ethnicist and even racist (Erder 2018: 128). Kemal Kirişçi, in his analysis of those articles of the 1934 Settlement Law which related to immigration policy and its implementation, points out that Turkish national identity has been Muslim, even Sunni-Hanafi, rather than Turkish (Kirişçi 2000).
78. On the construction and representation of this image, see Bozdoğan 2001. For a very thorough account of the feminist literature on the early republican period in Turkey, see Kılınç and Kılıçkıran 2022. For anti-veiling and anti-chador campaigns in the 1930s, see Adak 2022. For the idealised image of women in the early republic, see Kandiyoti 1987.
79. Nezihe Muhiddin was threatened, disregarded and discarded by a series of prosecutions by the state authorities. She died in a mental hospital in 1958 in Istanbul. On Nezihe Muhiddin (Tepedelengil), *Kadınlar Halk Fırkası* (Republican Women's Party) and *Kadın Birliği* (Women's Union), see Zihnioğlu 2003.
80. İsmet İnönü said that day in the parliamentary session, 'When the Turkish revolution is mentioned, it will be said that it is also the revolution for the emancipation of women' (*Milliyet*, 6 December 1934).

3

TRANSITION TO THE MULTI-PARTY REGIME

> After the overthrow of the dictatorship, the so-called liberals came to power; in fact, it was the merchant and industrialist circles looking for unlimited opportunities for profit, and the landlords who did not like the 'Land Law' even in its mild form.
>
> Atilla İlhan, *Kurtlar Sofrası* (1963)

The multi-party era in Turkey began in 1945 when a second party other than the ruling *Cumhuriyet Halk Partisi* (CHP), the *Milli Kalkınma Partisi* (National Development Party: 1945–58) led by Nuri Demirağ (1886–1957), was founded. Actually, there had been other parties since the establishment of the Republic, namely *Terakkiperver Cumhuriyet Fırkası* (1924–5) and the *Serbest Cumhuriyet Fırkası* (1930), but these parties had very short lives.

Turkish politics in the period 1946–60 can be read as the story of the disagreements over the rules of the game and their own positions within the regime between two groups: the military/civilian bureaucracy and its social allies, a group that sought to establish its legitimacy with the mission of creating the national state and modernizing society; and the new elites that came to power through elections and included many different groups that reacted to the first group. The political meaning of the DP's coming to power was to pave the way for the masses that had been excluded from political life during the consolidation of the republican regime, and to make their presence felt in the process of influencing the ruling bloc. (Demirel 2011: 396)

Cumhuriyet Halk Partisi in Power

In a speech on 1 November 1945, İsmet İnönü stated that the only shortcoming of democracy in Turkey was the lack of an opposition party.[1] He announced at the speech, instead of the existing two-stage system with electors, the 1947 general election was to be made direct.[2] The opposition that was awaited emerged in the CHP. On 7 June 1945, CHP members Celâl Bayar (1883–1986), Refik Koraltan (1889–1974), Adnan Menderes (1899–1961) and Fuat Köprülü (1890–1966) submitted a motion to be discussed openly in the parliamentary group. The aim of this memorandum (known as *Dörtlü Takrir*) was to transform Turkey from single-party rule to a multi-party regime, to hold free elections, to have academic autonomy for universities, a single-step election system, and to free the executive power from the patronage of the CHP. When Menderes and Köprülü publish critical articles in *Vatan* daily, they were both expelled from the party on 21 September 1945. This was followed by the expulsion of Refik Koraltan from the party. In line with the developing events, Celâl Bayar resigned from both his parliamentary seat and the party.

Founding the Demokrat Parti

Celal Bayar, a former prime minister, and his friends Adnan Menderes,[3] Refik Koraltan and Fuad Köprülü founded a new political party called the *Demokrat Parti* (Democrat Party/DP) on 7 January 1946. Celal Bayar was appointed the party's leader.[4] The party adopted a policy of liberalisation in economic and political areas. In its programme, the Democratic Party took a position in favour of 'greater respect' for religion. Article 14 of the programme stated that the party rejected the erroneous interpretation of *laiklik* that lead to a hostile attitude against religion, and advocated a clearer separation between religion and public affairs so that the government would not interfere in religious activities (Tunaya 1952: 663).

The 1946 Elections

For the first time in the history of the Republic of Turkey, a multi-party general election was held on 21 July 1946. However, the way the elections were held was not democratic at all: it was without judicial control, under gendarme pressure in rural areas, with open voting, secret counting and on the basis of the majority system. As a result, the CHP won the election with 395 of the 465 parliamentary seats. The DP managed to get sixty-one deputies into parliament. Four independent candidates from the DP list also won the election. After the results were announced,[5] DP claimed that there had been police pressure, fraud and corruption in the election. However, these objections were to no avail and the 1946 election became known as the shadiest election in Turkey's political history.

Seventh Congress of CHP and Following Steps

The seventh and last congress of the CHP as a single party was convened in Ankara on 17 November 1947. Other than re-regulating religious education, some other important decisions were taken at the congress. First of all, the practice of combining the Presidency and the CHP chairmanship in the same person was given a new form. Amendment to the bylaws provided that, as long as the party chairman remained the president, he was to delegate all his powers as chairman to the deputy chairman elected by the party congress. With other amendments made in bylaws, the party broke its traditional authoritarian and bureaucratic structure and prioritised internal democracy.

The party started to distance itself from the economic policy of statism (*devletçilik*) introduced in the 1930s and became more sympathetic to free enterprise. Also, at the congress it was decided to retract Article 17 of the Land Distribution Law, something the Assembly eventually did in 1950 (Uzun 2012: 126–7), though it was actually never applied.

Steps were taken on the *hac* (pilgrimage to Mekka) issue; foreign currency was allocated for those going on *hac*. Permission to go on pilgrimage, which caused great joy among the religious people, was first granted in 1947, but there was no organisation to make it happen. Nevertheless, despite all obstacles in travelling conditions many people managed to go on *hac* (Güran 1996).

These developments probably lead CHP to have Şemsettin Günaltay (1883–1961), an Islamic history professor known for his religious sensitivities, to serve from 15 January 1949 to 22 May 1950 as prime minister. Günaltay was instrumental in changing the party's rigid *laiklik* approach towards an accommodation with Islam. In his period as prime minister, the teaching of Islam was liberalised and a variety of other measures were taken to harmonise the government's policy with the belief system and Islamic practices of society (Karpat [2009] 2012: 221). On 1 March 1950 'shrines of Turkish dignitaries' and 'shrines with artistic value' were reopened for visitation.[6] An amendment to Article 163 of the Turkish Penal Code regulated making propaganda and forming an organisation in order to establish an Islamic state as a crime.

Throughout the congress, delegates did not refrain from strongly criticising the CHP's past practices.[7] Consequently, the issue of religious education and the re-evaluation of the conduct regarding religion paved the way for a serious break in the classical CHP approach. In time, steps were taken to address the demands voiced in the discussions, and *imam-hatip* (religious vocational) courses were opened in 1948. In 1949, elective religion classes were introduced in primary schools, and the Faculty of Theology at Ankara University was established in the same year to train teachers to teach in these schools.

The opposition group was mainly composed of Turkist, Islamist and leftist circles. The broad plebeian mass that both the ruling and opposition blocs were trying to appeal to, and whose support they sought, was the same: millions of peasants or people of rural origin living within the framework of conservative values (Aksakal 2017: 156). With religiously appealing steps, the CHP tried to rival the rising DP.[8] However, even all these efforts did not prevent it from losing power to the DP in the 1950 elections.

Millet Partisi

The opposition movement within the DP resulted in the establishment of the *Millet Partisi* (Nation Party) on 20 July 1948. Field Marshal Fevzi Çakmak[9] was the honorary president of the party. Starting from its foundation, the party criticised the ruling CHP and the opposition DP very harshly. The party strongly opposed the CHP's understanding of religion and *laiklik*, arguing that the DP was a party of collusion and that they were the real opposition. Even this party, according to Tarık Zafer Tunaya, was far from representing the Islamist movement that emerged in the Ottoman times after 1908 (Tunaya 1962: 191). The *Millet Partisi* was not very successful in the 1950 elections, receiving 3.1 per cent of the vote. Eventually, as a result of the lawsuit filed at the Ankara Third Criminal Court, it was concluded that the party was 'a party based on religious principles and hiding its aims' and the *Millet Partisi* was dissolved on 27 January 1954 (Ersel *et al.* 2005: 132).

Demokrat Parti in Power

The elections held on 14 May 1950 marked the end of the CHP's twenty-seven-year rule. DP came to power alone with 53.3 per cent of the votes and 408 deputies. Nevertheless, the post-war transition from a one-party to a multi-party regime was a state-led regime change. As Hakan Yılmaz puts it,

> No non-state actor (whether it be the bourgeoisie, the landlords, the small peasants, the urban lower classes, or any coalition of these) played a determinant role during the transition process ... the final outcome of the democratic transition was a reallocation of political power among the state actors: Political power was transferred from one group of the Kemalist ruling bloc (the civilianized Kemalist leaders, organized in the Republican People's Party) to the other group of the Kemalist ruling bloc (the civilian Kemalist leaders, organized in the Democrat Party). In other words, at the end of the democratic transition political power remained within the Kemalist ruling bloc and it did not pass into the hands of the political representatives of the social groups and classes. (Yılmaz 1997: 2–3)

Nevertheless, CHP apparently was not expecting to lose the elections. DP elected Celal Bayar as the president of Turkey, and Adnan Menderes became the prime minister. Rumours of a coup resulted in various changes in the armed forces; consequently, Menderes and Bayar, with the support of İsmet İnönü, managed to establish their authority over the military (Eroğul 1970: 67).[10]

The Ezan *in Arabic*

The *ezan* (call to prayer) to be recited in Turkish has been an issue of controversy and a topic for heated debates after the transition to a multi-party regime.[11] The first attempt by the DP to clear the criticized past was about the *ezan*. On 16 June 1950, the TBMM unanimously approved the draft law lifting the prohibition of Article 526 of the Turkish Penal Code on the Arabic *ezan* and *kamet*.[12] At the meeting, where no deputy spoke against the bill, Cemal Reşit Eyüpoğlu, speaking on behalf of the CHP Parliamentary Group, said, 'We will not oppose the removal of the Arabic call to prayer as a criminal matter, trusting that national consciousness will resolve this issue on its own.' The accepted amendment served as an amnesty for the persons under judicial processes alleged to violate Article 526 of the Penal Code.[13]

Waves of Internal Migration

The change in the predominantly self-sufficient closed village economy structure of rural areas in the years following World War II brought about internal migration, which started in 1945 and became a social phenomenon in the 1950s. In the period between 1945 and 1950, internal migration was mostly intra-regional. Since the cities in the region lacked the means to feed this new population, starting from 1950, they were directed towards large industrial and commercial centres. In the 1950s, when transportation facilities increased and the market developed, there was a great increase in the number of people migrating from villages to cities. Umut Azak links the general context of migration from the rural to urban areas with the anxiety of the Kemalist elite stemming from the perception of an endangered westernised, secular lifestyle (Azak 2010: 114).

DP's Reactions against Fundamentalist Conducts

Although the DP benefitted from Islamic or nationalist motives, it did not welcome the organised representation of these lines in the political or even civil sphere (Taşkın 2007: 86).[14] For instance, the increasing number of acts of vandalism targeting busts and statues of Atatürk led DP to enact the Law on Crimes Committed Against Atatürk on 24 July 1951.[15]

On 22 November 1952, Ahmet Emin Yalman, the editor-in-chief of *Vatan* daily newspaper was attacked and wounded by a bullet in Malatya. Yalman was one of the earliest critics of Atatürk's administration, for which he had been prosecuted and banned from publishing. Investigation revealed that that the assassination attempt was organised by a religious extremist group. In a speech he delivered in Adana on 6 December 1952, Menderes said, 'No one has the right to violate the freedom of conscience in the country . . . The Malatya incident has shown that those who want to use religion for various purposes work collectively.' Consequently, on 23 July 1953, 'the Law to Protect Freedom of Conscience and Assembly' was enacted to sanction 'use' of religion or religious feelings to obtain political or personal influence. Nevertheless, the failed assassination attempt on Yalman led to the crystallisation of the fear of *irtica* (violent reactionary Islam/religious fanaticism) in Kemalist circles.[16]

Samsun deputy Hasan Fehmi Ustaoğlu was expelled from the DP on 9 December 1952 due to an article he published in *Büyük Cihad* daily in

Samsun. The title of his article was, 'It is not true that the nation is indebted to Atatürk's reforms'. A number of publications with Islamist views were censored. Necip Fazıl Kısakürek, the editor-in-chief of *Büyük Doğu*, was sentenced to nine months and twelve days in prison in December 1952 for an article he published in the magazine, which was found to be against *laiklik* by the Press Court.[17] Eşref Edib (Fergan), the editor-in-chief of *Sebilürreşad*, was sentenced to five months in prison on 5 March 1953 for an article published in the magazine titled 'Black Fundamentalism, Yellow Fundamentalism, Red Fundamentalism'. On 23 January 1953, the Nationalists Association, a right-wing conservative association, was shut down. The president of the association, DP Isparta member of the parliament Sait Bilgiç, and his friend Tahsin Tola were served to the disciplinary board for expulsion.

On 11 February 1953, the editor-in-chiefs of newspapers published in Istanbul (Ahmet Emin Yalman from *Vatan*, Ali Naci Karacan from *Milliyet*, Falih Rıfkı Atay from *Dünya*) gathered at the Journalists' Association and decided to form a National Solidarity Front (*Milli Tesanüd Cephesi*) against *irtica* and racism. The call of the journalists attracted great interest and support from various segments of society. In his speech to the parliament two days later, Prime Minister Menderes expressed his satisfaction with the establishment of the National Solidarity Front.

DP Hardens

On 2 May 1954, the DP won an overwhelming majority in the general elections and at the very beginning of its second term in power, it enacted a series of laws to take measures to suppress the opposition. Among these laws was one aimed at penalising provinces that voted for the opposition. Kırşehir, which voted for the *Cumhuriyetçi Millet Partisi*, the successor of the Millet Party, was made a district.[18] Malatya, which voted for the CHP, was divided in two to form the province of Adıyaman. Dissident journalists were sentenced to long prison terms by various court decisions. The DP also displayed an intolerant attitude towards the opposition within the party; dissenting party members were expelled from the DP. These practices, which greatly restricted the independence of the judiciary, university autonomy, freedom of the press and the possibilities of opposition, led to a gradual hardening of relations between the opposition and the government. In the years following 1954, the DP adopted an even more repressive attitude.

Although the DP emerged victorious in the 1957 elections, its votes lagged behind the total votes of the opposition parties. After the elections, the opposition parties started to propagandise that the government had turned into a minority government and started to look for ways to overthrow it. Against this unity of the opposition, the DP launched a counter-attack by establishing a *Vatan Cephesi* (Homeland Front) in an effort to increase the number of DP supporters and thereby strengthen the party. Prime Minister Adnan Menderes mentioned the *Vatan Cephesi* for the first time in his speech at the DP Manisa Provincial Congress on 12 October 1958. He called on the DP's provincial, district and hearth organisations to join the *Vatan Cephesi*. The list of those who joined the *Vatan Cephesi*, which did not have a legal character, was regularly announced on the state radio every day. These long lists of names, read at news time, had a negative effect on the public and provoked a reaction. The gathering of the opposition in the unity front and the government in the *Vatan Cephesi* further increased the political tension in the country. The *Vatan Cephesi* initiative lasted until 27 May 1960, when the DP government came to an end.

The plane carrying Prime Minister Adnan Menderes and his delegation to London to attend the Tripartite Cyprus Conference crashed on 17 February 1959 near Gatwick Airport to the south of London. Menderes survived, but fourteen of the twenty-one people on board died in the crash. When he returned to Turkey, Menderes was cheered tremendously. Hundreds of sacrifices were made all over the country. Menderes himself immediately went to Eyüp Sultan and offered ten sacrifices. According to his close friend Samet Ağaoğlu, he himself attributed his salvation to divine protection (Ağaoğlu 1967: 43). From then on, even in group meetings in the Assembly, he would proudly declare that he was 'God's favourite person'. The same conviction spread rapidly among the public. After a one-day stay in Istanbul, Menderes arrived in Ankara the next day, where he was greeted with great enthusiasm, too.

Menderes's survival of the London plane crash was interpreted in some media as it happened, '*Allah'ın şanı uluhiyeti sayesinde* (thanks to the glory of Allah)'. Hence, due to this fact a group in the Assembly started arguing that the Constitution should include the clause 'The religion of the Turkish nation is Islam' and penal sanctions should be imposed on those who blaspheme the sacred. Allegedly, this was one of the factors that led the armed forces to take action to put an end to policies based on the abuse of religion (Tunaya 1962: 245).

In terms of relations between the government and the opposition, 1959 was an extremely tense year. This tension became even more severe in 1960. At the end of April 1960, clashes broke out between security forces and university students, resulting in casualties. There was also a subtle movement within the army against the ten-year DP rule. On 27 May 1960, a group of officers gathered under the name of the National Unity Committee, chaired by General Cemal Gürsel, announced the seizure of power on behalf of the Turkish armed forces. This announcement was made in a statement broadcast by radio on the morning of 27 May 1960. The declaration said, 'Due to the crisis our democracy has fallen into and upon the recent unfortunate events, in order to prevent fratricidal strife, the Turkish armed forces have taken over the administration of the country.'

Bediüzzaman Said-i Nursi and *Nur* (Light) Movement (*Nurculuk*)

Bediüzzaman Said-i Nursi (1876–1960), the founder of the Islamist movement known as *Nurculuk*, died on 23 March 1960 in Urfa during his domestic travels in Turkey,[19] and was buried in the Haliürrahman Mosque cemetery. On 13 July 1960, his grave was opened and his bones were buried in an unknown place near Isparta. His life has been divided into three periods in terms of his activism: (1) the Old Said (1876–1922), (2) the New Said (1922–50), and (3) the Third Said (1950–69) (Vahide 2005). These three periods overlapped with the main periods of modern Turkey's history. Each period of his life had different characteristics and strategies.

Born in 1876 in the village of Nurs to a Kurdish family in Bitlis, Said-i Nursi was unable to complete his studies in various madrasas due to his constant arguments with his schoolmates and teachers.[20] However, he had a wide knowledge of religious subjects, especially in the field of hadith. Hence, he was known as *Bediüzzaman* (the wonder of the age) from an early age. In 1894, Said-i Nursi travelled to Van; his dream was to realise a madrasa project called *Medresetü'z Zahra* in Van. The leaders of the *İttihat ve Terakki*, whom he contacted for this purpose, approached him cautiously. Nevertheless, he took part in the Balkan Wars and World War I on the side of the *İttihat ve Terakki*. In this period, Nursi became a member of the *Ittihad-i Muhammadiyya*, the committee that tried to unite Muslims under the Ottoman caliph (Reed 1999: 138; Vahide 2005). Nursi viewed politics as a means to solve the problems that (Ottoman) Muslims experienced (Kuru and Kuru 2008: 101).

In 1922, the transformation began from the 'old Said', who pursued a political way, to the 'new Said', who initiated a faith-based movement (Reed 1999: 212). Said-i Nursi, who was in Van between 1923 and 1925, was accused of participating in the Şeyh Said rebellion. He was tried by the Independence Court and sentenced to exile. He lived in exile in Burdur, Isparta, Barla, Kastamonu and Emirdağ. In 1934, he was arrested in Eskişehir, due to the increasing number of his disciples, that is 'Nur students' in Isparta. He was released in 1936. Meanwhile, copies of the *Risale-i Nur* corpus were spreading rapidly among his followers; copies made by hand and through the use of duplicating machines (Eickelman 2002: 124). In 1943, he was subjected to compulsory residence in Afyon/Emirdağ. In 1948, he was sentenced to twenty months in prison for establishing a politically motivated association; he was released after the DP's general amnesty in 1950.

In 1952, the Istanbul Prosecutor's Office filed another lawsuit against him for illegal religious propaganda. The subject of the case was his newly published book *Gençlik Rehberi* (Youth Guide). Said-i Nursi was acquitted of this case and another one in 1953. In 1956 he declared that his followers were obliged to support the DP. In 1958 he obtained permission to print *Risale-i Nur* (Epistles of Light) in Latin letters. Nursi was sending letters about political issues to political leaders, consequently Prime Minister Menderes and other politicians met with him. However, it should be underlined that Nursi never supported the use of Islam for political aims. He rejected the understanding of the Islamic state and political Islam, but rather he focused on Islamic beliefs and moral values; the ascetic aspect of Islam. He challenged the classical view on the so-called unity of *din-wa-dawla* (religion and state). For him, Islam is a religion; it does not belong to any group, and cannot be monopolised by any community. If any group uses Islam as a means for its own political aim, there is a possibility of limiting Islam to that group. According to Nursi, the state should be neutral and the servant of the people. Therefore, he always supported modern institutions and values such as the republican state, democracy, and the separation of state and religion (Karabaşoğlu 2004: 282–9).[21] Said Nursi was also an advocate of an intellectual and spiritual dialogue between Muslims and Christians (Michel 2008: 235–6).

Nurculuk, which spread rapidly after 1952 with the support of the DP, is based on some 130 booklets with various titles, with the general title of *Risale-i Nur*, which Said-i Nursi personally dictated. Even though Nursi apparently benefitted from Sufism, he cannot be defined as a Nakşibendi. Several scholars' mistake of defining him as such (Özdalga 2000;[22] Karpat 2001: 108, 113) mostly depend on their reference to Şerif Mardin's ground-breaking book titled *Religion and Social Change in Modern Turkey: The Case of Bediüzzaman Said Nursi*.[23] As Kuru and Kuru (2008) put it, 'despite its scholarly quality, Mardin's book misrepresents the Nur movement as an extension of the Naqshibandi tariqa'. Moreover, Nursi never identified himself with the Nakşibendi, or any other *tarikats* (Reed 1999: 39).[24] Although he was influenced by Sufism, he made it clear that his faith-based movement was something new and different from Sufism.[25] Nursi's goal was the survival of Islam as a living text, one embodied in daily experiences, without the support of political means and traditional orders (Yavuz 2003b: 157–62).

The Diyanet

The DP leadership never considered making any changes in the status of the Diyanet. Criticisers of the *laiklik* applications of the CHP did not have any problem with the official promotion of Sunni Islam; on the contrary they preferred to benefit from the opportunities offered by the state (Sitembölükbaşı 1995: 37–8, 71–2). During the transition period from single-party to multi-party regime there were two scholars of religion as the consecutive chairs of the Diyanet.

Ahmet Hamdi Akseki

Ahmet Hamdi Akseki (1887–1951) graduated from the Kalam branch of the *Medresetü'l Mütehassısin* in Istanbul in 1915. He gave lectures at various madrasas and schools and at Istanbul *Darülfünun*. Initially, in 1924, Akseki began working in Diyanet as a member of the *Müşavere Heyeti* (board of consultants). Between 1939 and 1947, he served as the deputy chair of Diyanet.

Upon the death of Şerefeddin Yaltkaya in 1947, he was appointed President of Diyanet, a position he held until his death. Hence, Akseki worked at Diyanet for more than a quarter of a century as one of the founders of the institution.

For the development of Islamic societies, Akseki advocated that religion should be purified from superstition and based on two basic sources, the Koran and the hadith. Akseki wrote works such as *Dini Dersler* (Lectures on religion, 1920, three volumes), *İslam Dini Fıtridir* (Islam is inborn, 1925) and *İslam Dini* (Islam Religion, 1933) in order to meet the public's need for religious knowledge. During the single-party years, publishing and publication of religious works was forced down to the lowest level, to the point of a few copies a year (Kara 2016: 415–500). Akseki, on the other hand, took advantage of the opportunities of his institution and position, and carried out exceptional religious publishing activity without clashing with the main policies of the republican ideology on religion, adapting to them conveniently. He also stretched and partially exceeded early republican policies aiming at simple knowledge and religious sensitivities. Akseki was also an influential intellectual in his own field and one of the most important representatives of Islamist thought in *Sırat-ı Müstakim* and *Sebilürreşad* circles, which transferred from the late Ottoman period to the Republic.[26]

Eyüp Sabri Hayırlıoğlu

Eyüp Sabri Hayırlıoğlu (1887–1960), who was elected as Konya deputy in the second term of the Grand National Assembly of Turkey (1923–7), advocated for the revision of the *Kanun-u Esasi* (Constitution) and the proclamation of the Republic in his speeches in the People's Party group meetings and in the TBMM. In addition, his proposal to celebrate the proclamation of the Republic and Atatürk's election as the Republic's president with 101 cannon shots was accepted. After failing to be elected as a member of the parliament in the third term, Hayırlıoğlu resumed his profession as a lawyer in Konya. In the meantime, he also engaged in trade. Upon the death of Ahmet Hamdi Akseki, Hayırlıoğlu was appointed as the Chair of the Diyanet (1951–60) and became the first president of the Diyanet to be allowed to wear 'spiritual outfit' outside the temple according to a Council of Ministers decision dated 22 November 1951.[27]

In his time as the Chair, a morality programme was aired at Ankara Radio beginning as of 6 March 1953, and the he delivered the first speech himself on

'The Relations between Faith and Action'. During his presidency, he became a party to a major polemic in the press of the time, on the occasion of a question addressed to him. The question was about whether it was permissible to print the Koran in the Arabic language but in Latin letters. Answering the question on 1 June 1958, Hayırlıoğlu stated that this would not be permissible, listing his reasons.[28] On 10 June 1960, he was dismissed from his post as the Chair of the Diyanet due to ill health; four months later he died.

The Non-Muslim Population

The DP was initially supported by non-Muslim communities. However, within a short period of time, the prosperity created by the DP's economic opportunities in the initial years in power would begin to decline, and non-Muslims would once again become targets at a time when unemployment increased in the cities and the gap in wealth widened (Kuyucu 2005: 372–3).

In 1938, the management of minority foundations was given by a law (no. 3513) to special administrators (single trustees) appointed by the *Vakıflar Genel Müdürlüğü* (General Directorate of Foundations) itself. Thus, minority communities were deprived of the opportunity to manage their own affairs. In 1949, this system was abolished and minority foundations were defined as community foundations whose management was to be formed through elections (Benlisoy 2019: 356).

Pogrom of 6–7 September 1955

Stalin began to use the Russian Orthodox Church to increase his influence both in the Balkans and the Middle East and questioned the ecumenical identity of the Fener Patriarchate.[29] In response, the US and the UK felt the need to elect a cleric to the Patriarchate with the calibre and power to counter this 'threat'. So Athinagoras, the archbishop of the North and South Americas, was made Turkish citizen at once and elected patriarch in 1948. Patriarch Athinagoras departed from the traditional Fener policy of his time and became the most ardent supporter of the Turkish–Greek rapprochement under the NATO umbrella. Hence the softened relations between Turkey and Greece helped the Greek Orthodox Patriarchate of Fener to flourish (Macar 2003: 183–95).

In August 1954, the Cyprus dispute began to flare up internationally.[30] At the end of June 1955, Britain invited Turkey and Greece to a conference on Cyprus. The talks began in London on 27 August 1955. According to the Turkish thesis defended by Foreign Minister Fatin Rüştü Zorlu, the island should be given to Turkey, while Greece insisted on *Enosis*.[31] In the meantime, in order for the government to demonstrate public support, the '*Kıbrıs Türktür Cemiyeti*' (Cyprus is Turkish Society) was established and the public was started to be made a party to the problem through the consciousness of Turkishness. *Türkiye Milli Talebe Federasyonu* (National Students Federation of Turkey) also launched rallies and demonstrations to raise national awareness and excitement about Cyprus (Akgönül 2007).

The events began on the evening of 6 September 1955 when initially state radio broadcasted at 13.00, and then the evening newspaper *Istanbul Ekspres*, known to be close to the DP, published the news that Atatürk's house in Thessaloniki had been bombed. As soon as the news was published, a large group of students, led by the Turkish Cypriot Association, gathered in Taksim Square in Istanbul and began to march. First, various Greek newspapers were burned, and then houses and shops belonging to non-Muslims, especially Greeks, were looted (Sezer-Şanlı 2019: 381–4). Menderes learned about the incidents in Istanbul when the governor of Istanbul called him between 16.30 and 17.00. He ordered the governor of Istanbul: 'You are aware of the necessity of resorting to military forces in case of need, you will strictly prevent even five people from gathering together in the amount you desire according to your estimates and discretions.'[32] When Menderes was informed that the events had reached a dangerous level, he called the commander in charge of the military units and gave the order to fire if necessary to maintain order.[33] When he learned that the events could not be brought under control, he immediately came to Istanbul. Nevertheless, the attacks continued not only in and around Beyoğlu, but also in districts far from Beyoğlu and each other, such as Beykoz, Kadıköy and Prince's Islands (Aktoprak 2010: 38). Depending on varying sources, different conclusions can be reached about the harm caused by the uprisings. According to a Turkish source, 4,214 houses, 1,004 workplaces, seventy-three churches, one synagogue, two monasteries, twenty-six schools, and 5,317 other establishments such as factories, hotels, pubs, etc., were attacked.[34] According to an American source, 59 per cent of the attacked workplaces, and 80 per cent of damaged houses belonged to Greek Orthodox. Seventeen per cent of all assaulted workplaces and 9 per cent of all damaged houses belonged to

Armenians. In addition to these, three out of thirty-three Armenian churches and four out of twenty-two Armenian schools were attacked. Twelve per cent of all attacked workplaces and 3 per cent of all destroyed houses belonged to Jewish residents according to this source.[35] In household attacks, Greek Orthodox women in particular were raped.[36]

In Izmir, there were attacks against the Greek Consulate and the Greek pavilion at the Izmir Fair, as well as against all non-Muslim minorities, including Greeks and Levantines. The fact that the events in Ankara were less violent than those in Istanbul was due to the smaller Greek population in this city (Güven 2005: 43). It should be underlined that the security forces did not intervene in the incidents, but martial law was declared in Istanbul and Izmir after midnight.

The government and military authorities blamed the communists for the events.[37] After the declaration of martial law, forty-five people, including Aziz Nesin, Kemal Tahir and Asım Bezirci, who had been previously labelled as communists, were detained and arrested as perpetrators of the attacks (Nesin 1986: 48). After the incidents, the Turkish Cypriot Association was closed down and eighty-seven people involved in the events were also arrested. All arrested would be acquitted after serving five or six months in prison (Üçüncü and Öksüz 2022: 274–301).

For the victims of 6–7 September, Menderes said,

> All citizens will work together. We will leave no trace of destruction. In order to compensate for the moral damages, we must show national solidarity, extend our hand of compassion and tell them that we want to live as brothers and sisters. We will quickly repair the temples and schools. We will open all the shops in a short time.

Under the auspices of the prime minister, a relief campaign was launched by a committee of leading industrialists (Demir 2007: 47).

An investigation in Greece revealed that the sound bomb planted in Atatürk's house had been given to an official at the Turkish consulate by a student from Western Thrace, who was said to be a member of *Milli İstihbarat Teşkilatı* (MIT/National Intelligent Organization). Despite the lack of witnesses, Menderes and Zorlu were found guilty of planning the events of September 6/7 at the Yassıada Court (Üçüncü and Öksüz 2022: 403–61). Speros Vryonis, in his 2005 book, documents the direct role of the DP organisation and government-controlled trade unions in amassing the rioters that swept Istanbul. Ten of Istanbul's eighteen branches of the 'Cyprus is Turkish' Association were run by DP officials (Vryonis 2005). Richard D. Robinson states in his 1965 book that a critic of the Menderes regime commented to him in 1962, 'It is now almost generally agreed that these riots were planned, organized, and started by Democratic leaders and local bosses, but developed into far beyond the original plan and intention' (Robinson 1965: 157). It seems that the demonstration was deliberately incited to unintended violence by other parties, the identity of whom still remains undisclosed. Local authorities, knowing of the government-sponsored demonstration, apparently did not know how to respond to the violence during the first few destructive hours. But there was no evidence to prove that Menderes deliberately planned the type of mass violence that in fact erupted.

After 1955 Pogrom

On 16 September 1955, the Turkish authorities interdicted the publication of the minority newspaper *Eleftheri Phoni* and arrested its publisher Andreas Lambikis, whom they imprisoned without a warrant or official charges for a period of three months in the military jail of Harbiye. From early 1957 to 1959 the Turkish authorities deported fifty-seven personalities of the Greek Orthodox minority in İstanbul, including reporter Dimitrios Kaloumenos, who had captured with his camera the vandalism of 6 September 1955. A campaign was also launched then, using psychological pressure on consumers, forcing them not to buy products from shops owned by Greeks. To that end, they distributed propagandist leaflets in front of the non-Muslim shops, with the slogan '*Bu dükkan gavurların malıdır. Yanındakine girin, çünkü Türkündür*' (This shop belongs to an infidel. Prefer the shop next door, it belongs to a Turk) (Kiratzopulos 2009: 192–3).

Dilek Güven characterises the 6/7 September 1955 pogrom as demographic engineering for two reasons. The first is the fact that the riots both directly and indirectly provoked the non-Muslim population of Istanbul

(Greek Orthodox, Armenians and Jews) to migrate from the country. Although the Greek Patriarchate and the Greek consulate in Istanbul tried to prevent migration, after the riots the number of Greek-speaking residents was reduced from 79,691 in 1955 to 65,139 in 1960. Between 1955 and 1960, 10,000 Jews left Istanbul for Israel. The British consulate reported a sudden increase of visa applications from non-Muslim minorities after the riots. For a majority of the non-Muslim residents, the events of 6/7 September was evidence that they were not recognised as Turkish citizens. The belief was that they would be subject to discrimination in the future regardless (Güven 2011: 14–15).[38]

On 14 May 1948, following the establishment of Israel as an independent state, the Jewish population had already begun to emigrate from Turkey to Israel as a result of the increasingly negative climate towards non-Muslim citizens in Turkey. The Jewish population in Turkey, which was around 51,000 in 1945, dropped to 33,000 in 1955 and 23,000 in 1960 (Bali 2003: 432).

Educational Institutions

The number of Greek-speaking community primary schools increased from forty-four to fifty-one during the DP era. After the 1952 Turkish–Greek Educational Agreement, school supplies of Greek origin were provided to students free of charge. During this period, a commerce section was opened at Zoğrafyon High School. The Seminary in Heybeliada had a higher education section in 1951 and started to provide education to students from various countries. As a result of these activities, the total number of students in Greek-speaking minority schools increased from 3762 of the 1945–6 academic year to 6912 in the 1956–7 academic year (Benlisoy 2019: 361–362).

An important development in terms of Armenian educational institutions was the opening of the Surp Haç Tıbrevank Seminary in Üsküdar, Istanbul, with a permit granted during the Democrat Party government. Opened in 1954, the first principal of the school was the abbot Karekin Kazancıyan, who would be elected patriarch in 1994. In the 1950s, the school authorities travelled in the central and eastern regions of Anatolia to recruit students; however, it was closed in 1969 due to lack of students. Thus, the school was renamed the Surp Haç Armenian High School and continued its education life as a minority school (Barış 2021: 57–58).

Women in the 1950s

Anne McClintock states that 'all nationalisms are gendered' as well as invented, and that 'no nation in the world gives women and men the same access to the rights and resources of the nation-state' (McClintock 1993: 61). Indeed, in the transition period towards democracy as well, women and men were not given the same access to the rights and resources of the nation state. The patriarchal nature of Kemalist modernisation is one of the main arguments in feminist literature. The main indicators of this character are the suppression of female sexuality, the control of the female body and the visibility of women as genderless citizens in the public sphere (Kandiyoti 1987: 317–39; Arat 1997: 95–112; Berktay 1998: 1–11). In this sense, the transition from the Ottoman Empire to the Republic was a transition from an Islamic patriarchy to a modern patriarchy (Arat 1998). Examples of this situation abound in the transition to a multi-party regime.

At the Seventh Congress of the CHP in 1947, Necati Akgün, a delegate from Gümüşhane, stated that working women in the cities whose husbands had profitable professions such as doctors and lawyers earned money 'for their personal desires and whims' and that he wanted these women to be replaced by young men, for them not to be victims of leftist currents. Akgün's suggestion was met with applause (CHP 1948, Yedinci Kurultayı – proceedings: 160). The only reaction to Akgün's remarks came from Seyhan deputy Makbule Dıblan. Dıblan said to Akgün, 'In the revolutionary congress of Atatürk's great party ... I am at a loss to understand the meaning of women's withdrawal from working life' (CHP 1948, Yedinci Kurultayı – proceedings: 189).

Women are the most important objects of control for patriarchy in the media.[39] For example, according to Peyami Safa (1899–1961), a journalist, columnist and novelist, there are male professions that require objective vision and cold-bloodedness, and it is both impossible and inaccurate for women to work like men:

> Most of our problems arise from the incompatibility between 'reason' and 'reality'. Reason wants women to work like men in society and at the same time manage to keep the characteristics of their body and soul. Reality does not allow this: In professions such as judges, lawyers, surgeons, etc., which require male qualities of thought and expression, objective vision and cold-bloodedness, it

would not be right, even if it were possible, for a woman to retain her extra tenderness and sensitivity. Especially a woman who gives birth every two or three years, and who has to stay with her baby for months at a time with each birth, cannot reconcile her maternal duties with her professional life ... The fact that there are more women students than men at the Universities of Paris shows that this cause is destined for a greater crisis in the West and arouses justified concerns in the European mind.[40]

On 13 April 1949, *Türk Kadınlar Birliği* (the Turkish Women's Union) was reopened with the aim of protecting the rights of women and promoting their cultural advancement. Mevhibe İnönü, the wife of President İsmet İnönü, became the honorary president of the association, and among the founding members of the association were women deputies of the CHP. Several other women associations were established in the following years of the DP period.[41] Zühal Kılıç argues that Kemalist women's organisations tried to overcome women's shortcomings instead of defending women's rights, and therefore it would be more accurate to call them *organisations for women* rather than women's organisations (Kılıç 1998: 350).

On 9 March 1956, three women members of the parliament from DP introduced a draft legislation in order to ban chador: Aliye Timuçin, Edibe Sayar and Nazlı Tlabar.[42] Campaigns have been running since the 1930s against the veil and chador (Adak 2022: 189–203). A legislative draft of 1956 stirred several arguments in the parliament and in the media (Kurt-Güveloğlu 2016: 17–23) The proposal did not receive support within the DP; male DP members of the parliament advised Timuçin, Sayar and Tlabar to withdraw their proposal. Eventually the draft was rejected.[43]

The 1950s were years in which women's presence in working life in Turkey was increasingly felt and women's work outside the home became an important topic of discussion. As Ahmet Makal points out in his study, 'Historical Origins of Women's Labour in Turkey: 1920–1960', the proportion of women engaged in agriculture in the general female labour force between 1945 and 1955 was 96 per cent (Makal 2012: 55). In the 1950s, women who were forced to work for low wages in the cities began to work as day cleaners in the homes of upper- and middle-class professional women who were unable to perform the care and housework expected of them. According to Cahit Talas, one of the reasons for the low wages of women workers in the

1950s was that women were more likely than men to be excluded from unions and had less collective bargaining power (Talas 1957).

While the women's movement in the 1950s adopted and reproduced the dominant patriarchal discourses on the one hand, on the other hand, it is seen that its actions and discourses prepared the ground for the feminist claims and demands that would be voiced by the women's movements of the following periods (Sarıtaş and Şahin 2019: 665).

Notes

1. *TBMM Zabıt Ceridesi*, Dönem VII, Toplantı III, c. 20 (1 Kasım 1945), 7.
2. *TBMM Zabıt Ceridesi*, Dönem VII, Toplantı III, c. 20 (1 Kasım 1945), 8–9.
3. For a short biography of Adnan Menderes, see Bora 2019.
4. Celal Bayar was an early member of the *İttihat ve Terakki*; he was among the first supporters of the National Movement during the Turkish War of Independence. During the Atatürk era, he most notably served as minister of the economy and later as prime minister at the time of Mustafa Kemal's death.
5. Numbers differ slightly in different sources since there has been several disputes over the outcomes and there exists no official numbers for 1946 general elections.
6. Gökçen Beyinli reads this step as a policy that uses 'chosen' shrines as tools to reattach Ottoman roots to Turkish national identity as 'Turks' and 'Muslims'. According to Beyinli, this policy was to reposition Turkey as a strong nation state in the new global order (Beyinli 2020). Visiting shrines and performing rituals thereof as a means of living their faith, especially for women; see Beyinli 2021.
7. For debates in the Assembly, see Gözaydın 2020: 34–5.
8. For a thorough analysis on the CHP Seventh Congress, see Uzun 2012. For changing religious policies of CHP and regarding debates, see Çevik and Dinçer 2018.
9. Fevzi Çakmak was among the most senior officers within the imperial army at the time of the Ottoman collapse. After serving with distinction during the Turkish War of Independence, he was appointed to head the Turkish General Staff, a position he held until 1944. Çakmak, who was known as a devout commander, was buried in Eyüp Cemetery attended by a large crowd amidst the sounds of *tekbirs* (magnification of God/God is greater: *Allahu akbar*), in a ceremony that turned into an anti-CHP demonstration on the grounds that national mourning had not been declared. For Çakmak's diaries covering the eleven-year period between 1 January 1911 and 31 December 1921, and his last days before his death on 10 April 1950, see Hatemi 2010. For his political career, see Çiftçi 2019.

10. Cem Eroğul, in his monography on DP, categorises the ten years of its power in three episodes: the rise (1950–4), the pause (1954–7); and the fall (1957–60) (Eroğul 1970). The DP era has not been much of a focus in Turkish literature. Atilla İlhan's *Kurtlar Sofrası* (Table of the Wolves) published in 1963 is one of the rare novels concentrating on those times.
11. For a thorough account of these debates, see Azak 2010: 68–76.
12. *Kamet* is the *ezan* for the ones in the mosque.
13. For a compilation of narratives against the call to prayer to be recited in Turkish, and praises for the *ezan* to be in Arabic, see Armağan 2010.
14. The 1950s were still times when religious education was under quite strict control. İhsan Arslan, one of the founders of the AKP, grew up in the 1950s in the village of Balbaşı in Siirt, where children from the surrounding area received madrasa education. In his memoires Arslan recalls, 'Soldiers used to travel in pairs. We called them *romi*. When the shepherds noticed the *romis*, they would send word back to their villages. The madrasah would empty. Almost all the students were draft evaders, not registered in the population registration. When the gendarmerie came, the students would go down to Zore Creek' (Arslan 2020: 23).
15. For the Law on Crimes against Atatürk and Ticanis, a fundamentalist religious group, see Tekin 2004: 261–3; Koca 2019.
16. For an analysis of the Malatya Incident as an accelerator of fear of reactionary Islam as violent threat, see Azak 2010: 85–114. Umut Azak scrutinises thoroughly '*irtica*' as a contested concept in her book *Islam and Secularism in Turkey*. See Azak 2010: 86–9.
17. For the journal *Büyük Doğu*, see Koçak 2002: 601–13; Cantek 2003: 645–55.
18. *Kırşehir Vilayetinin Kaldırılmasına ve Nevşehir Kazasında Nevşehir Adıyla Yeniden bir Vilayet Kurulmasına dair Kanun*. For discussions on the law draft, see *TBMM Tutanak Dergisi*, Dönem X, c. 1 (June 1954), 343–61.
19. For an analysis of the representations and perceptions of Said Nursi and *Nurculuk*, both in the press and the academic works of the period, with a special focus on the public debate on *laiklik* triggered by the visits of Said Nursi to the cities of Ankara, Konya and Istanbul in December 1959 and January 1960, see Azak 2010: 115–38.
20. For the early life of Nursi in a context that underlines his Kurdishness, see Ulugana 2022: 322–6.
21. Zeynep Akbulut Kuru and Ahmet Kuru argue that neither political Islamism nor Sufism truly reflects Nursi's teaching. 'The development of a new category, faith-based activism (*hizmet-i imaniye* or *iman hizmeti*, in Nursi's own words), is necessary to understand his thoughts and activism.' See Kuru and Kuru 2008: 100.

22. In a later work, Özdalga defines *Nurculuk* as 'developed partly independently from the other branches of the Nakşibendi order'; however, she still classifies it as Sufi-based as indicated in her title (Özdalga 2010: 80).
23. For a review of Şerif Mardin's reading of Nursi, see Arlı 2004: 124–35.
24. Akgündüz comments that, 'The *Risale-i Nur* movement is not a *tarikat*, it is not a society (gemeinschaft), it is not a political party, so when asked what it is, Bediüzzaman replied, "We are a community" (gemeinschaft)' (Akgündüz 2010: 75–6).
25. For Nursi's critique of Sufism and his faith-based activism, see Kuru and Kuru 2008: 106–8.
26. In the preface of a very thorough work on Akseki, İsmail Kara states that, 'Since he was an active participant in publishing movements in both periods and wrote many works, it becomes possible to follow, see and evaluate the possibilities and problems, changes and continuities, searches and interpretations of a thought and movement centred on religion through his texts and attitudes' (Kara and Gündoğdu 2019: 7).
27. For a short biography of Eyüp Sabri Hayırlıoğlu, see https://www.diyanet.gov.tr/tr-tr/Person/PresidentDetail/28/eyyup-sabri-hayirlioglu.
28. Hayırlıoğlu's considerations briefly were:
    - The sound and grammatical structure of Arabic does not allow the Holy Koran to be written in an alphabet other than the Arabic alphabet. The eleven different sounds in the Arabic alphabet are not present in the Turkish alphabet. The Koran printed in Latin letters by the Maarif Publishing is full of errors.
    - Adding some characters to the Turkish alphabet is not a solution to the problem. Such a practice would not make the job easier, as it would require additional instruction in pronunciation. The youth of middle and higher education can learn the Arabic alphabet very easily.
    - Those who insist on reading the Holy Koran in Latin script are free to read the Holy Koran in Latin script currently available, provided that they accept the misreading in advance.
    - The issue of writing the Holy Koran in Latin script has nothing to do with Atatürk's reforms. In 1932, a *sura* was written in Latin letters and presented to Atatürk, who did not agree with this practice and initiated an investigation with a written and urgent order dated 26/5/1932 and numbered 6/1446. The advisory committee conveyed to him its opinion that printing the Holy Koran in Latin letters would mean distorting it (M. Öztürk 2019: 68–9).
29. For the ecumenical identity of the Fener Patriarchate, see C. Aktar (ed.) 2011.

30. For previous events that lead to the Cyprus dispute, see Babaoğlu 2012: 17.
31. Enosis is a Greek term meaning unity, describing the Greek Cypriot movement for political union with Greece.
32. *TBMM Zabıt Ceridesi*, D. 10, İ. 23, v. IX, 83.
33. When the commander passed on the order to his subordinates, he said, 'Even though I have orders to fire, you can manage with the gun stocks.' The Governor of Istanbul ordered the troops to open fire, but that order was not executed (Burçak 1998: 317).
34. Archives of the *Tarih Vakfı*, Fahri Çoker file, 6 Eylül Hadiseleri index.
35. NARA 782.00/9-1255, General Consulate of Istanbul to State Department, 01.12.1955.
36. For wounded, raped and dead, see Güven 2011: 5.
37. Nureddin Aknoz, the Commander of the Martial Administration, summoned journalists in Istanbul and told them that all publications related to the events of 6 September would be blamed on Communists, and that if any contrary thesis was put forward, the newspaper would be shut down immediately (Güven 2005: 188).
38. For minority demography in the 1950s, see also Benlisoy 2019: 370–2.
39. For several examples of patriarchal narrative in the media of the late 1940s, see Cantek 2008: 92–9.
40. *Ulus* daily, 16 December 1949.
41. For these associations, see Sarıtaş and Şahin 2019: 633–8.
42. For Nazlı Tlabar, see Kurt-Güveloğlu 2016; Çolak 2021.
43. *TBMM Tutanak Dergisi*, Dönem X, c.10, Birleşim 49 (26 March 1956), 1276.

4

AFTER THE MILITARY COUP OF 1960 (1960–1980)

> The events that took place during the Second World War, especially towards the end of it, seem like fairy tales to today's generations. However, these seemingly fairy-tale years have played a major role in the contemporary situation. The İnönüs, the Mendereses, the Justice Party, the National Salvation Party, or the National Action Party – all of whom and which can be included in the scope of today's historical memory are not mushrooms that grew from the ground; they grew from the seeds sown by the conditions of the 1940–1950s.
>
> Niyazi Berkes 1997: 159

The 1960 coup was an expression of the reaction by groups, including the military, against the state bureaucracy having lost its position at the pinnacle of the social hierarchy as a result of the development of the market economy and the empowerment of new social strata created in the 1950s. Steps were quickly taken to ensure that the military coup did not turn into a military regime. Thus, the military government found its solution to the regime crisis in the drafting of a new constitution; a committee composed of members of the Law Faculty at Istanbul University was assigned the task of drafting a constitution. In addition, academics from the Faculty of Political Sciences at Ankara University also prepared a draft constitution. In terms of its regulations on state–religion relations, the constitution submitted for approval – and eventually approved – by a referendum favoured the text drafted by the Istanbul University Commission.[1]

The 1961 Constitution

The 1961 Constitution that came into force by dint of the referendum held on 9 July 1961[2] introduced important innovations vis-à-vis the regulation of fundamental rights and freedoms, the establishment and functioning of the government, and the exercise of judicial and parliamentary oversight. One of the new institutions it introduced was a Constitutional Court to control the legality of legislation. The basic principles to be followed by the state and society were defined as 'the qualities of the Republic'; namely: 'The Republic of Turkey is a national, democratic, *laik* and social state governed by the rule of law based on human rights and the fundamental principles set out in the "Preamble" (Article 2)'.

Freedom of Religion and Conscience

The article regulating freedom of conscience and religion proved to be one of the most controversial during the process of drafting the 1961 Constitution. Members of the Constitutional Commission defended the Kemalist understanding of *laiklik*, whereas the conservative group in the Constituent Assembly were essentially arguing from a position informed by the classical Western understanding of secularism. Their main demand was that the right to religious belief be guaranteed, which they argued the relevant article in the draft constitution failed to do. They insisted that the state should assist religion rather than interfere with it, and that religious education should be provided. The interesting point here was the conservatives, who had been highly critical of the institutions for 'coming from the West', actually adopted the Western understanding of secularism and explicitly defended it. Still more interesting was the fact that, while they presented the absolute separation of state and religious affairs as 'non-interference by the state in religion', they also demanded that the state support religion and that it organise and regulate religion where necessary. These contradictions were indicative of an innately statist mindset with no input from a civil society (Gözaydın 2020: 41–3).

Freedom of conscience and religion was regulated in Article 19 of the 1961 Constitution:

- Every individual is entitled to follow freely the dictates of their conscience, to choose their own religious faith and to have their own opinions

- Worship, religious rites and ceremonies which are not contrary to public order, public morals or regarding laws shall be free.
- No person shall be compelled to worship, or participate in religious ceremonies and rites, or to reveal their religious faith and belief. No person shall be reproached for their religious faith and belief.
- Religious education and teaching shall be subject to the individual's own will and volition, and in the case of minors, to their legally appointed guardians.
- No person shall be allowed to exploit and abuse religious feelings or things considered sacred by religion in any manner whatsoever for the purpose of political or personal benefit, or for gathering power, or for even partially basing the fundamental, social, economic, political and legal order of the State on religious dogmas. Those who violate this prohibition, or those who induce others to do so shall be punishable under the pertinent laws. In the case of associations and political parties the former shall be permanently closed down by order of authorized courts and the latter by order of the Constitutional Court.

A secular state must provide freedom from religion, as well as guarantees for freedom of religion. Putting in place the checks and balances needed to provide freedom of conscience and religion to all is the job of the constitutional judiciary. The definition of *laiklik* set out by the Constitutional Court in the 1971 *Din Hizmetleri Sınıfı Kararı* (religious services staff decision) of 1971 aims not to exclude social manifestations of religion completely, allowing for a measured limitation in accordance with the rule of law:

> The principle of secularism enshrined in the Constitution of the Republic of Turkey (may be defined as) specifically:
> a. adopts the principle that religion should not be dominant and influential in State affairs,
> b. takes religion under the protection of the Constitution by granting unlimited freedom, without discrimination, to that aspect of religious belief that relates to the spiritual life of individuals,
> c. adopts restrictions on, and prohibits the abuse and exploitation of, those aspects of religion which relate to acts and conduct which transcend the spiritual life of the individual and affect society, in order to safeguard public order, confidence and interests,
> d. gives the State, as the protector of public order and rights, the power to exercise control over religious rights and freedoms.[3]

The Diyanet

The Diyanet was regulated constitutionally for the first time in Article 154 of the 1961 Constitution, in accordance with which the institution 'fulfils the duties specified in its special law'. After long debates in parliament, the Diyanet bill finally passed into law on 22 June 1965 as Law No. 633 on the Establishment and Duties of the Diyanet. The duties were defined as 'to carry out affairs related to the beliefs, worship and moral principles of the Islamic religion, to enlighten society on religion, and to manage places of worship'. The law broke new ground in citing the 'moral principles', in which the state should not intervene, given its supposedly neutral stand.[4]

Since the establishment of the Diyanet in 1924, its personnel had had the status of civil servants. This had been criticised both for its incompatibility with the principle of *laiklik* and for breaching the principle of equality by providing the status to only Sunni clergy. In a controversial 1971 decision, the Constitutional Court found that the Diyanet and the civil servant status of its personnel were compatible with *laiklik*. The Court held that the civil servant status of the Diyanet's staff was necessitated by historical factors and other facts and circumstances relating to Turkey.[5]

The previous tendency for the heads of the Diyanet to serve in the position until the end of their lives changed after the 1960 coup, with subsequent administrations making several political appointments. After Eyüp Sabri Hayırlıoğlu was replaced by Ömer Nasuhi Bilmen, the Istanbul mufti, who remained in the post for just nine months, there were no fewer than eight more heads of the Diyanet between 1960 and 1980. These chairmen and the duration of their service were as follows: Hasan Hüsnü Erdem (1889–1974), two years five months; Tevfik Gerçeker (1898–1982), one year one month; İbrahim Elmalı (1903–94), eleven months; Ali Rıza Hakses (1892–1983), one year two months; Lütfi Doğan (as deputy) (1930–), four years seven months; Dr Lütfi Doğan (1927–2018) four years; Associate Professor Süleyman Ateş (1933–), one year six months; Tayyar Altıkulaç (1938–), eight years nine months (Kara [2008] 2017: 84–9).[6]

During a press conference, in reply to a question concerning the Diyanet recognition of the Alevi belief, İbrahim Elmalı, the Chair of the Diyanet, said that: 'The Alevi-Sunni issue had already faded away' (Azak 2010: 140, 156–62). This expression marked Elmalı's and the Diyanet's rejection of the Alevi faith as a valid interpretation of Islam.

The *Türkiye Diyanet Vakfı* (Turkish Diyanet Foundation/TDV) was founded in 1975 by senior Diyanet officials. Article 2 of its Foundation Deed states that the purpose of the institution is

> to assist and support the Diyanet in promoting the religion of Islam in its true identity and enlightening society about religion, building and equipping mosques where necessary, opening and operating treatment institutions for poor patients, and developing social aid and services by transferring the alms paid by Muslim citizens, such as *zakat* and *fitrah*, to those in need in society in accordance with their condition.[7]

As a private organisation in legal terms and hence not part of the Turkish official administration, the Foundation has flexibility in how it acquires and spends resources, accepting donations from sources barred to the Diyanet.

A Brief Overview of the Era

The 1960 military coup marked the start of a new era in the history of the Republic; in 1980, another military coup would bring this period to an end. In this twenty-year period bookended by coups, the political and institutional position of the Turkish armed forces would change step by step with the establishment of the multi-party system, society gradually attaining autonomy from the state, the new social and economic dynamism of the rapidly urbanising population, and the emergence of new actors on the political scene. This two-way influence–response dynamic may well have been the most important factor that drove Turkey from 1960 to 1980 (İnsel 2005: 2).

Capital Punishment and Executions

The Yassıada trials of DP politicians ended on 15 September 1961; of the fifteen death sentences handed out by the High Court of Justice, three were approved by the National Unity Committee: those of former Foreign Minister Fatin Rüştü Zorlu (1910–61), former Finance Minister Hasan Polatkan (1915–61) and Adnan Menderes. The first two were executed on 16 September 1961 by hanging on İmralı Island; Menderes was executed the following day.

Workers in Europe

In response to the demand arising from the labour shortage in the capitalist economies of Western Europe, and West Germany in particular, after World

War II, Turkey began to export labourers to these countries. On 13 June 1961, Turkey and West Germany signed a protocol regulating the principles governing how the workers would be sent. The first group of workers was sent to Germany on 24 June 1961. The protocol signed with West Germany was followed by agreements with Austria, the Netherlands and Belgium in 1964, France in 1965, and Sweden in 1967. This supply, which consisted of qualified workers in small numbers until 1963, would increase considerably over time. In response, Germany reduced its demand for labour in 1967, and the economic stagnation in Western Europe in the 1970s led to a further decline in the number of workers going abroad. In the period from 1961 to 1973, when labour recruitment was halted, up to one million Turkish workers were working abroad (Akgündüz 1993; İçduygu 2012).[8]

A Solution for Housing: Gecekondu

In the absence of a housing policy, and in the midst of the housing crisis that peaked in the post-war years, immigrants who flocked to big cities across the country as a result of the structural transformations of the 1950s found their own solutions to their housing problems. Migrants built makeshift dwellings on mostly public land without infrastructure, creating a new form of housing known as *gecekondu* (shantytowns: literally, 'built overnight'). Families lived in these dwellings themselves, and renting was rare. In the period 1960–70, *gecekondus* built to house the builders and their families began to give way to others built to generate rental income and additional financial gains. A Law on the Prevention and Rehabilitation of *Gecekondus* (no. 775) was enacted on 30 July 1966, but it failed to solve the problems.

In the 1970s, *gecekondu* construction became fully commercialised. In the early days, *gecekondus* were built by occupying land owned by the Treasury, public legal entities or private individuals; naturally, there were no deeds conferring legal ownership. However, land and capital owners were quick to realise that the main problem lay in the provision of cheap land and that there was strong demand for *gecekondu*. From the second half of the 1970s onwards, they divided the land they owned, or had acquired cheaply in areas where no planning restrictions were in place, into very small parcels, then sought to increase their profits by providing cheap land for *gecekondu* construction through a system known as *hisseli ifraz/tapu*, by which deeds of ownership were shared between multiple owners. In this way, *gecekondu* settlements were legalised in terms of ownership, but an unplanned urban sprawl of dubious legality had been created (Karpat 2009; Sabri Çakır 2011).

University Students' Protests

Around the world, 1968 was the year of youth uprisings. In Turkey, too, protests by university students in particular escalated rapidly. The *Fikir Kulübü* (Opinion Club) had been founded in 1956 by the students of the Faculty of Political Sciences in Ankara, and other such clubs had been organised in other universities in the following years which united to form the *Fikir Klüpleri Federasyonu* (Federation of Opinion Clubs) on 17 December 1965 (Ünüvar 2007a: 821–9). The most important actions undertaken by this group of young people, who adhered to an anti-imperialist leftist discourse, were the protests against the US Sixth Fleet that arrived in Istanbul in June 1967 and the student march from Istanbul to Ankara on 7–20 November 1967, demanding the nationalisation of private universities. In 1968, boycotts and occupations took place in many universities all over Turkey. On 15 July 1968, the US Sixth Fleet was once again the target of heavy protests by university students. On 16 February 1969, leftist youth demonstrating against the Sixth Fleet were attacked by a nationalist conservative group chanting the 'Muslim Turkey' slogan: two people were killed and 200 injured in the incident known as 'Bloody Sunday'.[9] This was the first mass participation by Islamist students and militants in a bloody, public clash with left-wingers.

Provocations, Assaults and Attacks

On 11 February 1968, in Osmaniye, a district in Adana province, there was a riot fuelled by news reports that later turned out to be untrue. The district governor prevented a rally organised by the Osmaniye Association for the Struggle Against Communism in response to the news story 'Koran burned in Kadıköy' published in the Istanbul daily *Bugün*,[10] owned by Mehmet Şevket Eygi, on the grounds that the news report was false. However, the crowd was determined to demonstrate and found another reason to protest, claiming that Ruhi Kılıçkıran, a student from Osmaniye in the Faculty of Theology at Ankara University, who had died a few days earlier, had been murdered by leftists.[11] Mingling with the congregation in the mosque, the crowd grew to include 2000 people. Shouting slogans such as 'damn communism ... we are losing our religion!', they were suppressed by police and gendarmerie forces.[12] It turned out that Kılıçkıran, who was described as a martyr to his faith by the partisan media, had been accidentally shot by his brother, a member of the *Adalet Parti*'s Ardeşen Organisation, not by leftists.[13] Speaking at the CHP's Ankara Provincial Congress on 18 February 1968, İsmet İnönü said: 'The events in Osmaniye show that the reactionary movement has reached a stage where it can both fabricate a lie and use that lie as a pretext for an attack. This development is evidence that the reactionary movement is emboldened by the state of the government.' Prime Minister Demirel responded by saying: 'Viewing and describing freedom of religion and conscience as *irtica* is called political oppression.'

On the night of 7 July 1969, when the congress of the Turkish Teachers' Union (TÖB-DER) convened in Kayseri, two mosques, the Turkish Cultural Association and an İmam Hatip school were bombed by unknown assailants. The governor of Kayseri cancelled the congress. The next day, thousands of people surrounded the Alemdar Cinema where the congress was being held and set the building on fire. The security forces were slow to deploy, and the events spread throughout the city. Leftist organisations were vandalised. The crowd, which numbered more than ten thousand, chanted the takbir and carried out various attacks against movie theatres and entertainment venues and the people in them. At a press conference in Ankara, union president Fakir Baykurt (1929–99) accused the government and the governor of Kayseri in strong language, thanked the Turkish armed forces and said, 'Teachers respect religion'. Prime Minister Demirel said, 'There are amateur and professional agitators in Turkey.'[14]

The funeral of İmran Öktem (1904–69), the President of the Court of Cassation, on 3 May 1969 at the Maltepe Mosque in Ankara was also the occasion for disturbances. In 1966, in his speech at the opening of the judicial year, his remarks about *Nurcus* had caused some reactions. Later, while commenting on *laiklik*, he quoted Voltaire and said 'God was also created by man', which caused further reactions. At his funeral, the clergy who worked in the mosque refused to perform their duties and the funeral prayer was led by a member of the congregation.[15]

The 'march and rally for the liberation of Jerusalem' organised by the MSP in Konya on 6 September 1980 turned into a demonstration at which demands were made for sharia. Slogans such as 'The godless state will be destroyed' and 'Sharia will come and the savagery will end' were chanted frequently at the rally. During the singing of the National Anthem, a group sat on the ground and protested the anthem. The rally, which was the subject of an investigation by the Konya Prosecutor's Office, was cited as one of the justifications for the September 12 coup.

Aydınlar Ocağı *and the Turkish–Islamic Synthesis*

Aydınlar Ocağı (Hearth of Literati) was founded in 1970 in İstanbul as a right-wing association (Copeaux 2006: 83–6). Its first president was İbrahim Kafesoğlu (1914–84), one of the founding ideologists of the Turkish–Islamic synthesis (Copeaux 2006: 91–103).[16] In the early 1960s, the conservative intellectuals who gathered around the *Türk Kültürü Araştırma Enstitüsü* (Turkish Culture Research Institute), which was established under the auspices of President Cemal Gürsel, and the *Türk Kültürü* (Turkish Culture) journal published by this institution, shaped the historical background of the Turkish–Islamic synthesis under the leadership of İbrahim Kafesoğlu. Although this idea was at first predominantly Turkist, it had become reconciled with Islam by the mid-1970s. The original thesis emphasised that Islam was an important component of Turkish identity. Turks had voluntarily accepted Islam and then restored it, and had flown the flag of Islam on three continents. The thesis did not only provide a reconciliation with the Ottoman past, it also sought to liberate Kemalism from the hegemony of the Left. As a result, Islamist intellectuals like Abdurrahman Dilipak rejected the Turkish–Islamic synthesis as a synthesis of Kemalism and Islam (Bora and Can 1991: 133–4). The timing of the founding of the *Aydınlar Ocağı* was significant, too, for its role in rapidly developing a movement to counter the rising leftist intelligentsia. 'The importation from abroad of ideas that were incompatible with the national culture was leading to leftist ideas and anarchic acts that were weakening the state in the Republic of Turkey and shaking the structure of the nation' (Alper and Göral 2003: 585). The *Aydınlar Ocağı*'s mission was clearly stated in its statute:

> The aim of the *Aydınlar Ocağı* is to spread the idea of Turkish nationalism by developing national culture and consciousness, to fight against the crisis of ideas and anarchy of concepts that are shaking our national well-being, and to keep alive and strengthen the elements that make up our national existence.[17]

Escalating Violence

On 11 June 1970, *Devrimci İşçi Sendikaları Konfederasyonu* (DİSK, Revolutionary Workers' Syndicates Confederation) and affiliated unions reacted strongly to legislation amending the Trade Union Law. Protests began on 15 June 1970. On 16 June 1970, 70,000 workers participated in the first day of demonstrations in Istanbul and Izmit. Participation rose to 150,000 on the second day, when demonstrations turned into armed clashes with the security forces. Protest marches were organised in Ankara, Izmir, Cologne and other cities in Germany. Over the course of the two days of events, three workers, one policeman and one shopkeeper were killed; nearly 200 people were injured, and hundreds of workers were detained. Law no. 1317, which had triggered the protests, was annulled by the Constitutional Court in February 1971 as unconstitutional (Sülker 2005).

The student movements that had started in the mid-1960s changed in nature in the early 1970s, with various groups turning to armed protests. Against this backdrop, on 12 March 1971, the leadership of the Turkish armed forces issued a warning to the government, which came to be known as the 12 March Memorandum. On 17 May 1971, the kidnapping of Efraim Elrom (1911–71), the Israeli Consul General in Istanbul, by the People's Liberation Front of Turkey (THKP-C), a Marxist-Leninist organisation led by Mahir Çayan (1946–72), led to a hardening of the government's stance.[18] On 23 May 1971, Elrom was found murdered in a house in Istanbul with three bullets in his head. The house where Mahir Çayan and Hüseyin Cevahir (1945–71), who were wanted for their involvement in Elrom's murder, took shelter was surrounded by security forces. On 1 June 1971, Hüseyin Cevahir was killed and Mahir Çayan was wounded in the ensuing operation. On 31 May 1971, *Türk Halk Kurtuluş Ordusu* (People's Liberation Army of Turkey/THKO) members Sinan Cemgil (1944–71), Kadir Manga (1947–71) and Alparslan Özdoğan (1946–71) were among six activists killed in a clash with security forces on Nurhak Mountain in Adıyaman. On 16 July 1971, the trial of Deniz Gezmiş (1947–72), the founder and leader of the THKO, and his friends began; this was followed by the trials of Mahir Çayan and his friends on 16 August 1971. On 9 October 1971, Deniz Gezmiş and seventeen of his friends were sentenced to death for attempting to change the constitutional regime by force. On 30 November 1971, Mahir Çayan and four of his friends escaped from Maltepe Military Prison by digging a tunnel. Meanwhile, on 20 September 1971, constitutional amendments were adopted that imposed major restrictions on fundamental rights and freedoms.

On 10 January 1972, the Military Court of Cassation upheld the death sentences of Deniz Gezmiş, Yusuf Aslan (1947–72) and Hüseyin İnan (1949–72). On 19 February 1972, Ziya Yılmaz (1938–2011), who had escaped with Çayan, was captured wounded and Ulaş Bardakçı (1947–72) was killed. On 27 March 1972, three British technicians working at the NATO air base in Ordu were kidnapped by Mahir Çayan and his friends. On 30 June 1972, an operation was launched against the activists, who were hiding in the village of Kızıldere in Niksar province. Ten activists, including Çayan, were killed in the operation, while Ertuğrul Kürkçü (1948–) was captured alive. British technicians were also killed during the clash. After the operation in Kızıldere, the security forces took control of the situation throughout the country. On 6 May 1972, Deniz Gezmiş, Yusuf Aslan and Hüseyin İnan were executed.

The struggle between right-wing and left-wing groups seeking to dominate in universities and dormitories had actually begun in 1968, but it escalated in 1974. On 17 December 1974, Şahin Aydın, a leftist student at Yıldız State Academy of Architecture and Engineering, was stabbed to death. In the first four months of 1976, no fewer than thirty-two people lost their lives as a result of attacks: of these, twenty-five were left-wing, five right-wing and two were security guards. Three of the five right-wingers were killed 'for abandoning the cause' by their own organisations. Two hundred and thirty-one people lost their lives in attacks and clashes in 1977. Of these, thirty-four people lost their lives on 1 May 1977 in Istanbul's Taksim Square, when demonstrators were fired upon by gunmen who have still to be identified. On 16 March 1978, seven students were killed when a bomb was thrown at students leaving the central building of Istanbul University. Nearly 900 people lost their lives as a result of the violent incidents that took place throughout 1978, which included the Bahçelievler massacre in Ankara in which seven students (members of TİP) were murdered by ultra-nationalists. The academics Bedrettin Cömert (1940–78), Bedri Karafakioğlu (1915–78) and Necdet Bulut (1938–78) were also killed, while Servet Tanilli (1931–2011) was condemned to a lifetime in a wheelchair after a bullet lodged in his spine. The next year witnessed a further escalation of violence. Among those killed in 1979 were Abdi İpekçi (1929–79), editor-in-chief of the *Milliyet* daily, and Ümit Doğanay (1929–79) and Cavit Orhan Tütengil (1921–79), faculty members at Istanbul University. In the twelve months between September 1979 and September 1980, approximately 3000 people fell victim to politically motivated violence. The vast majority of the victims were left-wing, but the dead also included right-wingers, members of the security forces, celebrities and ordinary citizens (Ersel *et al.* 2005: 262–4, 398–400). At the time, left and right divisions extended to state structures including the police forces (Gürel 2004).

The violence quickly subsided after the Turkish armed forces seized power directly down the chain of command on 12 September 1980, and largely ceased shortly thereafter.

Political Parties and their Leaders

Following the military intervention of 27 May 1960, the *Milli Birlik Komitesi* (National Unity Committee), the military junta which had previously exercised power alone, formed the Constituent Assembly on 13 December 1960, sharing power with the Assembly of Representatives, a civilian institution. The Assembly of Representatives was formed through a mixture of elections and appointments. The Committee announced that political parties had to complete their establishment procedures by 13 February 1961 at the latest in order to participate in the first general elections. After this announcement, new parties began to appear one by one on the political scene; however, only four parties met the organisational requirements for participation in the elections, two old (*Cumhuriyet Halk Partisi* and *Cumhuriyetçi Köylü Millet Partisi*/CKMP)[19] and two newly established (*Adalet Partisi* and *Yeni Türkiye Partisi*/YTP).[20] The elections were held on 15 October 1961 with 81 per cent of the potential voters casting their votes. The CHP received 36.7 per cent of the votes, the AP 34.8 per cent, the CKMP 14 per cent and the YTP 13.7 per cent. Thus formed, the Grand National Assembly of Turkey (TBMM) held its first session on 25 October 1961, bringing the military regime to an end. The TBMM elected Cemal Gürsel as president on 26 October 1961. The CHP–AP coalition government headed by İsmet İnönü took office on 20 November 1961.

On 10 October 1965, six parties participated in the general election. The AP received 52.9 per cent of the votes and won 240 of the House of Representatives seats. This number of deputies was enough for the AP to form a government on its own. The CHP's share of the vote was 28.7 per cent, the lowest since 1950, so it was represented in the Assembly with 134 seats. On 11 November 1965, the first Demirel government began to work. On 14 September 1966, Cemal Gürsel died and on 28 March 1966, Cevdet Sunay, former Chief of General Staff, was elected as president.

Süleyman Demirel resigned on 12 March 1971 on the grounds that the memorandum which the armed forces had issued to the government could not be reconciled with the constitution and the rule of law. On 26 March 1971, CHP deputy Nihat Erim (1912–80),[21] who had withdrawn from his post in the Republican People's Party (CHP) to sit as an independent member of parliament, was appointed to form a 'national unity' coalition government as a 'neutral and technocratic' prime minister. The interim 12 March regime continued after Nihat Erim with the governments of Ferit Melen and Naim Talu. On 6 April 1973, Fahri Korutürk, former First Admiral of the Turkish Naval Forces (1903–87), was elected president. The March 12 interim regime ended with the elections of 14 October 1973.

In 1974, CHP leader Bülent Ecevit formed a coalition government with the National Salvation Party (MSP), which held seven portfolios with Erbakan serving as deputy prime minister (25 January–17 November 1974). The coalition ended as the CHP and MSP's approaches to political, social and economic issues began to rapidly diverge. In the second half of the 1970s, two Nationalist Front administrations were led by Süleyman Demirel as prime minister (31 March 1975–21 June 1977; 21 July 1977–5 January 1978). On 25 November 1979, Demirel formed the last civilian government before the military intervention of 12 September 1980. The Demirel government announced its economic stabilisation programme on 24 January 1980. The programme, known as the 'January 24th decisions', ushered in a period of liberalisation in the Turkish economy.

Cumhuriyet Halk Partisi *(CHP)*

On 24 August 1961, one and a half months after the Constitution was submitted to the referendum and accepted, the fifteenth CHP Congress convened in Ankara. Kasım Gülek (1905–96), who competed with İsmet İnönü for the party leadership, suffered a heavy defeat. In the 1963 local elections, the CHP (36.22 per cent) fell behind the AP (45.48 per cent). In the 1965 general elections, the CHP's share of the votes declined drastically.

At the eighteenth CHP Congress, which convened in Ankara on 18–21 October 1966, those who adopted the 'left of centre' view emerged victorious (Ağtaş 2007: 194–221). Bülent Ecevit, an intellectual and a journalist who had led the group which formulated the left-of-centre view, was elected General Secretary (Alper 2007: 202–13).

The March 12 memorandum caused great turmoil within the CHP. As a result of internal party struggles, Bülent Ecevit was elected CHP chairman on 14 May 1972. Ecevit introduced profound changes to the CHP from the bottom up, moving it to a more left-of-centre position with repercussions that continued throughout the 1970s.

İsmet İnönü resigned from the CHP on 5 November 1972, declaring that he could not align himself with the party's new policy; he died on 25 December 1973.

Adalet Partisi *(AP)*

The *Adalet Partisi* (Justice Party/AP) was founded on 11 February 1961 under the leadership of Ragıp Gümüşpala (1897–1964), who was first appointed Chief of the General Staff by the *Milli Birlik Komitesi* and then retired. The AP's programme was largely similar to the DP's and was underpinned by a liberal approach.

At the AP's second congress, held in Ankara on 27–29 November 1964, Süleyman Demirel (1924–2015), who had not been well known to the public until then, was elected to the presidency, which had been left vacant by the death of Ragıp Gümüşpala. Demirel, who would leave his mark on Turkey's political life for many years to come, was an engineer bureaucrat who had served as the General Director of the State Hydraulic Works between 1955 and 1960 (Bora 2005: 550–77; 2009: 502–8).

The AP won the majority of the votes in both the 1965 (52.9 per cent) and 1969 (46.5 per cent) general elections. Süleyman Demirel served as prime minister in several governments between 1965 and 1980, including the last civilian administration before the 1980 coup.

Türkiye İşçi Partisi *(TİP)*

The TİP (The Workers' Party of Turkey) was a socialist party founded on 13 February 1961 by twelve trade unionists. The TİP failed to participate in the

1961 elections. In 1962, the founders invited intellectuals to join the party with the aim of bringing the working class and intellectuals together so they could jointly overcome the deadlock they were experiencing. Mehmet Ali Aybar (1908–95), Behice Boran (1910–87), Adnan Cemgil (1909–2001), Cemal Hakkı Selek (1902–96), Fethi Naci (1927–2008) and many other intellectuals became members of the party. Its founding chairman was Avni Erakalın (1925–2012), a trade unionist. When Erakalın resigned from the party to become a parliamentary candidate for the YTP, the party's founders offered the presidency to Associate Professor Mehmet Ali Aybar, who duly became chairman in February 1962. The Socialist Party of Turkey joined the TİP in May 1962. The Party's first congress, held in Izmir on 9–10 February 1964, was an important turning point in terms of clarifying the party's socialist political identity. According to the party statute adopted at the congress, quotas were set to include working class members.

The TİP programme of 1964 indicated that the party adhered to *laiklik* and supported freedom of conscience, religion and thought. The personal, religious and philosophical beliefs of all citizens were to be afforded the utmost respect, and the party wanted everyone to do the same. There were to be no restrictions on religion, and every kind of worship, ritual and religious ceremony was to be permitted, as long as it was not contrary to public order, general morality or laws. No one was to be compelled to join in worship or religious rituals ceremonies, or to reveal their religious and philosophical beliefs. No one could be put under pressure or reproached because of their religious and philosophical beliefs. The TİP programme proposed that the religious affairs of the Muslims were to be managed by the Diyanet, which would be absolutely neutral in its dealings with Alevis and Sunnis. The non-Muslim communities were to manage their own religious affairs in line with international agreements and the provisions of the 1961 Constitution, which granted freedom of religion and conscience. Complete respect was to be shown to non-Muslims' schools, temples, hospitals, graveyards, and other community foundations.[22] It is thus clear that the TİP programme was not only secularist, it also made detailed statements on issues of belief.

In the 1965 elections, the TİP won 2.97 per cent of the votes in fifty-four provinces and sent fifteen MPs to the TBMM; in the 1966 partial Senate elections, it won one senatorial seat and increased its parliamentary group to sixteen members. These deputies, who included Çetin Altan (1927–2015), played an effective role in opposition. Having an effective opposition marked a turning point in the development of representative democracy in Turkey. However, faced by the rise of the socialist movement, the government introduced electoral thresholds to prevent the presence of opposition elements in the TBMM. In addition, socialist deputies serving in the TBMM were subjected to various forms of repression, including physical attacks as well as legal attacks such as the removal of their immunity. Although the latter attempt was rejected by the Constitutional Court, the electoral thresholds ensured that the TİP was not represented in the TBMM in the years ahead.

In the partial Senate elections of 1968, the TİP increased its share of the vote to 4.7 per cent, but failed to win any seats. However, it did win Bahadın, Yozgat, in the local elections. In 1968, attacks on the TİP turned violent and Vedat Demircioğlu (1943–68), a university student, was murdered (Şener 2007: 362).

After the 1965 elections, the internal debates within the party moved to the *Fikir Klüpleri Federasyonu* (Federation of Opinion Clubs), which had been founded in parallel with the TİP. When the *Fikir Klüpleri Federasyonu* changed its name to *Türkiye Devrimci Gençlik Federasyonu* (Revolutionary Youth Federation of Turkey/Dev-Genç) at its congress in October 1969, the ties between the TİP and Dev-Genç were completely severed (Ünüvar 2007b: 830–3).

A split within the TİP between Mehmet Ali Aybar's view of fully independent, humanistic socialism (Özman 2007: 376–403) and Behice Boran's support of Soviet Russia (Atılgan 2007: 436–72) deepened with the Warsaw Pact's intervention in Czechoslovakia in 1968. In the 1969 elections, Aybar was forced to resign from the presidency after a fall in the TİP vote. Although the TİP received 3 per cent of the votes in the 1969 elections, it could only win two parliamentary seats (Mehmet Ali Aybar and Rıza Kuas) because the electoral law had been changed especially to block the TİP. In February 1971, Aybar also resigned from the party. The TİP was shut down on 21 July 1971, following the 12 March memorandum. Its leaders were arrested and sentenced to prison terms of up to fifteen years. Some of them were released with the 1974 amnesty (Silier 2007: 432–476). In 1975, the TİP reorganised under the leadership of Behice Boran, but it has not been successful in any election since.

Cumhuriyetçi Köylü Millet Partisi *(CKMP)*/Milliyetçi Hareket Partisi *(MHP)*

Weakened by the departure of Osman Bölükbaşı in the 1960s, the CMKP invited Alparslan Türkeş and his friends to join in the hope that they would help revive the party's fortunes; Türkeş would take over the party leadership at the extraordinary congress on 30 July 1965.

Türkeş's discourse in the 1963–6 period was dominated by a corporatist, developmentalist, Kemalist restoration plan. In the 1965–9 phase, he began to emphasise Turkism and fanatical anti-communism within a fascist discourse. By opposing the breaking up of large agricultural estates and arguing that the solution was to 'develop agriculture and shift landless peasants to other sectors', he ensured the continued support of large landowners close to the CKMP. In the 1965 elections, while the CKMP's average vote across Turkey was 2.2 per cent, it exceeded the 10 per cent threshold in five provinces due to the block votes controlled by large landowners. Meanwhile, the CKMP, which was organised in just twenty-five provinces in 1965, had increased its organised presence to sixty-one provinces by 1967. At the CKMP congress in November 1967, Türkeş's famous words 'shoot anyone who joins the cause and betrays it' were included for the first time in a leaflet distributed at this congress (Bora and Can 1991: 44–6).

Secularism was strongly defended in the CKMP's 1965 election programme and in all of Türkeş's writings and speeches. However, this discourse had begun to change by the late 1960s. Türkeş and the CKMP spokesmen began to describe Islam as 'an inseparable element of Turkish history'. In 1969, Türkeş famously said, 'We are as Turkish as the Tengri Mountain and as Muslim as the Hira Mountain. Both philosophies are our motto.'[23]

The party's Adana congress, convened on 8 February 1969, was an important turning point. First, the name of the CKMP was changed to the Nationalist Movement Party (MHP) at this;[24] second, the regulations institutionaliszed a hierarchical governance that greatly increased the authority of the central organs, and Türkeş in particular, over the organisation; third, the party's emblem was set as three crescents on a red background, and the emblem of its youth branches as a grey wolf with a crescent (Yanık and Bora 2017: 298–300). On 7 January 1969, Türkeş announced that the commandos also known as *bozkurtlar* (Grey Wolves), who had been undergoing training in camps since the summer of 1968, were helping the party to protect Turkey against communism. It is known that President Cevdet Sunay responded to the CHP leader İnönü, who drew attention to the terrorism committed by the Grey Wolves, by saying: 'My dear fellow, they are the boys who fight against communism' (Bora and Can 1991: 48). Thus, Turkism was blended with ever larger doses of Islam as the 1970s progressed (Bora 2009: 357).

Milli Nizam Partisi *(MNP)*/Milli Selamet Partisi *(MSP)*

On 26 January 1970, the Islamist political movement emerged in Turkey's political arena as the *Milli Nizam Partisi* (National Order Party/MNP), a political force distinct from the right-wing political parties in which Islamic forces had previously preferred to participate. Necmettin Erbakan (1926–2011), one of its founders, was appointed as the party's chairman.[25] The programme of the MNP, which was dominated by an Islamist discourse, placed great importance on national and spiritual development. It opposed the free market economic approach and the interest system, and argued that the economy should be regulated through state intervention. The party also opposed joining the European Economic Community and argued that heavy industrial investments in Turkey should be accelerated.

The MNP was supported by three social layers: (1) new elites who came from provincial religious families, were educated in the secular educational institutions of the Republic, and were generally self-employed; (2) religious entrepreneurs engaged in commerce and industry in the provinces; and (3) Sunni religious people with low incomes living in both provincial and big cities (Çakır 2004: 545). The MNP's religiously sensitive agenda was not well received by republican Turkey's establishment. On 5 March 1971, the chief of the Public Prosecutor's office filed a lawsuit against the MNP on the grounds that it was 'conducting activities against *laiklik*'. As a result, the Constitutional Court decided to dissolve the party on 21 May 1971.

On 11 October 1972, a new party was founded under the name *Milli Selamet Partisi* (National Salvation Party/MSP).[26] Erbakan officially joined the party in May 1973. On 20 October 1973, he was appointed party chairman. The MSP argued that an 'imitating' order had been created by the preference for westernisation in the name of development. The party insisted that the nation had to return 'to its roots and favour Islam once again'. The MSP made its first electoral breakthrough in the 1973 elections, winning 11.8 per cent of the votes and forty-eight parliamentary seats. As no single party was able to secure a majority in the elections, the MSP became a partner in government with the CHP.

The MSP also made its influence felt in the Diyanet through inter alia the appointment of Süleyman Ateş to chair the institution.[27] While in government, Necmettin Erbakan sought to pressure the Diyanet into promoting the party's agenda through various means, including an investigation of the Süleyman Efendi community with a view to its being declared un-Islamic, if necessary (Lord 2018: 14n). Tayyar Altıkulaç, a former chair of the Diyanet, confirms such conduct in his memoires (2011: 481–9).

Birlik Partisi/Türkiye Birlik Partisi

Stating their opposition to 'extreme right and left, discrimination and sectarianism', a group of Alevi origin founded the *Birlik Partisi* (Unity Party/BP) on 17 October 1966. Hasan Tahsin Berkman[28] was appointed as the party's chairman. The party's programme emphasised freedom of religion and conscience and called for freedom of worship that did not contravene public order, public morality or the law. Declaring themselves to be 'progressive, reformist and Kemalist', the party's founders chose a lion as the party's emblem, symbolising the Prophet Muhammed's son-in-law Ali, with twelve stars representing the twelve imams around him. Hüseyin Balan (1917–84) was elected president at their congress in 1967, and Mustafa Timisi (1936–) was elected to replace him at the congress in 1969. In the 1969 general elections, BP entered parliament with eight deputies. In 1970, five deputies from the BP supported Demirel in a crucial budget session in the parliament; the backlash from within the party was sufficient to bring the BP to an end:[29] in 1971, the BP was renamed the *Türkiye Birlik Partisi* (Unity Party of Turkey/TBP). As such, it was represented in parliament by a single deputy following the 1973 elections. The TBP did not win any parliamentary seats in the 1977 general elections (Çakmak 2020: 651–4). Following the decline of the TBP, the Alevi movement would make no further progress until the mid-1990s.

Religious Circles

Even though the religious lodges were closed down in 1925 and their activities banned, several religious circles remained in existence. In the 1970s, political and legal associations and foundations began to express explicitly Islamic demands. David Shankland defines *tarikat* as, 'a number of believers united by the respect that they show for a particular person of lineage, whom they regard as different from other human beings by virtue of their being favoured by God' (Shankland 1999: 64). The teachings of the founding figure of a *tarikat* are accepted by their followers as the correct path to achieve union with God. These religious circles are hierarchical and often exclusive. Since the 1970s, *tarikat* has become a very infrequently used group title replaced by 'community'. Islamic circles began to vigorously distinguish themselves from rightism and conservatism in the 1970s; for instance, the *Milli Türk Talebe Birliği* (National Union of Turkish Students), the most prominent right-wing student organisation, began to Islamise in this decade.[30]

Hizbu't-Tahrir

Breaking away from the Muslim Brotherhood, Al Nabhani (1909/1914?–77), an Islamic scholar from Jerusalem, founded *Hizbu't-Tahrir* in 1953. The launch in 1967 of the Turkish branch of *Hizbu't-Tahrir* was radical Islamism's first attempt at organising in Turkey. The trial of five people, some of them university students, arrested along with Ercüment Özkan (1938–95) on 5 August 1967 for being members of *Hizbu't Tahrir*, began on 11 April 1967.[31] This fundamentalist orientation, which Ercümend Özkan would continue independently from the 1970s onwards, targeted the Western capitalist system as a graver and more fundamental enemy than communism (Yanık and Bora 2017: 295–6).

Nur *Movement*

After Nursi, the search for a successor began. Those who had been around Nursi and attended his lectures assumed leadership roles within the community. In 1967, a group of university-educated 'Nurcus' decided to establish a publishing house and publish a magazine: Mihrap publishing house and the magazine *İttihad* (1968–71) were launched as a result. When the magazine was closed down in 1971, they decided to publish a daily newspaper under the name *Yeni Asya* and a publishing house of the same name was also set up.

A nationalist *Nur* movement formed around Mehmed Feyzi (Pamukçu) Efendi (1912–90) in Kastamonu. This shift towards nationalism was a product of the Cold War period, and Bekir Berk (1926–92), who was Nursi's lawyer in most of the cases against the *Nur* movement, played an important role in bringing the *Nurculuk* closer to the Nationalist Front, supported by the *Yeni Asya*. The new nationalist line would play a catalytic role in some Kurdish Nurcus separating from the movement.

In the early 1970s, Islamic groups that had previously supported the DP and AP faced a new situation with the establishment of the Naqshbandi-backed MSP. When a group of Nurcus decided to support the MSP, the movement split for the first time along party lines. The group's decision to support the MSP was also a reaction against the AP's support for big capitalist groups. However, their support for the MSP did not last long: differences emerged over Erbakan and the policies he implemented in coalitions, and the Nurcus left the MSP before the 1977 elections. The Nurcus lost confidence in the MSP and would subsequently support Demirel's AP (Yavuz 2004: 290–1).

Gülen Movement

The Gülen movement, which is also described as a neo-*Nurcu* movement, is an Islamic network organised around Fethullah Gülen (1941?/1944–).[32] In terms of its social base, the Gülen movement has always been made up of members of the middle class who are trying to make the most of new economic and social opportunities (Gözaydın 2009a). In the years between 1970 and 1983, when the movement was forming, the primary focus was on raising individuals with Islamic knowledge and aimed to serve Islam. 'In an attempt to synthesize tradition and modernity, religion and science' (Koyuncu-Lorasdağı 2010: 221), having resigned from the Diyanet in 1981, Gülen embarked on a series of activities to train students, starting with the Kestanepazarı Koran Course in Izmir and later expanding to include summer camps and student houses (Yavuz 2013: 35). The movement's target audience during this period were students at various levels, from middle school to university. At the centre of the movement then were *ışık evler* (light houses)[33] inspired by Said Nursi's *dershane* (classroom) model (Yavuz 2003b: 13–15). Gülen desired to raise a 'golden generation'[34] equipped with the knowledge of the age and intent on renewing the Turkish–Islamic tradition on the axis of the nation state. As implemented by Gülen, Said Nursi's individual-oriented faith service based on a renewal of Islamic thought became a project for social change.[35] The students who were recruited and trained in *ışık evler* during this period would later play a key role in realising Gülen's new projects and in establishing relations with the grassroots of the movement.

During these first years, Gülen made great efforts to stay away from politics, and especially from political organisations with Islamic points of reference. For Gülen, Koranic verses should never, under any circumstances, be used as slogans for a political purpose (Koyuncu-Lorasdağı 2010: 225). The fight against communism, on the other hand, was high on his agenda, and Gülen was among the founders of the Anti-Communist Association in Erzurum in the 1960s. In this early period, a group of shopkeepers who had gathered around Gülen helped in particular to meet the financial needs of the students who had begun to live in *ışık evler*. In return for the financial contributions made by the owners of these small and medium-sized businesses, the students organised lectures and *sohbetler* (meetings). The movement began publishing *Sızıntı* magazine, its first media organ, during this period, in 1979, by the efforts of the student residents of the *ışık evler*.

Süleyman Efendi Community

The Süleyman Efendi community is a religious circle formed around the teachings of the Koran and an Islamic scholar named Süleyman Hilmi Tunahan (1888–1959) (Özdamar 2008). Tunahan was a *şeyh* of the Nakşibendi order's Müceddidiyye branch. The title *Süleymancılık* emerged during the power struggles within the *Din Görevlileri Federasyonu* (Religious Officers Federation), which was established in 1962, when his rivals used the word pejoratively to refer to the members of the circle in question. 'Süleymancı (of Süleyman)' had been a reference to the *şeyh* – in the rivals' opinion disrespectfully – in his first name.[36]

Defined as a movement centred on courses designed to teach the Koran and a circle to organise their implementation, *Süleymancılık* dates back to the 1940s. Tunahan personally planned and directed the Koran courses from 1941 until his death in 1959. In 1956, the number of courses increased from seventy to 400, and by 1959 it was close to 1000. The circle's activities also expanded beyond Istanbul, with Alanya, Kütahya and Eskişehir becoming important centres (Aydın 2004: 311).

One of the important turning points for the Süleyman Efendi community came in 1965, when the Law on the Diyanet was enacted. By dint of this law, only graduates of the Imam Hatip schools, the Faculties of Theology and the Higher Islamic Institutes could be appointed as religious officials. The 1965 legislation, which made it impossible for those who attended the Süleyman Efendi courses to actually become religious officials, caused serious disturbances within the community. After 1965, the Süleyman Efendi circles established the Federation of Associations for the Establishment, Protection and Maintenance of Koran Courses. In 1971, the government that came to power through the 12 March coup issued a regulation demanding that 'all course buildings are to be transferred to the Diyanet'. The permits and licenses of courses that did not comply with this decision would be revoked. In response, the Süleyman Efendi community founded the Federation of Associations for Assisting Students of Koran Courses and Other Schools. At this point, in addition to organising its courses in the Koran, the Süleyman Efendi circles began to win disciples by providing dormitory services to young people studying in high schools and universities, and by providing religious information on demand. The movement, which had been led by an advisory board after Tunahan died, became a centralised structure after 1971, with Tunahan's son-in-law, Kemal Kaçar (1917–2000), assuming leadership. This led some disgruntled members to break away from the movement. The Süleyman Efendi community would remain in open conflict with the Diyanet throughout the 1970s, and this was reflected in the press.[37]

After the 12 March memorandum, the Süleyman Efendi community expanded to new spheres of activity abroad. Islamic Cultural Centres were established in Germany, where Turkish workers were concentrated, with Cologne as the centre. Centres of this sort were later opened in other countries.

Although *Süleymancılık* was founded in Istanbul by a member of the *ilmiye*, the movement has mostly appealed to lower middle groups socially, economically and culturally. It finds support in rural areas, too, though it is urban in terms of its organisational structure (Aydın 2004: 321).

İskender Paşa Community

The İskender Paşa community has been one of the most influential religious groups in the religious and political life of post-1970 Turkey.[38] As a result of the closure of the *tekkes* by a law enacted in 1925, the Gümüşhanevi *Dergah*, founded by Ahmed Ziyaeddin Gümüşhanevi (1813–94) within the Müceddidiyye-Halidi lineage of the Nakşibendi order, was forced to cease its activities. The dervish lodge's unofficial existence continued in the person of Şeyh Mustafa Fevzi Efendi (1851–1926), but was limited to the informal relations he formed around his person. The lineage relations formed the first mortar of the community. In 1952, Mehmed Zahid Kotku (1887–1980) became the *şeyh*, and the circle began to be known as İskender Paşa in reference to the mosque where he served as imam (Çakır 1990: 17–24).[39] His predecessor, Abdülaziz Bekkine (1895–1952), had left him a very valuable inheritance: a large circle which included university professors, students and bureaucrats – in brief, a well-educated group which was middle to upper-middle class socially, economically and culturally.

In the 1970s, prominent members of the community played active roles in founding both the MNP and the MSP. Professor İrfan Gündüz (1950–), a student of Kotku, argues that Mehmed Zahid Kotku always argued that 'Muslims' should govern the state.[40] In its early years, the MSP restricted its activities to within the boundaries set by Kotku. However, this did not last long, especially when, in the late 1970s, the MSP adopted a more radical line in parallel with the rise of political Islam around the world. Kotku did not remain silent in the face of these developments: he warned party officials and Erbakan himself, and demanded that the party close down the youth organisations that had begun to participate in the armed conflicts. Erbakan did not respond positively or negatively to these warnings. This period ended with the *coup d'état* of 12 September 1980, when the MSP was shut down along with other political parties. Mehmed Zahid Kotku died a month later (Yaşar 2004: 325–31).

Erenköy Community

The *Erenköy Cemaati* was named after Erenköy, the Istanbul neighbourhood in which the Zihni Paşa Mosque stands in which Mahmut Sami Ramazanoğlu (1892–1984), an accountant by profession and the leader of the Community, worked after 1955. Ramazanoğlu taught and influenced a sizable number of professors, journalists, intellectuals and businessmen (Yavuz 2003a: 144–5). He led talk-circles in Erenköy until 1979, when he left Turkey to go to Saudi Arabia. He died there in 1984.[41] A largely urban network, the Erenköy community is composed of middle and upper middle-class businessmen organised across all of Turkey.

İsmail Ağa Community

The İsmail Ağa community, which was established by Mahmut Ustaosmanoğlu (1929–2022), was named after the İsmail Ağa Mosque in Çarşamba-Fatih, Istanbul. Mahmut Ustaosmanoğlu, who is usually referred to as Mahmut Efendi and is known to his disciples as Efendi Hazretleri, was the imam of the mosque from 1954 until his retirement in 1997. This community differs from the previous ones in having had strict dress codes from the start: men should wear long beards and non-Western clothing, while women should wear black chadors. The community which Ruşen Çakır describes as 'the provinces in the metropolis' (Çakır 1990: 60), soon spread throughout Turkey. Although it appealed to the lower-income groups in society, it was not interested in anything beyond tackling spiritual deprivation and poverty. Mahmut Hoca contented himself with providing his followers with a network for economic cooperation within the community.

Menzil Community

The Menzil community was established by Abdülhakim Erol (1902–72) in Menzil, a village at Adıyaman, as a branch of the Nakşibendi order. Abdülhakim Erol was replaced by his son Muhammed Raşit Erol (1930–93) on his death. The Menzil community would become prominent in the 1970s, partly as a result of rumours that alcoholics and other addicts who had gone to Menzil had been cured of their addictions by the prayers of Şeyh Muhammed Raşit Erol and the soup he offered them.[42] In the 1970s, the community was known to be close to the MHP.

Milli Görüş *(National Vision)*

The intellectual foundations of the *Milli Görüş* movement were laid in the late 1960s. *Milli Görüş* was a political identity created mainly by Necmettin Erbakan which takes a domestic and Sunni Islamic approach to both international and daily affairs, from industrialisation to education (Çalmuk 2004: 554–8). The adjective 'national' carries a religious/Islamic emphasis rather than a temporal one. The title *Milli Görüş* was used to describe this political movement because the associations founded by Necmettin Erbakan to work with migrant workers in Europe bore the name *'milli görüş'*, and their umbrella organisation was called the *Avrupa Milli Görüş Teşkilatları* (European National Vision Organizations). The *Milli Görüş* movement founded the MNP, MSP, *Refah Partisi* (Welfare Party/RP), *Fazilet Partisi* (Virtue Party/FP) and *Saadet Partisi* (Felicity Party) over the years. The inclusion of the names of all five parties in the following sentence from the MNP's Founding Declaration provides symbolic proof that the *Milli Görüş* parties have always been heading in the same direction, despite all the changes and transformations they have undergone: 'The high morality and virtue in the nature of our nation will come to life, and through the proper mnp channels, it will begin to yield welfare, felicity and salvation across the whole country' (Çakır 2004: 544–5).

The Alevi Population

That the Alevi communities, and especially the younger generations of Alevi groups, took part in leftist movements in the 1960s made them a target for the *ülkücüs* (ultra-nationalists); this targeting became more pronounced in the latter half of the 1970s. However, stigmatising Alevis as perverts was actually a long-standing motif in anti-communist agitation. The discourse that identified communism with irreligion and immorality was used as a convenient way to appeal to Sunni conservatism (Bora 2017: 313). Urbanising Alevis who became business rivals in very many provinces was yet another factor underpinning the growing tension (Ozan 2015). In February 1975, there were attacks against Alevis and their businesses in Erzincan. In 1976, there were incitements against Alevis in the Pazarcık district of Kahramanmaraş and the Divriği district of Sivas on the grounds that the '*kızılbaş* and communists burned down the mosque'. On 18 April 1978, eight people were killed and hundreds injured in the events that began with the assassination of right-wing mayor Hamid Fendoğlu and the marking of Alevi and leftist houses (Çakmak 2020: 660). Resulting from various provocations, three pogroms and massacres against Alevis were still to come in 1970–80s, in various places in Turkey.

Sivas

On 3 September 1978, a fight broke out between children in a predominantly Alevi neighbourhood in Sivas (Alibaba); then, when their families joined in, the whole neighbourhood turned against each other. In the meantime, the rumour that 'Alevis are attacking mosques' started by the *ülkücüs* stirred some people up, and the incidents spread throughout the city. It was alleged that certain individuals drove through the streets with loudspeakers blaring: 'the leftists put bombs in mosques'.

During the incidents, the attackers shouted 'death to communists' and destroyed many businesses and houses belonging to CHP members and Alevis. Firefighters who went to put out fires in some neighbourhoods were threatened by the attackers and had to leave. Nine people were killed (officially, it is claimed by the Alevi community that up to seventeen people were killed) and more than 100 injured during these incidents (Çakmak 2020: 660).

The incidents petered out two days later, after troops were deployed to the city and a curfew was imposed. According to an investigation, 167 shops and over one thousand buildings were damaged.[43]

Kahramanmaraş

A total of 105 people were killed and 176 people were wounded in the violent incidents that broke out in Kahramanmaraş on 22–6 December 1978. Martial law was declared in thirteen provinces during the incidents. The incidents started with the bombing of a movie theatre on 19 December 1978. Seven people were injured, one of them seriously. As the rumour spread that 'Alevi communists threw a bomb into the cinema', a mob formed. The angry crowd threw stones at the CHP Provincial Centre and the TÖB-DER (leftist teachers association) building, breaking their windows. On the night of 21 December 1978, two teachers who supposedly threw the bomb into the movie theatre were shot and killed on their way home. The next day, when a leftist group of 4–5 thousand people arrived in front of the mosque for the teachers' funeral, they were met by a crowd of 8–10 thousand people who said 'Communists and Alevis cannot perform rituals in this mosque!' The crowd attacked the funeral procession with sticks and stones. After the clashes, the governor issued a statement saying that two people had been killed, thirty-nine injured and 300 businesses, the majority owned by Alevis and leftists, had been vandalised.

Then, on the morning of 23 December 1978, mobs shouting 'Muslim Turkey' and 'Army and nation hand in hand' terrorised the city. Armed with various weapons, these right-wing groups set fire to numerous buildings and workplaces belonging to leftist institutions. In the afternoon, the attackers spread throughout the city and headed into Alevi neighbourhoods. Armed with long-range weapons, the attackers surrounded these neighbourhoods, burning houses and committing massacres. Military units from neighbouring provinces were despatched to Kahramanmaraş. Despite a curfew, the attacks continued on 24 December 1978. The attackers also clashed with the soldiers. They opened fire on fire brigades, attacked the courthouse, and set fire to a police station. Finally, on 26 December 1978, the events were brought under control. Of those detained during the events, seventy-five people were arrested. After the incidents, many Alevi families left Kahramanmaraş and settled in other cities, in particular Mersin.

The defendants in the Kahramanmaraş pogrom were tried in military courts. At the trial that began in June 1979, the death penalty was sought for 330 of the 803 defendants. Ultimately, thirteen of the defendants were sentenced to death and executed in 1988 (Ersel *et al.* 2005: 452–3; Çakmak 2020: 660–7; Dinler 2020: 675–7).

Çorum

A total of forty-eight people were killed in the events that began in Çorum at the end of May 1980 and peaked in the first week of July. Following the assassination of the MHP deputy chairman, Gün Sazak, by unidentified assailants in Ankara on 27 May 1980, MHP supporters began demonstrating in Çorum on 29 May 1980. The demonstrators injured various left-wing individuals and destroyed their workplaces. Later that day, they began to attack the Milönü neighbourhood where Alevi and left-wing people lived. Barricades were set up and the clashes between leftists and MHP supporters spread throughout the city and continued until the first week of June.

However, although the situation seemed to have calmed down, violence erupted again on 1 July 1980. On the evening of 1 July, right-wingers called on the public to wage 'jihad' against Alevis and left-wing supporters and began to vandalise homes and businesses belonging to CHP supporters, left-wing individuals and Alevis. On 2 July 1980, although a curfew had been declared, events intensified and barricades were set up all over the city.

On 4 July 1980, after Friday prayers, right-wing activists spread a rumour that 'the mosque in Milönü has been bombed' and the events gained momentum. People streaming out of various mosques in the city attacked buildings belonging to Alevis and left-wingers; the clashes lasted for hours, despite the curfew that was imposed. Meanwhile, the city's electricity and water were cut off. On 5 July 1980, soldiers took control of the city and the clashes subsided to a significant extent. However, migration from the city began soon afterwards. In many places, the barricades could not be removed until 6 July 1980.

The death toll of the incidents, which continued intermittently between 29 May and 6 July 1980, was determined as forty-eight; there were rumours that the ears and noses of the wounded were cut off during the incidents. On 21 July 1980, Minister of Interior Mustafa Gülcügil resigned. It was also announced that those who had thrown bombs near Alaattin Mosque were right-wingers and had been captured (Ersel *et al.* 2005: 510–11; Dinler 2020: 677–87).

The Non-Muslim Population

Due to the continued violence against the Turkish community in Cyprus after December 1963 and Greece's unwillingness to cooperate with Turkey as a guarantor state to bring about a concrete solution to the problem, the Turkish government terminated the Convention on Residence, Trade and Navigation which it had signed with Greece. This decision by the Turkish government shocked the 12,000 Rum living in Istanbul. In the meantime, the deportation of the Greek Patriarch of Fener, Acting Greek Patriarch Emilyanos and Metropolitan Canavaris on 21 April 1964, on the grounds that they were active against Turkey, met with a reaction in Greece. The Papandreou government protested against Turkey before the signatory states of the Treaty of Lausanne, claiming that the provisions regarding the Greek Patriarchate of Istanbul had been violated. Meanwhile, 300 Greek nationals had been deported from Turkey by the end of June in the wake of Ankara's decision to annul the Convention, while the number of Greek nationals expelled from Turkey had reached 6,000 by August, following the intensification of the conflict in Cyprus in July and the bombing of the Greek Cypriot population by the Turkish air force.

By 16 September 1964, when the Convention was abrogated, this number had exceeded 7,200. The number of Greeks living in Istanbul dropped to fewer than 2,000 as those whose residency had expired at the end of 1964 and into 1965 gradually left Turkey (Romain Örs 2019).

Women in the 1960s and 1970s

Especially after 1965, women's voices began to be heard more in the labour and student movements, while woman also began to placed in more central roles in nationalist and Islamic contexts. Women with different identities had different issues and demands:

- Publications focusing on women's agendas (*Kadın Gazetesi* and *Kadın Sesi*) and women's associations (Turkish Women's Union, Turkish Association of University Women), most of which were actually founded in the 1950s, represented the modernising wing of the establishment.
- The socialist vision of the 1960s saw feminism as a bourgeois ideology designed to divide the socialist movement. The view of feminism and the struggles of socialist women in the 1960s, which emphasised progressivism and socialism, generally reflected this view. Although socialist women of the 1960s read feminist texts and identified inequality between men and women within the movement as well as in their relationships and social relations, they refrained from associating these observations and experiences with feminism (Akkaya 2011). Their view of women's issues was often shaped by basic Marxist texts. August Babel's *Women and Socialism*, in particular, seems to have been an important source in the adoption of the idea that discriminatory traditions and practices against women would end with socialism.[44]
- In the mid-1960s, women who embraced the nationalist and *ülkücü* doctrine began to come together around various organisations and publications. The *Milliyetçi Türk Kadınları Derneği* (Nationalist Turkish Women's Association) was one of these organisations. Although the *Milliyetçi Türk Kadınları Derneği* discourse underlined the participation of women (*hatunlar*) in governance and wars alongside men in Turkish history, the movement defined womanhood primarily in terms of maternal duties. The *Türk Ev Kadınları Derneği* (Turkish Housewives' Association), founded in 1966, is another nationalist association that aims to fight communism. Another medium through which nationalist women's voices were heard was the magazine *Ayşe*, founded by Halide Nusret Zorlutuna. Both Zorlutuna and *Ayşe*'s editor-in-chief Emine Işınsu Okçu were also founding members of the *Milliyetçi Türk Kadınları Derneği* (Şahin and Sarıtaş 2017: 741–4).
- In the second half of the 1960s, women in the Islamic movement raised their voices, creating new discourses on veiling and ideal femininity based

on veiling. On 15 April 1968, the first university boycott was organised at Ankara University's Faculty of Theology: when a female student, Hatice Babacan, refused to take off her headscarf and was suspended as a result, students protesting the decision first refused to attend classes[45] and then began a boycott.[46]

Women's education and family planning also entered the agenda of women's movements in the 1960s. Especially in the second half of the 1960s, the Association of University Women of Turkey collaborated with UNESCO and carried out various related activities. Starting with literacy courses, women's education was also an area in which nationalist women's circles became more active.

In the 1970s, women's organisations diversified and increased, and the struggle for gender equality gained momentum. Within the socialist women's movement, many local and national organisations were formed including the prominent *İlerici Kadınlar Derneği* (Progressive Women's Association/İKD), which was founded in 1975.[47] The struggle for women's rights became more critical in terms of its agenda and political discourse. The second wave of feminism began to make its presence felt in Turkey in the 1970s. In this context, Şirin Tekeli was an important influence. Tekeli's 1978 associate professorship thesis, which would be published as a book in 1982 entitled *Women and Political and Social Life*, is one of the first and most influential works of feminist literature in Turkey (Adak 2020).

Notes

1. Even though the coup administration was cautious legally and politically in terms of state–religion relations, the use of religious jargon and sentiments to fortify the new regime was striking. The '*devrim şehitliği*' (shrine of revolution) was a concept formulated by the media of the time, then a cemetery for martyrs of the revolution was built physically. The news reported by the Anadolu Agency on 10 June 1960 was that: 'Turan Emeksiz, Nedim Özpulat, Ersan Özey, Ali İhsan Kalmaz and Sökmen Gültekin, who died on 28 April and 27 May, were buried in the Cemetery for the Martyrs of the Revolution built on the slope of Anıtkabir (Atatürk's mausoleum)'. These young people were presented as having suffered at the hands of the former DP administration. Turan Emeksiz was a student in the Faculty of Forestry who was shot during protests at Istanbul University on 28 April 1960. Nedim Özpulat was a young man who lost his balance and fell off the

tank he was standing on during the university demonstrations of 30 April 1960, and was subsequently crushed to death by the tank. Ersan Özey was an eleven-year-old Ankara Maarif College student who went out on the streets with his father on the morning of the coup and was shot for disobeying the soldiers' order to stop. Sökmen Gültekin was a first-year cadet at the Military Academy who died on the morning of the coup when his own gun went off as he was finalising his preparations. Ali İhsan Kalmaz was a lieutenant in the military unit charged with controlling the Ulus Post Office, who was killed by an accidental bullet fired by a gendarme under his command during a clash with the police officers on duty there. Besides the use of the term '*şehitlik*' (martyrdom) being significant for its religious connotations, the funeral was a performance which made the utmost use of nationalism and religious sentiments. For a thorough analysis of these events, see Kaynar 2017: 37–46. Also, specifically on Turan Emeksiz, see Gülpınar 2014.

2. The 1961 Constitution was adopted after 61.5 per cent of the participants in the referendum voted 'yes'.
3. Constitutional Court, E.1970/53, K.1971/76, 21 October 1971; *Resmi Gazete*, 15 June 1972 – 14216. For an analysis of the decision, see Vural 2013: 136–7.
4. For discussions on the Diyanet fulfilling its duties vis-à-vis the moral principles of Islam, see Gözaydın 2020: 113–16, 168–70. For a different reading of the regulating of morality, see Kara [2008] 2017: 65–6.
5. Constitutional Court, E1970/53, N1971/76, 21 October 1971. *Constitutional Court Journal* 10, 60–70.
6. 'Until the tenth president, Lütfü Doğan, who took office in 1968, every Diyanet Chair . . . and the majority of the muftis, preachers, imams and Koran Course instructors who served in the institution until the 1950s and 1960s, were *muderris*, lecturers, hafiz, imams and so on who had grown up in the Ottoman period and had the religious understanding and upbringing of that period. Although they came of age in the period of Ottoman modernization and the religion–politics relations formed through a process of new religious understanding that included *laik*/secular elements, in the final analysis, they belonged to a world where there was a caliph and a *şeyhülislam*, where scholars and *şeyhs* had a widespread and accepted authority and prestige. In terms of their lives, claims, desires and expectations, they belonged to a more religious and spiritual world – in the technical sense' (Kara [2008] 2017: 109). For politics and the Diyanet, see Mert 2017: 267–359.
7. For an establishment narrative of the TDV, see Altıkulaç 2011: 254–62; for some significant projects undertaken by the TDV, see Altıkulaç 2011: 1111–75.

8. 'The German State has tried to grapple with the reality of immigration in a paradoxical manner, by not acknowledging its existence and yet trying to assimilate and integrate, or at times repatriate by offering financial incentives for those to leave. The stigma of being "foreign" and "guest worker" lives with the immigrant communities, many of whom reciprocate by refusing to integrate into a system that, to them, obviously does not want their presence' (Hussain 2010: 234). For other, similar situations in France, the Netherlands, Denmark, Belgium, Sweden and Austria, see Hussain 2010: 223–45.
9. *Cumhuriyet*, 'İşte "Cihad" çağrılarının Sonu: Kanlı pazar', 17 February 1969.
10. *Bugün*, 'Tüyler Ürpertici Alçaklık: Dinsiz Gençler Kur'anı Çiğnediler', 30 January 1968.
11. *Bugün*, 'İslâmiyeti Savunduğu İçin Solcular Tarafından Vurulan R. Kılıçkıran Adlı Talebe Öldü', 6 January 1968.
12. *Bugün*, 'Mukaddesata Yapılan Tecavüzleri Lânetleyen Osmaniye'de Halk Yürüyüş Yaptı', 12 February 1968; *Cumhuriyet*, 'Osmaniye'de Halk Kaymakamlık Binasını Taşladı', 12 February 1968; *Akşam*, 'Osmaniye Hükûmet Binası Dün Taşlandı', 12 February 1968; *Son Havadis*, 'Osmaniye'de Kuran'ın Çiğnenmesi Olayı Protesto Edildi', 12 February 1968.
13. *Akşam*, 'İlâhiyatçı Genci Vuran, Solcu Değil Bir AP'lidir', 14 February 1968.
14. See https://www.kemalyalcin.com/yazilar/genel-yazilar/800-ogretmeni-kayseride-yakmak-isteyenler-ve-tarihi-gercekler/; https://m.bianet.org/biamag/insan-haklari/139569-insanlari-yakarak-oldurmek.
15. See *Cumhuriyet*, 4 May 1969; https://www.derintarih.com/tarihci-gozuyle/cenazesi-ortada-kalan-yargitay-baskani/.
16. Necip Fazıl (Kısakürek/1904–83), one of the prominent constructors of nationalist-conservative ideology from the 1950s to the 1980s, influenced both the nationalists and Islamists in Turkey. Kısakürek is a typical example of the exchange between Turkishness and Islam that multiplies the fascistic character of the movement. Like the ideologists who constructed the so-called Turkish–Islamic synthesis, he combined Turkishness and Islam, deriving an essentialist–racist claim of superiority from the combination of the two. His political goal, which he defined as 'Islamic revolution', is clearly totalitarian and fascist in nature (Bora 2009: 361). On Aydınlar Ocağı and the Turkish–Islamic synthesis, also see Döşemeci 2013: 181–8; Ergüç 2020: 403–14.
17. *Aydınlar Ocağı Derneği Ana Nizamnamesi* (1971). İstanbul: Özal Matbaası, 3.
18. For armed struggle within the socialist movement in Turkey, see Kürkçü 2007: 494–9.

19. The Republican Peasants' Nation Party was founded on 17 October 1958 as the fusion of several smaller nationalist parties. One of these parties was the *Köylü Partisi* (Villagers Party), which had been founded on 16 May 1952; another was Osman Bölükbaşı's *Cumhuriyetçi Millet Partisi* (Republican Nation Party), which was founded on 27 January 1954. These parties merged to form the *Cumhuriyetçi Köylü Millet Partisi* (CKMP), which was led by Osman Bölükbaşı (1911–2002). In the 1950s, it had become a conservative, nationalist party of the rural middle classes with a populist discourse.
20. The *Yeni Türkiye Partisi* (New Turkey Party/YTP) was founded on 13 February 1961 under the leadership of Ekrem Alican (1916–2000) to claim the DP's legacy. The party programme was not very different from the AP programme. The YTP's share of the vote declined steadily in the 1965 and 1969 elections and it was dissolved on 19 March 1973.
21. Nihat Erim was assassinated on 19 July 1980; his murderer(s) were never identified.
22. *Türkiye İşçi Partisi Programı* (1964). İstanbul: Karınca Matbaası, 80–2.
23. '*Tanrı Dağı Kadar Türk Hira Dağı Kadar Müslüman*', attributed to the Serdengeçti Osman Yüksel (1917–83), became a slogan of the *ülkücüler* (ultranationalists), especially in the 1970s. It is hard to find another phrase that explains the relationship between Islam and nationalism in Turkey (Akgün and Çalış 2002: 597). Mt Tengri (God) is a mountain range in Central Asia. According to Turkish mythology, the shores of Lake Issyk-Kul on Mt Tengri are considered the Turkish homeland (*Kızılelma, Turan*). Mt Hira is a mountain a few kilometres from Mecca. Its original name was Jabal'un-Nur and Hira is the name of a cave near its summit. In Islam, the mountain and the cave are considered sacred because it is believed that the first verses of the Koran were revealed to the Prophet Muhammad here, after he retreated into seclusion in the cave. See Yaşlı 2009: 184–95.
24. On the MHP movement's socio-cultural grassroots, see Çalık 1995: 111–197.
25. On Necmettin Erbakan and his political activities, see Shankland 1999: 87–131.
26. On the MSP, see Alkan 1984: 79–102.
27. On the Diyanet in this period and the effects of RP politics on it, see Mert 2017: 241–63.
28. In Mustafa Timisi's words, 'Berkman is an Alevi general from a village in Çorum, an intelligence officer, a Kemalist, a statist. He's not somebody's person, that would be a wrong, unfair assessment' (Aydoğdu and Timisi Nalçaoğlu 2021: 74.
29. The conflict between the AP deputies, who were said to have 'sworn allegiance' to Demirel, and Saadettin Bilgiç, one of the important figures in the internal opposition within the party, and his supporters led to problems during the budget vote. The AP government, whose first budget proposal had failed to get

through parliament, was overthrown. Confronted by this difficult situation, the AP government asked the BP deputies for help. Responding positively, five BP MPs – Kazım Ulusoy, Yusuf Ulusoy, Ali Naki Ulusoy, Hüseyin Balan and Hüseyin Çınar – supported the budget in the vote (*Akşam*, 16 March 1970). For the negative repercussions of this incident in and for the Alevi community, see Çiçek, Aydın and Baran 2017: 36–9).

30. For an analysis of *Milli Türk Talebe Birliği* transforming from an ultra-right association into a pro-Islamic one, see Duman and Yorgancılar 2008.
31. Asım Öz states that this case demonstrated the emerging tendency for political formations to set the agenda outside the official arena that had previously been imposed by the state (Öz 2017: 602). According to Öz, the significance of the rupture caused by this case has not yet been sufficiently researched (Öz 2017: 632). He considers *Hizbu't Tahrir* to be the primary movement defending the Islamic cause in the 1960s (Öz 2017: 609).
32. For a biography of Fethullah Gülen, see Yavuz 2013.
33. These were accommodations for students provided by the Movement.
34. Fethullah Gülen contended that humanity required a new golden generation (*altın nesil*) of ideal humans who would strive to emulate the perfection of the Prophet Muhammad as they sought to replicate the model of his initial community of Muslims in seventh century Medina (Hendrick 2013: 79).
35. On Fethullah Gülen's thoughts on society, state, morality and authority, see Çobanoğlu 2012.
36. Tayyar Altukulaç, an ex-head of the Diyanet, mentions in his memoires that: 'I know that our friends who belong to this community, especially those who were students of the late Süleyman Hilmi Tunahan, do not like being called "Süleymancılar" and are uncomfortable with it . . . But even though I force myself not to use the term "Süleymancı", there is no doubt that the community will continue to be called "Süleymancılar"' (Altıkulaç 2011: 716). Sunier and Landman (2015) prefer to use 'Süleymanlıs'.
37. Nazlı Ilıcak (ed.), Interview with Kemal Kaçar: 'Sülaymancılar cevaplıyor (Süleymancıs answering)', *Tercüman*, 4–9 December 1989.
38. See http://www.iskenderpasacami.com/.
39. Fatih M. Şeker analyses republican ideology's reception of the *Nakşibendi* order by focusing on Şerif Mardin's readings. On Zahid Kotku, see Şeker 2007: 168–75. On the *Nakşibendi* order, the *İskenderpaşa Dergahı* and Kotku, see Yavuz 1999: 129–46. For accounts by people personally acquainted with Mehmed Zahid Kotku, see Özal 1999: 159–76; Gürdoğan 2004. For a memoire of Kotku for 1916–22, see Kırmızı 2022. See also Silverstein 2010.

40. 'Doç. Dr İrfan Gündüz 'Hocaefendi'yi anlatıyor: Bizi devlete talip olmaya yönlendirirdi' (Prof. İrfan Gündüz tells Kotku: He directed us to compete for the state), *Milli Gazete*, 14 November 1991, 12.
41. For thorough coverage of Ramazanoğlu and his works, see https://ramazanoglumahmudsamiks.com/.
42. For information on Muhammed Raşid Erol, including his works and wonders, see https://hasaneyn.org/ay/.
43. Ali Kenanoğlu, a HDP member of the parliament, who witnessed the incidents as a child, states in his interview on 2 July 2020 that: 'I was just a child, we went to the Alibaba neighbourhood. I remember that the eldest son of the family whose house we were visiting was on guard duty. It was the first time in my life that I had heard the concept of guard duty. It seemed strange and I must have asked what guard duty was ... That's how I remember it. At the entrance and exit of the neighbourhood, at various points, young people were on military guard duty with guns in their hands, I witnessed this. Now, it is not possible for people living in this sort of mental state to take part in the economy and politics of the city. Their acts were aimed at one thing, and one thing alone: protecting their lives.' Available at: https://hakikatadalethafiza.org/ali-kenanoglu-ile-soylesi-corumdan-madimaka-hatirlamak-ve-unutmak-uzerine/.
44. See the interview with Gönül Dinçer, in which she states that she first read Babel in 1965. Dinçer was among the founders of *İlerici Kadınlar Derneği*, a prominent socialist women's organisation of the late 1970s (Akal 2011). On *İlerici Kadınlar Derneği*, see Pervan 2021.
45. *Cumhuriyet*, 12 April 1968, 1.
46. *Cumhuriyet*, 15 April 1968, 1. Sibel Eraslan argues that the boycotts that began with the 'Hatice Babacan incident' were 'an important crossroads for women who could go out to gain visibility' (Eraslan 2005: 820).
47. For an account of a group of women affiliated with the *Kurtuluş* movement under the title *Yolu Kurtuluştan Geçen Kadınlar*, see Türkmen 2022.

5

AFTER THE MILITARY COUP OF 1980 (1980–2002)

The woman stares blankly at them. Her face is wrinkled, her eyes full of fear. Her clothes are in tatters, the shoes on her feet are shredded... 'Where do you come from? What happened here?'
'I come from the village,' she says calmly. 'From the village behind the river... Our village was the only one left, and they burned it down.'
'Who burned it?'
'They did... They burned our grain, too. My house is gone... *mala min, mala min*[1]... my hearth is gone.'
'Are those who burned your village still in the village?'
'No, they left, they left a few days ago. I've been on the road for days. I'm looking for my son. My son... *mala min, mala min*...'
...
'Where is my son? Have you seen him? I had three sons, the eldest was killed in the village square, one was taken away. The other one ran away to join you. Have you seen him? He is only fourteen years old. *Mala min, mala min*...'
Mehmed Uzun, *Ronî Mîna Evînê-Tarî Mîna Mirinê* (1998: 212–13)

Turkey began the 1980–2002 period with the neo-liberal intervention in the economy within the framework of the 24 January decisions, escalating political terror, and the military *coup d'état* of 12 September 1980.[2] The 1980s was a decade in which politicised social violence was suppressed by state violence, and in which attempts were made to restore the legitimacy of state authority, which was in crisis, through the use of violence. The policies pursued led to depoliticisation, with a consumer society replacing political activism as a result. The execution,[3] imprisonment and torture of hundreds of thousands of people after the military coup traumatised young people in particular.[4] However, as the saying goes, every cloud has a silver lining: the negativities regarding freedoms led to various human rights organisations being formed, growing and putting down roots from the late 1980s onwards. The individual right to petition the European Court of Human Rights was accepted by Turkey in 1987. Turkey signed the United Nations Convention Against Torture and Other Cruel, Inhuman or Degrading Treatment or Punishment on 25 January 1988.[5] The 1980s were also important for the rise of a new entrepreneurial middle class in Anatolia.

The most important issue that distinguishes the 1990s from other post-World War II decades was the end of the Cold War. In Turkey, the 1990s were marked by neo-liberalism and military tutelage. Since the concept of security was defined very broadly in this period to include ideological issues, the military was able to intervene in the country at every level through the *Milli Güvenlik Kurulu* (National Security Board). It was in the late 1990s that substantial changes were first made to the 1982 Constitution. On 23 July 1995, the parliament made several amendments, including omitting the reference to September12 in the preamble; including provisions providing freedoms for associations and unions; and reducing the age for voting and membership of political parties from twenty-one to eighteen.

From 1980 to 2002, there were four presidents of Turkey.[6] A referendum on the 1982 Constitution led to the election of Kenan Evren (1917–2015), former General Chief of Staff and head of the military junta, as the seventh president of Turkey. Turgut Özal (1927–93) was elected in the 1989 presidential election in parliament and served as the president from 1989 until his death in1993.[7] Süleyman Demirel was the ninth president of modern Turkey, and served from 1993 to 2000. The last president to serve during this period, from 2000 to 2007, was Ahmet Necdet Sezer (1941–), a former head of Turkey's Constitutional Court.

1982 Constitution

After the 12 September 1980 coup, the military regime continued for more than three years. During this time, 650,000 people were detained and questioned, 250,000 were arrested, and countless others were tortured, executed, or disappeared.[8] Parliament was dissolved, parliamentary immunities were abolished, fundamental rights and freedoms were suspended, and martial law was declared throughout the country. The engineers of the coup took the name *Milli Güvenlik Konseyi* (National Security Council), a General Secretariat was established, and Bülend Ulusu (1923–2015), a retired admiral, was appointed prime minister and formed a new government.

With a law passed on 29 June 1981, the *Milli Güvenlik Konseyi* established a Constituent Assembly endowed with the powers of the parliament to draft a new constitution. The first wing of this Constituent Assembly was the *Milli Güvenlik Konseyi*; the second was the Advisory Council appointed by the military government. The duty of drafting the constitution belonged to the Advisory Council, while the authority to finalise it belonged to the *Milli Güvenlik Konseyi*. On 23 October 1981, the Advisory Council held its first meeting and formed a fifteen-person Constitutional Commission chaired by Orhan Aldıkaçtı (1924–2006), a professor of constitutional law. Various institutions and organisations (universities, trade unions, high courts, etc.) were consulted for their opinions on the constitution. However, despite all these arrangements, Kenan Evren states in his *Memoirs* that the actual draft constitution was in the hands of the Council from the beginning: 'The draft constitution was more or less ready at the General Secretariat before the Advisory Council took up the Constitution' (Evren 1991: 55). On 7 July 1982, the draft constitution was placed on the agenda of the Constituent Assembly, where discussions were held on the draft. As a result of these discussions, with the amendments made to the draft, the draft constitution was adopted on 23 September 1982.

The Advisory Council then drafted the Law on Political Parties and the Electoral Law. These drafts were discussed in the *Milli Güvenlik Konseyi* and then finalised. The draft constitution adopted by the Advisory Council was examined by the *Milli Güvenlik Konseyi* members and a few civilians under the chairmanship of Evren. Some new articles were added as it was finalised. According to the new constitution, the duty of the Advisory Council would end before general elections were held.

A referendum was held on 7 November 1982 which ratified the constitution with a 91.37 per cent vote in its favour. The 1982 Constitution asserts that Turkey is a *laik* and democratic republic that derives its sovereignty from the Turkish nation, which delegates the power of legislation to an elected unicameral parliament, the Turkish Grand National Assembly.

Freedom of Religion and Conscience

Freedom of religion and conscience are regulated in five articles in the 1982 Constitution: articles 2, 10 14, 24 and 174. The principle of *laiklik* is listed among the characteristics of the Republic in Article 2 of the Constitution. Article 10 regulates the principle of equality and stipulates that everyone is equal before the law regardless of religion or sect.[9] Several provisions which function as restrictions on the rights to freedom of thought, conscience and religion are regulated in Article 24.[10]

Compulsory Religious Education

The 1982 Constitution contains a key provision regarding 'religious culture and ethics education', which differs from the 1961 Constitution. Article 24, paragraph 4 of the 1982 Constitution provides that:

> Education and instruction in religion and ethics shall be conducted under State supervision and control. Instruction in religious culture and moral education shall be compulsory in the curriculum of primary and secondary schools. Other religious education and instruction shall be subject to the individual's own desire, and in the case of minors, at the request of their legal representatives.[11]

The optional religious education and instruction mentioned in the article are the Koran courses regulated by the Diyanet.[12]

The content of the religious culture and ethics education are not specified in the 1982 Constitution.[13] Textbooks used for religious instruction at all levels of education reveal that the 'religious culture and ethics' course is predominantly focused on Sunni Islamic culture and ethics. This is supported by the fact that Christian and Jewish students, who are Turkish nationals studying in primary and secondary schools other than minority schools, are not required to take a course in religious culture and ethics, provided that they document their belonging to one of these religions. Should they wish to take the course, they are required to submit a written petition from their parents.[14] Textbooks also reveal that religious education is not taught from a religious studies approach, but from a theological perspective. Although the 1982 Constitution defines a religious studies approach, in practice, compulsory religious education in primary and secondary schools has predominantly taught the Sunni understanding of Islam (Gözaydın 2009b).

The Diyanet

The 1982 Constitution, like the 1961 Constitution, regulated the Diyanet. Article 136 states that:

> The Presidency of Religious Affairs, which is included within the general administration, fulfils the duties specified in its special law, in line with the principle of *laiklik*, by remaining outside all political views and opinions and aiming at the solidarity and integration of the nation.

In other words, the 1982 Constitution appoints the Diyanet to ensure national solidarity and integration, and to protect Turkish national identity. The Diyanet was strengthened still more by another law from this era, Law no. 2820 on Political Parties of 22 April 1983, Article 89 of which prohibits political parties from including statements in their programmes and statutes that may violate the existence of the Diyanet.

The statements of State Minister Kâzım Oksay of ANAP in his speech to the Grand National Assembly of Turkey on the 1987 Budget signify the state's perception of religious affairs: 'The services of the Diyanet are in line with the democratic and *laik* character of our Republic. Thus, the spiritual needs of our nation are met by the state itself, and realistic and rational measures are taken to prevent movements that may pose a danger to the democratic regime ...' The Minister also states that: 'Official courses are being made widespread, so as to prevent Turkish citizens from being obliged to seek other means', and outlines the purpose of the basic policy regarding official religious services: 'As the government, we consider religious services to be essential for survival and life. However, we also consider it an important and vital issue for the continuation of our existence that these services should be provided to society within the framework of the Constitution and laws, and that they should be provided with a consciousness and content that will disrupt actions and behaviours that may harm the state and the regime.'[15]

Religiously sensitive groups remained critical about the Diyanet into the 2000s. Adil Özdemir and Kenneth Frank's handbook on practices of Islam in Turkey expresses this sentiment as:

> The public itself is often not sympathetic to the main element in (Turkey's administrative) structure, the Department of Religious Affairs, because of

its hierarchical, centralized control ... its operation by decree kills the spirit. The Department of Religious Affairs comes across as an organization without a soul, a bureaucratic monolith that emphasizes formalism ... Its employees are expected not to oppose but to identify with and endorse state policies. (Özdemir and Frank 2000: 201–2)

İsmail Kara mentions the scope of the conflict between the Diyanet and some religious circles, which extends to not praying behind 'Diyanet imams', but also refers to some of the decisions taken by the Diyanet through the *Din İşleri Yüksek Kurulu* (Supreme Board of Religious Affairs) in the post-1980 period as 'serious and comprehensive decisions of historical value and importance' (Kara [2008] 2017: 114–18).

The Diyanet's services before the 1980s were restricted to within the borders of Turkey. The population of Turkish origin in Europe increased over the years, due to labour migration in the 1960s and 1970s. The Turkish state made no attempts to intervene in the affairs of its nationals in Europe during this first wave of migration. When some groups outside the Diyanet, such as the Süleyman Efendi community, founded mosques and embarked on religious activities in Europe (Sunier and Landman 2015: 57–67), the Diyanet also began to organise in Europe, but after the 1980s.[16] Turkey established a European annex of the Diyanet, the *Diyanet İşleri Türk İslam Birliği* (the Diyanet Turkish-Islamic Union/DİTİB).[17] The duties of Diyanet personnel appointed to positions abroad are laid out in a decision of the Council of Ministers from 1984:

The Overseas Organization of the Diyanet exists to enlighten our citizens and kin abroad about religion, to try to ensure the assistance of local media organs for this purpose; to assist their religious and spiritual needs in matters of worship, religious education, hospital, prison, family problems, marriage, burial, *mevlit* and similar rituals; to deal with the religious activities carried out by various workers' organizations (places of worship, Koran courses and similar activities); to provide guidance and direction in order to ensure that these organizations act within the limits of the legislation that applies in our country; to preach in places of worship and in places where our workers are collectively present; to organize sermons, religious-scientific seminars and conferences; to perform these duties in person when necessary; to follow the social developments in the countries where they are located from a religious point of view; to examine the effects of these developments on our citizens; to collect and evaluate information about activities and organizations related to the Islamic Religion abroad; to establish contact with educational and training institutions at all levels; to examine the new methods applied in religious education, how religious services are carried out by workers from other Muslim countries; and to make proposals to the Presidency on issues related to their duties, and to fulfil other duties to be assigned by the Presidency, Mission and Consulate Chiefs.[18]

By dint of a decree issued by the Council of Ministers in 1991,[19] which reorganised Turkey's official organisations abroad, the Diyanet was also reorganised and the positions of social assistant and administrative attaché were cancelled and new religious services attaché positions established.

In 1987, Tayyar Altıkulaç, the Head of the Diyanet during the September 12 period, caused an uproar when he claimed there was a Council of Ministers decree on the payment of the salaries of Turkish imams working in Western Europe between 1982 and 1984 by the *Rabitat'-ül-Alem'ul-Islam*.[20] The Prime Minister at the time, Bülent Ulusu, who initially claimed to know nothing about the matter, was later forced to concede that the decree did in fact exist. In the end, it was revealed that Cabinet Decree No. 8/2838 on the payment of salaries to Turkish imams by the *Rabıta* was issued on 28 April 1981, and that the decree bore the signatures of both President Evren and Prime Minister Ulusu.[21]

Tayyar Altıkulaç (1938– /1978–86), Mustafa Sait Yazıcıoğlu (1949– /1987–92) and Mehmet Nuri Yılmaz (1943– /1992–2003) served as the heads of the Diyanet between 1980 and 2002.

A Brief Overview of the Era

The 1980s in Turkey was a period in which the effects of the political and economic crises of the 1970s continued to be felt, poverty and inequality increased, and neo-liberal policies were imposed. Even though civil governments were formed, military tutelage was felt over every aspect of life from 1980 to 2002. Violence in the Kurdish-majority eastern and south-eastern areas of Turkey escalated, especially in the 1990s. Internal migration created new urbanisation issues spatially, economically, socially and culturally.[22]

A Paradigm Shift in the Economy

The 1979 crisis, the economic decisions taken on 24 January 1980 to restore the viability of the economy,[23] and the structural adjustment decisions taken in the decade until 1990 led to a paradigm shift in Turkey's economy and the economic policies implemented therein. One of the basic propositions of neo-liberal economic policies, the demand for the downsizing of the state and an emphasis on the functioning of the market, was largely realised in Turkey in the 1980–1989 period as the state withdrew from the economy.

The 1990s in Turkey reflect a very volatile and unstable period, with four separate crises in 1991, 1994, 1998–9 and 2001. The main factor that distinguishes the economy of the 1990s, the so-called second liberalisation period, from the first period of liberalisation in 1980–9 is the financial liberalisation that opened the country's economy up to uncontrolled capital movements; as a consequence, economic growth became dependent on capital inflows and outflows (Pirili and Uzbay 2017: 197–8).

The neo-liberal restructuring of the economy, which has placed the concept of market rationality at the centre of state–economy interactions, challenged both the state's dominant regulatory role in the economy and its national developmentalist ideology (Keyman 2011: 25).

New Institutions in Governing

The constitution drafted by the engineers of the military coup was obstructive and restrictive of freedoms. With the purging of leftist academic cadres (1402s)[24] and the establishment of the Council of Higher Education (*Yüksek Öğretim Kurumu*/YÖK), universities were also brought under control and largely deprived of academic freedom and production.

The state security courts (*Devlet Güvenlik Mahkemesi*/DGM), established to deal with crimes against the security of the state, officially began their work on 1 April 1984. The relevant law envisaged the establishment of DGMs in the provinces of Adana, Ankara, Diyarbakır, Erzurum, İstanbul, İzmir, Malatya and Van, but their jurisdiction extends to the whole country. In November 1992, a law was enacted which further expanded the scope of crimes that fell within the jurisdiction of the DGMs. In 1998, the DGM was found to be in violation of the European Convention on Human Rights in a case heard by the European Court of Human Rights. In 2004, the DGMs were abolished by dint of a constitutional amendment.

The Kurdish Question[25]

Abdullah Öcalan and those around him organised as the *Partiya Karkeren Kurdistane* (The Kurdistan Workers' Party/PKK) in the autumn of 1978. The PKK advocated a pan-Kurdist line with a socialist rhetoric. In May 1979, when a large number of PKK members were arrested in Elazığ, Öcalan left for Syria. The September 12 regime's inhumanity was mostly directed at the members of the Kurdish political movement. The mass tortures in Diyarbakır Prison and elsewhere in the region[26] provided a favourable environment for the PKK to flourish. In the face of escalating mutual violence, Turkey chose to pursue security policies in the political environment of the 1980s. Initially the 'village guards/*korucu*' system was established in 1985,[27] and the powers of state administrators were increased in the so-called fight against terrorism. Based on the powers granted, 905 villages and 2,523 hamlets were evacuated in the region where the 'state of emergency' had been declared (Bingöl, Diyarbakır, Elazığ, Hakkari, Mardin, Siirt, Tunceli and Van) and remained empty until 1998. In all, 378,355 people were evacuated from these settlements.[28] The state did not provide any assistance to the evacuated villagers in terms of food and resettlement. The majority of those uprooted in the 1990s from their villages in the 'state of emergency' region migrated to big cities such as Istanbul, Izmir, Antalya and Mersin. According to estimates, 1 million to 1,200,000 people migrated from fourteen provinces. 'Turkish–Kurdish tensions' existed, and occasional clashes took place, in Manisa, Antalya and Muğla, cities that had received migrants between 1993 and 1995 in the main.

Turgut Özal sided with taking positive steps on the Kurdish issue, saying 'We must recognize the Kurdish reality'.[29] At the Cabinet meeting of 25 January 1991, the ban on the Kurdish language was lifted. However, Tansu Çiller (1946–), who became prime minister after Özal's death, returned to the policy of a military solution. During this period, some groups within the state engaged in murderous practices that are unacceptable in a state with the rule of law. As of November 1993, the number of unsolved murders increased. Rumours that the *Jandarma İstihbarat Terörle Mücadele* (Gendarmerie Intelligence Counter Terrorism/JİTEM) organisation was behind these assassinations abounded, but official state channels initially actually denied the existence of JİTEM. Another organisation that used violence against members of the Kurdish movement during this period was Hizbullah, which was founded in the 1980s. Initially created to disseminate religious propaganda, it morphed into a violent organisation in the early 1990s.[30]

On 6 November 1993, Doğan Güreş (1926–2014), the Chief of the General Staff, announced that the armed forces had changed their strategy in the fight against terrorism and switched from defence to offence, saying: 'This is low-intensity warfare'. According to observers, this period associated with Doğan Güreş and Tansu Çiller, was a period of escalating violence and its knock-on effects.

Turkish pressure led to Öcalan being forced to leave Syria on 9 October 1998. Öcalan went first to Russia and then to Italy, but was obligated by the US and Turkey to go to the Greek embassy in Kenya. On 15 February 1999, Abdullah Öcalan was isolated by Kenyan security forces acting in accordance with US instructions, and handed over to Turkey. Öcalan was tried and sentenced to death on 29 June 1999 on the charges of establishing and leading an armed terrorist organisation. The sentence was commuted to life imprisonment in accordance with European Union harmonisation laws, and he was put into solitary confinement in İmralı prison.

Institutions common in eastern and south-eastern Anatolia and known as Kurdish madrasas or Eastern madrasas, although not all of them were Kurdish in terms of their staff or students, and headed by *muderris*/imams, *şeyhs* (mostly Halidi-Nakşi, some Kadiri), and sometimes aghas/property owners, depending on the region, have played an effective unofficial role in religious education and religious services. This tradition and understanding, which was transferred to the big cities by internal migration, was weakened by the events and terrorism in the region between the mid-1980s and the 2000s (Kara [2008] 2017: 75–9; Öztoprak 2003).

Voices of the Civil Society

Despite the appalling state of human rights in Turkey at the time, the late 1980s and 1990s also witnessed the emergence of various voices in civil society, either through the establishment of human rights organisations[31] or as new voices in the media.

Having overcome great difficulties and numerous obstacles, the *İnsan Hakları Derneği* (Human Rights Association/İHD) was finally officially founded in Ankara on 17 July 1986. The ninety-eight founders included intellectuals as well as relatives of prisoners and detainees. Campaigns were organised, books and reports were published on hunger strikes and torture in prisons. Signature campaigns, panels and conferences were organised across the country calling for a general amnesty and the abolition of the death penalty. When the 1991 General Assembly put the Kurdish issue on the national agenda, it was seen as the first step towards addressing the problems with democracy, and the İHD worked specifically towards this goal, so that the many other problems could be subsequently addressed. While defending human rights and freedoms, İHD executives and members were subjected to pressure. Over the years, twenty-three members and executives have lost their lives as a result of unsolved murders, while hundreds of members have been injured. In 1998 and 2002, the then chairs of the association were subject to armed and physical attacks at the İHD headquarters. Hundreds of executives and members of the association have been put on trial, sentenced to imprisonment, and fined for their activities in the field of human rights (https://www.ihd.org.tr/).

The *İnsan Hakları ve Mazlumlar için Dayanışma Derneği* (Association for Human Rights and Solidarity for the Oppressed/MAZLUM-DER) was founded in Ankara in January 1991 by a group of Islamist, intent on 'taking a stand on the side of the oppressed against oppressors, and defending human rights and freedoms against all forms of oppression and torture'. The association defends human rights and freedoms according to the principles of Islam and takes religion as its source of inspiration (https://www.mazlumder.org/; Kabasakal Arat 2013: 225).

The *Türkiye İnsan Hakları Vakfı* (Human Rights Foundation of Turkey/TİHV) was founded in 1990 in Ankara by İHD and thirty-two human rights defenders. The rationale for the establishment of the TİHV was that 'the struggle against torture does not prevent torture on the scale at which it is currently practiced, and that the treatment of torture survivors is a humanitarian duty that cannot be postponed' (https://tihv.org.tr/).

The *Helsinki Yurttaşlar Derneği* (Helsinki Citizens' Assembly Turkey/HYD) started its activities in 1990 in parallel with the founding of the international Helsinki Citizens' Assembly and was established in Istanbul in 1993 as a non-governmental organisation, recognised as an organisation which operated internationally by the Council of Ministers. The Helsinki Citizens' Assembly was renamed the Citizens' Assembly by decision of the General Assembly in 2016. The Assembly works on fundamental rights and freedoms, peace, pluralism, citizenship and democratisation. It aims to introduce into daily life values such as living with dignity; the rule of law and justice; accountable, transparent and participatory public administration; gender equality as enshrined in international conventions; an economy which does not destroy the texture and peace of society, cities and the planet; the resolution of conflicts and problems through peaceful negotiations, consultation and dialogue, and ensuring that these values are reflected by and disseminated through society (https://hyd.org.tr/en).

Sokak (Street) was a weekly magazine published from August 1989 to April 1990. Its thirty-two issues focused on human rights across a broad spectrum which covered inter alia environmental issues, labour problems, feminism and gender. Entertaining but also serious and critical, *Sokak* was a brief but very fresh breath of fresh air in the Turkish media.[32]

Açık Radyo (Open Radio) went on air on 13 November 1995 as a 'regional' radio station broadcasting to the metropolitan Istanbul area and its environs. It was founded as a private company as required by the Turkish Law on Radio and TV Broadcasting, but has always functioned in the manner of a non-profit media organisation. *Açık Radyo* works to promote the principles of pluralist democracy and the rule of law, and to protect and promote universal human rights and fundamental freedoms. It has survived for twenty-five years as a rare independent Turkish media institution, despite increasing pressure from the state (https://acikradyo.com.tr/).

A New Entrepreneurial Middle Class in Anatolia

A new entrepreneurial middle class began to emerge after the 1980s in Anatolia. This was actually a continuation of developments that had started in the 1950s. Turkish capitalism took shape in the early republican era, when it flourished and was dominated by a few companies, like the Koç and Sabancı groups, which enjoyed close connections with the state. This crony capitalism, which is similar to that of South Korea, excluded Anatolian businesses until the conservative Turgut Özal, and his so-called princes, opened the door to a new group of entrepreneurs. Between 1983 and 1990, during the Özal period, religious networks, particularly the Nakşibendis and Nurcus, mobilised to offer welfare services, communal solidarity and entrepreneurial access to these newly educated classes and new business owners.

The new social group has been referred to as 'Anatolian Tigers' (Demir, Acar and Toprak 2004); 'Anatolian capital/Islamic capital' (Demir 2004); and an 'Anatolian bourgeoisie' (Karatepe 2017). These terms have been used to refer to the industrialists and entrepreneurs that have emerged, along with their companies, in a group of cities and their surrounding regions whose contribution to Turkey's economy and industrial production has increased both rapidly and remarkably.[33] The *Müstakil Sanayici ve İş Adamları Derneği* (Independent Industrialists and Businessmen's Association/MÜSİAD), an association of these businesspeople, was founded in Istanbul in May 1990 with the status of a public benefit non-governmental organisation. MÜSİAD's mission, as defined on their website, is 'to increase the number of its members who adopts pre-determined principles and values, develop solidarity among its members, and to contribute to the material and moral development of our country by means of the unity and spirit of solidarity ensured within it' (https://www.musiad.org.tr/en).

Some of these firms operate in Anatolian cities where the Islamist identity is relatively stronger, such as Denizli, Kayseri and Gaziantep (Öniş 2009: 26). For this reason, these firms are also referred to as 'green capital' or 'Islamist capital' (Beriş 2008: 38). Islam is a unifying force in the work life of these business formations and in the institutionalisation of the harmonising of relations between labour and capital. Islamist discourse appears to have played a crucial role in reconciling the interests of the working class and the Anatolian bourgeoisie. An excerpt from the book *Islamic Persons in Business Life*, published in the 1994, may shed light on these arguments:

> In contrast to the capitalist (liberal or hybrid) system, Islam sets out a system of solidarity in which workers and employers work for each other's benefit and complement each other. Both parties are grateful to each other and give thanks to Allah, the Giver of sustenance. In this system, production is more efficient and peace and tranquility prevail in labour and social life. Instead of seeing work and development as a purely worldly activity, the parties see it as a means of testing and worship, whose results will be realized in the eternal life. The relationship therefore has both a material and a spiritual dimension. (Balcı 1994: 125)

It appears that, through Islamic values, mutual trust can be established between those who are unequal in status and class. Ayşe Buğra interprets this mutual trust as replacing the need for a formal labour law or unions in industrial relations in which Islam plays a role (Buğra 2002: 189).[34]

Engineering Attempts for a New System

A regulation banning beer advertisements on radio and television was approved by the board of directors of Turkish Radio and Television (*Türkiye Radyo ve Televizyonu*/TRT) on 8 May 1984. The proposal by the Minister for National Education, Youth and Sports at the time, Vehbi Dinçerler, to ban beer advertisements was approved by the parliament and came into force on 15 May 1984, despite full-page protest advertisements in newspapers by brewers.

On 25 March 1985, Vehbi Dinçerler sent to schools an opinion opposing Charles Darwin's theory of evolution. In his text, Vehbi Dinçerler stated that the theory of evolution should not be included in textbooks as if it were a law, arguing that there was no convincing evidence for Darwin's theory. On Dinçerler's instructions, creationist books published in the USA were translated into Turkish for the first time and creationism was included in the biology curriculum.

During the Ramadan of 1985, Mahmut Topuz, the ANAP mayor of Karaağa town in the Doğanpınar district of Konya, fined a citizen named Nihat Aytek 10,000 TL for 'publicly breaching fasting'. This fine had no legal basis, but was noteworthy as it reflected the mentality of an elected administrator.

A rally in Taksim Square on 10 April 1994 to protest the Serbian massacre in Gorazde turned into an anti-secularist demonstration. In response to a call made on several TV channels, groups gathered in Taksim within a short period of time and unfurled banners in Arabic. Social Democratic People's Party (SHP) members laying a wreath at the Atatürk Monument on the sixty-sixth anniversary of the adoption of *laiklik* were also attacked by people chanting 'The secular state will surely be destroyed'. On the same day, during demonstrations in Ankara, the headquarters of the United Nations and the True Path Party, as well as the US and Russian embassies, had stones thrown at them.

Oğuz Atak, who worked in a bar in Arnavutköy, Istanbul, was shot dead by two men on 5 May 1997 while walking his dog in the park in Bebek. A television channel had shown Oğuz Atak in its main news the day before, commenting: 'A bartender seems to be mocking beliefs. He has painted lips, polished nails, pierced ears and a freakish outfit. He lives the free life of democracies as he perceives it. In a bar where the alcohol flows like water, it is appalling that he mockingly carves the names of Almighty Allah on his back.' The murderers were sentenced to eighteen years and six months and six years and three months respectively. Atak's parents, who filed a lawsuit against the TV channel, were awarded 10 billion TL in compensation, which was equivalent to approximately to 30,000 US dollars at the time.

28 February 1997

On 31 January 1997, the *Refah Partisi* (Welfare Party) municipality in Sincan, a small conservative town very close to Ankara, organised a meeting called 'the Jerusalem Night'. The Iranian Ambassador attended the event at the invitation of Sincan's mayor, Bekir Yıldız, and made a speech praising the Iranian regime and criticising Turkey's secular state order. Anti-Israeli slogans and calls for *şeriat* in Turkey threatened and angered the military to such an extent that tanks were despatched to Sincan on 4 February 1997 (Sargın 2012). A number of prior events between 1995 and 1997 were also perceived as threatening by the military as the government formed after the 1995 general elections had the RP as the senior member of the governing coalition: the official visits of the RP leader and Prime Minister Erbakan to two radical Islamist countries, Libya and Iran; his appointment of Islamist allies to posts in the bureaucracy; and the increase in the number of İmam Hatip schools.

Following the National Security Council (*Milli Güvenlik Konseyi*/ MGK)[35] meeting of 28 February 1997, which at eight and a half hours was the longest in its history, it was reported that the 'National Military Strategy Concept' had been changed and a new concept had been accepted, whereby the *irticai* movement replaced the concept of separatism – which had been viewed as the primary threat since 1993 – as the main threat. In an official statement released by the MGK General Secretariat on 1 March 1997, it was stated that the meeting had reviewed, in particular, 'activities against the Republic of Turkey, which is defined as a democratic, secular and social state of law that adheres to the Constitution and Atatürk's nationalism'. The issue of *laiklik* was then emphasised specifically: 'In Turkey, *laiklik* not only guarantees the regime, it is also the guarantee of democracy and social peace, and a way of life.'

The text concluded with a warning: 'It has been concluded that behaviours contrary to these principles will cause new tensions and consequences that will disrupt peace and trust in our society, and the measures that have be taken in this regard have been deemed appropriate, and it has been decided to inform the Council of Ministers of these measures.'

The measures to be taken were not specified concretely in this text; they would be published in the media sometime later. The decisions consisted of eighteen articles, of which the most important concrete legal arrangement was the extension of primary education from five years to eight years without interruption. This meant the abolition of the middle section of *imam-hatip* schools. The MGK also demanded that Koranic courses be completely under the control of the Diyanet, that measures be taken to prevent the infiltration of the armed forces by religious extremists, and that all public institutions and organisations, especially universities, should strictly enforce the legal regulations on dress code.

The actual targets of these measures were Prime Minister Necmettin Erbakan and the RP. Erbakan did not initially sign the resolutions, as he found them too harsh. In a meeting with the MGK Secretary General, he said 'I will be in a difficult situation if the declaration comes out like this' and demanded that the articles on eight years of basic education, restrictions on Koran courses and *imam-hatip* schools, the ban on personnel discharged from the army being given jobs in municipalities, and the articles on foundations be softened. As the tension between the MGK and the government peaked, Erbakan signed the MGK decisions on 5 March 1997.

On 5 April 1997, General Çevik Bir, the deputy Chief of the General Staff, gave an interview to the *Washington Post* in which he noted that 'The fight against anti-*laik* movements has become the number one priority of the Turkish armed forces, overtaking the fight against the PKK'. In a briefing given to journalists at the General Staff headquarters in Ankara on 11 June 1997, it was announced that the *Batı Çalışma Grubu* (Western Working Group) had been formed within the General Staff, with all officers and non-commissioned officers as 'natural members'. According to the statement, the group was named 'West' in order to emphasise that 'against the threat from the East, the Republic faces West'. The main function of the Western Working Group was to monitor *irticai* movements. In the following days, it was reported that the

Western Working Group's attention was primarily focused on Islamic capital and its relations with the *Refah Partisi* municipalities, and that the group had suggested an embargo on certain 'Islamic companies'.

The 28 February process remained in force into the 2000s. In a circular dated 4 February 1998 sent by Prime Minister Mesut Yılmaz to governors and district governors, it was pointed out that there were subversive, separatist and *irticai* activities ongoing against the fundamental principles of the Republic, and it was asked that private schools, dormitories, hostels, pensions, courses, dershanes or other institutions operating under other names established, operated and managed by associations, foundations and other private law legal entities engaged in such activities, or where such activities were focused, be effectively monitored. At the MGK meeting of 27 March 1998, at which the main item on the agenda was *irtica*, the military wing of the council expressed the view that harsh measures should be taken, especially with regard to the headscarf and the Fethullah Gülen movement. They also drew attention to the *irticai* organisation within the Ministry of the Interior. On 20 July 1998, an *irticai* purge was carried out within the bureaucracy. In line with the reports prepared by the Prime Ministry's Monitoring Board and Ministry of Interior inspectors, after one year's work, 328 deputy governors and district governors were dismissed from their posts due to their *irticai* activities.[36]

On 11 October 1998, the largest-scale of the ongoing headscarf protests took place. Demonstrations took place across the country under the slogan 'A human chain, hand in hand for respecting belief and freedom of thought'; the police prevented the protests from taking place in some places, and many of the demonstrators were detained.

Political Parties and their Leaders

With a law issued on 16 October 1981, the MGK permanently closed down those political parties whose activities had been suspended on 12 September 1981. The assets of the political parties were transferred to the Treasury. On 2 June 1981, the MGK banned the leaders and members of the closed parties from making oral and written statements.

In April 1983, the MGK approved and brought into force the Law on Political Parties. In May 1983, permission was given for new political parties to be established. In June 1983, the new electoral law came into force and the first general elections were scheduled for 6 November 1983. Many parties were vetoed by the MGK, and only the *Milliyetçi Demokrasi Partisi*, *Anavatan Partisi* and the *Halkçı Parti* were allowed to participate. In the parliamentary elections held in November1983, the *Anavatan Partisi* came to power with 45.1 per cent of the votes and 211 deputies.

The 1990s was a decade of unstable governments and coalitions which faced constant political crises that pushed relations between the political parties of the Centre and their grassroots to breaking point.

Milliyetçi Demokrasi Partisi *(MDP)*

The *Milliyetçi Demokrasi Partisi* (Nationalist Democracy Party) was founded on 16 May 1983 by Turgut Sunalp (1917–99), a former general in the Turkish Military Forces, and forty of his friends. Sunalp was appointed the party's chairman. Immediately after its foundation, the MDP declared that it was the defender of the political line of the September 12 coup. The *Milliyetçi Demokrasi Partisi* was the party favoured by the engineers of the coup, but the electorate did not choose the MDP. In the elections of 6 November 1983, it received just 23.27 per cent of the votes, making it the third party with seventy-one parliamentary seats, five of which were won by independents on its list. The MDP was dissolved in 1986.

Anavatan Partisi *(ANAP)*

The *Anavatan Partisi* (Motherland Party) was founded by Turgut Özal (1927–93)[37] in 1983. He would lead the government without any interruption until 1991 as the leader of a single-party administration. Turgut Özal was the architect of the 24 January 1980 package of economic measures and had served as Deputy Prime Minister in charge of the economy for a spell during the September 12 period. The ANAP claimed to unite four political tendencies: the AP (centre right), MSP (Islamic), MHP (Turkish nationalist) and CHP (social democrat). It gave itself the appearance of a 'middle class party' by using the theme of the 'middle pillar', which included social strata such as workers, civil servants, farmers and tradesmen. It also received support from some big capital circles. In an environment in which old party organisations were disbanding, it managed to become a strong and widespread party organisation in a short time, thanks to its relatively young and dynamic staff and effective supporters. In its pre-election political discourse, it was moderate, focused on economic issues, opposed the bureaucracy, and emphasised the theme of 'the state exists for the nation'. In the economic sphere, it advocated a liberalism embodied in the January 24 decisions.

The lifting of the ban imposed on former politicians by the 12 September regime was added to the agenda during the process of full transition to civilian rule. The ANAP government put the issue to a referendum, and while Prime Minister Özal campaigned in favour of maintaining the bans, the referendum held on 6 September 1987 called by a very small margin for the bans to be lifted.

Turgut Özal was elected as the eighth president of Turkey in 1989. Yıldırım Akbulut (1935–2021) became the ANAP leader from 1989 to 1991. Mesut Yılmaz (1947–2020) was elected as the chairperson of ANAP in 1991. Turgut Özal died suddenly on 17 April 1993.[38] ANAP was part of several ruling coalitions between 1996 and 2002.

Halkçı Parti *(HP)* + Sosyal Demokrasi Partisi *(SODEP)* – Sosyal Demokrat Halkçı Parti *(SHP)* – Cumhuriyet Halk Partisi *(CHP)*

The *Halkçı Parti* (Populist Party/HP) was founded on 20 May 1983 by Necdet Calp (1922–98) who had served as Undersecretary to the prime minister's office after the 12 September 1980 coup, and who had also served as Cabinet Secretary to former CHP leader and Prime Minister İsmet İnönü in the early 1960s. In the November 1983 general elections, the HP received 30.46 per cent of the votes, securing 117 deputies in the 400-seat parliament and becoming the main opposition party. The party leadership changed on 29 June 1985 at the HP Grand Congress, and Aydın Güven Gürkan (1941–2006), who had previously served as the HP's General Secretary, became its leader.

The *Sosyal Demokrasi Partisi* (Social Democracy Party/SODEP) was founded on 6 June 1983 by Professor Erdal İnönü (1926–2007). However, due to the MGK's ongoing veto of the founders, SODEP was only able to complete its foundation on 8 September 1983 and could not therefore participate in the November 6 elections. Erdal İnönü, the first chairman of the party, was vetoed, but was eventually able to become leader of SODEP on 17 December 1983, when the MGK's power of veto was lifted. On 25 March 1984, SODEP participated in the local elections and became the second party after ANAP with

23.4 per cent of the votes. At the first SODEP Congress, convened on 13 April 1984, Erdal İnönü stated that it was essential to have just a single umbrella party on the Left. As a result of the following negotiations, the merger protocol of SODEP and the HP was signed on 16 September 1985. In November 1985, the two parties united under the name *Sosyal Demokrat Halkçı Parti* (Social Democratic Populist Party/SHP), and the initial leadership of Aydın Güven Gürkan. At the June 1986 Congress, Erdal İnönü was elected as the chairman of the SHP.

In the November 1987 elections, the SHP won 22 per cent of the votes and ninety-nine seats in the parliament. After becoming the first party in the March 1989 local elections, the SHP became a full member of the Socialist International in June 1989. In June 1992, the 'law preventing the reopening of closed political parties under the same name' enacted during the September 12 period was abolished. Deniz Baykal (1938–2023), the leading figure of the opposition wing within the SHP, and other former CHP politicians decided to bring the CHP back into political action. On 9 September 1992, the CHP was reopened and a group of deputies who had left the SHP joined the CHP. The eighty-eight seats the SHP won in the TBMM in the 1991 elections had dropped to fifty-two by the end of 1992. In June 1993, the SHP's chairman, Erdal İnönü, announced that he would be leaving politics. At the 1993 Congress, Murat Karayalçın (1943–) was elected to lead the SHP. At the SHP Congress on 18 February 1995, it was decided to dissolve the party and join the CHP. Hikmet Çetin (1937–) was unanimously elected as the CHP leader at the Congress; however, in September 1995, Deniz Baykal was re-elected chairman of the CHP, a position he would retain for another fifteen years. However, the most shocking result of all would come in the 1999 parliamentary elections, when the CHP failed to enter parliament.[39]

Demokratik Sol Parti *(DSP)*

The *Demokratik Sol Parti* (DSP/Democratic Left Party) was founded on 14 November 1985 under the leadership of Bülent Ecevit. On 29 December 1986, the party founded by the members of the parliament who left the SHP after the SODEP-HP merger dissolved itself and joined the DSP. Ecevit and his group parting ways with the CHP was the outcome of disagreements, with Baykal in particular, on what the CHP was, including its attitudes towards religion. The DSP entered the parliament with twenty-five deputies. In the general elections of 20 October 1991, the DSP won 10.75 per cent of the votes. Ecevit re-entered the parliament after eleven years as a deputy for Zonguldak. In the early general elections of 24 December 1995, the DSP increased its vote to 14.64 per cent and its deputies to seventy-six, making the DSP the largest party of the Left. On 11 January 1999, the DSP formed a minority government with the joint support of all the parties except the CHP and various democratic mass and civil society organisations. Bülent Ecevit became prime minister for the fourth time in nearly twenty years. At a time when economic and political corruption were on the rise, Ecevit's honest personality and the DSP's non-corrupt structure created excitement, hope and trust in society. In the 18 April 1999 elections, the DSP increased its votes from 14.65 per cent to 22.19 per cent and became the first party in the Assembly. The DSP formed a government with the ANAP and the MHP. Bülent Ecevit became prime minister for the fifth time in his political life. On 3 November 2002, early elections were held and the DSP and other coalition partners failed to pass the 10 per cent election threshold.

Doğru Yol Partisi *(DYP)*

The *Doğru Yol Partisi* (True Path Party) was founded in 1983 as a continuation of the AP, which had been shut down in the September 12 coup. The DYP, led first by Süleyman Demirel and then Tansu Çiller, remained in power without interruption in the various coalition governments formed between 20 October 1991 and 30 June 1997. From 30 June 1997 to 3 November 2002, the DYP continued to serve as an opposition party in the Turkish Grand National Assembly. After the 3 November 2002 general elections, it remained outside parliament and its legal existence ended in 2007 when its name was changed to *Demokrat Parti*.

Milliyetçi Çalışma Partisi *(MÇP)*/Milliyetçi Hareket Partisi *(MHP)*

The *Milliyetçi Çalışma Partisi* (Nationalist Labour Party) was established in 1983 as a continuation of the MHP, which was shut down in the September 12 coup. It changed its name back to MHP on 24 January 1993, at which point its legal existence as the MHP came to an end.

After the September 12 coup, five of the 389 persons who were tried in the case against the MHP and the ultra-nationalist (*ülkücü*) organisations were sentenced to death, nine to life imprisonment, and the remaining 219 to sentences of varying length. The MHP leader Alparslan Türkeş was sentenced to more than nine years in prison and actually spent four and a half years behind bars. In 1987, after the ban on former party leaders was lifted, Türkeş became the leader of the MÇP and then the MHP.

The MHP was quite successful in the 1994 local elections, but received just 8.2 per cent of the vote in the December 1995 general elections, failing to pass the 10 per cent electoral threshold. After the death of MHP leader Alparslan Türkeş in 1997, Devlet Bahçeli was elected chairman at the party congress. In the 1999 Turkish general elections, the MHP received 17.98 per cent of the votes, becoming the second party after the DSP with 129 parliamentary seats. In the DSP-ANAP-MHP coalition, the MHP became the second largest coalition partner, receiving twelve ministries, including the post of deputy prime minister.

Büyük Birlik Partisi *(BBP)*

On 7 July 1992, Muhsin Yazıcıoğlu (1954–2009), a former president of the *Ülkücü Gençlik Derneği* (Nationalist Youth Association) and MP for Sivas, resigned from the MÇP with his friends, criticising its adoption of the Turkish–Islamic synthesis, an ideology that emphasises Islamic identity over Turkishness. He went on to found the Great Unity Party (BBP).

Refah Partisi *(RP)*/Fazilet Partisi *(FP)*

Necmettin Erbakan was elected leader of the *Refah Partisi* (Welfare Party), the political party the *Milli Görüş* movement established after the September 12 coup in 1987. In the 1991 elections, the RP entered parliament. Then, in a surprise result, the RP emerged from the 1995 elections as the first party, with 21.37 per cent of the votes. In the deep transformation of Turkish society imposed by the military elite, Erbakan's RP represented the continuation of traditional values and the continuation of the economic stability which began with Özal. The political agenda of the RP was 'just order' (*adil düzen*), with an emphasis on fighting corruption, on providing good public services, and on social justice, as it had done in its previous incarnations as the MNP and MSP.[40]

Meanwhile, on 27 March 1994, Erbakan's party won 19 per cent of the votes in the local elections and two important metropolitan cities, Istanbul and Ankara, with its young candidates Recep Tayyip Erdoğan (1954–)[41] and Melih Gökçek (1948–). In 1997, Erbakan joined the coalition government, but the number of Islamic elements in his rhetoric worried the military elite. As a result, the RP was dissolved by the Constitutional Court on 16 January 1998 on the grounds that it had committed 'actions against the principle of the *laik* republic'. As a result of the closure case, the Constitutional Court decided to ban six members of the RP, including Erbakan, from politics for five years.

The *Fazilet Partisi* (Virtue Party) was founded on 17 December 1997, under the leadership of İsmail Alptekin (1943–), as a party in line with the National Vision in preparation for the probable shutting down of the RP. After the party was shut down, nearly 150 members of the parliament who became independents joined the FP. On 14 May 1998, Recai Kutan (1930–) was elected chairman by the FP Founders' Assembly. The FP was itself dissolved by the Constitutional Court on 22 June 2001.

Halkın Emek Partisi (HEP); *Demokrasi Partisi* (DEP); *Halkın Demokrasi Partisi* (HADEP)

In the 1989 local elections, the SHP included the candidates of the *Halkın Emek Partisi* (People's Labour Party/HEP), which was not able to participate in the elections, on its lists in the provinces of south-eastern Anatolia. After the elections, Kurdish members of parliament attempted to take their oath in Kurdish at the opening ceremony of the Grand National Assembly of Turkey. On 21 March 1992, as a result of the events that broke out on Nowruz, HEP members within the SHP resigned from the party. When a closure case was filed against the HEP, the *Demokrasi Partisi* (Democracy Party/DEP) was founded in 1991; however, both parties were later dissolved by the Constitutional Court. In 1994, members of HEP and DEP founded HADEP.

The *Halkın Demokrasi Partisi* (People's Democracy Party/HADEP) was founded on 11 May 1994 and received 4 per cent of the vote in Turkey's 1995 general elections. In the 1999 general elections, HADEP increased its share of the vote to 4.75 per cent, also winning thirty-seven municipalities in the local elections. On 13 March 2003, HADEP was dissolved by the Turkish Constitutional Court on the grounds that it was a 'centre of illegal activities'.

Özgürlük ve Demokrasi Partisi (ÖDP)

The process referred to as the Kuruçeşme Process or Kuruçeşme Meetings in Turkish leftist politics covers a series of discussions and meetings that brought together different sections of the Left after 1986 with the aim of ensuring unity on the Left, analysing the current problems and conditions facing socialism, and establishing a legal socialist party. Before 1980, the majority of leftist groups engaged in politics within different organisations under various names, and were often in fierce political competition with each other. However, most were included in the Kuruçeşme Process during this period, and the meetings provided an opportunity for socialist circles to interact with each other in an inclusive manner. Issues such as political Islam in Turkish politics, the Kurdish question, and the problems of Turkey's labourers were discussed and opinions were put forward for the establishment of an overarching party. On 20 January 1996, the Founders' Conference announced that the party would be named the *Özgürlük ve Demokrasi Partisi* (Freedom and Solidarity Party); Ufuk Uras (1959–) was unanimously elected party chairman, largely because he was not affiliated with any group. Sadun Aren (1922–2008) became the honorary chairman of the ÖDP, which was officially established on 22 January 1996.

Religious Circles

Özal's post-1980 policies and the changes in both the economic and political spheres in Turkey helped to increase the participation of Islamic circles in the public sphere through changes in the 'opportunity spaces'[42] that expanded their web of life. It also paved the way for the empowerment of a Muslim bourgeoisie that could finance the media, schools and tutoring centres through which the Islamic sector could construct its own identity (Komşuoğlu and Kurtoğlu-Eskişar 2009: 27–8).

A set of reactive movements spread after the 1980s in conservative circles, especially among university educated youth: instead of identifying with a religious community, some started to advocate movements which referred to the Koran directly. 'Islam is only the Koran'; 'Everything that may be said in the name of Islam is written in the Koran'; 'The Koran is sufficient; hadiths and other literature are unreliable'. Paradoxically, those who argued along these lines became leaders of their groups and thus producers of their own Koranic interpretations. Abdülaziz Bayındır (1951–), a professor in Istanbul University's School of Divinity and the founder of the Süleymaniye Foundation; Mehmet Okuyan (1965–), a professor of theology; and Mustafa İslamoğlu (1960–) were leading figures in movements of this sort.

The Nur Movement

The Nurcu community fragmented substantially in the 1970s and 1980s, and several groups derived their teachings from the Nurcu theology. The spectrum was wide, ranging from the *Yazıcılar* group (writers), who believe that Bediüzzaman's works should be disseminated in Arabic letters and copied by hand, to the *Okuyucular* group (readers), who accept the *Risale-i Nur* in the Latin alphabet and published form. Other Nurcu groups included the *Meşveret* (consultation)/ *Kırkıncılar* community led by Mehmet Kırkıncı (1928–2016);[44] the *Med-Zehra* group in Van, led by Muhammed Sıddık Şeyhanzade (Dursun) (1948–2017); the *Zehra* group, which has a Kurdish identity and was led by İzzettin Yıldırım (1946–2000); the *Tahşiyeci* (footnoters) group led by Muhammed Doğan (Molla Muhemmed el-Kersi) (1944–) in Muş-Varto; and the *Yeni Asya* group led by Mehmet Kutlular (1938–) (Yargı 2020: 584–5).

A deep division within the *Nur* community occurred at the time of the 1980 *coup d'état*. The 1982 constitutional debate within the community reinforced the division: while the majority of the *Nur* community voted 'yes' for the Constitution in the referendum, the *Yeni Asya* group voted 'no' by continuing to support the AP and Süleyman Demirel. This distanced them somewhat from the others.

The Kurdish–Turkish ethnic divide also led to a split over Nursi's *medresetuzzahra* project. The group organised under the leadership of Sıddık Dursun, who founded the Med-Zehra Foundation, published the *Dava* in 1989. The more nationalist Kurds founded the Zehra Education and Culture Foundation under the leadership of İzzettin Yıldırım and published a Kurdish–Kirman journal called *Nubihar* in 1992.

The Gülen Movement

Fethullah Gülen pioneered the establishment of the *Gazeteciler Yazarlar Vakfı* (Journalists and Writers Foundation) in 1994 'to promote dialogue and tolerance among all strata of society' (Yılmaz 2005: 399). The Gülen movement, with the support of the Özal, Demirel and Çiller governments, purchased the *Zaman* (Time) newspaper in 1986 and turned it into one of Turkey's leading dailies (Yavuz 2003b: 190). In addition to *Zaman*, the Gülen movement launched a national television channel named *Samanyolu* (Milkyway), and popular radio stations such as *Dünya* (World) and *Burç* (Horoscope). In a post-Cold War world in which Islam had replaced communism as the perceived main threat, the Gülen movement became a model of moderate Islam; with its modern and tolerant image, it could play a role across the entire Muslim geography.[45]

In 1999, as a result of an investigation initiated by the Chief Public Prosecutor's Office of the Ankara DGM, a lawsuit was filed against Fethullah Gülen on 22 August 2000. He was charged with aiming to establish a state based on religious rules by changing the *laik* state structure, and an arrest warrant was issued for him in absentia. Gülen had travelled to the USA at the time for health reasons. After a long judicial process, Gülen was unanimously acquitted by the General Assembly of the Court of Cassation in June 2008.

Süleyman Efendi Community

The 1980 coup further enhanced the Süleyman Efendi community networks, as the state had begun to regard the Turkish–Islamic synthesis as a new national identity (Yavuz 2003a: 147). The movement dominated religious student hostels, and opened its Koranic courses at this time. The Community sought to influence politics through their support of the ANAP of Turgut Özal (1983–93) and the RP of Necmettin Erbakan (1994–8).

İskenderpaşa Community

Mahmud Esad Coşan (1938–2001), Kotku's son-in-law and a professor of theology at Ankara University's School of Divinity, succeeded him as leader of the community in 1980. In Hakan Yavuz's words, Coşan 'reinvented the Gümüşhanevi order as a model for political associations and economic corporations' (Yavuz 2003a: 142–3). The community had channelled a significant part of its power to the MSP, and when the party was closed and its prominent leaders arrested, the İskenderpaşa group changed from a state-oriented Islamic movement to a society-oriented one, providing jobs in its own companies and financial opportunities to its followers in the expanding private economy of the 1990s. In 1990, Esad Coşan attempted to cut his community's ties to the MNP-MSP-RP line and its patronage and tutelage. He had fully supported them in the past, but the time had come for Coşan to 'break the circle of abuse and deception of the insincere RP senior executives' and establish his own party to achieve his goals (Çakır 1990: 37).⁴⁶ Coşan left Turkey in the 28 February process and died in Australia in 2001.

Erenköy Community

Mahmut Sami Ramazanoğlu died in Saudi Arabia in 1984. He had authorised Hacı Hasan Efendi (1914–87) to continue his teachings in Kayseri before he left Turkey, while a council of four headed by Musa Topbaş (1917–99), a wealthy businessman and a lawyer, now led the Erenköy community. Musa Topbaş was succeeded by his son, Osman Nuri Topbaş (1942–).⁴⁷ With the new economic opportunities of the 1990s, the Erenköy community distanced itself from politics and increasingly became a civil society-oriented Islamic movement, with its own publishing houses, charity foundations and educational networks (Yavuz 2003a: 145).

Menzil Community

Following the *coup d'état* of 1980, Muhammed Raşit Erol had to move, first to Gökçeada and then to Ankara, due to a forced residence judgement. He set up home in Pursaklar, near the airport, where the community developed further. Several bureaucrats and politicians including Muhsin Yazıcıoğlu of the BBP were said to be Erol's disciples. After Muhammed Raşit Erol's death in 1991, the community divided into two: one group was led by Abdülbaki Erol (1949–2023), his brother, in Menzil as the Semerkand community; Muhammed Raşit Erol's son Feyzettin Erol (1957–) led the other group in the village of Buhara in Eskişehir (S. Öztürk 2019).

Milli Görüş

At the 14 May 2000 Congress of the FP, the thirty-year-old *Milli Görüş* movement came to an important crossroads. Traditionalists loyal to the movement's founder and leader for thirty years, the former prime minister Necmettin Erbakan, were challenged for the first time by a younger generation of innovators led by Abdullah Gül (1950–). Bülent Arınç (1948–), Abdüllatif Şener (1954–) and Abdullah Gül voiced the views of the reformers at the Congress: 'For as long as we want democracy in Turkey, we cannot oppose it within our own ranks', Gül said, accusing the party's leaders of allying with the civilian extensions of February 28. A later congress would create two separate parties.

Alevi Population, Identity Formation and Political Structuring

'In the 1980s a diverse set of social movements emerged that became known in Turkey and abroad as the "Alevi revival", a flowering of public activism and advocacy that attracted the attention of the EU and the international human rights community' (Shakman Hurd 2015: 91). In late 1991, a meeting was organised by Diyanet officials to discuss the issue of Alevism with a group of Alevi and Sunni participants; the results of the talks were to be published in the January and February 1992 issues of the Diyanet's monthly magazine. The meeting and the discussions that followed gave rise to an assimilation agenda.[48] Referring to the statements by Süleyman Demirel, Prime Minister of the coalition government at the time, that 'from now on you will be able to say that you are Alevi with pride', Hamdi Mert (1942–2015), then Vice-President of the Diyanet, stated in the introduction to the magazine that 'even those in positions of responsibility are rowing with the current; they are taking approaches that will inflame the fire instead of extinguishing it ... It will not benefit anyone to open wounds that have been closed after the daily excitement has subsided' (Mert 1992). The debates show that the assertion of Alevi identity was perceived by Diyanet officials as being driven by ideological and political considerations. The Diyanet authorities, to whom the duty of 'securing the solidarity and integration of the nation' had been entrusted by the 1982 Constitution, understood Alevi identity as separatist politics.

In line with global trends, cultural identities became a constitutive element of political processes in Turkey in the 1990s. A social movement that took its reference from Alevism, the Alevi movement, emerged and Alevi identity politics was born (Ertan 2017: 72). Alevis began to exist in the public sphere with their Alevi identity.[49]

The Poles of Alevi Politisation

Among the many Alevi civil society organisations that emerged in the 1990s, two were significant for their representation in the ideological field: the *Pir Sultan Abdal Kültür Derneği* (Pir Sultan Abdal Culture Association) established in 1988, which approaches Aleviness as a life style and Alevism as a socialist resistance movement; and the *Cem Vakfı* (Cem Foundation) founded in 1995, which views Alevism as a Turkish interpretation of Islam (Tuğal 2004: 494–5; Küçük 2007: 918–19; Ertan 2017: 173–229).

On 1 September 1996, the *Demokratik Barış Hareketi* (Democratic Peace Movement/DBH), led by Ali Haydar Veziroğlu (1946–), an Alevi businessman, emerged with a stadium feast in Ankara under the slogan 'Our names are different, our surname is Turkey'. The DBH officially became a party one month later. The DBH faced a lawsuit in the Constitutional Court due to its programme including demands to abolish the Diyanet. The *Barış Partisi* (Peace Party) was founded to replace the DBH. This party then merged under its own umbrella with the *Yeni Demokrasi Hareketi* (New Democracy Movement), which Cem Boyner (1955–) had left as its leader. In the meantime, the Constitutional Court resolved not to dissolve the DBH; however, the party dissolved itself, since it had now been replaced by the BP (Ertan 2017: 247–68).

Sivas/Madımak Massacre

The Madımak massacre took place on 2 July 1993 during the Pir Sultan Abdal cultural festival organised by the Pir Sultan Abdal Culture Association. After Friday prayers, a group of radical Islamists gathered in front of the Sivas Cultural Centre, where the festival was being held. After launching initial attacks there, they moved towards the Madımak Hotel where the festival guests were staying. As the security forces did not intervene, the number of attackers increased. Temel Karamollaoğlu (1941–), the Mayor of the RP, made a speech to calm the crowd, but when he ended his speech with the words 'may your *gaza* (holy war) be blessed', the attacks and the participants increased. By 7.30 pm, the mob was almost 10,000 strong. The attackers set fire to the hotel and set up barricades to prevent those inside from escaping. Thirty-three festival participants and two hotel staff were trapped in the hotel and killed. The Prime Minister at the time, Çiller, stated that the situation was under control and that 'the citizens outside are safe'.[50]

The cases against the attackers ended in 1997 with death sentences for thirty-eight, which became life sentences when capital punishment was abolished in 2004.[51]

Karacaahmet Cemevi Incident

At midnight on 7 September1994, the at the time unfinished Karaca Ahmet Cemevi in Üsküdar, Istanbul, was marked for demolishion by the Istanbul Metropolitan Municipality, then led by Recep Tayyip Erdoğan of the RP as mayor, on the grounds that the construction was being carried out without a permit. After reactions, the municipality was forced to withdraw, and construction work continued and the building was completed (Yaman 2022: 91–2). This incident may be read as the first substantial civil disobedience on the part of the Alevi population in republican history.

Gazi and Ümraniye Events

On the evening of 12 March 1995, a group of unidentified armed men hijacked a cab and opened fire with automatic weapons on three coffeehouses in the Alevi-majority Gazi neighbourhood, then fled. An Alevi *dede* (religious guide)[52] was killed and twenty people were heavily wounded in the attack. The police officers at the police station next to the coffeehouse did not intervene in the attack and did not pursue the gunmen. Hundreds of people marched on the police station to protest the situation, but retreated to the Gazi *cemevi* after the police intervened. One person was killed and three others were wounded when the civil police opened fire. On 13 March, police opened fire on the crowd during the funeral, resulting in fifteen people losing their lives and hundreds being injured. Four people were also killed when police opened fire on Alevis protesting the situation in Ümraniye. The martial law declared in two neighbourhoods was lifted on 16 March. In all, twenty-two people lost their lives and more than 400 were injured. Only two policemen were found guilty at the trial, and were sentenced to four years in prison in 2002.

The Non-Muslim Population

On 6 September 1986, twenty-one Jewish citizens were killed and four were wounded in an attack on the Neve Şalom Synagogue in Kuledibi, Istanbul, during Shabbat. The Ministry of Interior announced that it was a suicide attack and that the two attackers had been blown to pieces in the explosion inside the synagogue. However, eyewitnesses claimed that the two attackers escaped from the back of the synagogue. Bomb disposal teams arrived at the synagogue after the raid and defused seven bombs that had not yet exploded. Individuals who phoned news agencies after the attack claimed responsibility for the Neve Shalom raid on behalf of the 'Islamic Resistance Organisation' and the 'Palestinian Revenge Organisation'. Israel claimed the attack was carried out by a terrorist organisation associated with the Palestinians (https://www.nevesalom.org/teror.html).

Hagop Hagopian, the leader of the ASALA (Armenian Secret Army for the Liberation of Armenia) terrorist organisation,[53] was shot dead in an armed attack in Athens in the early morning of 28 April 1988. A caller to the Paris bureau of the Agence France Pressé reported that the action was carried out by a rival Armenian organisation. The news of the murder was reported the next day by several Greek newspapers with headlines attributing the murder to Turkish agents. The Athens police focused on an intra-organisational showdown in their investigation. A column in the *Washington Post* by Jack Anderson stated that the CIA had learned in 1982 that Turkey was planning to kill Armenian leaders in Europe, and that Turkey was therefore most likely behind the Hagopian case. After the Susurluk incident[54] in 1996, some political party leaders attributed this act, which remained unsolved, to Abdullah Çatlı (Ersel *et al.* 2005 vol. 4: 254). After Hagopian's death the group became less active.

Dimitrios I, the 269th Ecumenical Patriarch of the Greek Orthodox Church, died in Istanbul on 2 October 1991. He was succeeded on 22 October 1991 by Dimitrios Arhondonis, metropolitan of Kadıköy, under the name Bartholomeos I (Macar 2021).

Women in the 1980s and 1990s

The Law on Population Planning (Law 2827, 14 April 1983) legalised induced abortion on demand during the first ten weeks of pregnancy, and after the tenth week in the event of an inconvenience to the health of the mother and the baby. The law also allowed for temporary sterilisation, and required the consent of the spouse for both abortion and sterilisation. Castration, which completely removes the ability to reproduce, would be performed in cases deemed medically necessary. This legislation was a significant juncture in Turkey in terms of women's global struggle for liberation.

The 1980s

After 1980, women's issues began to be discussed in Turkey from a feminist standpoint distinct from statist and leftist lines.[55] In 1986, due in part to feminist initiatives, Turkey ratified the International Convention on the Elimination of All Forms of Discrimination against Women on 24 July 1985. From May 1987 onwards, the feminist movement increased its visibility in the public sphere with campaigns such as 'end beatings', 'women exist', 'our bodies are ours'[56] and 'purple needles'. The penal code was also amended in response to protests that followed the reduction of the penalty in rape cases in which the raped woman was a prostitute (Gözaydın 2006).

The 1990s

The 1990s witnessed the institutionalisation of the feminist movement. Institutions such as the Women's Problems Research and Application Centre at Istanbul University (1989),[57] the *Mor Çatı* (Purple Roof Women's Shelter) Foundation (1990),[58] and the Women's Works Library and Information Centre in Istanbul (1990)[59] were established. A decree dated 20 April 1990 founded the General Directorate on the Status and Problems of Women within the Prime Minister's Office (Acuner 2002: 128–48). Another characteristic of the 1990s was that women who had not been part of the feminist movement in the 1980s developed feminist demands in relation to the Kurdish movement and the Islamic movement.[60] In the 1990s, feminism largely ceased to be a big city movement.

Civil Code Reform

After a decade of activism by women's organisations seeking the reform of the Civil Code, the coalition government finally prepared a draft integrating demands for full gender equality in 2000. Following opposition to the draft led by the MHP, an influential campaign by the women's movement helped attain parliamentary approval for the new Civil Code in November 2001, ensuring the equality of man and woman in marriage and other provisions called for by women's organisations (İlkkaracan 2014: 158–9).

The Headscarf Issue

On 16 July 1982, a legal regulation entitled 'Regarding the Dress Code for Personnel Working in Public Institutions and Organization' entered into force. The regulation not only contained provisions allowing female civil servants to be uncovered at work, but also regulated heel heights, hair and nail length, which became disciplinary issues in the same way they are in military environments.[61] On 30 December 1982, YÖK adopted a dress code requiring 'modern attire'. The circular in question stated that:

a. All staff and students in higher education institutions must wear civilized, simple, modest attire in accordance with Atatürk's revolutions and principles.
b. It is essential that the clothes, shirts and shoes of all male and female students, including foreign students, be clean, neat and plain; the head is to be uncovered on university premises.

Subsequently, students in some universities were refused admission because they covered their heads, while disciplinary penalties were imposed in others. In October 1990, an amendment was made to the Higher Education Law which provided that: 'Dressing and attire is free in higher education institutions, provided that it is not contrary to the laws in force'. This article meant that headscarves were now permitted in the universities. However, on 7 March 1989, upon an appeal lodged by President Kenan Evren, the Constitutional Court annulled the legal regulation that allowed students to be covered in the nation's universities. Even though there was some loosening of the application of the ban over time, veiling was strictly forbidden in the February 28 process.

In 1991, Nilüfer Göle's *Modern Mahrem: Medeniyet ve Örtünme* (The Forbidden Modern: Civilization and Veiling) was published in Turkish. Göle looked at female Islamist university students in Turkey. Her emphasis on different forms of modernisation in Europe and Turkey was significant: in Europe it was a process, while in Turkey it was a project. Since Turkish modernisation depended on imitation, it had lacked economic, political, social and cultural underpinnings. These deficiencies had been reflected in several issues during the republican era, including women's issues. By means of group interviews, Göle revealed not only differences between individual Islamist female students' intentions and positions, but also their symbolic visibility in the public realm. According to Nilüfer Göle, Muslim women are empowered by an Islamism that assigns them a militant, missionary political identity, and by a secular education that gives them a professional and intellectual legitimacy. These women students therefore symbolise both tradition and modernity, returning to old values in a new style.⁶²

On 2 May 1999, a veiled Merve Kavakçı (1968–), newly elected as an RP MP, tried to take her seat in the TBMM. 'The chamber broke into a pandemonium of outraged shouts, accusations, and counteraccusations' (White 2003: 145). She refused to unveil and was not allowed to take the oath and was escorted out. On the grounds that she had not informed the Turkish authorities about her US citizenship, she was later stripped of her Turkish citizenship; she regained it in 2017.

Notes

1. 'My home, my hearth' (Kurdish).
2. As Carter Vaughn Findley argues, Adalet Ağaoğlu's *Dar Zamanlar* (Hard Times) trilogy provides a powerful account of republican times through to the 1980s. 'It begins with *Ölmeye Yatmak* (Lying down to die, covering 1968–1971), continues with *Bir Düğün Gecesi* (A Wedding Evening, 1974–1978), and concludes with *Hayır...* (No ..., 1984–1987). The characters belong to two generations. The heroine Aysel Dereli, her siblings and schoolmates, are children of the early republic. The younger generation are "the sixty-eighters" as they come to be called in *Hayır...*' (Findley 2010: 390–403).
3. Executions, which had become de facto inapplicable after 1972, began to be carried out again after September 12. In response to the anti-death penalty campaigns, especially abroad, Kenan Evren said: 'Now, after I catch them, I will put them on trial and then I will not execute them, I will feed them in prison for years. Now, would you agree to that?' From 12 September 1980 to 25 October 1984, known as the September 12 period, forty-eight people who had previously been sentenced to death were executed (Yıldırım 1997: 121).
4. For the youth's perception of the September 12 regime, see Lüküslü 2017: 342–5.
5. Unfortunately, signing the Convention did not bring torture to an end. In addition to persistent inhuman conduct in Kurdish-majority areas in East and Southeast Turkey, the Manisa trial is just one example of the existence of torture and the state of human rights. Thus, twenty-six teenagers were apprehended in the Aegean town of Manisa on 26 December 1995. The police charged them for spraying graffiti on a train carriage with the words 'No to education fees' and with 'writing political slogans on walls, distributing illegal leaflets, throwing Molotov cocktails and being members of an illegal organization. For the next few days, policemen in the counter-terrorism department of Manisa tortured the sixteen

boys and girls, one of them as young as fourteen. Hüseyin Korkut, one of the Manisa teenagers, was a second-year student of electronics at the time. He stayed in prison for three and a half months. When he was asked in court to describe the torture he was subjected to, he requested to speak to the judge in private, because he was too ashamed to talk about it publicly' (Öktem 2011: 100).

6. İhsan Sabri Çağlayangil (1908–93) served for 160 days (after Fahri Korutürk's term expired on 6 April 1980), and Hüsamettin Cindoruk (1933–) served for thirty-three days (17 April 1993–16 May 1993) as acting presidents.

7. The idea of Neo-Ottomanism in foreign policy emerged during this period. It was proposed by Özal, the journalist Cengiz Çandar (who was described as his 'unofficial foreign policy advisor'), the academician Mustafa Çalık, and academics and journalists centred on the journal who described themselves as the *Cedit* group. The Neo-Ottomanists criticised Turkey's Cold War foreign policy as 'keeping the status quo' and wanted Turkey to take an active stance beyond its borders, especially in the Balkans, the Caucasus and Central Asia. On Özal and the neo-Ottomanists, see Özkan 2016: 406–17.

8. Amnesty International (1988), *Turkey: Human Rights Denied*, EUR/44/65/88. London: AI Index.

9. Based on Articles 2 and 10, the Constitutional Court annulled Law No. 3255, which discriminated between Abrahamic religions and non-Abrahamic religions by providing a broader legal protection for followers of the Abrahamic religions. Nevertheless, not only Abrahamic religions, but all belief systems enjoy equal protection (E.1986/11 K.1986/26, 4 November 1986). *Anayasa Mahhkemesi Kararları Dergisi* 22, 310–16. On the Constitutional Court's decision on Abrahamic religions, see Vural 2013: 124–6.

10. For restrictions, see Yıldırım 2015: 185–7.

11. Education and teaching/instruction, two different concepts used in the article, have been scrutinised in the *Campbell and Cosans* v. *United Kingdom* decision of the ECtHR in 1982 as, '[T]he education of children is the whole process whereby, in any society, adults endeavour to transmit their beliefs, culture and other values to the young, whereas teaching or instruction refers in particular to the transmission of knowledge and to intellectual development.' *Campbell and Cosans* v. *United Kingdom*, 25 February 1982, nos. 7511/76, 7743/76, para. 33.

12. On Koranic courses taught under the auspices of the Diyanet, and regarding debates in parliament, see Gözaydın 2020: 135–9.

13. This was later defined by jurisprudence. See the decision of the Council of State, Eighth Chamber, E2006/4107, K2007/481, 28 December 2007; E2007/679, K2008/1461, 29 February 2008.

14. On compulsory religion courses in the context of religious minorities, see Müftügil 2015.
15. *TBMM* (proceedings), v. 34, 40th session, 128–9.
16. The Diyanet-affiliated organisations and their activities began in Germany, but quickly spread to other countries in Europe with populations of Turkish origin. Two Diyanet-affiliated structures were legally established in the Netherlands in 1979 and 1982 and quickly gained control of 140 mosques in the country. For an assessment of the Diyanet and its activities in the Netherlands, see Sunier *et al.* 2011. See also Çıtak 2011 (Belgium); Çıtak 2013 (Austria); and Kahraman 2007 (Denmark). Also see Sunier and Landman 2015.
17. For an establishment narrative of the DİTİP and other foundations in Europe, see Altıkulaç 2011: 386–8.
18. Decision dated 19 October 1984, no. 84/8610
19. Decision dated 22 August 1991, no. 2219.
20. *Rabitat'-ül-Alem'ül-İslami* (Muslim World League) is an Islamic non-governmental organisation based in Saudi Arabia. The organisation was founded in 1962 and has been funded by the Saudi government since its establishment.
21. Uğur Mumcu published a series of articles about the *Rabıta* and relations with Turkey between 22 February and 15 March 1987 in the *Cumhuriyet* daily newspaper. See also Mumcu 1987.
22. A popular musical/cultural product of rapid urbanisation with undertones of class differences was the 'arabesk' genre. For 'arabesk' music and culture, see Özbek 1991 and Stokes 1994.
23. The draft of the January 24 decisions, which constituted the political economy of the September 12 coup and opened Turkey up to the neoliberal system, was shared with the public for the first time before the coup by Turgut Özal at an event organised by the Aydınlar Ocağı (https://www.birgun.net/haber/12-eylul-37-yildir-suruyor-179122). On the aftermath of the January 24 decisions, see Tekeli 2017: 9–21.
24. 1402 was the number of the martial law used as a legal base for the purge. For an account by an academic who was a victim of the 1402 purge, see Özen 2002.
25. On the Kurdish question in the context of Turkish modernisation, see Somer 2007: 103–35.
26. On 15 February 1994, Turkey agreed to pay the 300,000 francs in compensation asked for by the European Commission of Human Rights to villagers in the Yeşilyurt village of Cizre who claimed to have been fed faeces by a group of soldiers in January 1989.

27. Village guards, officially known as *Türkiye Güvenlik Köy Korucuları* (Security Village Guards of Turkey) are Gendarmerie General Command-aligned border guards involved in the Turkish–Kurdish conflict.
28. See the report of the TBMM Parliamentary Investigation Commission dated 14 January 1998.
29. In 1993, President Özal, describing himself as the Turkish son of a Kurdish mother, wrote a letter to Prime Minister Süleyman Demirel warning that a 'social earthquake could cut one part of Turkey (off) from the rest' (Findley 2010: 366). But Demirel continued to back the military approach.
30. On Hizbullah, its Islamic character, and its relations with organisations abroad as well as the Turkish state, see Çakır 2011. Also, for accounts relating to the history of Hizbullah and its ideological, political and organisational aspects, see Kurt 2015. In a series of nationwide operations that began with a raid by Istanbul police on a villa in Kavacık on 17 January 2000, fifty-seven tortured bodies and a large number of arms were found. The bodies included those of Izzettin Yıldırım, head of the Zehra Education and Culture Foundation, known for his Islamic-Nurcu identity, and Konca Kuriş (1961–98), an Islamist feminist kidnapped in Mersin in 1998. On Konca Kuriş, see Değer and Çamdereli 2020. Hizbullah suffered a serious blow to its operations in 2000, when its leader Hüseyin Velioğlu was killed and over 3000 of its activists detained throughout Turkey (Nugent 2004).
31. For an extensive list of the most influential human rights organisations in Turkey, see Keyman and Kancı 2014: 148–149.
32. For *Sokak*, see its Editor-in-chief Tuğrul Eryılmaz's memoires (Eryılmaz 2018: 172–83). Also see Elveren and Uncu 2022.
33. For a brief but an illuminating piece on government–business relations and private sector development in the 1980s and 1990s, see Hoşgör 2011.
34. For an evaluation of HAK-İŞ, a pro-Islamic confederation of unions established in 1975, see Karatepe 2017: 213–14. The years 1987–8 were marked by strikes by HAK-İŞ unions, which had never organised a strike until 1980. In 1990, May Day was celebrated for the first time by HAK-İŞ, whose chairman Necati Çelik said at a press conference that they accepted 'May 1st as a day when the workers of the world glorify freedom, peace and pro-labour sentiments, sanctify labour, and reject exploitation' (Ersel *et al.* 2005 vol. 3: 393). On the issue of 'an Islamic economy with class distinctions', see Özdemir 2004: 837–69.
35. MGK was an outcome of the 1960 military coup, and has been a part of the constitution since 1961. The role of the MGK was further strengthened with the 1982 constitution. See Cizre Sakallıoğlu 1997.

36. For a step-by-step account of the 28 February process, see Bayramoğlu 2001.
37. For a thorough survey on Turgut Özal, see Sezal and Dağı 2001. Also, for an interesting analysis of Turgut Özal, his unique personality and his vision, see Gürpınar 2013: 96–117.
38. For a comparison of the funeral services of Atatürk and Özal, see Seufert and Weyland 1994.
39. For a survey focusing on the years 1983–95, organised around the questions of how partisanship works in Turkish social democracy; what members understand by party activity; how the party functions in terms of immigrant groups in big cities and networks of fellow citizens, and to what extent is it determined by these networks; and what is the support of Alevi communities for Turkish social democracy at the level of electoral results, see Schüler 1999.
40. However, there were significant changes in the RP over the course of the 1990s. Ayşe Kadıoğlu states that, 'while moving away from an Islamic, closed image of a cadre party to a modern image of a mass party, RP lost some of its anti-state, civil societal characteristics' (Kadıoğlu 1998a: 14). For an analysis of the RP, see Çakır 1994.
41. Erdoğan was sentenced to ten months' imprisonment as a result of a lawsuit filed against him for 'inciting people to hatred and hostility based on class, race, religion, sect or regional differences' in relation to expressions he used in his speech at an open-air meeting in Siirt in December 1997, and to the verses by Ziya Gökalp which he read out. He was released from prison on 24 July 1999 after four months and ten days in prison.
42. 'Opportunity spaces', a concept coined by Hakan Yavuz (2003a), is very helpful in understanding and analysing the Islamic movements in Turkey after the 1980s.
43. For a very thorough analysis of this process, see Bora and Can 1991: 243–81.
44. For Kırkıncı and his group's preference for the AP over the MNP, see his memoires (Kırkıncı 2004: 223).
45. For an evaluation of the Gülen movement as an organisation along neo-*Nur* lines, see Bora 2017: 430–7.
46. For an account of the reasons underlying the rupture between the Iskender Paşa group and the MNP-MSP-RP line, see Esad Coşan's speech in Çakır 1990: 48–54.
47. For detailed information about Osman Nuri Topbaş including his works, see https://www.osmannuritopbas.com/.
48. For the whole process, see Coşkuner and Aslan 2020. For an analysis of the Diyanet's assimilative conduct towards the Alevis, see Massicard 2007: 182–3.

49. Elise Massicard justifiably distinguishes Aleviness, which cover the social fact, from Alevism, which designates the movement struggling for the recognition of Aleviness (Massicard 2006: 218). For a discussion of Alevi demands in the 1980s and 1990s in the context of citizenship, see Koçan and Öncü 2004.
50. For attitudes and conducts of the politicians of the time, see Mustafa Timisi's memoires (Aydoğdu and Timisi-Nalçaoğlu 2021: 184–7).
51. For the Madımak massacre and its social impact, see Bermek 2021.
52. For the institution of *dede*, see Shankland 2003.
53. ASALA was an organisation formed in 1975 to force the Turkish government to acknowledge the Armenian massacres of 1915 and pay reparations. Its activities, which have included acts of terrorism, have been directed against Turkish government officials and institutions (https://www.britannica.com/summary/Armenian-Secret-Army-for-the-Liberation-of-Armenia).
54. The scandal surfaced with a car–truck collision on 3 November 1996, near Susurluk, in the province of Balıkesir. Abdullah Çatlı (1956–96), a wanted killer and drug trafficker on Interpol's Red List, and Hüseyin Kocadağ (1944–96), a former deputy head of the Istanbul Police Department, were killed; in the same car, Sedat Bucak (1960–), the leader of a Kurdish village guard clan who also was an MP with the DYP, which was part of the RP-led coalition government at the time, was injured (Özdemir 1997).
55. For a compilation of articles reflecting the narratives of the feminist movement in the 1980s, see Kum *et al.* 2005.
56. See Altınay 2002: 324–5.
57. https://kadinarastirmalari.istanbul.edu.tr/tr/.
58. https://morcati.org.tr/.
59. http://kadineserleri.org/; see Davaz-Mardin 2002.
60. For a compilation of interviews with women from Islamist circles, see Çakır 2000; on an Islamist women's civil society organisation in Istanbul, see Çayır 2000; on Islamist women's NGOs, see Pusch 2000; Çakıl-Dinçer 2020. For a powerful critique expressing the Islamist woman's desire to be a woman beyond her ideological identity as a 'sister' in the 'cause', see Aktaş 2001. For a comprehensive compilation of writings on women and feminism by leading Islamist women writers from Turkey, see Ramazanoğlu 2000. For a critique of the patriarchal vein of Islamist discourse, see Şefkatli-Tuksal 2000.
61. See the *Official Gazette* of 25 October 1982, no. 17849.
62. For some other analytical evaluations on the veiling issue, see İlyasoğlu 1994; Özdalga 1998; Navarro-Yashin 2002: 82–90; Çınar 2005: 18–98.

6

UNDER AKP RULE (2002–23)

> As he put it, at least in Turkey there was 'hope'. When he said 'Lebanon doesn't even have that', he felt like crying for a moment. Nabil's story broke my heart, he was absolutely right in his anger. Of course, what he said was valid not only for Lebanon, but for the whole Middle East, including Turkey, and even the world in general. It was a similar anger that pushed me into the crowd on the streets during the Gezi Resistance a few years ago. I was born in June, and five years ago I celebrated my twentieth birthday with my friends among the resistance tents in Gezi Park. Yes, as Nabil said, there was and still is hope in Turkey.
>
> Selahattin Demirtaş, *Efsun* (2022)[1]

On 3 November 2002, early general elections were held in Turkey. In the election, for which the d'Hondt system was used with a 10 per cent national threshold, only the *Adalet ve Kalkınma Partisi* (Justice and Development Party/AKP) and the CHP were able to pass the threshold and win seats in parliament. With 34.3 per cent of the votes and 363 parliamentary seats, the AKP had won the largest majority in the Turkish Grand National Assembly enjoyed by any party since the 1950s.[2] This meant that 46.33 per cent of the votes cast in the 2002 general elections were not represented in parliament. Even though the AKP gained a majority in the parliament with these election results, it was over-represented in an undemocratic way due to the electoral system.

In Turkish politics, the early 2000s was a period in which political and economic crises forced the need for political change. The 2002 elections had renewed the actors in Turkish politics, and the AKP cadres would now embark on the pursuit of substantial transformation and a new regime.

A Brief Overview of the Era

On 12 September 1980, the Left was largely neutralised, while the 'return to life' operation in 2000[3] had marginalised the leftist movement that had begun to regroup in the 1990s. The Kurdish movement was put into a de facto period of non-conflict in 1999 when Abdullah Öcalan was captured by the US special operations units in Kenya and handed over to Turkey. The February 28 process divided the National Vision movement, largely neutralising its 'traditionalist' wing. With the imprisonment of IBDA-C leader Salih Mirzabeyoğlu (1950–2018) (Biçer 2017)[4] and the killing of Hizbullah leader Hüseyin Velioğlu (1952–2000), the space that had opened up for radical Islam in the 1990s was almost closed. The neo-liberal policies that Kemal Derviş (1949–2023)[5] was invited to implement after two financial crises in 2001 stabilised public finances and brought down inflation. The economy was back on a path to growth and hot money inflows financed this growth for a long time, causing enormous economic pain for many. In other words, a relative stability was already in place for the AKP to benefit from, especially in the early years of AKP power.

2002–7

In its first term in power, the AKP placed the EU accession process at the centre of its project to transform Turkey. The biggest difference between the AKP and previous governments that supported EU membership is that the AKP accepted the process of integration with the EU on the condition that Turkey would not give up its own 'civilizational identity' (Koyuncu 2014: 272–6). In a 2003 publication, Hakan Yavuz argues that

> The AKP's identity and ideology resembles a fabric that changes colour depending on the light. This eclectic aspect of the party is the reason for its broad appeal. It is simultaneously Turkish, Muslim and Western. This pluralist aspect is also very much a political necessity, given the diverse lifestyles in the

country. It seeks to provide a framework of civic peace in which various groups can live together. (Yavuz 2003a: 260)

ECtHR issued its chamber judgement in the *Leyla Şahin* v. *Turkey* case, whose focus was Turkish legislation banning the wearing of headscarves in universities, on 29 June 2004, and its Grand Chamber judgement on 10 November 2005; Turkey was found to not be in violation of the Convention. Both decisions were disappointing for women who faced the choice of being denied education or attending universities in a manner that offended their conscience.[6]

In the period between 2002 and 2007, while the AKP represented the majority in the parliament, it did not completely dominate the state bureaucracy. In this context, the AKP was in power but not fully capable of governing. The presence of the strict secularist Ahmet Necdet Sezer as President of the Republic, coupled with the military's great suspicion of the AKP, caused the party to act hesitantly. The AKP appears to have instrumentalised many international institutions during this period, and the EU in particular, to balance the secular and anti-AKP bloc.[7]

2007–13

The wish for a *coexistence pacifique* among different groups in Turkey was not fulfilled. The events that led to early parliamentary elections on 22 July 2007 show the degree of polarisation. The conflict between the AKP and its fierce secularist opponents reached crisis point over the election of a new president of the Republic. Several mass demonstrations were organised to protest against the AKP and its candidate for the presidency, Abdullah Gül, as a threat to the secular character of Turkey.[8] The presidential election of 2007 proved to be a turning point in the AKP's populist trajectory, resulting as it did in a landslide victory for the AKP. The 'controlled conflict' of 2002 to 2006 between the AKP and the higher echelons of the Turkish armed forces became a crisis in 2007,[9] which was followed by the army drawing back in 2007–8 (Cizre 2008; Hale and Özbudun 2010: 80–98). The Euro-enthusiasm of the early AKP years with regard to EU–Turkey relations turned into Euro-fatigue (Usul 2008).[10]

On 14 March 2008, the Public Prosecutor, Abdurrahman Yalçınkaya (1950–), forwarded a 162-page indictment to the Constitutional Court, requesting the closure of the AKP. The indictment accused the AKP and its leaders of violating the principles of *laiklik* defined in Article 2 of the Turkish Constitution. It cited as evidence speeches and statements by President Abdullah Gül, Prime Minister Recep Tayyip Erdoğan, and almost seventy other AKP officials. The court accepted Yalçınkaya's indictment by a unanimous vote of 11–0 on 31 March 2008.[11] Ultimately, however, the Court acknowledged the supremacy of the ballot box in a democratic order and did not hand down a decision to close the AKP. Nonetheless, concluding that the AKP was a major source of anti-*laik* activities, the court cut by half the amount the party received from the Treasury.[12]

The same year, 2008, witnessed a crisis between the civilian and military leadership in what came to be known as 'Ergenekon', the military code name for a series of military schemes and coup plots. The Ergenekon case officially concluded in 2013 when the 275 verdicts were delivered by the Supreme Court of Appeals, including life sentences for several senior military officers.[13]

A wide range of amendments to the 1982 Constitution arranged under twenty-six headings and addressing issues including freedom of expression, protection of privacy, labour rights and judicial reforms in line with EU requirements were approved by the Turkish Grand National Assembly and submitted to a referendum by President Abdullah Gül. The referendum of 12 September 2010 resulted in a 57.88 per cent vote for the amendments and a 42.12 per cent vote against; the constitutional amendments were subsequently adopted.[14]

By the time the 2011 parliamentary elections took place, the public discourses of mainstream political actors no longer framed the AKP as a threat against the republican regime (Aydın-Düzgit 2012). The organised opposition, which included the CHP, lacked the capacity to influence the government, let alone serve as an alternative to it (Çınar 2015: 189). The power struggle that enabled the AKP to establish itself as the dominant party 'had a detrimental impact on Turkey's unconsolidated democratic transition, gradually relegating civil liberties and the rule of law to calculations of political hegemony and revanchism' (Akkoyunlu 2017: 53).

2013–23

A peaceful protest by a handful of environmental activists in Taksim Square on 28 May 2013 against government plans to raze Istanbul's Gezi Park to make room for the construction of a replica of the nineteenth-century Ottoman artillery barracks escalated into a country-wide protest movement that lasted over three months.[15] The social opposition, which was not represented in the political arena and had not been taken into account by the AKP, manifested itself all over Turkey through the protests over Gezi Park. The Gezi protests grew because the AKP leaders thought they would appear weak if they backtracked on the party's declared policies. When the protests flared up in late May/early June, Prime Minister Erdoğan characterised the protesters as 'three or five thugs (*çapulcu*)'. Unable to develop a political reasoning based on democratic behaviour, Prime Minister Erdoğan and the AKP began to produce conspiracy theories claiming that there were hostile plans afoot directed by forces hostile to Turkey.[16] The aftermath of the Gezi events was catastrophic in terms of human rights violations.[17] Erdoğan and the governing AKP took the opportunity to construct a political hegemony with a language including '*benim polisim* (my police)', '*benim valim* (my governor)', and revanchism that went as far as imprisoning opponents like Osman Kavala and naming a bridge over the Bosphorus after Yavuz Sultan Selim, an Ottoman sultan known for massacring the Alevis in the sixteenth century.

If the Gezi protests were a very significant milestone, the so-called 17–25 December process was the zenith for Erdoğan and the AKP, paving the way towards authoritarianism. On 17 December 2013, a wave of arrests was made targeting businessmen, bankers and most notably the sons of four serving Cabinet ministers in Erdoğan's government in the context of an anti-corruption operation. This incident brought the escalating tension between the AKP and the Gülen movement into the open.[18] Actually, the falling out between the two parties began on 7 February 2012, when various public officials, including Hakan Fidan, the head of MİT (National Intelligence Organisation) at the time, were subpoenaed to testify on the Kurdish peace process. After the results of the local elections of 30 March 2014 had been determined, Erdoğan, prime minister at the time, went out onto the balcony of the AKP headquarters and greeted the fans while holding hands with the family members who had been mentioned in relation to the corruption allegations. If it had not been clear enough before, his speech that day made it quite clear that Turkey now had a 'one-man regime' (Gözaydın 2017: 259; Watmough and Öztürk 2018).

The heavy repression of freedoms in Turkey during this period may best be presented by the legal and judicial processes that followed the use of the right and freedom of expression through the addressing of a petition to the government regarding the Kurdish question. On 11 January 2016, a petition signed initially by 1,128 academics as 'Academics for Peace' seeking an end to state violence and the beginning of peace negotiations with the Kurdish political movement was published in the media. The reaction of President Erdoğan and the AKP revealed an intolerance for criticism which has no place in a democratic country. After more than three years of detentions, arrests and verdicts against the signatories, the Constitutional Court decided in July 2019 that the rights of the petitioners had been violated.[19]

The war between the AKP and the Gülen community resulted in the 15 July 2016 coup attempt, which Recep Tayyip Erdoğan blamed entirely on the Gülen party. The government had already branded Gülen circles as FETÖ (Fettullahist Terrorist Organisation) and a 'parallel structure'. The authorities made statements claiming that the failed coup attempt was the work of 'FETÖ within the army' (Taş 2018b). Tony Alaranta argues that, after the 15 July coup attempt, the AKP, as Turkey's elected government, feeling that it was not receiving sufficient support and solidarity from Europe and the US, formed an anti-Western narrative in response by articulating various nationalist discourses. This historical narrative, which Islamic conservative, Kemalist, extra right-wing nationalist and left-wing nationalist elements now all use, begins with the victory at Malazgirt (Manzikert) against Byzantium in 1071 and ends with Atatürk being embraced by the AKP as *Halâskar Gazi* (Liberator and Warrior for Islam)[20] (Alaranta 2016).[21] The coup attempt seems to have given Erdoğan the ideal opportunity to achieve what he had been yearning for all along: not an allegiance based on self-interest, convictions or even admiration but a love rooted in unconditional, unthinking, passionate devotion (Gözaydın 2017: 261)

A state of emergency (OHAL) was declared for 90 days on 20 July 2016 and extended seven times until it was finally lifted on 18 July 2018. The human rights violations caused by the OHAL were enormous in quantity and quality.[22] During the state of emergency, the government purged more than 125,000 state employees, the passports of thousands of state employees and civilians were cancelled, thousands of civil society and media organisations were closed, periods of custody were extended and access to defence counsel was restricted. Additionally, a total of 2,271 private-sector education institutions and 1,427 associations were dissolved; thirty-nine radio stations, thirty-four TV channels and seventy-three journals and newspapers were shut down; fifteen foundation-owned universities were closed; and trustees were assigned to run ninety-nine municipalities on behalf of the state, most of them in the Kurdish region and governed by the pro-Kurdish party (HDP); trustees were also assigned to 985 companies (Yılmaz 2020). People who were alleged to have links to the Gülen movement were subjected to widespread suspension, dismissal and arrest and suffered a loss of rights in other fields including torture while in custody and in prison. However, these operations have extended beyond targeting the Gülen movement and have begun to include anyone who is an opponent of the government. The operations have affected the whole of society, from the judiciary, police, gendarmerie and military to public servants, local administrators, teachers, academics, lawyers, journalists and the business community. Many companies have been closed down and their assets seized, or assigned to public institutions (Çınar and Şirin 2017). Uğur Özgöker and Zekeriya Alperen Bedirhan make a perfect *post factum* analysis as follows:

> The coup attempt on July 15th, 2016 was a breaking point in the constitutional, democratic, secular, republican state of Turkey. In the new Turkey, instead of rule of law and independence of the judiciary; arbitrary rules that depend on Erdoğan's decisions are being implemented by the justice keepers. Instead of meritocracy, equality, non-discrimination and fairness; obedience to Erdoğan and membership of AKP is sufficient to enter state cadres. Instead of freedom of speech and press, fictions of the pro-government media organizations work not only in the interest of their own companies but also to survival of the AKP. Instead of secularism and respect for minorities, rising privileges of Muslim and Islamisation are more crucial. Instead of scientific education with rationalism and humanism, religious dogmas and heroism are the new features of the Turkish national education system. Instead of human rights; torture, prohibition, threats, legitimization of violence are the new reality of Turkey. Instead of interest-based relations in international area; Turkey is losing its prestige in the rising tension with not only European countries like the 2017 Dutch–Turkish diplomatic incident and disturbing ties between Germany and Turkey because of the arrests of human defenders but also the US on the US pastor Andrew Brunson's arrest. (Özgöker and Bedirhan 2018: 39)

Recep Tayyip Erdoğan won his second term as president on 24 June 2018. The AKP–MHP alliance won an absolute majority in the parliament, and was thus able to switch officially from a parliamentary system to the so-called Turkish-type presidential system. With the introduction of the new governance system in 2018, President Erdoğan secured the power to intervene in the bureaucracy and judiciary, as well as controlling the military (Öztürk and Gözaydın 2017).[23]

On 24 July 2020, Ayasofya was desecularised and opened as a mosque. Markus Dressler reads the conversion and the re-opening ceremony as a form of symbolic politics: 'The revaluation of the Ottoman tradition goes hand in hand with a devaluation of the Kemalist heritage without attacking directly . . . Erdoğan thus delegitimises the Kemalist conversion of Hagia Sophia into a museum as an act of destruction of cultural heritage' (Dressler 2020).

The Crescendo Significance of the Diyanet

The AKP inherited the Kemalist institution of the Diyanet, and bestowed on the institution a role in which it supports Islam in society. In 2009, when he was still serving as Vice President of the Diyanet, Professor Mehmet Görmez said in an interview (Aslan 2009),

> In recent years, the Diyanet has begun to redefine its duties in the light of social changes. Realizing that the task of 'enlightening society about religion' assigned to it by law cannot be performed through existing information materials, preaching and hutbes alone. The Diyanet is making a serious attempt to produce information and share this information more widely with society. The Diyanet is trying to give Koran courses a more scientific basis. In the same way, the Diyanet is redefining the duty of 'Religious Service', which it endeavours to provide in a more socially-oriented form. The number of countries demanding services is rapidly increasing, and the number of services abroad has doubled. However, I would like to admit that we have experienced a quarter-century delay in projects, given the changes in society.

The new regulations introduced by the Law on the Diyanet dated 1 July 2010 were, in a sense, the codification of provisions relating to the organisation and duties of the Presidency, which had been introduced over the years in a number of decrees and other administrative acts (Gözaydın and Öztürk 2023: 206–7). In other words, on paper, there was no dramatic change in the structure of the Diyanet in 2010: it was provided by legislation that the three pillars of the Diyanet would remain the central organisation, the provincial organisation and the organisation abroad (Paşaoğlu 2019: 204–19).

Mehmet Nuri Yılmaz, appointed to the Diyanet Chair by Süleyman Demirel in 1992, was removed from office by Recep Tayyip Erdoğan in 2003 and replaced by Professor Ali Bardakoğlu (1952–), an academic from the Faculty of Divinity at Ankara University. On 11 November 2010, Prof. Dr Mehmet Görmez (1959–), who had served as the Vice-President of the Diyanet since 13 August 2003, was appointed to replace Prof. Ali Bardakoğlu, who had served as the Head of the Diyanet for seven years and left the post voluntarily. Until 1 August 2017, when he retired, Prof. Görmez's vision for the Diyanet, which is reflected in the performance programmes and annual reports produced since 2010, was 'to be the most effective and respected institution in Turkey and the world, which is taken as a reference in all matters related to the Islamic Religion'. On 17 September 2017, Dr Ali Erbaş (1961–) was appointed as the Chair of the Diyanet.[24]

Turkey's changing foreign policy during the AKP era, and in particular the strategy of Prof. Ahmet Davutoğlu (1959–), who was the designer and implementer of Turkey's foreign policy as Foreign Minister between 2009 and 2014 and Prime Minister between 2014 and 2016 and sought to make Turkey a protagonist in the international arena, led to the extension of the Diyanet's activities abroad.[25] Under the AKP and Davutoğlu, the Diyanet's activities in the international arena began to expand beyond the geographies where people of Turkish origin live (Çıtak 2017: 12; Öztürk and Gözaydın 2018).[26] The Diyanet's written statement on the minaret referendum in Switzerland, which appeared in the Turkish press on 1 December 2009, stating that 'the cancellation or violation of fundamental human rights cannot be made the subject of a referendum, nor can it be accepted that any nation, state or organ restricts or limits them in a way that could be construed as such', can be read as a first manifestation of this new global Diyanet (Gözaydın 2020: 348).

The statement 'We rush to the aid of the oppressed and victimized wherever they are in the world, especially in countries such as Syria, Iraq, Afghanistan, Arakan, Palestine, Yemen and Somalia, and we try to alleviate their suffering with our humanitarian aid efforts' on the website of the Turkish Diyanet Foundation also reflects this claim to be a global institution.[27] On 6 April 2010, an administrative unit called the Presidency for Turks Abroad and Related Communities (YTB) was established for citizens residing outside Turkey and groups called 'sibling communities'. The YTB has taken on the task of coordinating the international programme bringing scholarship students to Turkey to study, and developing the services and activities on offer in these areas. In this context, the Diyanet provides about 1,000 scholarships every year (Öktem 2012: 44). Although the Diyanet's activities, especially in the Balkans, have been criticised by some of its interlocutors in these geographies, it can also be said that religious representatives in the region choose to cooperate with Turkey.[28]

The instrumentalisation of the Diyanet in domestic politics as well as foreign policy increased after 2010. The 'civil Fridays', which can be read as the Kurdish people's reaction to the state's struggle for power through religion, started in 2011 with the people at Diyarbakır praying publicly behind the *meles*[29] and listening to the sermon in Kurdish. Consequently, Erdoğan announced in 2012 that 'a mosque with a capacity of ten thousand people' would be built in Diyarbakır, and nearly a thousand *mele* were appointed to serve as 'imams and Koran instructors' in eastern and south-eastern Anatolian provinces. On the night of the 15 July 2016 coup attempt, *selas*[30] were broadcast through the night by every minaret in the country.[31]

This was also a period in which efforts were made to increase the services provided for women. It was mainly for this reason that the Diyanet employed more women; 2018 saw the first female vice president appointed to the Diyanet.[32]

Delivering religious service in a social context was put into practice with activities such as providing guidance to citizens in prisons and detention centres,[33] juvenile detention centres, nursing homes and health institutions, as well as tackling religious issues concerning and of concern to the family, women and youth. The Diyanet established 'family and religious guidance' bureaus in the offices of the muftis[34] in every province and affiliated district in Turkey.[35] In addition, the Women, Family and Youth Centre (KAGEM), which was established in 1996 to deal specifically with women's and family issues under the umbrella of the Turkish Diyanet Foundation, an institution closely related to the Diyanet, was restructured in 2011, expanding its areas of competence. On

26 November 2011, a memorandum of cooperation was signed between the Diyanet and the Ministry of Family and Social Services in order to strengthen the family; to protect family structures and values and ensure that they are passed on to future generations in a healthy way; to raise awareness in society of the problems that threaten the family and the individual within the family; to increase the effectiveness of protective preventive social services; to raise awareness of the issues facing women, children, youth, elderly and disabled individuals; and to strengthen social support systems. Since then, the Diyanet has been assigned a number of duties and responsibilities vis-à-vis actions relating to women and the family in national action plans, while the Presidency has signed numerous memoranda with various ministries on these issues (Mutluer 2014: 12–13).[36]

During the AKP period, Diyanet initiatives have included a contested hadith compilation; Alo Fetva (an on-line religious information service);[37] issuing halal certificates; establishing media channels; organising celebrations (*Kutlu Doğum* – the Blessed Birth of the Prophet Muhammed); and obtaining the alternative, non-secular authority to perform weddings (Gözaydın 2020: 357–67; Çıtak 2020: 173–8). In addition, the *Diyanet Akademi* (The Diyanet Academy) was established on 24 March 2022 as a unit for training personnel with qualifications required by the Diyanet in the field of religious services and religious education.

Political Parties and their Leaders

In terms of the political parties represented in the parliament, the 2000s started with just the AKP and CHP; after the 2007 elections, the MHP managed to join them, followed by the HDP in the 2015 elections. Especially after the official switch from the parliamentary system to the so-called Turkish-type presidential system in 2018, the AKP's authoritarian politics led to the emergence of a collective opposition. The anti-AKP electoral alliance formed between the CHP, the nationalist *İYİ Parti* and the pro-Islamist *Saadet Partisi* – joined later by the *Demokrat Parti*, *Deva Partisi* and *Gelecek Partisi* – held their first meeting on 12 February 2022. This so-called *Altılı Masa* (Table of Six) or *Millet İttifakı* (Nation Alliance), which encompassed a broad base of secular republicans, nationalists and Islamists, favoured a return to parliamentary democracy.

Adalet ve Kalkınma Partisi/AKP *(Justice and Development Party)*

The AKP was established by a wide range of politicians from various political parties, plus a number of first-time MPs, in 2001. The core of the party was formed by the reformist faction of the FP: people like Abdullah Gül, Recep Tayyip Erdoğan and Bülent Arınç came from the *Milli Görüş* movement, which had reached an important crossroads in 2000. Traditionalists loyal to Erbakan were challenged for the first time by a younger generation of reformers led by Abdullah Gül, an economist with a PhD who worked in the Islamic Development Bank from 1983 to 1991. With Erdoğan still technically prohibited from holding political office due to his criminal record, the AKP's co-founder, Abdullah Gül, became Prime Minister in his place and subsequently had the political ban on Erdoğan annulled. But Recep Tayyip Erdoğan has been the leading figure in the AKP from the beginning.[38] Becoming a member of the parliament via a by-election in Siirt province in 2003, Erdoğan replaced Gül as prime minister.

Unlike RP and FP leaders, AKP politicians pursued a political incorporationist strategy including a performative discipline and competence from the establishment of the party in 2001 until the end of its second term in government in 2011 (Altınordu 2016: 162). Since then, the AKP has been mobilising religion by deepening and layering the Kemalist *laik* institutions that had already given religion a place at the constitutional level, and appropriating a politics of diversity that advances religion even deeper as the cement of society (Akan 2017: 535–606).[39] As Bill Park comments, the AKP enabled Turks 'to express their . . . identities as a Turkic, Muslim, Middle Eastern, post-Ottoman as well as a European people and society. The AKP has been "a beneficiary of . . . dissatisfactions and suppressed identities"' (Park 2012: 207).[40] The secular/religious distinction that underlines and animates Kemalism was refashioned (Shakman Hurd 2011: 181). Since the Gezi protests of mid-2013, Erdoğan has employed the politics of fear to rally his supporters around an imminent threat to the national security narrative, using securitisation, fear and trauma to repress the opposition (Yılmaz and Shipoli 2021). Military tutelage was ended but democratisation failed too (Akkoyunlu 2017: 51–5). A delegative democracy was created that eroded the democratic texture of the regime by destroying institutional mechanisms and eliminating political competition, establishing an informal rent-distributing system in its place to ensure loyalty (Taş 2015: 788).

The AKP managed to mobilise the urban poor on behalf of a neoliberal, capitalist project and incorporated them into the system (Tuğal 2009). However, the informal rent-distributing system that ensures loyalty also served to transform the welfare state into a charity state (Köse and Bahçe 2009).[41] As is well known, two practices of philanthropy are prominent in Islamic sources: zakat and charity. Philanthropy enables the unequal construction of the social, the articulation and construction of status differences and the institutionalisation of power differentials. According to Amy Singer, the author of one of the best studies on philanthropy in Islamic societies,

> Donations affected the texture of interpersonal relations and charitable giving created bonds of dependence and obligation, gratitude and subservience. These were a form of social glue. At the same time, the ability to give at a particular level is an important indicator of horizontal divisions in society, enabling people to identify their peers as those who give in similar ways and comparable amounts. (Singer 2008: 223)

Through state-sponsored philanthropy and limited social assistance, the AKP has built political capital that can be analysed in terms of patronage relations, hegemony and populism.[42] The switch to the so-called presidential system of government in Turkey in 2018 marked a serious turning point in the neo-liberal transformation of the state which has been ongoing since the 1980s. In the economic field, it led to the AKP's politicised, centralised and personalised management practices (Bedirhanoğlu 2021). Socially, a pious/conservative middle class was created, made up of people who had previously been informally excluded from such wealth and opportunity. As they ultimately gained in self-confidence and engaged with the secular on equal terms, this new pillar of the new Turkey is different from Turgut Özal's *esnaf* (small business people/tradespeople) middle class and may be argued to be Erdoğan's biggest success.

In line with the conservative democratic identity of the AKP when it came to power in 2002, the party's education policies until 2011 were meant to demonstrate an increasing pluralism. After 2011, the AKP government introduced a radical change with the new education system known as 4+4+4[43] (Gençkal-Eroler 2019: 130–64).[44] AKP governments shaped the education system in line with a neoliberal policy programme and a conservative religious ideology (Karapehlivan 2019).

The AKP, which criticised the existence of the Council of Higher Education (YÖK) when it was in opposition, embraced it and used it for its own goals when it came to power. It has also turned the higher education system into an apparatus of state. Between 2006 and 2008, forty-one universities have been opened in forty-one provinces, while the number of state universities increased from fifty-three when the AKP came to power to 109 by the end of 2015.[45]

The AKP's use of Islam as an umbrella identity sought to unify Muslim Turks and Kurds by providing a supra-identity; however, in practice, it blurred the conceptual ethnonational boundaries of Kurdishness by turning it into an ambiguous sub-cultural identity (Gürses 2023).[46] The legal framework in Turkey is still 'ethnic-blind' vis-à-vis the Kurds (Kurban 2014: 355).

In government, the AKP evolved into a replica of the CHP of the 1930s with commonalities including their collectivist character, a desire for state control as a vehicle for realising an ideology, intolerance of diversity and the criminalisation of other perspectives. The difference between the two parties lies in the CHP placing religion as morality in the private sphere and the AKP emphasising its social and cultural role in the public sphere.[47] The genealogy and political histories of Islamists in Turkey is reflected in the trajectory of the AKP. Thus,

> when the forces and constraints of domestic and external social, political and economic conditions disappeared and the opportunities derived from being Muslim Democrats no longer existed, the former Islamists easily returned to their original ideology, showing that despite assertions to the contrary their respect for democracy and pluralism had not truly been internalized. (Yılmaz, Barton and Barry 2017)

CHP

In the 2002 general elections, the CHP was the only party other than the AKP to enter parliament. In October 2003, Deniz Baykal was re-elected as CHP chairman at their congress. Despite the turmoil within the CHP, the party's share of the vote rose to almost to 21 per cent in the 2007 elections. On 10 May 2010, less than two weeks before the Congress was to be convened, the

CHP Chairman Deniz Baykal announced his resignation from his post which he had held for fifteen years and eight months, in a press statement following the airing on 7 May 2010 on a website *metacafe.com* of a sex tape allegedly involving himself and a female CHP deputy. On 22 May 2010, Kemal Kılıçdaroğlu (1948–) became the chairman of the CHP. In the 2011 general elections, the party achieved a moderate success, winning 25.98 per cent of the vote and securing 135 seats in parliament.[48] In the general elections held on 2015, the CHP received approximately 25 per cent of the vote, winning 132 parliamentary seats.

Between 15 June and 9 July 2017, a march for justice was organised from Ankara to Istanbul, led by Kılıçdaroğlu. Kılıçdaroğlu took the decision to march after the CHP MP for Istanbul, Enis Berberoğlu (1956–), was put on trial on 14 June 2017. Berberoğlu was charged with leaking footage of trucks allegedly belonging to the National Intelligence Organisation exporting guns to Syria, giving the footage to Can Dündar (1961–), the former editor-in-chief of the *Cumhuriyet* newspaper. Berberoğlu was sentenced to twenty-five years in prison on 13 June 2017. On 17 September 2020, the Constitutional Court ruled that Enis Berberoğlu's 'right to be elected and to engage in political activity' and 'right to personal liberty and security' had been violated, and he was reinstated as an MP on 11 February 2021.

In the local elections of 31 March 2019, the CHP increased its total vote share by 13.5 per cent compared to 2014 and won eleven of the nineteen municipalities it nominated candidates for. The biggest success was winning the mayorships of Istanbul and Ankara after thirty years. Thus, Turkey's three largest metropolitan cities, along with eight more cities, were now under the control of CHP mayors.[49] When the *Yüksek Seçim Kurulu* (High Election Committee) annulled the mayoral elections in Istanbul, İmamoğlu increased his votes even more in the new elections held on 23 June 2019, achieving a historic success with 54.22 per cent of the votes.

MHP

In the 2002 elections, the MHP fell below the electoral threshold and was not represented in the TBMM; however, it has won a place in parliament at every general election since 2007. After the 2015 elections, Devlet Bahçeli was challenged by a group of MHP members, but rejected their demands to stage an extraordinary congress. This was followed by several resignation. In the 2018 general elections, the nationalist MHP formed the so-called *Cumhur İttifakı* (Peoples' Alliance) with the AKP. In the 2018 presidential election, the MHP did not put forward a candidate and supported Recep Tayyip Erdoğan for the Presidency of the Republic of Turkey; it took part in the 2023 general elections as part of the Peoples' Alliance.

Halkların Demokratik Partisi *(Peoples' Democratic Party/HDP)*

Aiming to challenge the Turkish–Kurdish divide as a pro-minority party in Turkish politics, the HDP was founded in 2012 as the political wing of the Peoples' Democratic Congress, a union of numerous left-wing movements that had previously fielded candidates as independents. In the 2015 elections, the HDP succeeded in passing the 10 per cent election threshold, winning more than 13 per cent of the votes and becoming the third largest parliamentary group in the TBMM. Though most of the politicians in the HDP are secular pro-Left Kurds, the HDP candidate list has also included devout Muslims, Alevis, Armenians, Assyrian Christians, Circassians, Laz, Roma and LGBTI+ activists. Currently, the HDP is represented by fifty-six MPs and is co-chaired by Pervin Buldan (1967–) and Mithat Sancar (1963–).[50]

The HDP has always been the target of judicial and political threats and sanctions from the establishment. Selahattin Demirtaş (1973–), who was elected co-chair of the HDP with Figen Yüksekdağ (1971–) in 2014 and nominated by his party for the 2018 presidential election, has been in prison since 4 November 2016. After the 2019 local elections, Diyarbakır Metropolitan Mayor Adnan Selçuk Mızraklı, Mardin Metropolitan Mayor Ahmet Türk and Van Metropolitan Mayor Bedia Özgökçe Ertan were dismissed by the Ministry of Interior and replaced with trustees. There is also a case pending before the Constitutional Court seeking the closure of the HDP.[51]

İyi Parti *(Good Party)*

Following the November 2015 general elections, some MHP members of parliament and party members criticised their leader Devlet Bahçeli's failure in the elections and formed a strong opposition within the party. Meral Akşener (1956–), Ümit Özdağ (1961–), Sinan Oğan (1969–) and others started collecting delegate signatures to take the MHP to an extraordinary congress. However, when the party could not stage an extraordinary congress for legal reasons, it expelled some of its members, including Meral Akşener. Subsequently, Meral Akşener, Koray Aydın (1955–), other deputies expelled from the MHP and a founding team of 200 people established the *Iyi* Party in October 2017. Although the list of founding members consists in the main of people with MHP and *ülkücü* origins, there are also people who were members of and/or represented the RP, ANAP, DYP and DSP.

Saadet Partisi *(Felicity Party/Saadet)*

Saadet Party, the political wing of the *Milli Görüş* movement, was founded on 20 July 2001; Recai Kutan (1930–) became its founding chairman. After the closure of the FP by the Constitutional Court, nearly half of the 105 deputies who remained independent joined the *Saadet*. Necmettin Erbakan was elected chairman in 2003, but in December 2003, the Chief Public Prosecutor's Office of the Court of Cassation demanded that Erbakan resign from party membership due to his prison sentence. Recai Kutan became acting chairman and remains in that post in 2023.

The Felicity Party won 4.77 per cent of the vote in the 2004 local elections, winning sixty-three mayorships. The party received 2.34 per cent of the vote in the 2007 general elections. After several elected general presidents, Temel Karamollaoğlu (1941–), who was involved in the founding of the *Saadet* and served as mayor of Sivas 1989–95, was elected chairman in 2016. The party participated in the 2017 referendum, 2018 general elections and 2019 local elections under Karamollaoğlu's leadership.[52]

Others in the 'Nation Alliance'

The *Demokrasi ve Atılım Partisi* (Democracy and Progress Party/DEVA) was founded on 9 March 2020 under the leadership of Ali Babacan, who resigned from the AKP in 2019, having served as Minister for Foreign Affairs and Economics Minister for thirteen years. The *Gelecek Partisi* (Future Party) was founded on 12 December 2019 by former Foreign Minister (2009–14) and Prime Minister (2014–16) Ahmet Davutoğlu. Davutoğlu was opposed to the government's intention to change Turkey's form of government from a parliamentary to a presidential system. His differences with Erdoğan resulted in Davutoğlu resigning as prime minister on 22 May 2016. Davutoglu resigned from the AKP on 13 September 2016. The Democratic Party was founded when the DYP changed its name and logo on 27 May 2007. The *Demokrat Parti* merged with ANAP in 2009, and is currently represented in the parliament by two MPs.

Religious Circles

Religious circles became much more visible in the 2000s and 2010s. However, Tayfun Atay, an academic known for his studies in the field of religion and politics, points out that religious groups, communities and circles now have Erdoğan as their *meşihat makamı* (religious leader). He comments: 'It could be argued that we have entered a period in which all the religious circles could be seen as being in a melting pot under Erdoğan'.[53] Various religious circles did not melt into the Erdoğan pot in this period, but their support for him has been constant and virtually all-encompassing, with the exception of the Gülen movement after 2013, Yeni Asya, Furkan Vakfı and İhsan Eliaçık.[54]

Nur *Movement*

Different groups within the *Nur* movement remained present into the 2000s. In a questions and answers section on the *Risale-i Nur* website, the answer dated 8 June 2009 to the question 'The Nur community is divided into "writers" and "readers": why is such a distinction made and what are the differences between these branches?' is,

> Conflict is a human reality. Each group of Nur followers has taken on a mission: some read, some write, others try to serve through radio, others still through TV and the internet. All together, they constitute a great and massive force, like the parts of a body, and in this way, at every stage of life, they fight both debauchery and immorality, as well as irreligion and so on. So, yes, on the surface there is a separation in the Nur communities. But there is no separation in this separation. Because the goal is one, the purpose is the same. There may only be some small differences in the method of service. In this way, different temperaments can be employed in different groups.[55]

Within the *Nur* movement, the *Yeni Asya* group has a different political stance from the others. This group sees the DP, AP, DYP and today's Democrat Party as links to the same tradition and supports them. Because of this stance, there have been ideological disagreements with other *Nur* communities from time to time. This situation came to a head in the 12 June 2011 parliamentary elections, when Said Nursî's living disciples issued a statement announcing their support for the AKP.[56] This support has certainly been mutually beneficial: Islamic groups have provided personnel for the AKP to fill civil service posts, while having cadres in public office has made it easier for these groups to expand, both financially and politically (Çelik 2017: 108–9).

Gülen Movement

Erdoğan and the AKP's most volatile relationship has been with Fethullah Gülen and his followers. The convergence and alliance between the two sides was interest- and power-oriented and the result of a common objective: removing the army's tutelage over the state structure. The Gülenists were the most prominent Islamic group related to the AKP between 2002 and 2011.[57] However, different approaches to the Kurdish question and the Gezi protests led to the *dershane* crisis[58] and the bursting out of long-festering frictions. Corruption allegations made by the Gülenists on 17 and 25 December 2013 saw the government respond with actions taken against pro-Gülen media in December 2014 and the Koza İpek Group in October 2015; these, in turn, led to a war (Taş 2018a). The alleged contribution of pro-Gülenists in the military to the coup attempt of 15 July 2016 resulted in a witch-hunt: hundreds of thousands of police officers, judges, public prosecutors, academics and business people considered sympathetic to Gülen were taken into custody, arrested, and faced inhumane treatment without respect being paid to their human rights.[59]

İskenderpaşa Community

Emin Coşan's son Nureddin Coşan (1963–), who has a bachelor's degree in Business Administration from the State University of New York–College of Saint Rose is the current head of the group, which also has substantial business interests. Their movement is known for the balance they try to create between tradition and modernity. Closely interested in politics, prominent names in the community played an important role in establishing the MNP and its successor, the MSP, which initiated the first explicitly pro-religious bodies in republican Turkey in the 1960s and 1970s. Currently, the community appears to be closer to political parties with more nationalistic-religious agendas, including one they themselves established as the *Sağduyu Partisi* (Common Sense Party) in 2002, though it has never organised at the national level.

İsmailağa Community

Currently the İsmailağa community runs private schools, Koran courses and various media organs. Religious education appears to be their focus at three levels: Arabic and *hafız*[60] students, regular madrasas and specialised madrasas. They also have an on-line system to answer questions from the public. This community differs from the others in imposing strict dress codes: men have long beards and wear non-Western clothing, while women are obliged to wear black chadors.[61] Recep Tayyip Erdoğan is known to maintain close relations with their leader, Mahmut Ustaosmanoğlu; Erdoğan paid a highly publicised visit to Ustaosmanoğlu the night before the elections in 2014.

Menzil Community

Currently, Fevzeddin Erol (1957–), a brother of Muhammet Raşit Erol, leads the community. The Menzil community has experienced significant growth since the coup attempt of 15 July 2016. When the Gülen movement's public sector cadres were purged, they were replaced by people close to the Menzil group; the community is especially well-represented and organised within the Ministry of Health. The former Minister for Energy and Natural Resources, Taner Yıldız, and the former Minister for Health, Recep Akdağ, are both said to be from the *Menzil Cemaati* (Çelik 2017: 109).

The Menzil group, like many other religious circles, announced their support for the Peoples' Alliance in the 2019 and 2023 elections. The sect has many structures including foundations, associations and business organisations; due to its close ties with the government, these structures often receive significant amounts of public funds. In addition, the group has companies under the names Semerşah Tourism and Erşah Tourism, which organise hajj and umrah. The Samarkand Foundation and Beşir Association, which signed the statement of support for the Peoples' Alliance, came to the fore during the AKP era. In 2013, the Beşir Association was granted the status of a public benefit association by decision of the Council of Ministers. This gave the association the right to collect financial donations without permission.[62]

Süleyman Efendi Community

The Süleyman Efendi community have been highly active in politics in Turkey in association with various right-wing parties. After Kemal Kaçar's death in 2000, Arif Ahmet Denizolgun (1955–2016), Tunahan's grandson, became the leader of the community. Denizolgun had an undergraduate degree in architecture and a graduate degree in Business Administration from Wagner College–Staten Island, New York. He was an RP member of the parliament in 1996–9 and served as Minister for Transport (1998–9). After his death in 2016, Alihan Kuriş (1979–), another one of Tunahan's grandsons, became leader of the community. Kuriş is also an architect, a graduate of Istanbul Technical University. According to Süleymancı thought, Allah and *kul* (servant/human being) cannot be in touch directly, and Tunahan is believed to serve as the intermediary/vessel. They are a very closed community and known to have a ritual called *rabıta* (connectedness), which means to create an affinity with Tunahan. Only a small elite are thought to warrant this spiritually, as they are 'chosen that actually know the real meanings in the Koran and hadiths'. It is also claimed that others can create that bond by looking at Tunahan's picture. The community only perform *namaz* following imams of their own.

Rıfai Group and Cemalnur Sargut

Turkey's religious structures are a world of men, but a woman, Cemalnur Sargut (1952–), leads a substantial Nakşibendi movement. Sargut's mother was a disciple of Kenan Rıfai (1867–1950), the leader of the Rıfai branch of Nakşibendis. Born in Thessaloniki and a graduate of the Galatasaray Lyceé in Istanbul, Kenan Rıfai later went to Medina and became a disciple of Seyyid Hamza-er Rıfai. After four years, he was authorised by his *şeyh* to move back to Istanbul to manage his activities in the lodge in Fatih, Istanbul (Ümmü Kenan Dergahı), which his mother had built in 1908. After the banning of the lodges in 1925, he continued his talks but to a small, closed circle. Upon his death, the community's leader became a woman, Semiha Ayverdi (1905–93/Kubbealtı Foundation). The community is currently led by Sargut, a chemical engineer who worked as a chemistry teacher for twenty years. Sargut and her community endowed the Kenan Rıfai Distinguished Professorship of Islamic Studies at the University of North Carolina in 2009. They have also endowed a chair at Peking University in Beijing, China. They have also contributed to establish the Kenan Rıfai Centre for Sufi Studies at Kyoto University.

Furkan Foundation

In Islamic circles, the Furkan Foundation established by Alparslan Kuytul (1965–) has been a rare opponent to the AKP and Erdoğan. An engineer by education, Kuytul furthered his studies at Al-Azhar University in Egypt, studying Islamic Law in the Theology Faculty. Kuytul founded the Furkan Foundation, based in Adana, in 1994 while he was still at Al-Azhar.[63]

After Erdoğan called on religious circles to stand behind him after the 17–25 December operations, a video in which Alpaslan Kuytul said that the AKP government wanted to neutralise all congregations was widely shared on social media. The Furkan Foundation also campaigned for 'No' in the 2018 constitutional referendum. Since 2018, the Foundation and Kuytul have been subjected to various legal sanctions and judicial processes by the government.

Anti-Capitalist Muslims and İhsan Eliaçık

Recep İhsan Eliaçık (1961–) leads a community that advocates a 'socialist' reading of Islam. They claim that the Koran's message on unification has been corrupted by traditional Islamic structures and that Islam, which they say was created to defend the underclasses, has become capitalistic. The so-called anti-capitalist Muslims ground their claims in some verses in Koran that criticise private property.

During the Gezi Park protests in which Eliaçık participated, he used expressions such as 'dictator', 'provocateur', 'arrogant' and 'liar' to describe Recep Tayyip Erdoğan on Twitter. As a result, Recep Tayyip Erdoğan filed a lawsuit against him for 50,000 TL in compensation. As an outspoken critic of the AKP and Erdoğan, İhsan Eliaçık has also been subjected to various legal sanctions and judicial processes by the government.

The Alevi Population: Legal Struggles

Alevi Openings

In June 2009, the AKP government began initiatives widely known as the Alevi 'openings' and consisting of seven workshops and three meetings. Getting the parties involved to participate was one of the problems facing the workshops: of the seven only two had significant Alevi representation, and diaspora Alevi organisations were not part of the process at all.[64] The final report on the process was issued in 2010 by the convener of the openings, Dr Necdet Subaşı (1961–), and presented to the public in 2011 by the Minister for State at the time, Faruk Çelik (1956–), at a ceremony at the Dolmabahçe Palace. Unfortunately, the Alevi opening produced no significant outcome.[65]

Judicial Processes Before the ECtHR

The 2010s witnessed a number of significant legal gains with regard to establishing the Alevi identity and faith before the ECtHR. The case, which was announced by the ECtHR on 2 February 2010 and resulted in Turkey's first conviction for violating Article 9 of the European Convention on Human Rights (ECHR; *Sinan Işık*, 21924/05, 02.02.2010), was filed by an Alevi citizen who did not want to have Islam written in the 'religion' section of his identity card. Until 2006, it was a requirement that the holder's religion be included on their identity card; however, in 2006, the right was granted to ask for this part to be left blank. After the domestic legal processes were completed, the case was taken to the European Court of Human Rights and the Court concluded by a majority decision that Turkey had violated Article 9, on the grounds that:

> The fact that it is necessary to apply to the official authorities in writing to delete the expression of religion in identity records, identity cards, etc., the fact of an identity card with an empty religion section, obliges the individual to disclose information about his personal beliefs and religious views against his consent. Undoubtedly, this is against the freedom of the person not to reveal their religion and belief.

The Court emphasised that the violation was due to the presence of a religion section on the identity cards, and not to which religion was written there. Although there has been no visible religion section on identity cards renewed since January 2017, the religion section remains hidden in the chip of the ID cards and provides the information in question to the authorities. Pursuant to Article 6 of the Personal Data Protection Law dated 24 March 2016 and numbered 6698, by dint of the provision that

Personal data on race, ethnic origin, political opinion, philosophical belief, religion, sect or other beliefs, dress, membership of associations, foundations or unions, health, sexual life, criminal convictions and security measures, and biometric and genetic data are sensitive personal data. It is forbidden to process sensitive personal data without the explicit consent of the person concerned

the inclusion of the expression 'Personal data other than health and sexual life listed in the first paragraph may be processed without seeking the explicit consent of the person concerned, in cases stipulated by the laws'[66] disables the regulation. When such applications are combined with the fact that the identity card chips can be scanned by the authorised institutions, it cannot be said that the Sinan Işık decision of the European Court of Human Rights has been fully implemented by Turkey.

Two cases in which Turkey was found to have behaved unfairly by the ECtHR in providing compulsory religious culture and morality courses are significant. One of them is the case of Hasan and *Eylem Zengin* v. *Turkey*, which was concluded in 2007, and the other is *Mansur Yalçın and others* v. *Turkey*, which was decided in 2014. In both cases, the Court concluded that the Turkish educational system did not meet the requirements of objectivity and pluralism and that insufficient content was provided in the case of non-Sunni Muslims to respect parents' beliefs. There is a difference between the two decisions regarding implementation: the Zengin decision envisages a change in the curriculum; namely, making textbooks objective and critical vis-à-vis all religions. In the Yalçın decision, the Court went one step further and concluded that the course should no longer be compulsory, if the situation did not improve through the implementation of the necessary changes. It should be underlined that religious education in Turkey, like other religious services, is based on a Sunni Hanefi school of practice, and is implemented in an indoctrinating manner.[67] Especially since 2012, increasing the number of İmam-Hatip schools, which are religious vocational schools, at the secondary and high school level has been part of the AKP's education policy. The increase in the number of these schools, and the addition of three allegedly optional religion courses[68] to the curriculum in addition to the compulsory religious culture and ethics courses, are a result of sectarian education policies. Although Turkey stated in its Action Plan for 2019 that the new curriculum introduced in 2018 met the criteria of objectivity and pluralism, the Sunni Islam perspective continues to dominate the curriculum, despite some minor developments.[69] In fact, there has been a clear regression recently in the implementation of the relevant ECHR decisions.[70] There is no educational institution for the training of religious officials who will provide religious services to Alevis.

The ECtHR's *Cumhuriyetçi Eğitim ve Kültür Merkezi* (32093/10) decision of 2014 concerns a violation of the right to freedom of religion and Article 14 taken in conjunction with Article 9 of the Convention, in that Alevi places of worship (*cemevis*) were not granted an exemption from the payment of illumination costs provided for places of worships by the Diyanet. Following the decision, some CHP municipalities initiated practices for exempting *cemevis* from such payments in their jurisdictions. Even though the judiciary currently decides on behalf of the *cemevis* as plaintiffs making claims based on their exemptions, there is still no general regulative legislation.

On 26 April 2016, in the light of the case of İzzettin Doğan and Others (application no. 62649/10), the Grand Chamber of the ECtHR concluded that Turkey had violated Article 9, which protects the right to freedom of religion or belief, and Article 14, which prohibits discrimination in conjunction with Article 9. The Cem Foundation, the initial domestic plaintiff, filed a petition complaining that the Diyanet did not provide public services so as to include Alevis and other beliefs. The demands made by the foundation included the granting of legal status to Alevism, the recognition of *cemevi* as places of worship (shrines), access to public funds for the operation of *cemevis*, and the granting of civil servant status to Alevi clergy. All these demands were rejected by the recipient Office of the Prime Minister on 19 August 2005. The Office stated that the Diyanet approaches all religions 'equally'. Having exhausted domestic judicial processes, a case was filed with the European Court of Human Rights. The case began in 2013; given its scope and importance, the court sent the file to the seventeen-judge Grand Chamber, whose decisions are final, rather than a small chamber of seven judges. As a result of the trial, the European Court of Human Rights defined Alevis' inability to benefit from any public service as 'religious discrimination'. The ECtHR concluded that the state's failure to officially recognise Alevis and provide them with legal status constituted a violation of Article 9 of the

ECHR regarding freedom of religion and conscience. The ECtHR, which also rejected the justification of the denial of Alevi belief on the basis of 'protecting the secular state', noted that the legal structure regarding religion and beliefs in Turkey is not based on 'neutral' criteria and this causes some beliefs to be exposed to discrimination. Defining the state's approach to religion and beliefs in Turkey as 'disproportionate to the target', the ECtHR concluded that the practice against Alevis is not based on a 'reasonable and objective basis' and therefore 'religious discrimination' is made against Alevis (Yıldırım 2016). Since the decision was made by the Grand Chamber, there was no possibility of appeal. The decision set an example not only for Alevis, but for all beliefs that were unable to receive public service from the state. However, no serious steps have been taken in Turkey towards implementing this legally binding decision.

An Action Plan concerning the execution of the above-mentioned judgements was submitted to the Committee of Ministers on 29 March 2023, in which it was claimed that all the requirements of the ECtHR had been fulfilled by Turkey. The establishing of the Presidency of Alevi-Bektaşi Culture and Cemevis within the Ministry of Culture and Tourism by a presidential decree published in the *Official Gazette* on 9 November 2022 is yet another expression of the AKP government's insistence on it being culture that distinguishes Alevism from Sunnism, not a different interpretation of Islam.[71] However, the people of Turkey have not forgotten that, at a political rally before the March 2014 local elections, Erdoğan denounced CHP leader Kılıçdaroğlu by saying 'You know he is an Alevi', prompting the crowd to boo his rival. At other rallies, he berated his rival Demirtaş as a 'Zaza' (Alevi Kurdish) (Somer 2015: 39).

The Non-Muslim Population

Today, non-Muslims constitute far less than 1 per cent of the total Turkish population of over 80 million.[72] No accurate statistics on non-Muslims have been produced recently by the Turkish state. According to the estimates of the United States State Department's 2021 report on religious freedom internationally, non-Muslim religious groups are mostly concentrated in Istanbul and other large cities, as well as in the southeast. Exact figures are not available; however, these groups self-report as approximately 90,000 Armenian Apostolic Orthodox Christians (including migrants from Armenia), 25,000

Roman Catholics (including migrants from Africa and the Philippines), and 12,000–16,000 Jews. There are also approximately 25,000 Syrian Orthodox Christians (also known as Syriacs), 15,000 Russian Orthodox Christians (mostly immigrants from Russia who hold residence permits), and 10,000 Baha'is. Estimates of other groups include 7,000–10,000 members of Protestant and evangelical Christian denominations, 5,000 Jehovah's Witnesses, fewer than 3,000 Chaldean Christians, fewer than 2,500 Greek Orthodox Christians, and fewer than 1,000 Ezidis. There are also small, undetermined numbers of Bulgarian Orthodox, Nestorian, Georgian Orthodox, Ukrainian Orthodox, Syriac Catholic, Armenian Catholic, Chaldean Catholic and Maronite Christians. The Church of Jesus Christ of Latter-day Saints (Church of Jesus Christ) estimates its membership at 300 individuals.[73]

There were some improvements after the 2002 general elections, particularly towards non-Muslim groups. However, after 2013, the momentum in the process of negotiating issues regarding non-Muslims has been lost, to a significant degree (Akgönül 2014: 370–2; Beylunioğlu 2017: 141). Discourse emphasising the superiority of Islam over other religions pronounced by Erdoğan[74] himself facilitates the frequent use of hate-speech against non-Muslim groups (Gözaydın 2021a: 99). Meanwhile, even though it is unlikely to prove sufficient as an overall solution to issues facing minority foundations, the introduction of a Law of Foundations is eminent. Nevertheless, violence against the non-Muslim population has been aimed at various groups.

On 15 and 20 November 2003, Istanbul became the target of Islamist terror attacks. Four suicide-bombers detonated explosives outside the Neve Shalom and Şişli Synagogues, the British Consulate and the Turkish liaison of HSBC Bank. The attacks claimed sixty-two lives and left more than 500 injured. The attacks were by members of the terrorist organisation *İslami Büyük Doğu Akıncıları Cephesi* (İBDA-C).[75]

On 19 January 2007, Hrant Dink (1954–2007), a prominent Armenian-Turkish journalist and the founder and director of *Agos*, an Armenian-Turkish weekly, was shot in Istanbul in broad daylight, in front of the newspaper's headquarters. The killer, a young Turkish nationalist, was quickly arrested, but justice has not yet been done, with many questions still left unanswered.[76]

On 18 April 2007, the German national Tilmann Ekkehart Geske, Necati Aydın and Uğur Yüksel, who worked at Zirve Publishing House, a Christian publishing house in Malatya, were murdered, having their throats slit. The suspects were caught at the scene. In September 2016, they were sentenced to three aggravated life sentences each. The Zirve Publishing House massacre was included in the Ergenekon investigation in March 2011. In September 2016, the court acquitted eight soldiers and two civilians, who were later included in the case, of all charges.

The Halki Seminary (Heybeliada Theological School) was founded on a supranational base to educate clergy in 1844. The school was legally closed in 1971 in response to an act reorganising higher education and prohibiting the operation of privately owned schools. The 1970s was a decade of friction between Turkey and Greece over Cyprus. Since then, the Halki Seminary has been the subject of political bargaining between the two states. Preventing the re-opening of the seminary, which is crucial for training the future patriarchs and prelates, is an intersecting violation of religious and educational rights (Gözaydın 2021a: 99).

Gender Issues in Turkey in the First Quarter of the Twenty-first Century[77]

On 25 May 2012, attending the closing session of the 2012 International Conference of Parliamentarians on the Programme of Action of the United Nations International Conference on Population and Development, Recep Tayyip Erdoğan, Prime Minister of Turkey at the time, said: 'I am against caesarean section, I see abortion as murder. Whether you kill a child in the womb or after it is born. There is no difference.' His statement sparked an intense debate on the issue in Turkey (Gözaydın 2013b: 146–51). This was not the first time that Erdoğan had made such statements. In 2010, he repeatedly stated that he did not believe in equality between men and women (İlkkaracan 2014: 154). The AKP's attempts to produce policies on inter alia abortion, artificial insemination, caesarean section, 'at least three children for every family', and – especially – on issues concerning women's bodies and their control over them, were other steps in its efforts to socially engineer the society of its imagining.

I think that the sermon of the Head of the Diyanet on 24 April 2020, the first Friday of Ramadan in 2020, and the varying reactions that followed provide important insights into religion, relations between state and society, law, human rights and politics in today's Turkey. The *hutbe*, which focused on health issues in the light of the pandemic, stated,

> O people! Islam considers adultery one of the biggest harams. It condemns homosexuality. What is the outcome of this. It brings diseases and rots the generation. Hundreds of thousands of people a year are exposed to the HIV virus caused by this great haram, which is called fornication in the Islamic literature of illegitimate and unmarried life. Come, let us fight together to protect people from such evils.[78]

I believe that the statement requires evaluation in terms of its language and content.

To begin with, such sentiments are clearly incompatible with the 'right to equality of all' and the 'prohibition of discrimination' within the framework of the Turkish Constitution and international human rights treaties that Turkey, as a state party, is legally obliged to abide by, as well as the legal regimes for the protection of human rights at the universal and regional level in general. Moreover, as a discourse, it disregards a number of scientific findings and facts that have been medically demonstrated, and can be interpreted as neglecting the rule that everyone should benefit equally from the 'right to equality before the law', which is among the basic components of the concept of 'human dignity'; it also clearly ignores the 'prohibition on discrimination'.[79]

Women's Rights

In the 2011 elections, the AKP not only increased its votes, strengthening its power, it also increased its female representation in parliament to the highest level in republican history so far. Yeğenoğlu and Coşar interpret this fact as stemming from amendments on behalf of women in the Turkish Criminal Code in 2004, which required municipalities with populations over 50,000 to open women's shelters, and founded an equal opportunity commission in the parliament (Yeğenoğlu and Coşar 2014: 160). However, the changes introduced immediately after the 2011 elections, which included the abolition of the State Ministry for Women's Issues and Women's Status and the establishing of the Ministry of Family and Social Services, alter this reading drastically. Characterisations of the AKP's gender politics as the zenith of the alliance between neoliberalism and conservatism are thus very apt (Yeğenoğlu and Coşar 2014: 175–81).

The Council of Europe Convention on Preventing and Combating Violence against Women and Domestic Violence of 2011, better known as the Istanbul Convention, ceased to be effective in Turkey on 1 July 2021, following its denunciation on 20 March 2021, primarily as a result of campaigning by religious circles.[80] No comment could shed a more eloquent light on the AKP's mindset vis-à-vis gender issues.

Headscarf Issue

Edibe Sözen, in a 2006 article on the AKP's gender politics, states that the triple issues of the headscarf, the public sphere and secularism constitute the three obstacles to the AKP's gender policies, associating them with the tension between the AKP and other state institutions (Sözen 2006: 277). Ironically, the AKP delayed tackling the headscarf issue, which can be conceptualised as a symbol of reception in a polarised Turkey, until the 2010s. Tür and Çıtak's 2009 analysis, based on interviews with AKP women's branches, reveals the fears: 'The party's policy on the veiling issue has the potential to alienate women, and women who worked for representation for covered women, in particular, from the party' (Tür and Çıtak 2009: 629).

As Alev Çınar puts it:

> Both the evolution of a secular public sphere under the surveillance of the state and recent Islamist appropriations of the public sphere have depended upon the production and manipulation of proliferating images of women, unveiled and re-veiled, as a technology of controlled inclusion that enhances the political agency of men, while seriously constraining women. (Çınar 2012: 43)

Limits on the acceptance of women's rights discourse by Islamist men (Yılmaz 2015: 163–5); religious circles' insistence on keeping women invisible in mosques[81] and funeral rituals (Yılmaz 2015: 207–20); and defining the home as the primary space for women[82] are the politics of the AKP as well as other religious circles.

LGBTI+ Rights

Against all odds, the LGBTI+ movement was a social movement that became increasingly vocal in the struggle for gender equality in Turkey in the 2000s and 2010s (İlkkaracan 2014: 169–71). The opposition have been more supportive of LGBTI+ rights than the AKP. The CHP attempted to amend the constitution to include sex orientation as a specific category (Engin 2015: 841) and gay quotas were considered for employees in a local municipality (Shaheen 2017). The HDP and the party's former leader Selahattin Demirtaş have been much more supportive (Muedini 2021: 137–8). Meanwhile, the narratives of the AKP authorities[83] and the AKP government's conduct has remained hostile. Even though pride marches were begun in 2015, they have been banned each year and the authorities have done all they could to oppress civil disobedience in relation to the bans by brutal police violence. A number of LGBTI+ individuals have been assassinated in Turkey (Şansal 2021: 147–9). Nevertheless, a group under the name AK LGBTİ is active in social media under several accounts (Deniz and Anık 2016).

Notes

1. *Efsun* is a novel written in prison by Selahattin Demirtaş (1973–), a politician and former chairman of the *Halkların Demokratik Partisi*/HDP, who has been kept in prison since November 2016 despite ECtHR rulings.
2. For an analysis of the AKP's election victory, see Özel 2003. See also Keyman and Öniş 2007: 161–77.
3. 'Operation Return to Life' is the official name given to the operations carried out by approximately 10,000 members of the security forces on 19 December 2000 in twenty prisons in response to hunger strikes that had begun on 20 October 2000 to resist the F-type cell system and the practice of isolation. In all, thirty-two people were killed (two soldiers and thirty prisoners) and hundreds injured (Sevimli 2010). For a collection of articles that begin with Ömer Laçiner's question, 'Can we really call the naming of the operation against the hunger strikes a "return to life": a cruel, blood-curdling irony?', see *Birikim* 142–3 (2001), 10–52.
4. IBDA-C is an Islamic militant organisation which follows the *Büyük Doğu* (Great East) ideology of Necip Fazıl Kısakürek. On 22 July 2014, Istanbul's Fourteenth High Criminal Court ordered the release of Mirzabeyoğlu, who had been sentenced to life imprisonment in an F-type prison after the death penalty was abolished in 2001.
5. Kemal Derviş was an economist and former head of the UN Development Programme. He took office as Minister of State for Economic Affairs in 2001 in the cabinet formed by Prime Minister Ecevit. Derviş was the architect of Turkey's successful three-year economic recovery programme launched in that year.

6. Following the introduction in 1998 of a ban on university students in Turkey wearing headscarves in class or examinations, the applicant left Istanbul University and continued her education in Austria. The Court noted that the ban existed when the applicant entered the university and that she should have known she would be prevented from going into class or examinations if she continued to wear a headscarf. The Court also stated that consideration should be given to the effect the wearing of a headscarf might have on those who did not wear headscarves. The Court, therefore, found that, within the State's margin of appreciation, the measure could be seen as 'necessary in a democratic society' in accordance with paragraph 2 of Article 9 of ECtHR (Çınar 2021: 120–1). However, in recent judgments of the ECtHR in cases such as Eweida and others, it is significant that the Court has stressed the need for a balance between the interests of society and the individual. Hence, the Constitutional Court in Turkey has taken referrals to the ECtHR into account when reaching judgments (Çınar 2021: 131). For the significance of the distinction between the plaintiff being a public service provider and a public service receiver in similar cases, and an analysis of the *Leyla Şahin* v. *Turkey* case, see Arslan 2005: 81–96. Also, see Borovalı 2009.
7. Hakan Yavuz questions whether the AKP was genuine in its desire to join the EU, or if it was intended as a tactical move to undermine the Kemalist state structure (Yavuz 2018).
8. For fierce secularists, Abdullah Gül's wife Hayrünnisa Gül's (1965–) veiling was an issue. For a series of efforts launched by Turkey's *ancien régime* against the AKP in 2007–8, see Gözaydın 2017: 257–8. On 'republican meetings', see Yavuz and Özcan 2007: 122–5.
9. On the April 2007 'e-memorandum', see Gözaydın 2017: 257–8.
10. For an insightful analysis of Turkey–EU relations from 2005, when the accession negotiations began, to the EU becoming a near non-issue in Turkey, see Arısan-Eralp and Eralp 2012.
11. However, four members of the Court objected to the inclusion of President Gül in the indictment, in the light of the provision in Turkish law that the President can only be indicted for treason.
12. For a thorough analysis of the case and judgement, see Sevinç 2010.
13. Serdar Kaya tests an academic theory by applying its parameters to the Turkish 'deep state' through the Ergenekon case (Kaya 2009). For another thorough reading of the Ergenekon crisis, this one by a former high-ranking CIA official, see Fuller 2014: 74–88. Most of the cases were overturned.
14. During the 2010 referendum process, a campaign emerged that would later become the subject of much debate, especially among intellectuals and the Left:

'Not Enough but Yes'. A group of intellectuals, writers, lawyers, jurists, artists, lecturers and political activists launched a campaign arguing that the new constitution, although not fully satisfactory, was a step forward in terms of democratic rights and freedoms in Turkey.

15. For a very thorough source on Gezi events, see Özkırımlı 2014.
16. For an insightful analysis of Gezi events, see Çınar 2015: 189–202. 'From 2014 on – in the aftermath of the Gezi events – he (Erdoğan) came to be classified as "very populist", his score well exceeding those of Viktor Orbán, Silvio Berlusconi, and Donald Trump' (Altınordu 2020: 89).
17. According to a report by Nils Muižnieks, Commissioner for Human Rights of the Council of Europe, following his visit to Turkey from 1 to 5 July 2013, six persons had thus lost their lives as a result of the events, including one police officer and a demonstrator shot to death by a police officer. While the number of injuries is a point of contention, the Turkish Medical Association stated on 15 July 2013 that 8,163 demonstrators in thirteen provinces had sought medical attention in the context of the Gezi events, with sixty-three serious injuries (three of which were in critical condition), 106 cases of head trauma, eleven persons losing an eye, and one splenectomy.
18. For a history of the conflict between the AKP and Gülen, see Çakır and Sakallı 2014; Taş 2018a; S. Öztürk 2019: 90–3.
19. For a brief history of the case of Academics for Peace, see Human Rights Foundation of Turkey 2019. See also Başer, Akgönül and Öztürk 2017; Sertdemir-Özdemir, Mutluer and Özyürek 2017; Özkırımlı 2017; Sözeri 2017: 217–31.
20. During the War of Independence, after the victory at Sakarya in 1921, the Grand National Assembly granted Mustafa Kemal the title *Halâskar Gazi* (Liberator and Warrior for Islam). The AKP made use of the Islamic connotation.
21. On the 'July 15 saga' and national narcissism as myth creation in the spirit of the neo-Ottomanist narrative, see Tokdoğan 2018: 221–61. For an article that picks up on the theme of martyrdom and specifically on the attempt to shape subjects who are ready to die for the state in the aftermath of the failed coup of 15 July 2016, see Yanık and Hisarlıoğlu 2019.
22. For the human rights situation in Turkey after 15 July 2016, see Balcıoğlu 2021: 39–43.
23. For a detailed report on the presidential system after two years of implementation, see Adar and Seufert 2021.
24. 'Ali Erbas, who took the baton of directorship from Mehmet Görmez in September 2017, was determined to continue his predecessor's pro-AKP agenda. The new director's commencement address is symbolic of what he planned to achieve during his

tenure. His symbolic use of a sword during his initial address, which he held in a traditional Ottoman fashion, and addressing of the *ummah* (as opposed to the citizens of Turkey) coincided with Erdoğan's pursuit of transnational neo-Ottomanism' (Mutluer 2018).

25. For a critical analysis of Davudoğlu and the AKP's foreign policy, see Gözaydın 2013a; Özkan 2015.
26. On the AKP's foreign policies in the Balkans and the Diyanet as its executive agent, see Öztürk 2021. Overall, Turkish foreign policy in the 2010s has been highly securitised and de-Europeanised, losing the soft power character that had been its trademark from the early 2000s. In this regard, for the AKP and Diyanet's policies in the Balkans in the 2010s, see Alpan and Öztürk 2022.
27. https://tdv.org/tr-TR/faaliyetlerimiz/.
28. On the role of religion in Turkey's international relations, see Gözaydın 2021b.
29. *Mele* means imam in Kurdish. On the impact of the republican experience among Kurdish *meles* and civilian Fridays, see Kurt 2016: 364–78; Koyuncu 2014: 227–8.
30. *Sela* is chanted in mosques on some special occasions before the call to prayer or to announce the funeral prayer about to be performed. The purpose of the *sela* is to announce and inform.
31. For an evaluation of the Diyanet's conduct on 15 July 2016, see Rosli 2022: 18–19.
32. On *vaizes* (women preachers), see Maritato 2020. For an account of Fatma Bayram, who has been a preacher in the Diyanet since 1990, see Bayram 2010. Also see Hassan 2011.
33. For religious assistance in prisons, see Öztürk and Gözaydın 2020.
34. The Diyanet has a representative in every city (Turkey is currently divided into eighty-one administrative units called cities); this representative is known as the *mufti*.
35. For a comparative analysis of the Vatican's and the Diyanet's public policies in relation to religious pluralism and family-related issues, see Ozzano and Maritato 2019.
36. For a journalistic source on the Diyanet; the Diyanet's budget; activities of the Turkish Diyanet Foundation; the Diyanet's various activities on family, women, children and youth; policies produced under AKP governments applied by the Diyanet; and the Diyanet's messages given to the public via its media, see Karakaş 2021. For a reading of the Diyanet under AKP governments through Friday *hutbes*, see Yılmaz and Albayrak 2022.
37. For the on-line service on religious issues especially by women preachers (*vaizes*), see Kalpaklıoğlu 2023.

38. Erdoğan constructed his own image from the start of his political career with a narrative of being a representative of the pious and conservative people, the silent majority from the Anatolian heartland, against a culturally alien and self-serving elite who have monopolised cultural authority, political power and economic resources. His claim to be 'of the people' is made credible not only through his rhetorical skills, but also through his social background. Erdoğan grew up in Kasımpaşa, a poor neighbourhood of Istanbul known for its traditional 'tough guy' culture. As a youth, he worked as a street vendor to support his education and developed a passion for soccer – and would have pursued a professional career in the sport if it were not for his father's strict opposition (Çakır and Çalmuk 2001: 11–25). On Erdoğan and the narrative of New Turkey, see Yavuz 2021. On Erdoğan as the constitutive symbol of the neo-Ottomanist narrative and his pathos, see Tokdoğan 2018: 95–220. Istanbul has been the symbolic space of this narrative. On Erdoğan's neo-Ottomanism, also see Yavuz 2020: 144–78.
39. Jeffrey Haynes, focusing on politics, identity and religious nationalism in Turkey from Atatürk to the AKP period, argues that neither Islam nor secularism per se is the one defining characteristic of the Turkish identity. Rather, he claims, it is a pronounced, perhaps even xenophobic, fear of outsiders, including not only Westerners but also some Muslim non-Turks (Haynes 2010). I agree with the analysis, but I would use 'dislike' instead of 'fear', thereby underlining the element of narcissism.
40. For the AKP's ability to perpetuate its rule via an anti-Western civilisational populist narrative, see Yılmaz and Morieson 2023.
41. For the concept of charity in Islamic societies, see Singer 2008.
42. For an excellent reading of AKP through paternalism, destitution, charity and gratitude strategies, see Yılmaz 2018. Sevinç Doğan also analyses the impact of AKP's local organisation on the dynamics of socialisation, the mechanism it establishes through patronage/protective relations, and thus the dynamics of reproduction of AKP power in a case study of Sanayi, a worker and a *gecekondu* neighbourhood of İstanbul-Kağıthane (Doğan 2016). For another micro analysis focusing on the Ankara Çukurambar neighbourhood and formation of a conservative upper-middle class habitus, see Akçaoğlu 2018.
43. Four years of primary school, four years of secondary school; four years of high school.
44. The AKP's relationship with the Gülen movement, which was one of its important components in the early years of AKP rule, led first to tension, then to crisis, and finally to rupture. For how these developments impacted the educational field, see Gençkal-Eroler 2019: 164–89.

45. For an impressive survey of universities under the AKP, see Tekerek 2023.
46. For the AKP using Islamic elements in the peace process of 2013–15, see Merdjanova 2018.
47. Hakan Yavuz asserts that Turkish secularism and Islamism have shaped one another, and that each is currently seeking to impose itself on the other (Yavuz 2019).
48. For a comparison of the AKP and CHP's pre-election promises and post-election behaviour, see Gürleyen 2014.
49. Ankara: Mansur Yavaş (1955–); İstanbul: Ekrem İmamoğlu (1971–); İzmir: Tunç Soyer (1959–).
50. Secular and sensitive to gender equality, HDP operates a co-presidential system of leadership, with one chairman and one chairwoman.
51. On Kurds and elections under AKP rule, see Çiçek 2017: 167–85.
52. On Temel Karamollaoğlu's memoirs, see Karamollaoğlu 2022.
53. Atay 2017: 180–1.
54. Emrah Çelik lists the supportive groups thus: the Menzil group, İskenderpaşa community, İsmailağa community, Erenköy community, Yahyalı group, Kadiris, Halveti Şabanniye group, the Kurdish *şeyhs* of Tillo and Norşin, the Işık group, the Kurdish Islamists, Haznevis, the Adnan Hoca group, Galibis, and the Süleyman Efendi community. He states that the Nurcu groups, such as Okuyucus, Yazıcıs, Kırkıncı Hoca, and the close friends of Said Nursi, such as Mehmet Fırıncı and Said Özdemir, have also been strong supporters of the AKP (Çelik 2017:108).
55. https://sorularlarisale.com/nur-cemaati-yazicilar-ve-okuyucular-olarak-ikiye-ayriliyor-neden-boyle-bir-ayrim-yapiliyor-ve-bu-kollarin-birbirinden.
56. For an interview dated 3 June 2021 in which Ruşen Çakır talks about Yeni Asya, see 'Nurculuğun ana omurgası: Yeni Asya', available at https://www.pressreader.com/turkey/yeni-asya/20210603/281556588751494.
57. Ömer Şahin, 'Erdoğan-Gülen kavga ediyor peki ya diğer dini gruplar?' *Al-Manitor*, 30 December 2014. Available at: https://www.al-monitor.com/tr/contents/articles/originals/2014/12/turkey-erdogan-gulen-war-benefit-lesser-known-islamic-groups.html.
58. *Dershane* here means 'privately run university preparation schools'. Many of them were run by the Gülen movement and the government proposed a law to close them in December 2013.
59. On judicial activities concerning 15 July 2016, see Çalıkuşu 2023.
60. *Hafız* is someone who memorises the Koran in its entirety.
61. https://www.ismailaga.org.tr.

62. A book edited by an Oktay Yıldırım was published in 2019 under the title 'Diyanet's confidential report on the *tarikats*' (*(Gizli) Diyanet'in Tarikatlar Raporu*). On Menzil, see 219–23.
63. https://furkanvakfi.org/.
64. For a critical evaluation of the process, see Yalçınkaya 2009. For the Diyanet's interventions against Alevism and the privileging of Sunni Islam, see Lord 2018: 151–62.
65. Şener Aktürk argues that the Alevi initiative, but also others undertaken by the AKP in relation to Kurds and non-Muslims, serve an Islamic conceptualisation of a new religious-national identity. Invoking overwhelmingly religious justifications was both the main motivation for, and the main limitation of, allegedly reformist initiatives. Aktürk underlines Erdoğan's statement in July 2013: 'If being Alevi means loving Ali, then I am an Alevi par excellence', reading it as an attempt to merge Alevi and Sunni into a singular, ecumenical Muslim identity (Aktürk 2018: 13–17).
66. https://www.mevzuat.gov.tr/MevzuatMetin/1.5.6698.pdf.
67. The implementation of compulsory religious courses in Turkey have been a case of providing a confessional religious course in Sunni-Hanefi Islam. Confessional religious education in public schools should be given in such a way that different religions and religious interpretations can offer up their own versions. The obligation to follow a confessional course violates Toledo rules in that the state is not neutral and not *laik*/secular, and hence does not equally protect the freedom of conscience of every citizen.
68. An administrative regulation issued in 2012 introduced three new 'optional' courses, one of which at least has been mandatory de facto ever since: The Rudiments of Religion; The Koran; The Life of the Prophet Mohammed. Needless to say, all these courses are given from the Sunni (Hanefi) perspective.
69. Only twenty pages mentioning Alevism have been added to the 1782 pages of the religious culture and ethics textbooks used over the nine years from the last year of primary school through to the last year of high school. On Alevism in textbooks, see Yaman 2021.
70. The Constitutional Court of Turkey found compulsory religious education to be in violation of both the Constitution and the Turkish Civil Code in 2022 (2014/15345) (*Official Gazette*, 28 July 2022, no. 31906).
71. In the Hasan and Eylem Zengin case, representing the claimant, the advocate Kazım Genç, president of the Alevi Pir Sultan Abdal Cultural Association, declared at the ECtHR hearing that 'Alevism is both in regards of its teaching/

philosophy as well as in regards of its religious practices totally different from Islam; an entity for itself'. However, the ECtHR situated Alevism broadly within the Islamic tradition. See Dressler 2011: 199.

72. In the 1927 census, when the total population was approximately 13.5 million, non-Muslims numbered 339,486, or 2.5 per cent of the total population (Oran 2011: 26).
73. https://www.state.gov/reports/2021-report-on-international-religious-freedom/turkey/.
74. 'Erdoğan: bizim tek derdimiz var, İslam, İslam, İslam' (we have only one concern: Islam, Islam, Islam). See https://m.bianet.org/kurdi/siyaset/166454-erdogan-bizim-tek-derdimiz-var-islam-islam-islam.
75. A report by Frankfurt's Peace Research Institute reads these attacks as repercussions of a partial cooperation between Turkey and the US: Turkey granted the US overflight rights for Turkish airspace, but denied the American request to use US military bases in Turkey for air raids against Iraq (Karakaş 2007: 31).
76. On the commemoration and aftermath of the assassination, see Rosati 2015: 213–45.
77. For a comparison of changing gender relations among Alevis and Sunnis in Turkey, see Shankland 2006: 109–23.
78. https://www.gazeteduvar.com.tr/gundem/2020/04/24/ali-erbastan-nefret-soylemi-escinsellik-nesli-curutuyor; https://kaosgl.org/haber/diyanet-in-cuma-hutbesinde-nefret-islam-escinselligi-lanetliyor; https://kaosgl.org/haber/insan-haklari-derneginin-ne-isi-olur-ki-acaba-escinsellikle.
79. For Erdoğan's reactions, see https://www.yenisafak.com/gundem/cumhurbaskani-erdogandan-ankara-barosuna-herkes-haddini-bilecek-3536791; https://www.aa.com.tr/tr/politika/cumhurbaskani-erdogan-bu-zorlu-surecten-alnimizin-akiyla-cikmayi-basardik/1820109.
80. On international solidarity against denunciation, see https://istanbulsozlesmesi.org/dayanisma-mesajlari/; on campaigns against the denunciation, see https://united4istanbulconvention.medium.com/.
81. Since October 2017, under the name 'women in mosques', a group of Muslim women activists have been attempting to observe their rituals outside the section allocated to women. See Parlak 2020.
82. Organisational activities among women in religious circles have always taken place in homes (Yılmaz 2015: 220–31).
83. Aliye Kavaf, former state minister for family affairs, 'homosexuality is a biological disorder, a disease, . . . something that needs to be treated' (2011); Recep Tayyip

Erdoğan: 'a sexual preference incompatible with the culture of Islam in Turkey' (2013); Türkan Dağoğlu, former AKP member of parliament, 'a woman marrying a woman, or a man marrying a man is not a right' (2013); Melih Gökçek, former Ankara mayor, 'I hope to God that in Turkey there will not be a gay and there should not be'(2016). See Muedini 2021: 135.

CONCLUSION: WHAT NEXT FOR TURKEY?

People gradually became content by believing they have attained what they want, instead of thinking and weighing. Maybe they don't yet realize that they are gradually side-lining the act of figuring out, of trying to see what is really happening. By the time they do realize, it will be dark. Even if the sun seems to rise again in the morning, it will be dark. Even if it seems to lighten up again, the darkness of the night will never completely dissipate.

Bilge Karasu, *Gece* (1985)

General elections took place in Turkey on 14 May 2023. Presidential elections were held to elect the President of Turkey for a five-year term using a two-round system. Simultaneously, parliamentary elections were held to elect 600 members of parliament to the Grand National Assembly of Turkey. Prior to the election, the electoral threshold for a party to enter parliament was lowered from 10 per cent to 7 per cent by the AKP. The elections were contested by a total of twenty-four political parties. Some parties decided to participate in the elections as part of an electoral alliance, many of which had been formed for the previous 2018 election and had since grown. The governing AKP led the Peoples' Alliance, which also included the MHP, the BBP and the New Welfare Party (*Yeni Refah Partisi*). The largest opposition alliance, called the Nation Alliance, was headed by the main opposition party, the CHP, and included five other parties: the *İYİ Parti*, *Saadet*, the *Demokrat*

Parti, DEVA and *Gelecek Partisi*. The pro-Kurdish HDP opted to run on the lists of the *Yeşiller ve Sol Gelecek Partisi* (Party of Greens and the Left Future) in the light of a potential closure case before the Constitutional Court. They formed the Labour and Freedom Alliance with the Workers' Party of Turkey (*Türkiye İşçi Partisi*/TİP).

The Peoples' Alliance retained its majority in the parliament with 322 MPs. The AKP won the highest percentage of the vote with 36 per cent, though this was its worst result since 2002. The MHP, the second largest party in the People's Alliance, outperformed expectations and won 10.1 per cent of the votes. Overall, the alliance won just under 50 per cent of the vote. The Nation Alliance only marginally improved on its 2018 vote, winning a combined 34 per cent and 213 MPs. The Labour and Freedom Alliance suffered a fall in their vote, winning just over 10 per cent and sixty-six seats. No other electoral alliance won seats. The election resulted in seven parties entering parliament, which is a record in Turkish politics.[1]

In the first round of the presidential elections, Recep Tayyip Erdoğan received 49.5 per cent, Kemal Kılıçdaroğlu 44.9 per cent and Sinan Oğan 5.2 per cent; Oğan would endorse Erdoğan in the second one. Erdoğan was re-elected President of Turkey on 28 May 2023 with 52.18 per cent of the votes compared with 47.82 per cent for Kılıçdaroğlu.[2] Recent opinion polls reveal that the most intense feelings of opposition voters are anxiety, anger and disappointment. Opposition voters seem to have shifted from feeling that 'Erdoğan will not leave, even if he wins the election' to feeling that 'we cannot win the election against Erdoğan'. Turkey does not seem very happy and satisfied with its life, and opposition voters carry an even heavier emotional burden. As a result, however, the ties binding a large segment of the society to either the ruling party or the opposition are becoming a little weaker, as these groups distance themselves from politics.[3]

Throughout this book, I have tried to fill in the background to the politics of Turkey today in order to show that nothing happens overnight. As in the rest of the world, waves of modernisation in the nineteenth century inevitably paved the way for modern Turkey and a population polarised in terms of life styles, sensibilities and world-views through the twentieth century and up to the centennial of the Republic of Turkey. Envisioning their ideal state, half the population have longed for the 'mythical past', while the other half have turned to face 'the imaginary West'. Despite these contrasting attitudes, common ground has been provided by fear of becoming like the other; fear of hybridisation; fear of being excluded from one's own group; fear of becoming an infidel or a bigot. These worries, like an all-consuming fire, have been escalating and covering Turkey with ash, converting the nation into a wasteland.[4]

The Ottoman ruling class was recruited from Muslim and non-Muslim elements from the Balkans and the Caucasus. Those living in the provinces could not find a place in the centre; as a result, migration and the goal of becoming a first-class citizen by settling in the centre are important elements in understanding Turkey's right-wing population, in particular. The republican reforms pushed the provincial population further away from the centre. Migrations after the 1950s from the countryside into the cities caused huge changes over time. By the end of the twentieth century, the old urban, well-educated, middle-class culture had been overwhelmingly replaced by another, this one dynamic but provincially minded. Populist politics both nourished this culture and benefitted from it.

Emerging in the early twentieth[h] century and growing with the Republic, Turkification policies became a means of state-aided capital formation and enrichment. Massacres and enforced expulsions of Christians by successive Ottoman and Turkish governments and their Muslim agents over thirty years (1894–1924) enabled capital to change hands to the benefit of the Muslim population. Pogroms in the 1930s in Thrace and in 1955 in Istanbul, with the arbitrary Wealth Tax of 1942 helping pave the way, allowed Muslim potential entrepreneurs to accumulate wealth. The rural populations that arrived in urban areas in waves of migration after the 1950s became property owners in big cities through the legalising of the occupation of publicly owned lands through zoning amnesties. The distribution of the economic cake through enrichment via the state has always been a tool for political powers, regardless of their ideological stance. The lack of a strong civil society in either Ottoman or republican Turkey may be seen as a factor in the absence of independent entrepreneurs who do not rely on the state for business privileges.

Provincial businesses in Anatolia were empowered by governmental tenders and other state-aided financial means, especially after the 1980s. The AKP came to power in 2002 by representing a portion of the population that had felt neglected, especially by early republican governments. Having enabled the establishing of new business conglomerates, especially after the 2010s, the governing political power escalated in order to nourish them with various financial opportunities in Turkey and abroad. The MNP and its various successors (MSP, RP, FP, SP) promoted a self-sufficient command economy through its National Vision. Erdoğan and his colleagues, who actually emerged through such an economic vision, had switched by the late 1990s to a liberal global capitalistic approach. Empowered ever more by state subsidiaries, new business groups became powerful allies to Erdoğan and the AKP. Replacing the welfare state with one that distributes charity to its loyal voters gave the poor a slice of the economic cake, too.

In the modern world of nations as imagined communities, to use Benedict Anderson's term, belonging to religious *tarikats*, carrying ethnic identities and being fellow countrymen have prevailed sociologically in the creation of bonding and networks of solidarity and business. Although some of the current Islamic groups root their genealogies in historic Islamic orders (especially those claiming a Nakşibendi lineage), they are actually new religious and spiritual movements that have adapted themselves to, and legitimised themselves in, a modern world. The business enterprises in the form of the companies and groups of companies which each and every religious group in Turkey today run and operate reveal the financial aspect of their existence.

I read the processes and the outcome of the latest elections as an escalating nationalism usurping religious sensitivities. Over the AKP years, corruption, forced morally empty religious education, escalating temporality, and frustrations stemming from several other causes have eroded faith in political Islam.[5] Religiosity appears to have been squeezed into a set of rituals enacted within preferred networks (*tarikats*). Nevertheless, it appears that nationalism with a Sunni Islamic core that fuses with authoritarianism and pragmatism will be a significant part of Turkish society and politics for the foreseeable future. Nationalism is highly prevalent on the laic front, as well. However, there do seem to be some major emphases with regard to religious impositions.

As a political organisation Hüda-Par, with which the AKP chose to run in the recent elections, comes with a lot of baggage. Hüda-Par is a political party founded in December 2012 by Mehmet Hüseyin Yılmaz, the chairman of Mustazaf-Der, an association which was shut down on the grounds that it was associated with Turkey's Hizbullah organisation, the most visible actor in Islamist violence in Turkey. After the 17 January 2000 İstanbul/Beykoz police operation, the perception that Hizbullah had been put to an end was proved wrong by a new shock one year later, when Gaffar Okkan, Diyarbakır's police chief, was ambushed with other police officers in the middle of the city and assassinated. In 2006, Hizbullah began to show a different face at the rallies attended by tens of thousands of people protesting against the Prophet Muhammad cartoons. With the civil organisation Mustazaf-Der first, and the political organisation Hüda-Par later, the Kurdish/Islamists developed projects to counter poverty and deprivation in the region, attempted to mobilise the masses, and created an alternative to the PKK-led Kurdish movement. Hüda-Par, or *Hür Dava Partisi* (Free Cause Party), the AKP's vehicle for reaching the pious Kurdish vote, is an Islamist Kurdish political party. The AKP's approach to Hüda-Par also reveals pragmatism on the part of Erdoğan in courting both Turkish religious nationalism and Kurdish religious nationalism, which are actually anathema to one another, through the bridge provided by Islam. The Kurdish ethnic identity of Hüda-Par appears to be just as significant as its religious Sunni Islamic identity. It should come as no surprise, however, that an orthodox Islamic and Kurdish nationalist political movement should have emerged in lands that have been powerfully influenced by Nakşibendi-Halidi *şeyhs* for a couple of centuries now. Hüda-Par's escalating social, economic and political power in the region seems likely to diffuse an intense Sunni influence there in the near and foreseeable future. In terms of human rights violations, women socially and women's NGOs politically are likely to be major targets of this intensified conservatism.

The continuation of the assault on LGBTI+ groups and individuals constitutes another serious human rights infringement. I think the sermon given by the President of the Diyanet on 24 April 2020, the first Friday of Ramadan that year, and the reactions to it shed light on religion, the relationship between the state and society, law, human rights and politics in Turkey today and for the foreseeable future. The sermon, which focused on health issues in the light of the then ongoing Covid pandemic, included the following statements: 'O people! Islam considers adultery one of the greatest sins. It condemns homosexuality. Where is the wisdom in this? These practices cause diseases and rot the population. Hundreds of thousands of people a year are exposed to the HIV virus which was brought into being by this great haram. Fornication in Islam is illegitimate. Come, let us join together and fight to protect people from such evils.'[6] Such sentiments are clearly incompatible with the 'right to equality of all' and the 'prohibition of discrimination' in particular, which are enshrined in the Turkish Constitution and the international human rights treaties which Turkey is legally obliged to respect as a state party, as well as with the legal regimes for the protection of human rights at the universal and regional level. Moreover, as a discourse, it disregards a number of scientific findings and facts that refute its content, and can be interpreted as neglecting the rule that everyone benefits equally from the right to equality before the law, which is a basic component of the concept of human dignity; it also ignores the prohibition on discrimination. Like other autocratic leaders of our era, such as Orban and Putin, Recep Tayyip Erdoğan has focused his discourse less on religion and more on protecting the family. The criticism levelled by the AKP MP for İzmir, Ceyda Bölünmez Çankırı, on the İzmir Bar Association's Pride events are yet another indicator of ongoing violations: 'LGBT is a clinically diagnosed illness. LGBT is the primary cause of the devaluation of women and damages our most sacred family structure.'[7] Pride events were initiated in 2015, but have been banned each year; civil disobedience in relation to these bans has been met with brutality by the police.

My assumption for another emphasis in terms of the use of Islam concerns international relations, specifically in the Balkans. Over the course of the AKP period, Turkey has shifted its foreign-policy identity, describing itself as the inheritor of a long-standing Ottoman cultural tradition and attempting to influence former Ottoman territories more actively. This sort of instrumentalisation of Turkish history, culture and religion has been most visible in the Balkans. Under AKP rule, Turkey has made increasing transnational use of what is allegedly 'soft' power, transcending its borders by means of key state apparatuses such as the Diyanet, as well as formally non-governmental but actually state-sponsored organisations (GONGOs) and faith-based bodies that are also affiliated to the Turkish state. Turkey's policies in the Balkans reveal that 'the incipient elite in Ankara tends to believe that countries and local groups share the Balkan idealization in the Turkish capital' (Öztürk 2021: 219). Even though these perceptions and their consequent practices have had a polarising effect in the recipient region, it seems that the use of Islam in foreign relations by the hegemonic and authoritarian governments of the AKP will carry on for the near and foreseeable future, especially in the Balkans.

In Turkey, where the rule of law is one of the fundamental principles enshrined in the Constitution, the related legal requirements have not been duly applied, especially over the last decade, at the insistence of the executive – which is to say, the political – power. For some time now, there has been no independence in the functioning of the judiciary, which is the main power in the provision of legal protection. The political power has not fulfilled its commitments under Article 46 of the European Convention on Human Rights, namely to abide by finalised ECtHR judgements. Selahattin Demirtaş and the defendants in the Kobani Case, as well as the defendants in the Osman Kavala and Gezi cases have been kept in prison unlawfully, despite ECtHR judgements in favour of each, which found Turkey to be violating Article 18 of ECHR, and remain prisoners on political grounds. The political power never misses an opportunity to repeat that Osman Kavala and Selahattin Demirtaş cannot be released; prosecutors, judges and courts act accordingly. Similarly, another Gezi case defendant, Can Atalay, a lawyer, human rights defender, political activist and MP elected by the people of Hatay province in 2023, has not been released despite constitutional provisions that require it. Hundreds of seriously ill prisoners are kept in prisons. Despite the Constitutional Court's ruling on the violation of the Saturday Mothers' right to seek justice for their lost offspring, they are still denied the freedom of assembly. The quality of education in law faculties and among some legal professionals is so low that a prosecutor has the impudence to file an appeal against an acquittal with a single sentence: 'Acquitting the defendant, who is an instructor and academic in the faculty of Law, without taking into account their determination to commit a crime, when a verdict of conviction should have been reached is contrary to the procedure and the law.' There is no indication as to how and by whom 'the defendant's determination to commit a crime' is to be ascertained; Kafkaesque absurdities prevail. In short, the law, which everyone will need one day, is currently a farce.

State intervention has been fuelled by the concentration of mainstream media ownership in the hands of a few business conglomerates with close economic ties to the government. Since 2008, close friends and associates of Erdoğan have acquired large shares in television and print news, creating a conflict between real news and what AKP officials consider acceptable news. Many journalists and columnists have lost their jobs, with many others becoming political targets. The media monopoly has become a key concern vis-à-vis the citizens' right to unbiased information as well as an obstacle to fair election processes.

'What is a Nation?', an 1882 lecture in which the French historian Ernest Renan (1823–92), argues that nations are based as much on what people jointly forget as on what they remember. A sense of a shared past is obviously vital for a nation; however, the fact that both the Turkish right-wing and neo-Kemalist ideologies read Turkey's history in entirely different ways is in itself an indication that they have some problems with the truth. Their different perceptions of history place their trusted and traitorous actors in diametrically opposed positions. Thus, a body blow has been dealt to the will to live together, which is another requirement for the continuation of a nation. Nevertheless, the existence of a democratic legitimacy appears to permit a *coexistence pacifique*. Unfortunately, in Turkey, neither a common ethics nor a moral philosophy, both indispensable elements for strengthening conscience and justice socially and individually, are present. Moreover, neither half of Turkey's highly polarised society trusts the other. In the final analysis, neither the Kemalists in the past nor the Erdoğanists now can endure the Other, but coexistence and dialogue are *sine quibus non* for a democracy. I also believe that a secular system is a prerequisite for democracy in Turkey. However, this should not be an authoritarian or assertive secularism, but rather one in which the state distances itself from all beliefs.

> 'I am like dregs in my own memory . . .'
> Hilmi Yavuz, 'ben için sonnet' in *Ayna Şiirleri* (1992)

Notes

1. For the parliamentary election results in detail, see the official Supreme Election Council of Turkey website: https://www.ysk.gov.tr/doc/dosyalar/docs/14Mayis2023CBSecimIstatistik.pdf.
2. For the presidential election results in detail, see the official Supreme Election Council of Turkey website: https://www.ysk.gov.tr/doc/dosyalar/docs/28Mayis2023CBSecimiIkinciOylamaBulteni.pdf.

3. For a very insightful analysis of the 2023 elections, but also of Turkey as 'a nation with a complex socio-political landscape, . . . characterized by a fundamental division between the conservative, Islamo-Turkish sector and the secular-Western citizenry', see Yavuz 2023, 4.
4. Critical thinking and constructive criticism have never been a forte in Turkey's society. For an illuminating critical reading of 'the right wing', see A. Tarık Çelenk's *Türk Sağı: Mahalle, Kriz ve Kritik* (Turkish Right: Neighbourhood, Crisis and Critique; 2022). Emin Alper's film *Kurak Günler* (Burning Day; 2022) is an excellent metaphorical representation of hypocrisy, polarisation, and violence in politics and society.
5. 'Islam has arguably become personalized and to some extent commercialized as the post-1980's Muslim bourgeoisie has developed a market for Muslim leisure and fashion, literature, music, and lifestyle – not all religion-referenced. Political Islamism has been replaced by cultural Muslimhood' (White 2013: 182).
6. https://www2.diyanet.gov.tr/DinHizmetleriGenelMudurlugu/Sayfalar/HutbelerListesi.aspx (accessed on 21 June 2023).
7. https://www.haberler.com/politika/ak-parti-izmir-milletvekili-lgbt-etkinliklerine-tepki-gosterdi-16042328-haberi/ (accessed on 18 June 2023).

REFERENCES

Abou-El-Haj, Rifa'at (2005) *Formation of the Modern State. The Ottoman Empire Sixteenth to Eighteenth Centuries.* Syracuse: Syracuse University Press.

Abu-Manneh, Butrus (1992) 'Shaykh Ahmad Ziyauddin el-Gumushanevi and Ziya-i Khalid Suborder', in Frederick de Jong (ed.), *Shi'a Islam, Sects and Sufism: Historical Dimensions*. Utrecht: M. Th. Houtsma Sticting, 105–17.

Abu-Manneh, Butrus (1994) 'The Islamic roots of the Gülhane rescript', *Dir Welt des Islam* 34, 173–203.

Abu-Manneh, Butrus (2001) *Studies on Islam and the Ottoman Empire in the 19th Century (1826–1876)*. Istanbul: The ISIS Press.

Abu-Manneh, Butrus (2015) 'Two concepts of state in the Tanzimat period: the Hatt-ı Şerif of Gülhane and the Hatt-ı Hümayun', *Turkish Historical Review* 6, 117–37.

Acuner, Selma (2002) '90'lı Yıllar ve Resmi Düzeyde Kurumsallaşmanın Doğuş Aşamaları', in Aksu Bora-Asena Günal (ed.), *90'larda Türkiye'de Feminizm*. İstanbul: İletişim, 125–58.

Adak, Hülya (2003) 'National myths and self-na(rra)tions: Mustafa Kemal's *Nutuk* and Halide Edib's *Memoirs* and the *Turkish Ordeal*', in Sibel Irzık and Güven Güzeldere (eds), *Relocating the Fault Lines: Turkey beyond the East-West Divide* (*The South Atlantic Quarterly* special issue – 102/2-3), 647–61.

Adak, Sevgi (2020) 'Yetmişli Yıllarda Kadın Hareketi: Yeni Bir Feminizmin Ayak Sesleri', in Mete Kaan Kaynar (ed.), *Türkiye'nin 1970'li Yılları*. İstanbul: İletişim, 609–29.

Adak, Sevgi (2022) 'Kemalist Modernleşmeye kadınların Öznelliği Üzerinden Bakmak: Peçe ve Çarşaf Karşıtı Kampanyalar Odağında bir İnceleme', in Sevgi Adak and

Alexandros Lamprou (eds), *Tek Parti Dönemini Yeniden Düşünmek: Devlet, Toplum ve Siyaset*. İstanbul: Tarih Vakfı Yurt Yayınları, 183–219.

Adar, Sinem and Günter Seufert (2021) *Turkey's Presidential System After Two and a Half Years: An Overview of Institutions and Politics*. Stiftung Wissenschaft und Politik (SWP) Research Paper 2. Berlin: Centre for Applied Turkey Studies (CATS).

Adıvar, Halide Edip ([1922] 2007) *Ateşten Gömlek*. İstanbul: Can Yayınları.

Adıvar, Halide Edip ([1962] 2007) *Türk'ün Ateşle İmtahanı: İstiklal Savaşı Hatıraları*. İstanbul: Can Yayınları.

Agai, Bekir (2007) 'Islam and education in secular Turkey: state policies and the emergence of the Fethullah Gülen group', in Robert W. Hefner and Muhammad Qasim Zaman (eds), *Schooling Islam: The Culture and Politics of Modern Muslim Education*. Princeton, NJ: Princeton University Press, 149–71.

Agoston, Gabor and Bruce Masters (2009) *Encyclopaedia of the Ottoman Empire*. New York: Facts on File, Inc.

Ağaoğlu, Samet (1967) *Arkadaşım Menderes*. İstanbul: Baha Matbaası.

Ağtaş, Özkan (2007) 'Ortanın Solu: İsmet İnönü'den Bülent Ecevit'e', in Murat Gültekingil (ed.), *Modern Türkiye'de Siyasi Düşünce: Sol*, vol. 8. İstanbul: İletişim, 194–221.

Ahdar, Rex and Ian Leigh (2005) *Religious Freedom in the Liberal State*. Oxford: Oxford University Press.

Ahmad, Feroz (1993) *The Making of Modern Turkey*. London: Routledge.

Ahmad, Feroz (2003) *Turkey: The Quest for Identity*. Oxford: Oneworld.

Ahmed, Shahab (2016) *What is Islam? The Importance of Being Islamic*. Princeton, NJ: Princeton University Press.

Ahmed, Yakoob (2020) 'Why should Ottoman History be taught as Islamic History?' [podcast], 14 August 2020. Available at: https://podcast.isar.org.tr/12-why-should-ottoman-history-be-taught-as-islamic-history-yakoob-ahmed-history-society/.

Akal, Emel (2011) *Kızıl Feministler: Bir Sözlü Tarih Çalışması*. İstanbul: İletişim.

Akan, Murat (2017) *The Politics of Secularism: Religion, Diversity, and Institutional Change in France and Turkey*. New York: Columbia University Press.

Akçam, Taner (2004) *From Empire to Republic: Turkish Nationalism and the Armenian Genocide*. London: Zed Books.

Akçam, Taner and Ümit Kurt (2012) *Kanunların Ruhu: Emval-ı Metruke Kanunlarında Soykırımın İzini Sürmek*. İstanbul: İletişim.

Akçaoğlu, Aksu (2018) *Zarif ve Dinen Makbul: Muhafazakar Üst-Orta Sınıf Habitusu*. İstanbul: İletişim.

Akçura, Yusuf ([1904] 2016) *Üç Tarz-I Siyaset*. İstanbul: Ötüken Neriyat.

Akgönül, Samim (2007) *Türkiye Rumları, Ulus-Devlet Çağından Küreselleşme Çağına Bir Azınlığın Yok Oluş Süreci*. İstanbul: İletişim.

Akgönül, Samim (2014) 'Non-Muslim minorities in the Turkish democratization process', in Carmen Rodriguez, Antonio Avalos, Hakan Yılmaz and Ana I. Planet (eds), *Turkey's Democratization Process*. London: Routledge, 361–75.

Akgün, Birol and Şaban H. Çalış (2002) 'Tanrı Dağı Kadar Türk, Hira Dağı Kadar Müslüman: Türk Milliyetçiliğinin Terkibinde İslamcı Doz', in Tanıl Bora (ed.), *Modern Türkiye'de Siyasi Düşünce: Milliyetçilik*, vol. 4. İstanbul: İletişim, 584–600.

Akgündüz, Ahmet (1987) '1274/1858 Tarihli Osmanlı Ceza Kanunnamesinin Hukuki Kaynakları, Tatbik Şekli ve Men-i İrtikâb Kanunnamesi', *Belleten* 51/199, 153–92.

Akgündüz, Ahmet (1993) 'Labour migration from Turkey to Western Europe (1960–1974): an analytical review', *Capital and Class* 17/3, 153–94.

Akgündüz, Ahmet (2010) *Bilinmeyen bir Dahi: Bediüzzaman Said Nursi*. İstanbul: Bilge.

Akiba, Jun (2018) 'Shari'a judges in the Ottoman Nizamiye courts, 1864–1908', *Osmanlı Araştırmaları/The Journal of Ottoman Studies* 51, 209–37.

Akkaya, Gülfer (2011) *Sanki Eşittik: 1960–1970'li Yıllarda Devrimci Mücadelenin Feminist Sorgusu*. İstanbul: Kumbara Sanat Atölyesi ve Toplumsal Dayanışma Derneği Yayınları.

Akkoyunlu, Karabekir (2017) 'Electoral integrity in Turkey: from tutelary democracy to competitive authoritarianism', in Bahar Başer and Ahmet Erdi Öztürk (eds), *Authoritarian Politics in Turkey: Elections, Resistance and the AKP*. London: I. B. Tauris, 47–63.

Aksakal, Hasan (2017) *Türk Muhafazakarlığı: Terennüm, Tereddüt, Tahakküm*. İstanbul: Alfa.

Aksan, Virginia H. (2007) *Ottoman Wars 1700–1870: An Empire Besieged*. London: Routledge.

Aksoy, Gürdal (2016) *Dersim: Alevilik, Ermenilik, Kürtlük*. İstanbul: İletişim.

Akşin, Sina (1997) *Ana Çizgileriyle Türkiye'nin Yakın Tarihi I*. İstanbul: Cumhuriyet Yayınları.

Aktar, Ayhan (2009) '"Turkification" policies in the early republican era', in Catharina Dufft (ed.), *Turkish Literature and Cultural Memory: Multiculturalism as a Literary Theme after 1980*. Wiesbaden: Harrassowitz Verlag.

Aktar, Ayhan (2021a) *Nationalism and Non-Muslim Minorities in Turkey, 1915–1950*. London: Transnational Press.

Aktar, Ayhan (2021b) *Varlık Vergisi ve Türkleştirme Politikaları*. Expanded edn. İstanbul: Aras.

Aktar, Ayhan (2021c) 'İttihat Terakki ve aşiretler: Fihristü'l Aşair üzerine . . .', *K 24*, 9 September. Available at: https://t24.com.tr/k24/yazi/ittihat-terakki-ve-asiretler-fihristu-l-asair-uzerine,3346.

Aktar, Cengiz (ed.) (2011) *Tarihi, Siyasi, Dini ve Hukuki Açıdan Ekümenik Patrikhane*. İstanbul: İletişim.

Aktaş, Cihan (2001) *Bacıdan Bayana: İslamcı Kadınların Kamusal Alan Tecrübesi*. İstanbul: Pınar.

Aktoprak, Elçin (2010) 'Bir "Kurucu Öteki" Olarak: Türkiye'de Gayrimüslimler', *İnsan Hakları Çalışma Metinleri: XVI*. Ankara: Ankara Üniversitesi Siyasal Bilgiler Fakültesi İnsan Hakları Merkezi.

Aktürk, Şener (2018) 'One nation under Allah? Islamic multiculturalism, Muslim nationalism and Turkey's reforms for Kurds, Alevis and non-Muslims', *Turkish Studies* 19/4, 523–51. Available at: https://doi.org/10.1080/14683849.2018.1434775.

Alaranta, Toni (2011) 'The Enlightenment idea of history as a legitimation tool of Kemalism in Turkey', unpublished PhD thesis, University of Helsinki.

Alaranta, Toni (2016) 'Turkish Islamism and Nationalism before and after the failed coup attempt', *The Turkey Analyst*. Available at: https://turkeyanalyst.org/publications/turkey-analyst-articles/item/569-turkish-islamism-and-nationalism-before-and-after-the-failed-coup-attempt.html.

Algar, Hamid (1990) 'A brief history of the Naqshbandi Order', in Marc Gaborie Au-Alexandre Popovic and Thierry Zarcone (eds), *Naqshbandis: Historical Developments and Present Situation of a Muslim Mystical Order* (Proceedings of the Sévres round-table, 2–4 May 1985). Istanbul: Éditions ISIS, 9–49.

Alkan, Türker (1984) 'The National Salvation Party in Turkey', in Metin Heper and Raphael Israeli (eds), *Islam and Politics in the Modern Middle East*. New York: St Martin's Press, 79–102.

Alpan, Başak and Ahmet Erdi Öztürk (2022) 'Turkish foreign policy in the Balkans amidst "soft power" and "de-Europeanisation"', *Southeast European and Black Sea Studies* 22/1, 45–63. doi:10.1080/14683857.2022.2034370.

Alper, Emin (2007) 'Bülent Ecevit', in Murat Gültekingil (ed.), *Modern Türkiye'de Siyasi Düşünce: Sol*, vol. 8. İstanbul: İletişim, 202–13.

Alper, Emin and Özgür Sevgi Göral (2003) 'Aydınlar Ocağı', in Ahmet Çiğdem (ed.), *Modern Türkiye'de Siyasi Düşünce: Muhafazakarlık*, vol. 5. İstanbul: İletişim, 583–9.

Altıkulaç, Tayyar (2011) *Zorlukları Aşarken*. 3 vols. İstanbul: Ufuk.

Altınay, Ayşe Gül (2002) 'Bedenimiz ve Biz: Bekâret ve Cinselliğin Siyaseti', in Aksu Bora-Asena Günal (ed.), *90'larda Türkiye'de Feminizm*. İstanbul: İletişim, 125–58.

Altınordu, Ateş (2016) 'The political incorporation of anti-system religious parties: the case of Turkish political Islam (1994–2011)', *Qualitative Sociology* 39/2, 147–71.

Altınordu, Ateş (2020) 'Uncivil populism in power: the case of Erdoğanism', in Jeffrey C. Alexander, Giuseppe Sciortino and Peter Kivisto (eds), *Populism in the Civil Sphere*. Cambridge: Polity, 74–95.

Anderson, Benedict ([1983] 1991) *Imagined Communities: Reflections on the Origins and Spread of Nationalism*. Expanded edn. London: Verso.

Anscombe, Frederick F. (2010) 'Islam and the age of Ottoman reform', *Past and Present* 208, 159–89.

Anscombe, Frederick F. (2014) *State, Faith and Nation in Ottoman and Post-Ottoman Lands*. New York: Cambridge University Press.

Arai, Masami (1992) *Turkish Nationalism in the Young Turk Era*. Leiden: E. J. Brill.

Arat, Yeşim (1997) 'The project of modernity and women in Turkey', in Sibel Bozdoğan and Reşat Kasaba (eds), *Rethinking Modernity and National Identity in Turkey*. Seattle: University of Washington Press, 95–112.

Arat, Zehra (1998) 'Kemalizm ve Türk Kadını', in Ayşe Berktay Hacımirzaoğlu (ed.), *75 Yılda Kadınlar ve Erkekler*. İstanbul: Tarih Vakfı Yayınları, 51–70.

Arı, Kemal (1995) *Büyük Mübadele: Türkiye'ye Zorunu Göç (1923–1925)*. İstanbul: Tarih Vakfı Yurt Yayınları.

Arısan-Eralp, Nilgün and Atilla Eralp (2012) 'What went wrong in the Turkey-EU relationship', in Kerem Öktem, Ayşe Kadıoğlu and Mehmet Karlı (eds), *Another Empire? A Decade of Turkey's Foreign Policy under the Justice and Development Party*. Istanbul: Istanbul Bilgi University Press, 163–83.

Arlı, Alim (2004) *Oryantalizm Oksidentalizm ve Şerif Mardin*. İstanbul: Küre yayınları.

Armağan, Mustafa (2010) *Türkçe Ezan ve Menderes: Bir Devrin Yazılamayan Gerçekleri*. İstanbul: Timaş.

Arpaguş, Hatice (2014) *Osmanlı ve Geleneksel İslam*. İstanbul: M.Ü. İlahiyat Fakültesi Vakfı Yayınları.

Arslan, M. İhsan (2020) *Aklımda Kalan*. Edited by Ayşe Karabat. İstanbul: Kapı Yayınları.

Arslan, Zühtü (2005) *Avrupa İnsan Hakları Sözleşmesinde Din Özgürlüğü*. Ankara: Liberal Düşünce Topluluğu Yayını.

Artanian, Vartan (1988) *The Armenian Constitutional System in the Ottoman Empire, 1839–1863: A Study of its Historical Development*. Istanbul: ISIS.

Asad, Talal (1993) *Genealogies of Religion: Discipline and Reasons of Power in Christianity and Islam*. Baltimore: Johns Hopkins University Press.

Asad, Talal (2003) *Formations of the Secular: Christianity, Islam, Modernity*. Stanford: Stanford University Press.

Asad, Talal (2006) 'Responses', in Charles Hershkind and David Scott (eds) *Powers of the Secular Modern: Talal Asad and his Interlocutors*. Stanford: Stanford University Press, 206–41.

Asad, Talal (2018) *Secular Translations: Nation-state, Modern Self and Calculative Reason*. New York: Columbia University Press.

Aslan, Ali (2009) 'Söyleşiyorum: Mehmet Görmez', *Anlayış*, November. Available at: http://www.anlayis.net/makaleGoster.aspx?dergiid=&makaleid=2213.

Aslan, Şükrü (2021) 'Cumhuriyetin ilk yasalarında inanç kimlikleri', *Birgün*, 17 March. Available at: https://www.birgun.net/haber/cumhuriyet-in-ilk-yasalarinda-inanc-kimlikleri-337822 (accessed on 4 February 2023).

Aslanmirza, Burak (2021) *İttihat ve Terakki Cemiyeti'nin Kızıl Konak Evrakı*. İstanbul: Tarih Vakfı Yurt Yayınları.

Atacan, Fulya (2006) 'Explaining religious politics at the crossroad: AKP-SP', in Ali Çarkoğlu and Barry Rubin (eds), *Religion and Politics in Turkey*. London: Routledge, 45–57.

Atalay, Onur (2018) *Türke Tapmak: Seküler Din ve İki Savaş Arası Kemalizm*. İstanbul: İletişim.

Atatürk, Mustafa Kemal (1997) *Atatürk'ün Söylev ve Demeçleri I-III: T.B.M. Meclisinde ve C.H.P. Kurultaylarında (1919–1938)*, 5th edn. Ankara: Atatürk Kültür, Dil ve Tarih Yüksek Kurumu Atatürk Araştırma Merkezi Yayınları.

Atay, Tayfun (2017) *Parti, Cemaat, Tarikat: 2000'ler Türkiyesi'nin Dinbaz-Politik Seyir Defteri*. İstanbul: Can Sanat Yayınları.

Atılgan, Gökhan (2007) 'Behice Boran', in Murat Gültekingil (ed.), *Modern Türkiye'de Siyasi Düşünce: Sol*, vol. 8. İstanbul: İletişim, 436–72.

Aybars, Ergun (1975) *İstiklal Mahkemeleri*. İstanbul: Bilgi Yayınevi.

Aydın, Bilgin (1998) 'Osmanlı Devleti'nde Tekkeler Reformu ve Meclis-i Meşâyih'in Şeyhülislâmlık'a Bağlı Olarak Kuruluşu, Faaliyetleri ve Arşivi', *İstanbul Araştırmaları* 7, 93–109.

Aydın, Cemil (2017) *The Idea of the Muslim World: A Global Intellectual History*. Cambridge MA: Harvard University Press.

Aydın, Mustafa (2004) 'Süleymancılık', in Yasin Aktay (ed.), *Modern Türkiye'de Siyasi Düşünce: İslamcılık*, vol. 6. İstanbul: İletişim, 308–22.

Aydın-Düzgit, Senem (2012) 'No crisis, no change: the third AKP victory in the June 2011 parliamentary elections in Turkey', *South European Society and Politics* 17/2, 329–46.

Aydın-Düzgit, Senem (2014) 'Human rights in Turkey', in Carmen Rodriguez, Antonio Avalos, Hakan Yılmaz and Ana I. Planet (eds), *Turkey's Democratization Process*. London: Routledge, 312–29.

Aydın Düzgit, Senem (2019) 'The Islamist–Secularist divide and Turkey's descent into severe "polarization"', in Thomas Carothers and Andrew O'Donohue (eds), *Democracies Divided: The Global Challenge of Political Polarization*. Washington, DC: Brookings Institution Press, 17–37.

Aydoğdu, Hatice and Nilüfer Timisi Nalçaoğlu (2021) *Mustafa Timisi Anlatıyor: Biz Varız Dün Bugün Yarın*. Ankara: Dipnot.

Azak, Umut (2010) *Islam and Secularism in Turkey: Kemalism, Religion and the Nation State*. London: I. B. Tauris.

Babaoğlu, Resul (2012) 'Türkiye Rum Cemaati ve 6/7 Eylül 1955 Olayları', *History Studies* 4/4, 15–34.

Baer, Marc David (2010) *The Dönme: Jewish Converts, Muslim Revolutionaries, and Secular Turks*. Stanford, CA: Stanford University Press.

Balcı, Yusuf (1994) 'İslamda Çalışma İlişkileri', in MÜSİAD/Hüner Şencan (ed.), *İş Hayatında İslâm İnsanı (Homo Islamicus): İslami Duyarlılıkla Yönetilen Firmalarda Örgütsel Davranış Biçimleri*. İstanbul: MÜSİAD Araştırma Raporları, 113–27.

Balcıoğlu, Ercan (2021) 'Human rights in Turkey: past, present and future', in Hasan Aydın and Winston Langley (eds), *Human Rights in Turkey: Assaults on Human Dignity*. Cham: Springer, 23–48.

Bali, Rıfat N. (1999) *Bir Türkleştirme Serüveni (1923–1945). Cumhuriyet Yıllarında Türkiye Yahudileri*. İstanbul: İletişim.

Bali Rıfat N. (2003) *Cumhuriyet Yıllarında Türkiye Yahudileri – Aliya: Bir Toplu Göçün Öyküsü (1946–1949)*. İstanbul: İletişim.

Bali, Rifat N. (2006) 'The politics of Turkification during the single party period', in Hans-Lukas Kieser (ed.), *Turkey Beyond Nationalism Towards Post-Nationalist Identities*. London: I. B. Tauris.

Baltacıoğlu-Brammer, Ayşe (2021) 'The emergence of the Safavids as a mystical order and their subsequent rise to power in the fourteenth and fifteenth centuries', in Rudi Mathee (ed.), *The Safavid World*. London: Routledge.

Bardakoğlu, Ali (2004) '"Moderate perception of Islam" and the Turkish model of the Diyanet: The President's statement', *Journal of Muslim Minority Affairs* 24/2 (October), 367–74.

Barış, Linda (2021) *Türkiye'de Ermeni Okulları ve Ermeni Kimliği*. İstanbul: İletişim.

Barkey, Karen (2008) *Empire of Difference: The Ottomans in Comparative Perspective*. New York: Cambridge University Press.

Barkey, Karen (2012) 'Rethinking Ottoman management of diversity: what can we learn for modern Turkey?', in Ahmet T. Kuru and Alfred Stepan (eds), *Democracy, Islam, & Secularism in Turkey*. New York: Columbia University Press, 12–31.

Barutçu, Ahmet Faik (2001) *Siyasi Hatıralar: Milli Mücadeleden Demokrasiye*, 21. Ankara: Yüzyıl Yayınları.

Baş, Mustafa (2005) *Türk Ortodoks Patrikhanesi*. Ankara: Aziz Andaç Yayınları.

Başer, Bahar, Samim Akgönül and Ahmet Erdi Öztürk (2017) '"Academics for Peace" in Turkey: a case of criminalising dissent and critical thought via counterterrorism policy', *Critical Studies on Terrorism* 10/2, 274–96.

Batur, Enis (1985) *Alternatif: Aydın*. İstanbul: Hil Yayın.

Bauer, Thomas (2021) *A Culture of Ambiguity: An Alternative History of Islam*. Translated by Hinrich Biesterfeldt and Tricia Tunstall. New York: Columbia University Press.

Bayram, Fatma (2010) *Bir Vaizenin Günlüğü*. İstanbul: Kaknüs Yayınları.

Bayramoğlu, Ali (2001) *28 Şubat: bir müdahalenin güncesi*. İstanbul: Birey Yayıncılık.

Bedirhanoğlu, Pınar (2021) 'Economic management under the presidential system of government in Turkey: beyond the depoliticization versus repoliticisation dichotomy', *Journal of Balkan and Near Eastern Studies* 24/1, 97–113. Available at: https://doi.org/10.1080/19448953.2021.1992183.

Bein, Amit (2011) *Ottoman Ulema Turkish Republic: Agents of Change and Guardians of Tradition*. Stanford: Stanford University Press.

Benlisoy, Foti (2019) 'Ellili Yıllar Türkiyesi'nin Tarihi: Azınlıkların Tarihi', in Mete Kaan Kaynar (ed.), *Türkiye'nin 1950'li Yılları*. İstanbul: İletişim, 355–76.

Benlisoy, Foti and Stefo Benlisoy ([2016] 2022) *Türk Milliyetçiliğinde Katedilmemiş bir Yol: 'Hristiyan Türkler' ve Papa Eftim*, 2nd edn. İstanbul: Istos.

Beriş, H. Emrah (2008) 'Türkiye'de 1980 Sonrası Devlet Sermaye İlişkileri ve Parçalı Burjuvazinin Oluşumu', *Ekonomik Yaklaşım* 19/69, 33–45.

Bermek, Doğan (ed.) (2021) *Madımak ve Toplumsal Değişim; Öncesi ve Sonrası ile Madımak: Sönmemiş Ateş*. İstanbul: Alevi Düşünce Ocağı (ADO) Yayını.

Berkes, Niyazi ([1964] 1998) *The Development of Secularism in Turkey*. London: Hurst & Company.

Berkes, Niyazi (1997) *Unutulan Yıllar*. Edited by Ruşen Sezer. İstanbul: İletişim.

Berktay, Fatmagül (1998) 'Cumhuriyet'in 75 Yıllık Serüvenine Kadınlar Açısından Bakmak', in Ayşe Berktay Hacımirzaoğlu (ed.), *75 Yılda Kadınlar ve Erkekler*. İstanbul: Tarih Vakfı Yayınları, 1–11.

Berktay, Fatmagül (2003) *Tarihin Cinsiyeti*. İstanbul: Metis.

Beydilli, Kemal (1995) 'II. Mahmud Devri'nde Katolik Ermeni Cemaati ve Kilisesi'nin tanınması (1830) [Recognition of the Armenian Catholic Community and the Church in the Reign of Mahmud II (1830)]', in Şinasi Tekin and Gönül Alpay Tekin (eds), *Turkish Sources XXIV*. Cambridge, MA: Department of Near Eastern Languages and Civilizations, Harvard University.

Beydilli, Kemal (2000) 'Osmanlı Döneminde Kilise Siyasetinden bir Kesit: II. Mahmud Devrinde Kilise Tamiri', *Tartışmalı İlmi Toplantılar Dizisi* 33, 255–66. Available at: https://www.academia.edu/16498890/Osmanl%C4%B1_D%C3%B6neminde_Kilise_Siyasetinden_Bir_Kesit_II_Mahmud_Devrinde_Kilise_Tamiri.

Beyinli, Gökçen (2020) 'Reframing Turkey, Istanbul and national identity: Ottoman history, "chosen people" and the opening of shrines in 1950', *Nations and Nationalism* 28/4, 1428–31.

Beyinli, Gökçen (2021) *İslam ve Sair Halk: Laik Türkiye'de Hurafeler, Kadınlar, Türbeler*. İstanbul: Kitap Yayınevi.

Beylunioğlu, Anna Maria (2017) 'Recasting the parameters of freedom of religion in Turkey: non-muslims and the AKP', in Bahar Başer and Ahmet Erdi Öztürk (eds), *Authoritarian Politics in Turkey: Elections, Resistance and the AKP*. London: I. B. Tauris, 141–56.

Biçer, Ramazan (2017) 'İBDA-C (İslami Büyük Doğu Akıncılar Cephesi)', in *Güvenlik Terimleri Sözlüğü*, Ankara: TC. İçişleri Bakanlığı Kamu Düzeni ve Güvenliği Müsteşarlığı Yayınları, 300–2.

Binder, Leonard (1988) *Islamic Liberalism: A Critique of Development Ideologies*. Chicago: University of Chicago Press.

Birand, Kâmıran ([1957] 1998) 'Aydınlanma Devri Devlet Felsefesinin Tanzimata Tesirleri', in *Kâmıran Birand Külliyatı*. Ankara: Akçağ, 1–76.

Birge, John Kingsley ([1937] 1994) *The Bektashi Order of Dervishes*. London: Luzac.

Bora, Tanıl (2005) 'Süleyman Demirel', in Murat Yılmaz (ed.), *Modern Türkiye'de Siyasi Düşünce: Liberalizm*, vol. 7. İstanbul: İletişim, 550–77.

Bora, Tanıl (2009) 'Türkiye'de Faşist İdeoloji: "Hürriyet Değil Faşizm Gibi Bir İdare İstiyoruz"', in Ömer Laçiner (ed.), *Modern Türkiye'de Siyasi Düşünce: Dönemler ve Zihniyetler*, vol. 9. İstanbul: İletişim, 482–507.

Bora, Tanıl (2013) '1930'lardan 1950'lerte Resmi Milliyetçiliğin Dersim'e Bakışı: Asimilasyonizmin Kırılganlığı', in Zeliha Hepkon, Songül Aydın and Şükrü Aslan (eds), *Dersim'i Parantezden Çıkarmak: Dersim Sempozyumu'nun Ardından*. İstanbul: İletişim, 77–96.

Bora, Tanıl (2017) *Cereyanlar: Türkiye'de Siyasi İdeolojiler*. İstanbul: İletişim.

Bora, Tanıl (2019) 'Adnan Menderes', in Mete Kaan Kaynar (ed.), *Türkiye'nin 1950'li Yılları*. İstanbul: İletişim, 331–47.

Bora, Tanıl (2021) *Hasan Âli Yücel*. İstanbul: İletişim.

Bora, Tanıl and Kemal Can (1991) *Devlet, Ocak, Dergâh: 12 Eylül'den 1990'lara Ülkücü Hareket*. İstanbul: İletişim.

Bordewich, Fergus M. (2008) 'A monumental struggle to preserve Hagia Sophia', *Smithsonian Magazine*, December. Available at: https://www.smithsonianmag.com/travel/a-monumental-struggle-to-preserve-hagia-sophia-92038218/.

Borovalı, Murat (2009) 'Islamic scarves and slippery slopes', *Cardozo Law Review* 30/6, 2593–611.

Bozdoğan, Sibel (2001) *Modernism and Nation Building: Turkish Architectural Culture in the Early Republic*. Seattle: University of Washington Press.

Brisku, Adrian (2017) *Political Reform in the Ottoman and Russian Empires: A Comparative Approach*. London: Bloomsbury.

Buğra, Ayşe (2002) 'Labour, capital, and religion: harmony and conflict among the constituency of political Islam in Turkey', *Middle Eastern Studies* 38/2, 187–204.

Buğra, Ayşe and Osman Savaşkan (2014) *New Capitalism in Turkey: The Relationship Between Politics, Religion and Business*. Cheltenham: Edward Elgar.

Buğra, Tarık (1963/2003) *Küçük Ağa*. İstanbul: İletişim.

Burçak, Rıfkı Salim (1998) *On Yılın Anıları (1950–1960)*. Ankara: Nurol Matbaacılık.

Cady, Linell E. and Elizabeth Shakman Hurd (eds) (2010) *Comparative Secularisms in a Global Age*. New York: Palgrave Macmillan.

Cagaptay, Soner (2006) *Islam, Secularism, and Nationalism in Modern Turkey: Who is a Turk*. London: Routledge.

Candan, Rabia Beyza (2015) '1840 Tarihli Ceza Kanunname-I Hümayunu İncelemesi', *Anadolu Üniversitesi Hukuk Fakültesi Dergisi* 1/1, 63–81.

Cantek, Levent (2003) 'Büyük Doğu', in Ahmet Çiğdem (ed.), *Modern Türkiye'de Siyasi Düşünce: Muhafazakarlık*, vol. 5. İstanbul: İletişim.

Cantek, Levent (2008) *Cumhuriyetin Büluğ Çağı: Gündelik Yaşama Dair Tartışmalar (1945–1950)*. İstanbul: İletişim.

Capoccia, Giovanni and R. Daniel Kelemen (2007) 'The study of critical junctures: theory, narrative, and counterfactuals in historical institutionalism', *World Politics* 59/3, 341–69.

Casanova, Jose (1994) *Public Religions in the Modern World*. Chicago: University of Chicago Press.

CHP (1948) *Yedinci Kurultay Tutanağı* [Proceedings 7th General Meeting of Cumhuriyet Halk Partisi 1947]. Ankara: Ulus Basımevi.

Cihan, Ahmet (2004) *Reform Çağında Osmanlı İlmiyye Sınıfı*. İstanbul: Birey.

Cizre Sakallıoğlu, Ümit (1997) 'The anatomy of the Turkish military's political autonomy', *Comparative Politics* 29/2, 151–66.

Cizre, Ümit (2008) 'The Justice and Development Party and the military: recreating the past after reforming it?', in Ümit Cizre (ed.), *Secular and Islamic Politics in Turkey: The making of the Justice and Development Party*. London: Routledge, 132–71.

Copeaux, Etienne (2006) *Tarih Ders Kitaplarında (1931–1993) Türk Tarih Tezinden Türk-İslam Sentezine*. Translated by Ali Berktay. İstanbul: İletişim.

Coşkuner, Murat and Seçil Aslan (2020) 'İktidarın Dinsellik Temsili: Dinsel İktidar Kurumu Olarak Diyanet İşleri Başkanlığı'nın Alevilik Temsili', *Ankara Üniversitesi SBF Dergisi* 75/2, 463–87.

Çakıl-Dinçer, Gülşen (2020) 'Feminizmle İlişkisi Bağlamında Türkiye'de İslamcı Kadın Hareketi', in Feryal Saygılıgil and Nacide Berber (eds), *Modern Türkiye'de Siyasi Düşünce: Feminizm*, vol. 6. İstanbul: İletişim, 239–49.

Çakır, Ruşen (1990) *Ayet ve Slogan*. İstanbul: Metis.

Çakır, Ruşen (1994) *Ne Şeriat Ne Demokrasi: Refah Partisini Anlamak*. İstanbul: Metis.

Çakır, Ruşen (2000) *Direniş ve İtaat: İki İktidar Arasında İslamcı Kadın*. İstanbul: Metis.

Çakır, Ruşen (2004) 'Milli Görüş Hareketi', in Yasin Aktay (ed.), *Modern Türkiye'de Siyasi Düşünce: İslamcılık*, vol. 6. İstanbul: İletişim, 544–9.

Çakır, Ruşen (2011) *Derin Hizbullah: İslamcı Şiddetin Geleceği*, extended 2nd edn. İstanbul: Metis.

Çakır, Ruşen and Fehmi Çalmuk (2001) *Recep Tayyip Erdoğan: Bir Dönüşüm Öyküsü*. İstanbul: Metis.

Çakır, Ruşen and Semih Sakallı (2014) *100 Soruda Erdoğan x Gülen Savaşı*. İstanbul: Metis.

Çakır, Sabri (2011) 'Türkiye'de Göç, Kentleşme/Gecekondu Sorunu ve Üretilen Politikalar', *SDÜ Fen Edebiyat Fakültesi Sosyal Bilimler Dergisi* 23, 209–22.

Çakmak, Yalçın (2020) 'İtikattan Kimliğe: Dinamikler ve Karşı Dinamikler Bağlamında Yetmişli Yıllarda Aleviler', in Mete Kaan Kaynar (ed.), *Türkiye'nin 1970'li Yılları*. İstanbul: İletişim, 645–69.

Çalık, Mustafa (1995) *MHP Hareketi – kaynakları ve gelişimi – 1965–1980*. Ankara: Cedit Neşriyat.

Çalıkuşu, Figen (2023) *101 Soruda 15 Temmuz Yargısı*. İstanbul: Zoe.

Çalmuk, Fehmi (2004) 'Necmettin Erbakan', in Yasin Aktay (ed.), *Modern Türkiye'de Siyasi Düşünce: İslamcılık*, vol. 6. İstanbul: İletişim, 550–67.

Çayır, Kenan (2000) 'İslamcı bir Sivil Toplum Örgütü: Gökkuşağı İstanbul Kadın Platformu', in Nilüfer Göle (ed.), *İslamın Yeni Kamusal Yüzleri*. İstanbul: Metis, 41–67.

Çelenk, A. Tarık (2022) *Türk Sağı: Mahalle, Kriz ve Kritik*. İstanbul: Beyoğlu Kitapevi.

Çelik, Emrah (2017) 'Power and Islam in Turkey: the relationship between the AKP and Sunni Islamic groups, 2002–16', in Bahar Başer and Ahmet Erdi Öztürk (eds), *Authoritarian Politics in Turkey: Elections, Resistance and the AKP*. London: I. B. Tauris, 99–119.

Çetinsaya, Gökhan (1999) 'Rethinking nationalism and Islam: some preliminary notes on the roots of "Turkish-Islamic Synthesis" in modern Turkish political thought', *The Muslim World*, LXXXIX/3–4 (July–October), 350–75.

Çevik, Abidin and Fahriye Dinçer (2018) 'Cumhuriyet Halk Partisi'nin Değişen Din Siyaseti: 1947 Kurultayı', *Turkish Studies Current Debates in Social Sciences (CUDES-2018)* 13/23, 25–36.

Çınar, Alev (2005) *Modernity, Islam, and Secularism in Turkey: Bodies, Places and Time*. Minneapolis: University of Minnesota Press.

Çınar, Alev (2012) 'Subversion and subjugation in the public sphere: secularism and the Islamic headscarf in Turkey', in Alev Çınar, Srirupa Roy and Maha Yahya (eds), *Visualising Secularism and Religion: Egypt, Lebanon, Turkey, India*. Ann Arbor: University of Michigan Press, 25–46.

Çınar, Menderes (2015) *Vesayetçi Demokrasiden 'Milli' Demokrasiye*. İstanbul: Birikim Kitapları.

Çınar, Özgür Heval (2021) *Freedom of Religion and Belief in Turkey: Religion, Society and Politics*. London: Palgrave (Pivot) Macmillan.

Çınar, Özgür H. and Tolga Şirin (2017) 'Turkey's human rights agenda', *Research and Policy on Turkey* 2/2, 133–43.

Çıtak, Zana (2011) 'Religion, ethnicity and transnationalism: Turkish Islam in Belgium', *Journal of Church and State* 53, 222–4.

Çıtak, Zana (2013) 'The institutionalization of Islam in Europe and the Diyanet: the case of Austria', *Middle Eastern Studies* 5, 167–82.

Çıtak, Zana (2017) 'National conceptions, transnational solidarities: Turkey, Islam and Europe', *Global Networks* 18/3, 377–98. Available at: https://doi.org/10.1111/glob.12184.

Çıtak, Zana (2020) 'The transformation of the state-religion relationship in Turkey under the AKP: the case of the Diyanet', in Pınar Bedirhanoğlu, Çağlar Dölek, Funda Hülagü and Özlem Kaygusuz (eds), *Turkey's New State in the Making: Transformations in Legality, Economy and Coercion*. London: Zed Books.

Çiçek, Atıl Cem, Selçuk Aydın and Hüseyin Baran (2017) 'Gelenekle Sol Arasına Sıkışmış bir Siyasal Hareket: (Türkiye) Birlik Partisi', *SİYASAL: Journal of Political Sciences* 26/2, 27–52. Available at: http://dx.doi.org/10.26650/siyasal.2017.26.2.0002.

Çiçek, Cuma (2017) 'Kurds and elections under the AK party's rule: the shifting internal and external borders of the Kurdish political region', in Bahar Başer and Ahmet Erdi Öztürk (eds), *Authoritarian Politics in Turkey: Elections, Resistance and the AKP*. London: I. B. Tauris, 157–88.

Çiftçi, Ali (2019) 'Mareşal Fevzi Çakmak'ın 1946–1950 Yılları Arasındaki Siyasal Faaliyetleri', *Trakya Üniversitesi Sosyal Bilimler Dergisi* 21/2, 967–85.

Çiğdem, Ahmet (2004) 'İslamcılık ve Türkiye Üzerine Bazı Notlar', in Yasin Aktay (ed.), *Modern Türkiye'de Siyasi Düşünce: İslamcılık*, vol. 6. İstanbul: İletişim, 26–33.

Çobanoğlu, Yavuz (2012) *'Altın Nesil' in Peşinde: Fethullah Gülen'de Toplum, Devlet, Ahlak ve Otorite*. İstanbul: İletişim.

Çolak, Filiz (2021) 'Demokrat Parti'nin İlk Kadın Milletvekili: Hatice Nazlı Tlabar (1913–1971)', *Tarih İncelemeleri Dergisi* XXXVI/1, 53–90.

Dalacoura, Katerina (2019) '"Islamic civilization" as an aspect of secularization in Turkish Islamic thought', *Historical Social Research* 44/3, 127–49.

Danforth, Nick (2016) 'The Ottoman Empire from 1923 to today: in search of a usable past', *Mediterranean Quarterly* 27/2, 5–27.

Davaz-Mardin, Aslı (2002) 'Görünmezlikten Görünürlüğe: Kadın Eserleri Kütüphanesi ve Bilgi Merkezi Vakfı', in Aksu Bora-Asena Günal (eds), *90'larda Türkiye'de Feminizm*. İstanbul: İletişim, 183–204.

Davison, Andrew (1998) *Secularism Revivalism in Turkey: A Hermeneutic Reconsideration*. New Haven: Yale University Press.

Davison, Andrew (2003) 'Turkey, a "secular" state? The challenge of description', *The South Atlantic Quarterly* 102/2, 333–50.

Davison, Roderic (1963) *Reform in the Ottoman Empire: 1856–1876*. Princeton, NJ: Princeton University Press.

Değer, Ayşegül and Rümeysa Çamdereli (2020) 'Konca Kuriş', in Feryal Saygılıgil and Nacide Berber (eds), *Modern Türkiye'de Siyasi Düşünce: Feminizm*, vol. 6. İstanbul: İletişim, 224–30.

Demir, Ömer (2004) 'Anadolu Sermayesi ya da İslamcı Sermaye', in Yasin Aktay (ed.), *Modern Türkiye'de Siyasi Düşünce: İslamcılık*, vol. 10. İstanbul: İletişim, 870–86.

Demir, Ömer, Mustafa Acar and Metin Toprak (2004) 'Anotolian tigers or Islamic capital: prospects and challenges', *Middle Eastern Studies* 40/6, 166–88.

Demir, Şerif (2007) 'Adnan Menderes ve 6/7 Eylül Olayları', *Yakın Dönem Türkiye Araştırmaları* 12, 37–63.

Demirdirek, Aynur (1998) 'In pursuit of the Ottoman Women's Movement', in Zehra F. Arat (ed.), *Deconstructing Images of the Turkish Women*. London: Macmillan, 65–81.

Demirel, Ahmet (1994) *Birinci Meclis'te Muhalefet: İkinci Grup*. İstanbul: İletişim.
Demirel, Ahmet (2014) 'Liste delmeyi başaran beş mebus', *Taraf*, 20 April, 9.
Demirel, Fatmagül (2007) *Adliye Nezareti: Kuruluşu ve Faaliyetleri (1876–1914)*. İstanbul: Boğaziçi Üniversitesi Yayınevi.
Demirel, Tanel (2011) *Türkiye'nin Uzun On Yılı: Demokrat Parti İktidarı ve 27 Mayıs Darbesi*. İstanbul: İstanbul Bilgi Üniversitesi Yayınları.
Demirtaş, Selahattin (2022) *Efsun*. İstanbul: Dipnot.
Deniz, A. Çağlar and Evrim Viyan Anık (2016) 'Muhafazakar Eşcinseller: AK LGBTİ', in A. Çağlar Deniz (ed.), *Öteki Muhafazakarlık*. Ankara: Phoenix Yayınevi, 305–50.
Deniz, Dilşa (2020) 'Re-assessing the genocide of Kurdish Alevis in Dersim, 1937–38', *Genocide Studies and Prevention* 14/2, 20–43. Available at: https://doi.org/10.5038/1911-9933.14.2.1728.
Derin, Haldun (1995) *Çankaya Özel Kalemini Anımsarken (1933–1951)*. Edited by Cemil Koçak. İstanbul: Tarih Vakfı Yurt Yayınları.
Deringil, Selim (1989) *Turkish Foreign Policy During the Second World War*. Cambridge: Cambridge University Press.
Deringil, Selim (1991) 'Legitimacy structures in the Ottoman state: the reign of Abdülhamid II (1876–1909)', *International Journal of Middle Eastern Studies* 23/3, 345–59.
Deringil, Selim (1993) 'The Ottoman origins of Kemalist nationalism: Namik Kemal to Mustafa Kemal', *European History Quarterly* 23, 165–91.
Deringil, Selim (1998) *The Well-Protected Domains: Ideology and Legitimation of Power in the Ottoman Empire, 1876–1909*. London: I. B. Tauris.
Deringil, Selim (2000) '"There is no compulsion in religion": on conversion and apostasy in the late Ottoman Empire: 1839–1856', *Society for Comparative Study of Society and History* 40, 547–75.
Deringil, Selim (2007) *Simgeden Millete: II Abdülhamid'den Mustafa Kemal'e Devlet ve Millet*. İstanbul: İletişim.
Deringil, Selim (2009) '"The Armenian question is finally closed": mass conversions of Armenians during the Hamidian massacres of 1895–1987', *Comparative Studies in Society and History* 51, 344–71.
Deringil, Selim (2012) *Conversion and Apostasy in The Late Ottoman Emire*. New York: Cambridge University Press.
Devereux, Robert (1963) *The First Ottoman Constitutional Period: A Study of the Midhat Constitution and Parliament*. Baltimore: Johns Hopkins Press.
Dinler, Veysi (2020) 'Yangın Yeri, Katliam: Maraş ve Çorum', in Mete Kaan Kaynar (ed.), *Türkiye'nin 1970'li Yılları*. İstanbul: İletişim, 671–87.

Doğan, Sevinç (2016) *Mahalledeki AKP: Parti İşleyişi, Taban Mobilizasyonu ve Siyasal Yabancılaşma*. İstanbul: İletişim.

Döşemeci, Mehmet (2013) *Debating Turkish Modernity: Civilization, Nationalism, and the EEC*. New York: Cambridge University Press.

Dressler, Markus (2010) 'Public-private distinctions, the Alevi question, and the headscarf: Turkish secularism revisited', in Linell E. Cady and Elizabeth Shakman Hurd (eds), *Comparative Secularisms in a Global Age*. New York: Palgrave Macmillan, 121–41.

Dressler, Markus (2011) 'Making religion through secularist legal discourse: the case of Turkish Alevism', in Markus Dressler and Arvind-Pal S. Mandair, *Secularism and Religion-Making*. Oxford: Oxford University Press, 187–208.

Dressler, Markus (2013) *Writing Religion: The Making of Turkish Alevi Islam*. Oxford: Oxford University Press.

Dressler, Markus (2015) 'Rereading Ziya Gökalp: "Secularism and Reform of the Islamic State in the Late Young Turk Period"', *International Journal of Middle East Studies* 47, 511–31.

Dressler, Markus (2020) 'Interpreting the desecularisation of the Hagia Sophia: Islamisation, neo-Ottomanism, anti-Imperialism or preservation of cultural heritage?', *University of Leipzig Multiple Secularities Bulletin*, Leipzig. Available at https://www.multiple-secularities.de/bulletin/interpreting-the-desecularisation-of-the-hagia-sophia-islamisation-neo-ottomanism-anti-imperialism-or-preservation-of-cultural-heritage/?filter2=all.

Dressler, Markus, Armando Salvatore and Monika Wohlrab Sahr (2019) 'Islamicate secularities: new perspectives on a contested concept', *Historical Social Research* 44/3, 7–34.

Duman, Doğan and Serkan Yorgancılar (2008) *Türkçülükten İslamcılığa Milli Türk Talebe Birliği*. Ankara: Vadi Yayınları.

Eickelman, Dale F. (2002) 'Islam and ethical pluralism', in Sohail H. Hashmi (ed.), *Islamic Political Ethics: Civil Society, Pluralism and Conflict*. Princeton, NJ: Princeton University Press, 115–34.

Eickelman, Dale F. and James Piscatori (1996) *Muslim Politics*. Princeton, NJ: Princeton University Press.

Ekinci, Ekrem Buğra (2004) *Tanzimat ve Sonrası Osmanlı Mahkemeleri*. İstanbul: Arı Sanat Yayınevi.

Eldem, Ethem (2022) 'Tanzimat Hatt-ı Hümayunu'nu (1839) baştan okuma', *Tarih ve Toplum Yeni Yaklaşımlar* 20 (Fall), 9–97.

Elveren, Merve and Erman Ata Uncu (2022) '"Love is anarchist": the short-lived experiment in Turkey's oppositional press, Sokak (1989–1980).' *mezofera.org*.

Available at http://mezosfera.org/love-is-anarchist-the-short-lived-experiment-in-turkeys-oppositional-press-sokak-1989-1990/.

Emrence, Cem (2006) *99 Günlük Muhalefet: Serbest Cumhuriyet Fırkası*. İstanbul: İletişim.

Emrence, Cem (2011) *Remapping the Ottoman Middle East: Modernity, Imperial Bureaucracy and the Islamic State*. London: I. B. Tauris.

Engin, Ceylan (2015) 'LGBT in Turkey: policies and experiences', *Social Sciences* 4, 838–58.

Eraslan, Sibel (2005) 'İslamcı Kadının Siyasette Zaman Algısı Üzerine', in Yasin Aktay (ed.), *Modern Türkiye'de Siyasi Düşünce: İslamcılık*, vol. 6. İstanbul: İletişim, 818–25.

Erdem, Ufuk (2021). "Türkiye Büyük Millet Meclisinin Açılma Süreci ve Meclisin Açılış Günü (23 Nisan 1920)", *Fırat Üniversitesi Sosyal Bilimler Dergisi* 31/2, 1055–68.

Erder, Sema (2018) *Zorla Yerleştirmeden Yerinden Etmeye: Türkiye'de Değişen İskân Politikaları*. İstanbul: İletişim.

Ergin, Osman (1977) *Türk Maarif Tarihi*, vol. 5. İstanbul: Eser Matbaası.

Ergüç, Veysel (2020) *Aydınlar Ocağı ve Türk-İslâm Sentezi*, in Mete Kaan Kaynar (ed.), *Türkiye'nin 1970'li Yılları*. İstanbul: İletişim, 403–14.

Eroğul, Cem (1970) *Demokrat Parti: Tarihi ve İdeolojisi*. Ankara: Ankara Üniversitesi Siyasal Bilgiler Fakültesi Yayınları.

Ersel, Hasan, Ahmet Kuyaş, Ahmet Oktay and Mete Tunçay (eds) (2005) *Cumhuriyet Ansiklopedisi 1941–1960*, 5th edn /4 vols. İstanbul: Yapı Kredi Yayınları.

Erşahin, Seyfettin (1999) 'The Ottoman ulema and the reforms of Mahmud II', *Hamdard Islamicus* 22/2, 19–40.

Ertan, Mehmet (2017) *Aleviliğin Politikleşme Süreci: Kimlik Siyasetinin Kısıtlılıkları ve İmkanları*. İstanbul: İletişim.

Ertür, Başak (2022) *Spectacles and Specters: A Performative Theory of Political Trials*. New York: Fordham University Press.

Eryılmaz, Tuğrul (2018) *68'li ve Gazeteci* (interview: Asu Maro). İstanbul: İletişim.

Evren, Kenan (1991) *Kenan Evren'in Anıları*, vol. 3. İstanbul: Milliyet Yayınları.

Findley, Carter V. (1980) *Bureaucratic Reform in the Ottoman Empire*. Princeton, NJ: Princeton University Press.

Findley, Carter V. (1989) *Ottoman Civil Officialdom: a Social History*. Princeton, NJ: Princeton University Press.

Findley, Carter Vaughn (2010) *Turkey, Islam, Nationalism and Modernity: A History, 1789–2007*. New Haven: Yale University Press.

Finkel, Caroline (2005) *Osman's Dream*. New York: Basic Books.

Fortna, Benjamin (2002) *Imperial Classroom: Islam, the State, and Education in the Late Ottoman Empire*. Oxford: Oxford University Press.

Fox, Jonathan and Shmuel Sandler (2005) 'The question of religion and world politics', *Terrorism and Political Violence* 17/3, 293–303.

Frierson, Elizabeth B. (2005) 'Woman in the Late Ottoman intellectual history', in Elizabeth Özdalga (ed.), *Late Ottoman Society Intellectual Legacy*. London: RoutledgeCurzon, 135–62.

Fuller, Graham E. (2014) *Turkey and the Arab Spring: Leadership in the Middle East*. Lexington: Bozorg Press.

Gençkal-Eroler, Elif (2019) *'Dindar Nesil Yetiştirmek' Türkiye'nin Eğitim Politikalarında Ulus ve Vatandaş İnşası (2002–2016)*. İstanbul: İletişim.

George, Alexander L. and Andrew Bennett (2005) *Case Studies and Theory Development in the Social Sciences*. Cambridge, MA: MIT Press.

Gerber, Haim (1987) *Social Origins of the Modern Middle East*. Boulder: L. Rienner.

Geyikdağı, Mehmet Yaşar (1984) *Political Parties in Turkey: The Role of Islam*. New York: Praeger.

Gezik, Erdal (2012) *Dinsel, Etnik ve Politik Sorunlar Bağlamında Alevi Kürtler*. İstanbul: İletişim.

Gingeras, Ryan (2019) *Eternal Dawn: Turkey in the Age of Atatürk*. Oxford: Oxford University Press.

Gondicas, Dimitri and Charles Issawi (eds) (1999) *Ottoman Greeks in the Age of Nationalism*. Princeton, NJ: Darwin.

Göçek, Fatma Müge (1996) *Rise of the Bourgeoise, Demise of the Empire: Ottoman Westernization and Social Change*. Oxford: Oxford University Press.

Göçek, Fatma Müge (2006) 'Reading genocide: Turkish historiography on the Armenian deportations and massacres of 1915', in Israel Gershoni, Amy Singer and Y. Hakan Erdem (eds), *Middle East Historiographies: Narrating The Twentieth Century*. Seattle: University of Washington Press, 101–27.

Gökaçtı, Mehmet Ali (2005) *Türkiye'de din eğitimi ve imam hatipler*. İstanbul: İletişim.

Gökalp, Ziya ([1918] 2023) *Türkleşmek, İslamlaşmak, Muassırlaşmak*. İstanbul: Ötüken.

Gökberk, Ülker (2020) *Excavating Memory: Bilge Karasu's İstanbul and Walter Benjamin's Berlin*. Boston: Academic Studies Press.

Göknar, Erdağ (2003) 'Ottoman past and Turkish future: ambivalance in A. H. Tanpınar's *Those Outside the Scene*', in Sibel Irzık and Güven Güzeldere (eds), *Relocating the Fault Lines: Turkey beyond the East–West Divide* (*The South Atlantic Quarterly* special issue 102/2–3), 647–61.

Göle, Nilüfer (1991) *Modern Mahrem: Medeniyet ve Örtünme*. İstanbul: Metis.

Gölpınarlı, Abdülbaki (1969) *100 soruda Türkiye'de Mezhepler ve Tarikatlar*. İstanbul: Gerçek yayınevi.

Gözaydın, İştar B. (2002) 'Türkiye Hukukunun Batılılaşması', in Uygur Kocabaşoğlu (ed.), *Modern Türkiye'de Siyasi Düşünce: Modernleşme ve Batıcılık c. III*. İstanbul: İletişim, 286–97.

Gözaydın, İştar (2006) 'Adding injury to injury', in John T. Parry (ed.), *Evil, Law and the State: Perspectives on State Power and Violence*. Amsterdam: Rodopi Press, 59–70.

Gözaydın, İştar B. (2009a) 'The Fethullah Gülen movement and politics in Turkey: a chance for democratization or a Trojan horse?', *Democratization* 16/6, 1214–36.

Gözaydın, İştar (2009b) 'Türkiye'de Din Kültürü ve Ahlak Bilgisi Ders Kitaplarına İnsan Hakları Merceğiyle Bir Bakış', in Gürel Tüzün (ed.), *Ders Kitaplarında İnsan Hakları II: Tarama Sonuçları*. İstanbul: Tarih Vakfı Yayınları.

Gözaydın, İştar (2013a) 'Ahmet Davutoğlu: role as an Islamic scholar shaping Turkey's foreign policy', in Nassef Manabilang Adiong (ed.), *Islam and International Relations: Diverse Perspectives*. Newcastle upon Tyne: Cambridge Scholars Publishing, 50–9.

Gözaydın, İştar (2013b) 'Kürtaj ve Yaşam Hakkı', in Zafer Üsküll and O. Serkan Gülfidan (eds), *Doğuş Üniversitesi Hukuk Fakültesi İnsan Hakları Konferansları I–II: Türkiye'de İnsan Hakları – Yaşam Hakkı*. İstanbul: Legal Yayınevi.

Gözaydın, İştar (2014) 'Management of religion in Turkey: the *Diyanet* and beyond', in Özgür Heval Çınar and Mine Yıldırım (eds), *Freedom of Religion and Belief in Turkey*, Newcastle upon Tyne: Cambridge Scholars Publishing, 10–35.

Gözaydın, İştar (2017) 'Epilogue: The desire is there', in Bahar Başer and Ahmet Erdi Öztürk (eds), *Authoritarian Politics in Turkey: Elections, Resistance and the AKP*. London: I. B. Tauris, 256–66.

Gözaydın, İştar (2020) *Diyanet: Türkiye Cumhuriyeti'nde Dinin Tanzimi*. İstanbul: İletişim Yayınları.

Gözaydın, İştar (2021a) 'Discrimination based on religion: a complex story in Turkey', in Hasan Aydın and Winston Langley (eds), *Human Rights in Turkey: Assaults on Human Dignity*. Cham: Springer, 89–107.

Gözaydın, İştar (2021b) 'Religion and Turkey's international relations', in Jeffrey Haynes (ed.) *Handbook on Religion and International Relations*. London: Edward Elgar.

Gözaydın, İştar and Ahmet Erdi Öztürk (2023) 'The Presidency of Religious Affairs (the Diyanet) and the organization of the secular state', in Alpaslan Özerdem and

Ahmet Erdi Öztürk (eds), *A Companion to Modern Turkey's Centennial Political, Sociological, Economic and Institutional Transformations since 1923*. Edinburgh: Edinburgh University Press, 194–212.

Grigoriadis, Ioannis N. (2013) *Instilling Religion in Greek and Turkish Nationalism: A 'Sacred Synthesis'*. New York: Palgrave Macmillan.

Gülpınar, Turgay (2014) 'Turan Emeksiz: Bir Simgenin Doğuşu ve Yok Edilişi', in Serdar M. Değirmencioğlu (ed.), *'Öl Dediler Öldüm': Türkiye'de Şehitlik Mitleri*. İstanbul: İletişim, 133–46.

Gündoğan, Kazım (2022) *Aleviles(tiril)miş Ermeniler: Dersimli Ermeniler 2 – 'Biz İsa'ya Tabiyiz, Ali'ye Mecburuz'*. İstanbul: Ayrıntı.

Güran, Kemal (1996) 'Cumhuriyet Döneminde Hac', *İslam Ansiklopedisi*. Available at: https://islamansiklopedisi.org.tr/hac#7-cumhuriyet-donemi.

Gürdoğan, Ersin Nazif (2004) *Görünmeyen üniversite*. İstanbul: İz Yayıncılık.

Gürel, Burak (2004) '"Communist Police!" the State in the 1970s Turkey', *Journal of Historical Studies* 2, 1–18.

Gürleyen, Işık (2014) 'What did they promise for democracy and what did they deliver? The AKP and the CHP 2002–11', in Carmen Rodriguez, Antonio Avalos, Hakan Yılmaz and Ana I. Planet (eds), *Turkey's Democratization Process*. London: Routledge, 109–29.

Gürpınar, Doğan (2013) *Düne Veda: Türkiye'de Liberalizm ve Demokratlık (1980–2010)*. İstanbul: Etkileşim Yayınları.

Gürses, Mehmet (2023) 'Kurdish question: a century later', in Alpaslan Özerdem and Ahmet Erdi Öztürk (eds), *A Companion to Modern Turkey's Centennial Political, Sociological, Economic and Institutional Transformations since 1923*. Edinburgh: Edinburgh University Press, 252–63.

Gürün, Kâmuran (2010) *Türk-Sovyet İlişkileri (1920–1953)*. Ankara: Türk Tarih Kurumu Yayını.

Güven, Dilek (2005) *Cumhuriyet Dönemi Azınlık Politikaları Bağlamında 6/7 Eylül Olayları*. İstanbul: Tarih Vakfı Yurt Yayınları.

Güven, Dilek (2011) 'Riots against the non-Muslims of Turkey: 6/7 September 1955 in the context of demographic engineering', *European Journal of Turkish Studies* 12, 1–18.

Hale, William and Ergun Özbudun (2010) *Islamism, Democracy and Liberalism in Turkey: The Case of the AKP*. London: Routledge.

Hanioğlu, M. Şükrü (2001) *Preparation for a Revoluton: The Young Turks, 1902–1908*. New York: Oxford University Press.

Hanioğlu, M. Şükrü (2008) *A Brief History of the Late Ottoman Empire*. Princeton, NJ: Princeton University Press.

Hanioğlu, M. Şükrü (2011) *Atatürk: an Intellectual Biography*. Princeton, NJ: Princeton University Press.

Hassan, Mona (2011) 'Women preaching for the secular state: official female preachers (*bayan vaizler*) in contemporary Turkey', *International Journal of Middle East Studies* 43, 451–73.

Hatemi, Nilüfer (2010) *Mareşal Fevzi Çakmak ve Günlükleri*. İstanbul: Yapı Kredi Yayınları.

Haynes, Jeffrey (2010) 'Politics, identity and religious nationalism in Turkey: from Atatürk to the AKP', *Australian Journal of International Affairs* 64/3, 312–27.

Hendrick, Joshua D. (2013) *Gülen: The Ambiguous Politics of Market Islam in Turkey and the World*. New York: New York University Press.

Hoşgör, Evren (2011) 'Islamic capital/Anatolian tigers: past and present', *Middle Eastern Studies* 47/2, 343–60.

Hourani, Albert (1981) 'Sufism and modern Islam: Mavlana Khalid and the Naqshbandş order', in Albert Hourani (ed.), *The Emergence of the Modern Middle East*. Basingstoke: Palgrave Macmillan.

Hourani, Albert (1991) *Islam in European Thought*. Cambridge: Cambridge University Press.

Human Rights Foundation of Turkey (2019) *Academics for Peace: A Brief History – January 11, 2016 – March 15, 2019*. Ankara: HFRT Academy.

Hussain, Dilwar (2010) 'The Holy Grail of Muslims in Western Europe: representation and their relationship with the State', in John L. Esposito and François Burgat (eds), *Modernizing Islam: Religion in the Public Sphere in Europe and the Middle East*. New Brunswick: Rutgers University Press, 215–50.

Hür, Ayşe (2013) 'İttihatçı ve Kemalistlerin Alevi-Bektaşi Politikaları', *Radikal Daily*, 30 June, 18–19.

İçduygu, Ahmet (2012) '50 Years after the labour recruitment agreement with Germany: the consequences of emigration for Turkey', *Perceptions* XVII/2, 11–36.

İlhan, Atilla ([1963] 1975) *Kurtlar Sofrası*, 2 vols, 2nd edn. İstanbul: Bilgi Yayınevi.

İlkkaracan, Pınar (2014) 'Democratization in Turkey from a gender perspective', in Carmen Rodriguez, Antonio Avalos, Hakan Yılmaz and Ana I. Planet (eds), *Turkey's Democratization Process*. London: Routledge, 154–76.

İlyasoğlu, Aynur (1994) *Örtülü Kimlik: İslamcı Kadın Kimliğinin Oluşum Öğeleri*. İstanbul: Metis.

İnal, İbnülemin Mahmud Kemal ([1940] 1969) *Osmanlı Devrinde Son Sadrazamlar I. Cüz*. İstanbul: Millî Eğitim Bakanlığı Devlet Kitapları.

İnalcık, Halil (2017) *The Ottoman Empire and Europe: The Ottoman Empire and its Place in European History*. İstanbul: Kronik Books.

İnsel, Ahmet (2005) 'Demokrasinin sancılı yılları', in Hasan Ersel, Ahmet Kuyaş, Ahmet Oktay and Mete Tunçay (eds) (2005) *Cumhuriyet Ansiklopedisi 1961–1980*, vol. 3, 5th edn. İstanbul: Yapı Kredi Yayınları.

İslamoğlu-İnan, Huricihan (ed.) (1987) *The Ottoman Empire and the World-Economy*. Cambridge: Cambridge University Press.

İslamoğlu, Huricihan (2021) *Dünya Tarihi ve Siyaset*. İstanbul: İletişim.

Jackson, Sherman A. (2017) 'The Islamic secular', *American Journal of Islamic Social Sciences* 34/2, 1–31.

Joseph, John (1983) *Muslim-Christian Relations and Inter-Christian Rivalries in the Middle East: The Case of the Jacobites in an Age of Transition*. Albany: State University of New York Press.

Kabasakal Arat, Zehra F. (2013) *Human Rights in Turkey*. Philadelphia: University of Pennsylvania Press.

Kadıoğlu, Ayşe (1998a) 'Republican epistemology and Islamic discourses in Turkey in the 1990s', *The Muslim World* 88, 1–21.

Kadıoğlu, Ayşe (1998b) 'Laiklik ve Tütkiye'de Liberalizmin Kökenleri', *Defter* 11/33, 41–63.

Kadıoğlu, Ayşe (2010) 'The pathologies of Turkish republican laicism', *Philosophy and Social Criticism* 36/3–4, 489–504.

Kafadar, Cemal (1995) *Between Two Worlds: The Construction of the Ottoman State*. Berkeley: University of California Press.

Kahraman, Fatma Zeliha (2007) 'Diyanet İşleri Başkanlığı'nın Yurt Dışı Din Hizmetleri: Danimarka Örneği', unpublished MA thesis, Sakarya Üniversitesi Sosyal Bilimler Enstitüsü.

Kalpaklıoğlu, Burcu (2023) *Fetvayla Yol Göstermek: Alo Fetva Hattı, Vaizeler, Gündelik Hayat Tavsiyeleri*. İstanbul: İletişim.

Kamouzis, Dimitris (2012) 'Elites and the formation of national identity: the case of the Greek Orthodox *millet* (mid-nineteenth century to 1922)', in Benjamin C. Fortna, Stefanos Katsikas, Dimitris Kamouzis and Paraskevas Konortas (eds), *State Nationalisms in the Ottoman Empire, Greece and Turkey: Orthodox and Muslims 1830–1945*. London: Routledge, 13–46.

Kandiyoti, Deniz (1987) 'Emancipated but unliberated? Reflections on the Turkish case', *Feminist Studies* 13/2, 317–39.

Kandiyoti, Deniz (1988a) 'Bargaining with patriarchy', *Gender and Society* 2/3, 274–90.

Kandiyoti, Deniz (1988b) 'Women and the Turkish state: political actors or symbolic pawns?', in Nira Yuval Davis and Floya Anthias (eds), *Woman-Nation-State*. London: Macmillan.

Kaplan, Abdurrahman (2011) *İki Devirde bir Din Adamı: Mehmet Rıfat Börekçi*. Ankara: Net Ofset.

Kaplan, İsmail (1999) *Türkiye'de Milli Eğitim İdeolojisi ve Siyasal Toplumsallaşma Üzerindeki Etkisi*. İstanbul: İletişim.

Kara, İsmail ([1986] 2020) *Türkiye'de İslamcılık Düşüncesi 1: Metinler Kişiler*, 4th edn. İstanbul: Dergâh.

Kara, İsmail (1998) *Şeyhefendinin Rüyasındaki Türkiye*. İstanbul: Dergâh.

Kara, İsmail (2000) *Kutuz Hoca'nın Hatıraları: Cumhuriyet Döneminde bir Köy Hocası*. İstanbul: Dergâh.

Kara, İsmail (2002) 'Meclis-i Meşâyih, Ulema-Tarikat Münasebetleri ve İstanbul'da Şeyhlik Yapmış Beş Zatın Kendi Kaleminden Terceme-i Hâli', *Kutadgubilig* 1/186, 202–3.

Kara, İsmail (2003) *Din ile Modernleşme Arasında: Çağdaş Türk Düşüncesinin Meseleleri*. İstanbul: Dergâh.

Kara, İsmail (2004) 'Diyanet İşleri Başkanlığı', in Yasin Aktay (ed.), *Modern Türkiye'de Siyasi Düşünce: İslamcılık*, vol. 6. İstanbul: İletişim.

Kara, İsmail (2005) 'Turban and fez: ulema as opposition', in Elizabeth Özdalga (ed.), *Late Ottoman Society: The Intellectual Legacy*. London: RoutledgeCurzon, 163–202.

Kara, İsmail ([2008] 2017) *Cumhuriyet Türkiyesi'nde Bir Mesele Olarak İslam 1*, 8th edn. İstanbul: Dergâh.

Kara, İsmail (2014) *İslamcıların Siyasi Görüşleri 1: Hilafet ve Meşruiyet*, 3rd edn. İstanbul: Dergâh.

Kara, İsmail (2016) *Cumhuriyet Türkiyesi'nde Bir Mesele Olarak İslam II*. İstanbul: Dergâh.

Kara, İsmail (2021) *Bir Düşünce Tarihi Metni Olarak İstiklal Marşı*. İstanbul: Dergâh.

Kara, İsmail (2023) 'Hutbe Zaten Türkçe Değil mi idi?', *Derin Tarih* 131 (February), 2–7.

Kara, İsmail and Rabia K. Gündoğdu (2019) *Diyanet İşleri Başkanı Ahmet Hamdi Akseki: Hayatı Mücadelesi ve Eserleri*. İzmir: Diyanet İşleri Başkanlığı Yayınları.

Kara, Mustafa (1977) *Din, Hayat, Sanat Açısından Tekkeler ve Zaviyeler*. İstanbul Dergâh.

Kara, Mustafa (1985) 'Tanzimat'tan Cumhuriyet'e Tasavvuf ve Tarikatlar', in *Tanzimat'tan Cumhuriyet'e Türkiye Ansiklopedisi*. İstanbul: İletişim, 978–94.

Karabaşoğlu, Metin (2004) 'Said Nursi', in Yasin Aktay (ed.), *Modern Türkiye'de Siyasi Düşünce: İslamcılık*, vol. 6. İstanbul: İletişim, 271–89.

Karabatak, Halûk (1996) '1934 Trakya Olayları ve Yahudiler', *Tarih ve Toplum* 146 (February).

Karabekir, Kâzım (1933–51) *İstiklal Harbimizin Esasları*. İstanbul: Sinan Matbaası ve Neşriyat Evi.

Karadeniz Teknik Üniversitesi Rize İlahiyat Fakültesi (2006) *İlahiyat Fakülteleri Kelam Anabilim Dalı VIII. Koordinasyon toplantısı ve Dini Otorite Sempozyumu*. İstanbul: Ensar Neşriyat.

Karakaş, Burcu (2021) *'Biz Her Şeyiz': Diyanet'in İşleri*. İstanbul: İletişim.

Karakaş, Cemal (2007) *Turkey: Islam and Laicism Between the Interests of State, Politics, and Society*. PRIF Reports No. 78. Frankfurt: Peace Research Institute.

Karal, Enver Ziya (1970) *Osmanlı Tarihi V. Cilt: Nizam-ı Cedit ve Tanzimat Devirleri (1789–1856)*, 3 baskı. Ankara: Türk Tarih Kurumu Yayınevi.

Karal, Enver Ziya (1976) *Osmanlı Tarihi VI. Cilt: Islahat Fermanı Devri (1856–1861)*, 2 baskı. Ankara: Türk Tarih Kurumu Yayınevi.

Karaman, Tuğba (2016) 'Recasting Late Ottoman women: nation, press and Islam (1876–1914)', unpublished PhD thesis, University of Manchester.

Karamollaoğlu, Temel (2022) *Son Tanık: Hayatı – Hatıratı-Mücadelesi* (interview by Mustafa Yılmaz). Ankara: Milli Gazete Ankara Kitap Kulübü.

Karapehlivan, Funda (2019) *Constructing a 'New Turkey' Through Education: An Overview of the Education Policies in Turkey under the AKP Rule*. Istanbul: Heinrich Böll Stiftung. Available at: https://tr.boell.org/en/2019/10/01/constructing-new-turkey-through-education.

Karasu, Bilge ([1980] 2003) 'Where the tale also rips suddenly', in *The Garden of Departed Cats*. Translated by Aron Aji. New York: New Directions Publishing.

Karasu, Bilge (1985) *Gece*. İstanbul: İletişim.

Karatepe, İsmail Doğa (2017) '1980'li Yıllarda Anadolu Burjuvazisinin Yükselişi', in R. Funda Barbaros and Erik Jan Zurcher, *Modernizmin Yansımaları: 80'li Yıllarda Türkiye*. Ankara: Efil Yayınevi, 203–24.

Kardeş, Salâhaddin (2008) *'Tehcir' ve Emval-I Metrûke Mevzuatı*. Ankara: T. C. Maliye Bakanlığı Strateji Geliştirme Başkanlığı.

Karpat, Kemal H. (1972) 'The transformation of the Ottoman state, 1789–1908', *International Journal of Middle East Studies* 3/3, 243–81.

Karpat, Kemal H. (1985) *Ottoman Population 1830–1914: Demographic and Social Characteristics*. Madison: University of Wisconsin Press.

Karpat, Kemal H. (2001) *The Politicization of Islam: Reconstructing Identity, State, Faith, and Community in the Late Ottoman State*. New York: Oxford University Press.

Karpat, Kemal (2009) *The Gecekondu: Rural Migration and Urbanization*. New York: Cambridge University Press.

Karpat, Kemal H. ([2009] 2012) *Elites and Religion: From the Ottoman Empire to Turkish Republic*, 3rd edn. İstanbul: Timaş.

Kasaba, Reşat (1988) *The Ottoman Empire and the World Economy – The Nineteenth Century*. Albany: State University of New York Press.

Kaya, Serdar (2009) 'The rise and decline of the Turkish "Deep State": the Ergenekon case', *Insight Turkey* 11/4, 99–113.

Kayalı, Hasan (1997) *Arabs and Young Turks – Ottomanism, Arabism and Islamism in the Ottoman Empire, 1908–1918*. Berkeley: University of California Press.

Kaynar, Mete Kaan (2017) 'Türkiye'nin Altmışlı Yılları Üzerine Bazı Notlar', in Mete Kaan Kaynar (ed.), *Türkiye'nin 1960'lı Yılları*. İstanbul: İletişim, 23–58.

Kaynar, Reşat (1954) *Mustafa Reşit Paşa ve Tanzimat*. Ankara: Türk Tarih Kurumu Yayınevi.

Keyder, Çağlar (1987) *State and Class in Turkey: a Study in Capitalist Development*. London: Verso.

Keyder, Çağlar and Faruk Tabak (eds) (1991) *Landholding and Commercial Agriculture in the Middle East*. Albany: State University of New York Press.

Keyman, E. Fuat (2011) 'Nationalism in Turkey: modernity, state and identity', in Ayşe Kadıoğlu and E. Fuat Keyman (eds), *Symbiotic Antagonisms: Competing Nationalisms in Turkey*. Salt Lake City: University of Utah Press, 10–32.

Keyman, E. Fuat and Tuba Kancı (2014) 'Democratic consolidation and civil society in Turkey', in Carmen Rodriguez, Antonio Avalos, Hakan Yılmaz and Ana I. Planet (eds), *Turkey's Democratization Process*. London: Routledge, 133–53.

Keyman, E. Fuat and Ziya Öniş (2007) *Turkish Politics in a Changing World: Global Dynamics and Domestic Transformations*. Istanbul: Istanbul Bilgi University Press.

King, Pamela Ebstyne (2003) 'Religion and identity: the role of ideological, social, and spiritual contexts', in James L. Furrow and Linda M. Wagener (eds) *Beyond the Self*. New York: Routledge, 197–204.

Kiratzopulos, Vasilis (2009) *Kayıt Olunmamış Soykırım: İstanbul Eylül 1955 Yeni Dünya Düzeninin İtinayla Sakladığı Utanç Uygulaması*. Translated by Sonya Özzakar. İstanbul: Pencere Yayınları.

Kirişçi, Kemal (2000) 'Disaggregating Turkish citizenship and immigration practices', *Middle Eastern Studies* 36/3, 1–22.

Kirişçi, Kemal and Gareth M. Winrow (1997) *The Kurdish Question and Turkey: An Example of a Trans-State Ethnic Conflict*. London: Frank Cass Publishers.

Kılıç, Zülal (1998) 'Cumhuriyet Türkiyesi'nde Kadın Hareketine Genel bir Bakış', in Ayşe Berktay Hacımirzaoğlu (ed.), *75 Yılda Kadınlar ve Erkekler*. İstanbul: Tarih Vakfı Yayınları, 347–60.

Kılınç, Doğan (2013) *Azınlık Hakları*. Ankara: Yetkin Yayınları.

Kılınç, Kıvanç and Didem Kılıçkıran (2022) 'Modernliğin Diğer Kadınları: 1930'ların Kız Okulları Üzerinden Sınıf, Toplumsal Cinsiyet ve Mekana dair bir Okuma', in Sevgi Adak and Alexandros Lamprou (eds), *Tek Parti Dönemini Yeniden Düşünmek: Devlet, Toplum ve Siyaset*. İstanbul: Tarih Vakfı Yurt Yayınları, 155–81.

Kırkıncı, Mehmet (2004) *Hayatım Hatıralarım*. İstanbul: Zafer.

Kırmızı, Abdülhamit (2019a) '19. Yüzyılı Laiksizleştirmek: Osmanlı-Türk Laikleştirme Anlatısının Sorunları', *Cogito* 94, 1–17.

Kırmızı, Abdülhamit (2019b) '(Vefayat/Obituary) – Şeriat, Tarikat, Tanzimat: Butrus Abu-Manneh (1932–2018)', *İslam Araştırmaları Dergisi* 42, 189–93.

Kırmızı, Abdülhamit (2021) 'Şer'an Olamadığı Halde Kanunen ve Nizamen: Osmanlı Uleması ve Tanzimat', *Sahn-ı Semân'dan Dârülfünûn'a: XIX. Yüzyıl Osmanlı'da İlim ve Fikir Dünyası*. İstanbul: Zeytinburnu Belediyesi Kültür Yayınları, 31–71.

Kırmızı, Abdulhamit (2022) 'Günlükten Sonra Hayat: Bir Asker Günlüğünün Biyografiyle İlişkisi', *Toplumsal Tarih Akademi* 1, 40–62.

Klein, Janet (2011) *The Margins of Empire Kurdish Militias in the Ottoman Tribal Zone*. Stanford: Stanford University Press.

Koca, Selçuk (2019) 'Atatürk'ü Koruma Kanunu', in Mete Kaan Kaynar (ed.), *Türkiye'nin 1950'li Yılları*. İstanbul: İletişim, 321–30.

Koçak, Cemil (2002) 'Türk Milliyetçiliğinin İslam'la Buluşması: Büyük Doğu', in Tanıl Bora (ed.), *Modern Türkiye'de Siyasi Düşünce: Milliyetçilik*, vol. 4. İstanbul: İletişim.

Koçan, Gürcan and Ahmet Öncü (2004) 'Citizen Alevi in Turkey: beyond confirmation and denial', *Journal of Historical Sociology* 17/4, 464–89.

Koçunyan, Aylin (2018) *Negotiating the Ottoman Constitution 1839–1876*. Paris: Peeters Paris.

Komşuoğlu, Ayşegül and Gül M. Kurtoğlu-Eskişar (2009) 'İslamcılık ve Türkiye Üzerine Karşılaştırmalı bir Değerlendirme', in Ayşegül Komşuoğlu and Gül M. Kurtoğlu Eskişar (eds), *Siyasal İslamın Farklı Yüzleri*. İstanbul: Profil Yayıncılık.

Koyuncu, Büke (2014) *'Benim Milletim...' AK Parti İktidarı, Din ve Ulusal Kimlik*. İstanbul: İletişim.

Koyuncu-Lorasdağı, Berrin (2010) 'The prospects and pitfalls of the religious nationalist movement in Turkey: the case of Gülen movement', *Middle Eastern Studies* 46/2, 221–34.

Köker, Levent (1990) *Modernleşme, Kemalizm ve Demokrasi*. İstanbul: İletişim.

Köker, Levent (1997) 'National identity and state legitimacy: contradictions of Turkey's democratic experience', in Elizabeth Özdalga and Sune Persson (eds),

Civil Society, Democracy and the Muslim World. Swedish Research Institute in Istanbul Transactions, vol. 7, Istanbul: Swedish Research Institute, 63–72.

Köksal, Duygu and Anastasia Falierou (eds) (2013) *A Social History of Ottoman Women: New Perspectives*. Leiden: Brill.

Köprülü, M. Fuat (1931) 'Bizans müesseselerinin Osmanlı müesseselerine te'siri hakkında bazı mülahazalar', *Türk Hukuk ve İktisat Tarihi Mecmuası* 1, 165–314.

Köroğlu, Erol (2007) *Ottoman Propaganda and Turkish Identity: Literature in Turkey During World War I*. London: Tauris Academic Studies.

Köse, Ahmet Haşim and Serdal Bahçe (2009) '"Hayırsever" Devletin Yükselişi: AKP Yönetiminde Gelir Dağılımı ve Yoksulluk', in İlhan Uzgel and Bülent Duru (eds), *AKP Kitabı: Bir Dönüşümün Bilançosu*. Ankara: Phoenix, 492–509.

Kratochvíl, Petr (2019) 'Religion as a weapon: invoking religion in secularized societies', *The Review of Faith & International Affairs* 17/1, 78–88.

Kreiser, Klaus ([2010] 2018) *Atatürk: Bir Biyografi*. Translated by Dilek Zaptçıoğlu. İstanbul: İletişim.

Kum, Berivan, Fatma Gülçiçek, Pınar Selek and Yeşim Başaran (2005) *Özgürlüğü Ararken: Kadın Hareketinde Mücadele Deneyimleri*. İstanbul: Amargi Yayıncılık.

Kurban, Dilek (2014) 'The Kurdish question: law, politics, and the limits of recognition', in Carmen Rodriguez, Antonio Avalos, Hakan Yılmaz and Ana I. Planet (eds), *Turkey's Democratization Process*. London: Routledge, 345–60.

Kurt, Mehmet (2015) *Din, Şiddet ve Aidiyet: Türkiye'de Hizbullah*. İstanbul: İletişim.

Kurt, Mehmet (2016) 'Ulus-Devlet Ümmetçiliğine Dindar Muhalefet: Kürt Muhafazakârlıkları', in A. Çağlar Deniz (ed.), *Öteki Muhafazakarlık*. Ankara: Phoenix Yayınevi, 351–84.

Kurt-Güveloğlu, Gülşah (2016) 'Demokrat Parti'nin Kadın Milletvekillerinden Nazlı Tlabar (1950–1960)', *Tarih ve Gelecek Dergisi* 2/2, 9–35.

Kuru, Ahmet T. (2009) *Secularism and State Policies toward Religion: The United States, France and Turkey*. New York: Cambridge University Press.

Kuru, Ahmet T. (2019) *Islam, Authoritarianism and Underdevelopment: A Global and Historical Comparison*. New York: Cambridge University Press.

Kuru, Zeynep Akbulut and Ahmet T. Kuru (2008) 'Apolitical interpretation of Islam: Said-Nursi's faith based activism in comparison with political Islamism and Sufism', *Islam and Christian-Muslim Relations* 19/1, 99–111.

Kushner, David (1987) 'The place of the Ulema in the Ottoman Empire during the Age of Reform (1839–1918)', *Turcica* 19, 51–74.

Kutay, Cemal (2022) *Kurtuluşun ve Cumhuriyetin Manevi Mimarları*. Ankara: Diyanet İşleri Başkanlığı Yayını.

Kuyucu, Ali Tuna (2005) 'Ethno-religious "unmixing" of "Turkey": 6–7 September riots as a case in Turkish nationalism', *Nations & Nationalism* 11/3, 361–80.

Küçük, Murat (2007) 'Türkiye'de Sol Düşünce ve Aleviler', in Murat Gültekingil (ed.), *Modern Türkiye'de Siyasi Düşünce: Sol*, vol. 8. İstanbul: İletişim, 896–934.

Kürkçü, Ertuğrul (2007) 'Türkiye Sosyalist Hareketine Silahlı Mücadelenin Girişi', in Murat Gültekingil (ed.), *Modern Türkiye'de Siyasi Düşünce: Sol*, vol. 8. İstanbul: İletişim, 494–9.

Kürkçügil, Masis (2023) *Bir Başka Tarih Mümkün müydü? Ermeni Meselesi Üzerine Yazılar*. İstanbul: Ayrıntı.

Laçiner, Ömer (2001) 'Hayata dönüş', *Birikim* 142–3, 10–52.

Lerner, Hanna (2014) 'Critical junctures, religion, and personal status regulations in Israel and India', *Law and Social Inquiry* 39/2, 387–415.

Levi, Avner (1996) '1934 Trakya Yahudileri Olayı: Alınmayan Ders', *Tarih ve Toplum* 151 (July).

Levy, Avigdor (ed.) (1994) *The Jews of the Ottoman Empire*. Princeton, NJ: Darwin.

Lewis, Bernard (1961) *The Emergence of Modern Turkey*. London: Oxford University Press.

Lewis, Bernard (1988) *The Political Language of Islam*. Chicago: University of Chicago Press.

Lewis, Bernard (2002) *What Went Wrong: Clash Between Islam and Modernity in the Middle East*. New York: Perennial.

Lewis, Bernard (2004) *The Crisis of Islam: Holy War and Unholy Terror*. London: Phoenix.

Lewis, Geoffrey (1999) *The Turkish Language Reform: A Catastrophic Success*. Oxford: Oxford University Press.

Lord, Ceren (2018) *Religious Politics in Turkey: From the Birth of the Republic to the AKP*. Cambridge: Cambridge University Press.

Lüküslü, Demet (2017) '12 Eylül Rejiminin Gençlik Algısı', in R. Funda Barbaros and Erik Jan Zurcher (eds), *Modernizmin Yansımaları: 80'li Yıllarda Türkiye*. Ankara: Efil Yayınevi, 338–47.

Macar, Elçin (2003) *Cumhuriyet Döneminde İstanbul Rum Patrikhanesi*. İstanbul: İletişim.

Macar, Elçin (2021) *İmroz'dan İstanbul'a: Patrik Bartholomeos*. İstanbul: Doğan Kitap.

Macauley, Melissa (2009) 'A world made simple: law and property in the Ottoman and Qing Empires', in Huri İslamoğlu and Peter C. Perdue (eds), *Shared Histories of Modernity: China, India and the Ottoman Empire*. New Delhi: Routlege, 273–98.

Mahoney, James and Dietrich Rueschemeyer (2003) *Comparative Historical Analysis in the Social Sciences*. New York: Cambridge University Press.

Makal, Ahmet (2012) 'Türkiye'de Kadın Emeğinin Tarihsel Kökenleri: 1920–1960', in Ahmet Makal and Gülay Toksöz (eds), *Geçmişten Günümüze Türkiye'de Kadın Emeği*. Ankara: Ankara Üniversitesi Yayınları, 38–116.

Mango, Andrew (1999) *Atatürk*. London: John Murray.

Mann, Michael (2005) *The Dark Side of Democracy: Explaining Ethnic Cleansing*. New York: Cambridge University Press.

Mardin, Şerif (1962) *The Genesis of Young Ottoman Thought: A Study in the Modernization of Turkish Political Ideas*. Princeton, NJ: Princeton University Press.

Mardin, Şerif (1973) 'Center-periphery: a key to Turkish politics', *Deadalus* 102, 169–90.

Mardin, Şerif (1981) 'Religion and secularism in Turkey', in Ali Kazancıgil and Ergun Özbudun (eds), *Atatürk: Founder of a Modern State*. London: Hurst & Company.

Mardin, Şerif (1984) '"Aydınlar" Konusunda Ülgener ve Bir İzah Denemesi', *Toplum ve Bilim* 24, 9–15.

Mardin, Şerif (1989) *Religion and Social Change in Modern Turkey: The Case of Bediüzzaman Said Nursi*. Albany: State University of New York Press.

Mardin, Şerif (1991) 'The just and the unjust', *Deadalus* 120, 113–29.

Mardin, Şerif (1997) 'The Ottoman Empire', in Karen Barkey and Mark von Hagen (eds), *After Empire:Multi-Ethnic Societies and Nation-Building: the Soviet Union and Russian, Ottoman and Habsburg Empires*. Boulder: Westview Press, 115–28.

Mardin, Şerif (2006) *Religion, Society, and Modernity in Turkey*. Syracuse: Syracuse University Press.

Maritato, Chiara (2020) *Women, Religion, and the State in Contemporary Turkey*. Cambridge: Cambridge University Press.

Markova, Zina (1983) 'Russia and the Bulgarian-Greek Church question in the seventies of the 19th century', *Etudes Historiques* 11, 159–97.

Massicard, Elise (2006) 'Claiming difference in an unitarist frame: the case of Alevism', in Hans-Lukas Kieser (ed.), *Turkey Beyond Nationalism: Towards Post-Nationalist Identities*. London: I. B. Tauris, 74–82.

Massicard, Elise (2007) *Türkiye'den Avrupa'ya Alevi Hareketin Siyasallaşması*. Translated by Ali Berktay. İstanbul: İletişim.

Massicard, Elise (2013) 'Aleviler: Cumhuriyet Tarihyazımında Unutulan Özneler?', in Bülent Bilmez (ed.), *Cumhuriyet Tarihinin Tartışmalı Konuları*. İstanbul: Tarih Vakfı Yurt Yayınları, 140–50.

Matschke, Klaus-Peter (2002) 'Research problems concerning the transition to *Tourkokratia:* the Byzantinist standpoint', in Fikret Adanır and Suraiya Faroqhi (eds), *The Ottomans and the Balkans: A Discussion of Historiography*. Leiden: Brill, 79–114.

Mavrogordatos, George H. (2003) 'Orthodoxy and Nationalism in the Greek case', in John T. S. Madeley and Zsolt Enyedi (eds), *Church and State in Contemporary Europe: The Chimera of Neutrality*. London: Frank Cass, 117–36.

McClintock, Anne (1993) 'Family feuds: gender, nationalism and the family', *Feminist Review* 44, 61–80.

McPherson, David (2018) 'Three rival versions of the relationship of religion to modernity', *Journal of Religion & Society* – Supplement Series 17, 11–31.

Mecellem, Jessica G. (2016) 'Human rights trials in an era of democratic stagnation: the case of Turkey', *Law & Social Enquiry* 43/1, 119–51.

Meeker, Michael (2002) *A Nation of Empire: The Ottoman Legacy of Turkish Modernity*. Berkeley: University of California Press.

Meinardus, Otto (1999) *Two Thousand Years of Coptic Christianity*. Cairo: American University in Cairo Press.

Merdjanova, Ina (2018) 'Islam and the Kurdish peace process in Turkey (2013–2015)', in Emel Elif Tuğdar and Serhun Al (eds), *Comparative Kurdish Politics in the Middle East: Actors, Ideas and Interests*. New York: Palgrave Macmillan, 137–62.

Meriç, Nevin (2014) 'Siyaset Fetva İlişkisi: Birinci Dünya Savaşında Cihat Fetvası', Akdeniz Üniversitesi Birinci Dünya Savaşının 100. Sempozyumu: Savaşan Devletlerin Tarihçilerinin Gözüyle 100. Yılında I. Dünya Savaşı. Akdeniz Üniversitesi online publication.

Mert, Hamdi (1992) 'Kapak Gündemi', *Diyanet Aylık Dergi* 13.

Mert, Hamdi (2017) *Din ü Devlet Mülk ü Millet: Bir Ömrün Hikayesi*. Edited by Hicret K. Toprak. Ankara: Sistem Ofset Basım Yayın.

Michel, S. J. Thomas (2008) 'Peaceful movements in the Muslim world', in Thomas Banchoff (ed.), *Religious Pluralism, Globalization, and World Politics*. Oxford: Oxford University Press.

Millas, Herkül (ed.) (2001) *Göç: Rumlar'ın Anadolu'dan Mecburi Ayrılışı (1919–1923)*. Çev. Damla Demirözü. İstanbul: İletişim.

Miller, Ruth (2005) *Legislating Authority: Sin and Crime in the Ottoman Empire and Turkey*. New York: Routledge.

Modood, Tariq (2010) 'Moderate secularism, religion as identity and respect for religion', *The Political Quarterly* 81/1, 4–14.

Morris, Benny and Dror Zeevi (2019) *The Thirty-Year Genocide: Turkey's Destruction of its Christian Minorities 1894–1924*. Cambridge, MA: Harvard University Press.

Muedini, Fait (2021) 'Justice and Development (AKP) attitudes towards the LGBTI community in Turkey', in Hasan Aydın and Winston Langley (eds), *Human Rights in Turkey: Assaults on Human Dignity*. Cham: Springer, 131–40.

Mumcu, Uğur (ed.) ([1977] 2006) *Kazım Karabekir Anlatıyor*. 24th edn. Ankara: um:ag Vakfı Yayınları.

Mumcu, Uğur (1987) *Rabıta*. İstanbul: Tekin Yayınevi.

Mutluer, Nil (2014) 'Yapısal, Sosyal ve Ekonomi Politik Yönleriyle Diyanet İşleri Başkanlığı', *Sosyo-Ekonomik Politikalar Bağlamında Diyanet İşleri Başkanlığı: Kamuoyunun Diyanet'e Bakışı, Tartışmalar ve Öneriler*. İstanbul: Helsinki Yurttaşlar Derneği Yayınları.

Mutluer, Nil (2018) 'Diyanet's role in building the "*Yeni* (New) *Milli*" in the AKP era', *European Journal of Turkish Studies* 27. Available at: https://doi.org/10.4000/ejts.5953.

Müftügil, Ayşe Seda (2015) 'Education and religious minorities in Turkey: the story behind the introduction of compulsory religion courses', in Michael Rectenwald, Rochelle Almeida and George Levine (eds), *Global Secularisms in a Post-Secular Age*. Boston: De Gruyter, 189–204.

Nadi, Yunus (1957) *Birinci Türkiye Büyük Millet Meclisinin Açılışı ve İsyanlar*. İstanbul: Sel Yayınları.

Navarro-Yashin, Yael (2002) *Faces of the State: Secularism and Public Life in Turkey*. Princeton, NJ: Princeton University Press.

Nesin, Aziz (1986) 'Aziz Nesin'in 6/7 Eylül (Hapishane) Anıları', *Tarih ve Toplum* 7/34, 48.

Neumann, Christoph ([1994] 1999) *Araç Tarih Amaç Tanzimat: Tarih-i Cevdet'in Siyasi Anlamı*. Translated from the German by Meltem Arun. İstanbul: Tarih Vakfı Yurt Yayınları.

Neumann, Christoph (2002) 'Bad times and better self: definitions of identity and strategies for development in late Ottoman historiography, 1850–1900', in Fikret Adanır and Suraiya Faroqhi (eds), *The Ottomans and the Balkans: A Discussion of Historiography*. Leiden: Brill, 57–78.

Nugent, John T. Jr (2004) 'The defeat of Turkish Hizbollah as a model of counter-terrorism strategy', *Middle East Review of International Affairs* 8/1, 69–75.

Ocak, Ahmet Yaşar ([1980] 2000) *Babailer İsyanı: Aleviliğin Tarihsel Altyapısı yahut Anadolu'da İslam-Türk Heterodoksisinin Teşekkülü*. İstanbul: Dergâh Yayınları.

Ocak, Ahmet Yaşar (1999) *Türkler, Türkiye ve İslam: Yaklaşım, Yöntem ve Yorum Denemeleri*. İstanbul: İletişim.

Ocak, Ahmet Yaşar (2021) *Osmanlı İmparatorluğu ve İslam: Bir İmparatorluk Bir Din*. İstanbul: Alfa.

Oktay-Uslu, Zeynep (2020) 'Alevism as Islam: rethinking Shahab Ahmed's conceptualization of Islam through poetry', *British Journal of Middle Eastern Studies* 49/2, 1–22.

Okyar, Fethi (1980) *Üç Devir'de bir Adam*. Edited by Cemal Kuntay. İstanbul: Tercüman Yayınları.

Okyar, Ali Fethi (1987) *Serbest Cumhuriyet Fırkası Nasıl Doğdu, Nasıl Fesh Edildi?* İstanbul: Ketebe Yayınları.

Oppong, Steward Harrison (2013) 'Religion and identity', *American International Journal of Contemporary Research* 3/6, 10–16.

Oran, Baskın (2004) *Türkiye'de azınlıklar: Kavramlar, Teori, Lozan, İç Mevzuat, İçtihat, Uygulama*. İstanbul: İletişim.

Oran, Baskın (2011) *Türkiyeli Gayrımüslimler Üzerine Yazılar*. Edited by Ülkü Özen. İstanbul: İletişim.

Ortaylı, İlber (1999) 'The policy of the Sublime-Porte towards Naqshibendis and other *tariqas* during the Tanzimat period', translated from Turkish by Sylvia Zeybekoğlu, in Elizabeth Özdalga (ed.) *Naqshbandis in Western and Central Asia* (papers read at a conference held at the Swedish Research Institute in Istanbul, 9–11 June 1997), Swedish Research Institute in Istanbul Transactions, vol. 9, 67–72.

Ortaylı, İlber (2021) *The Empire's Longest Century*. Translated by Jonathan Ross. Istanbul: Kronik Books.

Ozan, Ebru Deniz (2015) 'İki Darbe Arasında Kriz Sarmalı', in Gökhan Atılgan (ed.), *Osmanlı'dan Günümüze Türkiye'de Siyasal Hayat*. İstanbul: Yordam Kitap, 658–746.

Ozzano, Luca and Chiara Maritato (2019) 'Patterns of political secularism in Italy and Turkey: the Vatican and the Diyanet to the test of politics', *Politics and Religion* 12, 457–77.

Öcal, Mustafa (ed.) (2008) *Tanıkların Dilinden Cumhuriyet Dönemi Din Eğitimi ve Dini Hayat*. İstanbul: Ensar Neşriyat.

Ökte, Faik (1951) *Varlık Vergisi Faciası*. İstanbul: Nebioğlu Yayınevi.

Öktem, Kerem (2011) *Angry Nation: Turkey since 1989*. London: Zed Books.

Öktem, Kerem (2012) 'Global Diyanet and multiple networks: Turkey's new presence in the Balkans", *Journal of Muslims in Europe* 1/1, 27–58.

Ökten, Nazlı (2006) 'An endless death and an eternal mourning: November 10 in Turkey', in Esra Özyürek (ed.), *Politics of Public Memory: Production and Erasure of the Past in Turkey*. Syracuse: Syracuse University Press, 95–113.

Öngider, Seyfi (2009) 'Kemalist Rejimin İnşası: Takrir-i Sükûn Kanunu', in Ömer Laçiner (ed.), *Modern Türkiye'de Siyasi Düşünce: Dönemler ve Zihniyetler*, vol. 9. İstanbul: İletişim, 312–18.

Öniş, Ziya (2009) 'Conservative globalism at the crossroads: the Justice and Development Party and the thorny path to democratic consolidation in Turkey', *Mediterranean Politics* 14/1, 21–40.

Öz, Asım (2017) 'Manevi İmar ile İslam İnkılabı Arasında: Altmışlı Yıllarda İslam Davası Etrafındaki Vaziyet Alışlar Üzerine', in Mete Kaan Kaynar (ed.). *Türkiye'nin 1960'lı Yılları*. İstanbul: İletişim, 591–632.

Öz, Eyüp (2019) *Serbest Cumhuriyet Fırkası ve Muhalif Ege: Ege Gezisinden Menemen Olayı'na Güçlü bir Seferberliğin Sosyopolitik Tarihi*. İstanbul: İletişim.

Özal, Korkut (1999) 'Twenty years with Mehmed Zahid Kotku: a personal story', in Elizabeth Özdalga (ed.), *Naqshbandis in Western and Central Asia: Change and Continuity*. Swedish Research Institute in Istanbul Transactions, vol. 9. İstanbul: Swedish Research Institute, 159–85.

Özbek, Meral (1991) *Popular Kültür ve Orhan Gencebay Arabeski*. İstanbul: İletişim.

Özbudun, Ergun (2012) 'Turkey – plural society and monolithic state', in Ahmet T. Kuru and Alfred Stephan (eds), *Democracy, Islam and Secularism in Turkey*. New York: Columbia University Press.

Özdalga, Elizabeth (1998) *The Veiling Issue, Official Secularism and Popular Islam in Modern Turkey*. London: RoutledgeCurzon.

Özdalga, Elizabeth (2000) 'Worldly asceticism in Islamic casting: Fethullah Gülen's inspired piety and activism', *Critique* 17, 83–104.

Özdalga, Elizabeth (2008) 'The Alevis – a new religious minority? Identity politics in Turkey and its relation to the EU integration process', in Dietrich Jung and Catharina Raudvere (eds), *Religion, Politics, and Turkey's EU Accession*. New York: Palgrave Macmillan.

Özdalga, Elizabeth (2010) 'Transformation of Sufi-based communities in modern Turkey: the Nakşibendis, the Nurcus, and the Gülen community', in Celia Kerslake, Kerem Öktem and Philip Robins (eds), *Turkey's Engagement with Modernity: Conflict and Change in the Twentieth Century*. London: Palgrave Macmillan (in association with St Antony's College, Oxford), 69–91.

Özdalga, Elizabeth (2022) *Pulpit, Mosque and Nation: Turkish Friday Sermons as Text and Ritual*. Edinburgh: Edinburgh University Press.

Özdamar, Mustafa (2008) *'Hadim-ül Kur'an' Üstaz Süleyman Hilmi Tunahan*. İstanbul: Kırk Kandil.

Özdemir, Adil and Kenneth Frank (2000) *Visible Islam in Modern Turkey*. London: Macmillan.

Özdemir, Şennur (2004) 'MÜSİAD ve Hak-İş'I Birlikte Anlamak: Sınıflı bir 'İslami Ekonomi' mi?', in Yasin Aktay (ed.), *Modern Türkiye'de Siyasi Düşünce: İslamcılık*, vol. 6. İstanbul: İletişim, 837–69.

Özdemir, Veli (1997) *İfade Tutanakları: Susurluk Belgeleri*, 2 vols. İstanbul: Scala Yayıncılık.
Özdemirci, İlbey C. N. (2022) *Fötr Şapkalı Şıh: Cumhuriyet Sekülerleşmesi ve Taşra*. İstanbul: İletişim.
Özel, Soli (2003) 'Turkey at the polls: after the tsunami', *Journal of Democracy* 14/2, 80–94.
Özen, Haldun (2002) *Entellektüelin Dramı 12 Eylül'ün Cadı Kazanı*. Ankara: İmge Kitapevi.
Özgöker, Uğur and Zekeriya Alperen Bedirhan (2018) 'Relations between the EU and Turkey after 2016 Turkish coup d'état attempt', *Journal of International Relations and Foreign Policy* 6/2, 33–41.
Özkan, Behlül (2014) *From the Abode of Islam to the Turkish Vatan: The Making of a National Homeland in Turkey*. New Haven: Yale University Press.
Özkan, Behlül (2015) 'Abdühamid'in ruhunu beklerken: restorasyon, medeniyet ve Davudoğlu', *Birikim* (January–February), 309–10.
Özkan, Behlül (2016) 'Yeni Osmanlıcılık ve Pan-İslamcılık', in Evren Haspolat and Deniz Yıldırım (eds), *Türkiye'de Yeni Siyasal Akımlar (1980 Sonrası)*. Ankara: Siyasal Kitapevi.
Özkırımlı, Umut (2011) 'The changing nature of nationalism in Turkey: actors, discourses, and the struggle for hegemony', in Ayşe Kadıoğlu and E. Fuat Keyman (eds), *Symbiotic Antagonisms: Competing Nationalisms in Turkey*. Salt Lake City: University of Utah Press, 82–100.
Özkırımlı, Umut (ed.) (2014) *The Making of a Protest Movement in Turkey: #occupygezi*. New York: Palgrave (Pivot) Macmillan.
Özkırımlı, Umut (2017) 'How to liquidate a people? Academic freedom in Turkey and beyond', *Globalizations* 14/6, 1–6.
Özkırımlı, Umut and Spyros A. Sofos (2008) *Tormented by History: Nationalism in Greece and Turkey*. London: Hurst.
Özman, Aylin (2007) 'Mehmet Ali Aybar', in Murat Gültekingil (ed.), *Modern Türkiye'de Siyasi Düşünce: Sol*, vol. 8. İstanbul: İletişim, 376–403.
Özoğlu, Hakan (2001) 'Nationalism and Kurdish notables in the late Ottoman–early republican era', *International Journal of Middle East Studies* 33, 383–409.
Özoğlu, Hakan (2011) *From Caliphate to Secular State: Power Struggle in the Early Turkish Republic*. Santa Barbara: Praeger.
Özteke, Fahri (2019) 'İbadet Dilinin Sadeleştirilmesine Din Adamlarının Verdiği Refleksler (Tanzimat, Meşrutiyet ve Milli Mücadele Dönemlerinde)', in Burak Kocaoğlu (ed.), *Tarih Yolunda Bir Ömür: Prof. Dr. İsmail Özçelik'e Armağan*. Ankara: Berikan Yayınevi.

Öztığ, Laçin İdil and Umut Can Adısönmez (2023) 'Sovereignity, power and authority: understanding the conversion of Hagia Sophia from a performative perspective', *Southeast European and Black Sea Studies*, doi:10.1080/14683857.2023.2189543.

Öztoprak, Sadreddin (2003) *Şark Medreselerinde Bir Ömür*. İstanbul: Beyan Yayınları.

Öztürk, Ahmet Erdi (2019) 'An alternative reading of religion and authoritarianism: the new logic between religion and state in the AKP's new Turkey', *Southeast European and Black Sea Studies* 19/1, 79–98.

Öztürk, Ahmet Erdi (2021) *Religion, Identity and Power: Turkey and the Balkans in the Twenty-first Century*. Edinburgh: Edinburgh University Press.

Öztürk, Ahmet Erdi and İştar Gözaydın (2017) 'Turkey's constitutional amendments: a critical perspective', *Research and Policy on Turkey* 2/2, 210–24.

Öztürk, Ahmet Erdi and İştar Gözaydın (2018) 'A frame for Turkey's foreign policy via the Diyanet in the Balkans', *Journal of Muslims in Europe* 7/3, 331–50.

Öztürk, Ahmet Erdi and İştar Gözaydın (2020) 'Turkey: religious assistance in prisons – state monopoly of religious service', in Julia Martinez-Arino and Anne-Laure Zwilling (eds), *Religion and Prison: An Overview of Contemparary Europe*. Cham: Springer, 391–400.

Öztürk, Ahmet Erdi and Semiha Sözeri (2018) 'Diyanet as a Turkish foreign policy tool: evidence from the Netherlands and Bulgaria', *Politics and Religion* 11/3, 624–48.

Öztürk, Mahmut (2019) 'Diyanet İşleri Başkanı Eyüp Sabri Hayırlıoğlu ile Yaşanan Latince Kur'an Polemiği', *İSTEM* 33, 65–87.

Öztürk, Saygı (2019) *Menzil: Bir tarikatın iki yüzü*. İstanbul: Doğan Kitap.

Özyürek, Esra (2006) *Nostalgia for the Modern: State Secularism and Everyday Politics in Turkey*. Durham, NC: Duke University Press.

Pamuk, Şevket (1987) *The Ottoman Empire and European Capitalism, 1820-1913: Trade, Investment and Production*. Cambridge: Cambridge University Press.

Park, Bill (2012) *Modern Turkey: People, State and Foreign Policy in a Globalized World*. London: Routledge.

Parla, Taha (1985) *The Social and Political Thought of Ziya Gökalp 1876–1924*. Leiden: Brill.

Parla, Taha (1991a) *Türkiye'de Siyasal Kültürün resmi Kaynakları v. 1: Atatürk'ün Nutuk'u*. İstanbul: İletişim.

Parla, Taha (1991b) *Türkiye'de Siyasal Kültürün resmi Kaynakları v. 2: Atatürk'ün Söylev ve Demeçleri*. İstanbul: İletişim.

Parlak, Deniz (2020) 'Paravanın Arkasından Çıkıp Mekanı Dönüştürmek: Kadınlar Camilerde', in Feryal Saygılıgil and Sacide Berber (eds), *Modern Türkiye'de Siyasi Düşünce: Feminizm*, vol. 10. İstanbul: İletişim, 251–9.

Paşaoğlu, Mehmet Talha (2019) *Din, Devlet, Millet: Diyanet İşleri'nin 95 Yıllık Hikayesi*. İstanbul: Libra.

Pervan, Muazzez (2021) *İlerici Kadınlar Derneği (1975–1980): 'Kırmızı Çatkılı Kadınlar'ın Tarihi*. İstanbul: Tarih Vakfı Yurt Yayınları.

Philliou, Christine (2011) *Biography of an Empire: Governing Ottomans in an Age of Revolution*. Berkeley: University of California Press.

Philpott, Daniel (2007) 'Explaining the political ambivalence of religion', *American Political Science Review* 101/3, 505–25.

Pierson, Paul (2000) 'Increasing returns, path dependence, and the study of politics', *American Political Science Review* 94/2, 251–67.

Pirili, Mustafa and Meneviş Uzbay (2017) '1990'lı yıllarda Türkiye'de Siyaset: Devlet ve Hegemonya Krizi', in R. Funda Barbaros and Erik Jan Zurcher (eds), *Modernizmin Yansımaları: 90'lı Yıllarda Türkiye*. Ankara: Efil Yayınevi, 180–208.

Pusch, Barbara (2000) 'Stepping into the public sphere: the rise of Islamist and religious-conservative women's non-governmental organizations', in Stephan Yerasimos, Gunter Seufert and Karin Vorhoff (eds), *Civil Society in the Grip of Nationalism*. İstanbul: Orient-Institut, Istanbul and Institut Français d'Etudes Anatoliennes publication, 475–505.

Quataert, Donald (2005) *The Ottoman Empire, 1700–1922*. New York: Cambridge University Press.

Rahman, Fazlur (1982) *Islam and Modernity: Transformation of an Intellectual Tradition*. Chicago: University of Chicago Press.

Ramazanoğlu, Yıldız (ed.) (2000) *Osmanlıdan Cumhuriyete Kadının Tarihi Dönüşümü*. İstanbul: Pınar.

Reed, Fred A. (1999) *Anatolia Junction: A Journey into Hidden Turkey*. Burnaby: Talonbooks.

Robinson, Richard D. (1965) *The First Turkish Republic: A Case Study in National Development*. Cambridge, MA: Harvard University Press.

Romain Örs, İlay (2019) *İstanbullu Rumlar ve 1964 Sürgünleri: Tütk Toplumunun Homojenleşmesinde Bir Dönüm Noktası*, 2nd edn. İstanbul: İletişim.

Rosati, Massimo (2015) *The Making of a Postsecular Society: A Durkheimian Approach to Memory, Pluralism and Religion in Turkey*. Aldershot: Ashgate.

Rosli, Nurhidayu (2022) 'Transformation of religious institution in Turkey from the Ottoman Sheik ul-Islam to the modern *Diyanet* institution', *Journal of Islamic Thought and Civilization* 12/1, 1–22.

Rubin, Avi (2011) *Ottoman Nizamiye Courts: Law and Modernity*. New York: Palgrave.

Salmoni, Barak A. (2000) 'Islam in Turkish pedagogic attitudes and education materials: 1923–1950', *The Turkish Studies Association Bulletin* 24/2, 23–61.

Sancar, Serpil (2012) *Türk Modernleşmesinin Cinsiyeti: Erkekler Devlet Kadınlar Aile Kurar*. İstanbul: İletişim.

Sargın, Güven Arif (2012) '*Sincan*, a town on the verge of *civic* breakdown: the spatialization of identity politics and resistance', in Alev Çınar, Srirupa Roy and Maha Yahya (eds), *Visualizing Secularism and Religion: Egypt, Lebanon, Turkey, India*. Ann Arbor: University of Michigan Press, 258–80.

Sarıçoban, Gülay (2019) 'The second group in the first Turkish Grand National Assembly', *Gaziantep University Journal of Social Sciences* 187/4, 1574–91.

Sarıtaş, Ezgi and Yelda Şahin (2019) 'Ellili Yıllarda Kadın Hareketi', in Mete Kaan Kaynar (ed.), *Türkiye'nin 1950'li Yılları*. İstanbul: İletişim, 627–65.

Satterthwaite, Joseph C. (1972) 'The Truman Doctrine: Turkey', *The Annals of the American Academy of Political and Social Science* 401, 74–84.

Schüler, Herald (1999) *Türkiye'de Sosyal Demokrasi: Particilik, Hemşehrilik, Alevilik*. Translated by Yılmaz Tonbul, edited by Tanıl Bora. İstanbul: İletişim.

Sertdemir-Özdemir, Seçkin, Nil Mutluer and Esra Özyürek (2017) 'Exile and plurality in neoliberal times: Turkey's Academics for Peace', *Public Culture* 31/2.

Seufert, Günter and Petra Weyland (1994) 'National events and the struggle for the fixing of meaning: a comparison of the symbolic dimensions of the funeral services for Atatürk and Özal', *New Perspectives on Turkey* 11, 71–98.

Sevimli, A. Güçlü (2010) *Hayata Dönüş Operasyonu: Koğuştan Hücrelere*. İstanbul: Çağdaş Hukukçular Derneği Yayınları.

Sevinç, Murat (2010) 'AKP'nin Kapatılma Davası', in İlhan Uzgel and Bülent Duru (eds), *AKP Kitabı: Bir Dönüşümün Bilançosu*, 2nd edn. Ankara: Phoenix, 264–79.

Sezal, İhsan and İhsan Dağı (eds) (2001) *Özal: Siyaset, İktisat, Zihniyet*. İstanbul: Boyut Kitapları.

Sezer-Şanlı, Ayşem (2019) 6–7 Eylül 1955: Türkiye'de Bir "Pogrom" Yaşandı', in Mete Kaan Kaynar (ed.), *Türkiye'nin 1950'li Yılları*. İstanbul: İletişim, 377–92.

Shaheen, Kareem (2017) 'Turkish LGBTI activists "illegal" ban on events in Ankara', *The Guardian*, 20 November. Available at: https://www.theguardian.com/world/2017/nov/20/turkey-bans-lgbti-events-ankara-public-order.

Shakman Hurd, Elizabeth (2011) 'A suspension of (dis)belief: the secular-religious binary and the study of international relations', in Craig Calhoun, Mark Juergensmeyer and Jonathan Van Antwerpen (eds), *Rethinking Secularism*. Oxford: Oxford University Press, 166–84.

Shakman Hurd, Elizabeth (2015) *Beyond Religious Freedom: The New Global Politics of Religion*. Princeton, NJ: Princeton University Press.

Shankland, David (1999) *Islam and Society in Turkey*. Huntingdon: The Eothen Press.

Shankland, David (2003) *The Alevis in Turkey: The Emergence of a Secular Islamic Tradition*. London: Routledge.

Shankland, David (2006) *Structure and Function in Turkish Society: Essays on Religion, Politics and Social Change*. Istanbul: ISIS Press.

Shaw, Stanford and Ezel Shaw (1977) *History of the Ottoman Empire and Modern Turkey, v. II: Reform, Revolution and Republic – the Rise of Modern Turkey, 1808–1974*. Cambridge: Cambridge University Press.

Sırma, İhsan Süreyya (2022) *Sultan II. Abdülhamid Dönemi Şeyhülislamları ve Şeyhülislamlık Müesesesi*. İstanbul: Beyan.

Silier, Orhan (2007) 'TİP'in İkinci Dönemi: "Daha İyi Yenilmek" Olanaklı mıydı?', in Murat Gültekingil (ed.), *Modern Türkiye'de Siyasi Düşünce: Sol*, vol. 8. İstanbul: İletişim, 432–76.

Silverstein, Brian (2010) *Islam and Modernity in Turkey*. New York: Palgrave.

Singer, Amy (2008) *Charity in Islamic Societies*. Cambridge: Cambridge University Press.

Sitembölükbaşı, Şaban (1995) *Türkiye'de İslamın Yeniden İnkişafı (1950–1960)*. Ankara: Türkiye Diyanet Vakfı Yayınları.

Smith, Jonathan Z. (1998) 'Religion, religions, religious', in Mark C. Taylor (ed.), *Critical Terms for Religious Studies*. Chicago: University of Chicago Press, 269–84.

Soane, Ely Bannister (1912) *To Mesopotamia and Kurdistan in Disguise: with Historical Notices of the Kurdish Tribes and the Chaldeans of Kurdistan*. London: Maynard and Company.

Somay Bülent (2014) *The Psychopolitics of the Oriental Father: Between Omnipotence and Emasculation*. London: Palgrave Macmillan.

Somel, Selçuk Akşin (1987) 'Sırat-ı Müstakim: Islamic Modernist Thought in the Ottoman Empire, 1908–1912', MA thesis, Boğaziçi Üniversitesi Sosyal Bilimler Enstitüsü.

Somel, Selçuk Akşin, Christoph K. Neumann and Amy Singer (2011) 'Introduction: Re-sounding silent voices', in Amy Singer, Christoph K. Neumann and Selçuk Akşit Somel (eds), *Untold Histories of the Middle East: Recovering Voices from the 19th and 20th Centuries*. London: Routledge, 1–22.

Somer, Murat (2007) 'Defensive and liberal nationalisms: the Kurdish question and modernization/democratization', in E. Fuat Keyman (ed.), *Remaking Turkey: Globalization, Alternative Modernities and Democracy*. Plymouth: Lexington Books.

Somer, Murat (2015) 'Whither with secularism or just undemocratic *laiklik*? The evolution and future of secularism under the AKP', in Valeria Talbot (ed.), *The Uncertain Path of The 'New Turkey'*. Milan: ISPI – Istituto per gli Studi di Politica Internazionale.

Soysal, Mümtaz and Fazıl Sağlam (1983) 'Türkiye'de Anayasalar', in *Cumhuriyet Dönemi Türkiye Ansiklopedisi*. İstanbul: İletişim, 17–52.

Söyler, Mehtap (2013) 'Informal institutions, forms of state and democracy: the Turkish deep state', *Democratization* 20/2, 310–34.

Sözen, Edibe (2006) 'Gender politics of the JDP', in M. Hakan Yavuz (ed.), *The Emergence of a New Turkey: Democracy and the AK Parti*. Salt Lake City: University of Utah Press, 258–80.

Sözeri, Efe Kerem (2017) 'Freedom of information in Turkey: the death of the free press and the case of Academics for Peace', in Bahar Başer and Ahmet Erdi Öztürk (eds), *Authoritarian Politics in Turkey: Elections, Resistance and the AKP*. London: I. B. Tauris, 213–27.

Stokes, Martin (1994) 'Turkish arabesk and the city: urban popular culture as spatial practice', in Akbar S. Ahmed and Hastings Donnan (eds), *Islam, Globalization and Postmodernity*. London: Routledge, 21–37.

Sunier, Thijl and Nico Landman (2015) *Transnational Turkish Islam: Shifting Geographies of Religious Activism and Community Building in Turkey and Europe*. London: Palgrave Macmillan.

Sunier, Thjil, Nico Landman, Helen van der Linden, Nazlı Bilgili and Alper Bilgili (2011) *The Turkish Directorate for Religious Affairs in a Changing Environment*. Amsterdam/Utrecht: Vrije Universiteit van Amsterdam en Universiteit Utrecht.

Suny, Ronald Grigor (2015) *'They Can Live in the Desert but Nowhere Else': A History of the Armenian Genocide*. Princeton, NJ: Princeton University Press.

Sülker, Kemal (2005) *15–16 Haziran: Türkiye'yi sarsan iki uzun gün*. İstanbul: İleri Yayınları.

Şahin, Yelda and Ezgi Sarıtaş (2017) 'Altmışlı Yıllarda Kadın Hareketi: Süreklilikler, Kopuşlar ve Çeşitlenme', in Mete Kaan Kaynar (ed.), *Türkiye'nin 1960'lı Yılları*. İstanbul: İletişim, 727–58.

Şansal, Barbaros (2021) 'LGBTQ rights in Turkey: do not touch my body!', in Hasan Aydın and Winston Langley (eds), *Human Rights in Turkey: Assaults on Human Dignity*. Cham: Springer, 141–55.

Şapolyo, Enver Behnan (1964) *Mezhepler ve Tarikatlar Tarihi*. İstanbul: Türkiye Yayınevi.

Şar, Edgar (2019) 'Laiklik and nation-building: how state-religion-society relations changed in Turkey under the Justice and Development Party', in Rasim Özgür Dönmez and Ali Yaman (eds), *Modernization: Islam, Islamism and Nationalism in Turkey*. Maryland: Lexington Books, 111–45.

Şefkatli-Tuksal, Hidayet (2000) *Kadın Karşıtı Söylemin İslam Geleneğindeki İzldüşümleri*. Ankara: Kitabiyat.

Şeker, Fatih M. (2007) *Cumhuriyet İdeolojisinin Nakşibendilik Tasavvuru: Şerif Mardin Örneği*. İstanbul: Dergâh yayınları.

Şener, Mustafa (2007) 'Türkiye İşçi Partisi', in Murat Gültekingil (ed.), *Modern Türkiye'de Siyasi Düşünce: Sol*, vol. 8. İstanbul: İletişim, 356–417.

Şimşir, Bilal N. (1992) *Türk Yazı Devrimi*. Ankara: Atatürk Kültür, Dil ve Tarih Yüksek Kurumu Türk Tarih Kurumu Yayınları.

Taglia, Stefano (2015) *Intellectuals and Reform in the Ottoman Empire: Young Turks and the Challenges of Modernity*. London: Routledge.

Taglia, Stefano (2016) 'Ottomanism then and now: historical and contemporary meanings', *Die Welt des Islams* 56/3–4, 279–89.

Tahir, Kemal ([1965] 2016) *Yorgun Savaşçı*. İstanbul: Ithaki.

Talas, Cahit (1957) *Sendika Hürriyeti*. Ankara: Ankara Üniversitesi Siyasal Bilgiler Fakültesi Yayınları.

Tanpınar, Ahmet Hamdi (1961) *Saatleri Ayarlama Enstitüsü*. İstanbul: Remzi Kitabevi.

Taş, Hakkı (2015) 'Turkey – from tutelary to delegative democracy', *Third World Quarterly* 36/4, 776–91.

Taş, Hakkı (2018a) 'A history of Turkey's AKP-Gülen conflict', *Mediterranean Politics 23/3*, 395–402.

Taş, Hakkı (2018b) 'The 15 July abortive coup and post-truth politics in Turkey', *Southeast European and Black Sea Studies* 18/1, 1–19.

Taşkın, Yüksel (2007) *Anti-Komünizmden Küreselleşme Karşıtlığına Milliyetçi Muhafazakar Entelijensiya*. İstanbul: İletişim.

Tekeli, İlhan (2017) '1980'li Yıllarda Türkiye Ekonomisinde Dönüşüm, Modernitenin Aşınması ve Planlama', in R. Funda Barbaros and Erik Jan Zurcher (eds), *Modernizmin Yansımaları: 80'li Yıllarda Türkiye*. Ankara: Efil yayınevi, 7–48.

Tekeli, Şirin (1991) 'Tek Parti Döneminde Kadın Hareketi de Bastırıldı', in Levent Cinemre and Ruşen Çakır (eds), *Sol Kemalizme Bakıyor*. İstanbul: Metis.

Tekerek, Tuğba (2023) *Taşra Üniversiteleri: AK Parti'nin Arka Kampüsü*. İstanbul: İletişim.

Tekin, Mustafa (2004) 'Ticanilik', in Yasin Aktay (ed.), *Modern Türkiye'de Siyasi Düşünce: İslamcılık*, vol. 6. İstanbul: İletişim, 260–3.

Tezcan, Baki (2010) *The Second Ottoman Empire. Political and Social Transformation in the Early Modern World*. New York: Cambridge University Press.

Thelen, Kathleen (2000) 'Timing and temporality in the analysis of institutional evolution and change', *Studies in American Political Development* 14/1, 101–8.

Tokdoğan, Nagehan (2018) *Yeni Osmanlıcılık: Hınç, Nostalji, Narsizm*. İstanbul: İletişim.

Topal, Alp Eren (2021) 'Ottomanism in history and historiography: fortunes of a concept', in Johanna Chovanec and Olof Heilo (eds), *Narrated Empires: Perceptions of Late Habsburg and Ottoman Multinationalism*. New York: Palgrave, 77–98.

Toprak, Hicret K. (2019) *Mihrap, Minber ve Devlet: Tek Parti Döneminde Diyanet İşleri Başkanlığı*. İstanbul: Küre Yayınları.

Toprak, Zafer (1996) '1934 Trakya Olaylarında Hükümetin ve CHP'nin Sorumluluğu', *Toplumsal Tarih* 34 (October), 19–25.

Torpey, John (2010) 'A (post-) secular age? Religion and the two exceptionalisms', *Social Research* 77/1, 269–96.

Tuğal, Cihan (2004) 'İslamcılığın Dini Çoğulluk Alanındaki Krizi: Alevilik Açmazı Hakkında Bazı Açılımlar', in Yasin Aktay (ed.), *Modern Türkiye'de Siyasi Düşünce: İslamcılık*, vol. 6. İstanbul: İletişim, 493–502.

Tuğal, Cihan (2009) *Passive Revolution: Absorbing the Islamic Challenge to Capitalism*. Stanford: Stanford University Press.

Tunaya, Tarık Zafer (1952) *Türkiye'de Siyasi Partiler (1859–1952)*. İstanbul: Doğan Kardeş Yayınları.

Tunaya, Tarık Zafer (1962) *İslamcılık Cereyanı: Meşrutiyet'in Siyası Hayatı Boyunca Gelişmesi ve Bugüne Bıraktığı Meseleler*. İstanbul: Baha Matbaası.

Tunaya, Tarık Zafer (1991) *İslamcılık Akımı*. İstanbul: İstanbul Bilgi Üniversitesi Yayınları.

Tunçay, Mete (2005) *Türkiye Cumhuriyeti'nde Tek Parti Yönetiminin Kurulması: 1823–1931*. İstanbul: Tarih Vakfı Yurt Yayınları.

Tunçay, Mete and Haldun Özen (1984) '1933 Tasfiyesinden Önce Dârülfünun', *Yapıt* 7 (October–November), 5–28.

Turner, Bryan S. with Berna Zengin Arslan (2013) 'State and Turkish secularism: the case of Diyanet', in Bryan S. Turner (ed.), *The Religious and the Political: A Comparative Sociology of Religion*, Cambridge: Cambridge University Press, 206–23.

Tür, Özlem and Zana Çıtak (2009) 'AKP ve Kadın: Teşkilatlanma, Muhafazakarlık ve Türban', in İlhan Uzgel and Bülent Duru (eds), *AKP Kitabı: Bir Dönüşümün Bilançosu*. Ankara: Phoenix, 614–29.

Türkmen, Emir Ali (ed.) (2022) *Yolu Kurtuluştan Geçen Kadınlar:* Kurtuluş *Kendini Anlatıyor 9*, Ankara: Dipnot Yayınları.

Türköne, Mümtaz'er (1991) *Siyasi İdeoloji olarak İslamcılığın Doğuşu*. İstanbul: İletişim.

Ulugana, Sedat (2022) *Kürt-Ermeni Coğrafyasının Sosyopolitik Dönüşümü (1908–1914): Halidiler, Hamidiyeliler, Bedirhaniler ve Taşnaklar*. İstanbul: İletişim.

Us, Hakkı Tarık (1954) *Meclis-i Meb'usan 1293–1877*. İstanbul: Vakit Kütüphanesi.

Usul, Ali Resul (2008) 'The Justice and Development Party and the European Union: from euro-scepticism to euro-enthusiasm and euro-fatigue', in Ümit Cizre (ed.), *Secular and Islamic Politics in Turkey: The Making of the Justice and Development Party*. London: Routledge, 175–98.

Uzun, Hakan (2012) 'İktidarını Sürdürmek İsteyen Bir Partinin Kimlik Arayışı: Cumhuriyet Halk Partisi'nin 1947 Olağan Kurultayı', *Çağdaş Türkiye Tarihi Araştırmaları Dergisi/Journal Of Modern Turkish History Studies* 12/25, 101–39.

Uzun, Mehmet ([1998] 2020) *Aşk Gibi Aydınlık Ölüm Gibi Karanlık*. Translated by Muhsin Kızılkaya. İstanbul: Sel Yayıncılık.

Uzunçarşılı, İsmail Hakkı (1985) *Midhat Paşa ve Taif Mahkumları*. Ankara: Türk Tarih Kurumu.

Üçüncü, Uğur and Hikmet Öksüz (2022) *6-7 Eylül 1955 olayları: Yakın Dönem Türkiye tarihinin Sis Perdesi*. İstanbul: Timaş.

Ünlü, Barış (1918) *Türklük Sözleşmesi: Oluşumu, İşleyişi ve Krizi*. Ankara: Dipnot Yayınları.

Ünüvar, Kerem (2007a) 'Fikir Kulüpleri Federasyonu (1965–1969)', in Murat Gültekingil (ed.), *Modern Türkiye'de Siyasi Düşünce: Sol*, vol. 8. İstanbul: İletişim, 821–9.

Ünüvar, Kerem (2007b) 'Türkiye Devrimci Gençlik Federasyonu (1970–1971)', in Murat Gültekingil (ed.), *Modern Türkiye'de Siyasi Düşünce: Sol*, vol. 8. İstanbul: İletişim, 830–3.

Vahide, Şükran (2005) *Islam in Modern Turkey: An Intellectual Biography of Bediuzzaman Said Nursi*. Albany: State University of New York Press.

van Bruinessen, Martin (1992a) *Ağa, Şeyh, Devlet*. Translated by Banu Yalkut. İstanbul: İletişim.

van Bruinessen, Martin (1992b) *Kürdistan Üzerine Yazılar*. Translated by Nevzat Kıraç, Bülent Peker, Leyla Keskiner, Selda Somuncuoğlu and Levent Kafadar. İstanbul: İletişim.

Vryonis, Speros (2005) *The Mechanism of Catastrophe: The Turkish Pogrom of September 6–7, 1955, and the Destruction of the Greek Community of Istanbul*. New York: Greekworks.com.

Vural, Hamza Semih (2019) 'Sultan II. Abdülhamid'in Tarikatlarla Münasebetleri', MA thesis, T. C. Sakarya Üniversitesi Sosyal Bilimler Enstitüsü.

Vural, Hasan S. (2013) *Türkiye'de Din Özgürlüğüne İlişkin Anayasal Güvence*. Ankara: Seçkin.

Watmough, Simon P. and Ahmet Erdi Öztürk (2018) 'From "diaspora by design" to transnational political exile: the Gülen Movement in transition', *Politics, Religion & Ideology* 19/1: 33–52.

White, Jenny B. (2003) 'State Feminism, Modernization, and the Turkish Republican Woman', *The National Women's Studies Association Journal (NWSA Journal)* 15, 145–59.

White, Jenny B. (2005) *Islamist Mobilization in Turkey: A Study in Vernacular Politics*. Seattle: University of Washington Press.

White, Jenny B. (2013) *Muslim Nationalism and the New Turks*. Princeton, NJ: Princeton University Press.

Yakut, Esra (2005) *Şeyhülislamlık: Yenileşme Döneminde Devlet ve Din*. İstanbul: Kitap Yayınevi.

Yalçınkaya, Ayhan (2009) 'Siyaset, Din, Alevilik ve Özgürlük Hayaleti', in Ömer Laçiner (ed.), *Modern Türkiye'de Siyasi Düşünce: Dönemler ve Zihniyetler*, vol. 9. İstanbul: İletişim, 785–804.

Yaman, Ali (2021) 'Education on Alevism in Turkish public schools', in Ednan Aslan and Marcia Hermansen (eds), *Religious Diversity at School: Educating for New Pluralistic Contexts*. Vienna: Springer, 417–38.

Yaman, Ali (2022) *Şah-ı Merdan'a Talip Olanlar: Kızılbaşlar, Aleviler, Bektaşiler*. Ankara: Kitap Yayınları.

Yanarocak, Hay Eytan Cohen (2017) 'My rival is my teacher: Erdoğan in the footsteps of Atatürk.' Available at: https://dayan.org/content/my-rival-my-teacher-erdogan-footsteps-ataturk.

Yanık, Aybars and Tanıl Bora (2017) 'Altmışlı Yıllarda Türkiye'nin Siyasi Düşünce Hayatı', in Mete Kaan Kaynar (ed.), *Türkiye'nin 1960'lı Yılları*. İstanbul: İletişim, 275–300.

Yanık, Lerna K. and Fulya Hisarlıoğlu (2019) '"They wrote history with their bodies": necrogeopolitics, necropolitical spaces and the everyday spatial politics of death in Turkey', in Banu Bargu (ed.), *Turkey's Necropolitical Laboratory: Democracy, Violence and Resistance*. Edinburgh: Edinburgh University Press, 46–70.

Yar, Erkan (2016) *Alevi İnanç Sistemi*. İstanbul: ADO (Alevi Düşünce Ocağı) Yayınları.

Yargı, Abdullah (2020) 'Nurculuk Hareketi İçerisindeki Vakıf Bireylerin Vakıflıktan Ayrılmasındaki Toplumsal Etkenler', *Ondokuz Mayıs Üniversitesi İlahiyat Fakültesi Dergisi* 49, 567–92.

Yaşar, M. Emin (2004) 'Dergah'tan Parti'ye, Vakıf'tan Şirket'e Bir Kimliğin Oluşumu ve Dönüşümü: İskenderpaşa Cemaati', in Yasin Aktay (ed.), *Modern Türkiye'de Siyasi Düşünce: İslamcılık*, vol. 6. İstanbul: İletişim, 323–40.

Yaşlı, Fatih (2009) *'Kinimiz Dinimizdir' Türkçü Faşizm Üzerine bir İnceleme*. Ankara: Tan.

Yavuz, Hakan (1999) 'The matrix of modern Turkish Islamic movements: the Naqshibandi Sufi order', in Elizabeth Özdalga (ed.), *Naqshbandis in Western and*

Central Asia (papers read at a conference held at the Swedish research Institute in Istanbul 9–11 June, 1997), Swedish Research Institute in Istanbul Transactions, vol. 9. Istanbul: Swedish Research Institute, 129–46.

Yavuz, M. Hakan (2000) 'Cleansing Islam from the public sphere', *Journal of International Affairs* 54, 21–42.

Yavuz, M. Hakan (2003a) *Islamic Political Identity in Turkey*. Oxford: Oxford University Press.

Yavuz, M. Hakan (2003b) 'Islam in the public sphere: the case of the Nur movement', in M. Hakan Yavuz and John L. Esposito (eds), *Turkish Islam and the Secular State: The Gülen Movement*. Syracuse: Syracuse University Press.

Yavuz, M. Hakan (2004) 'Bediüzzaman Said Nursi ve Nurculuk', in Yasin Aktay (ed.), *Modern Türkiye'de Siyasi Düşünce: İslamcılık*, vol. 6. İstanbul: İletişim, 264–94.

Yavuz, M. Hakan (2009) *Secularism and Muslim Democracy in Turkey*. Cambridge: Cambridge University Press.

Yavuz, M. Hakan (2013) *Toward an Islamic Enlightenment: The Gülen Movement*. Oxford: Oxford University Press.

Yavuz, M. Hakan (2018) 'A framework for understanding the ıntra-Islamist conflict between the AK Party and the Gülen movement', *Politics Religion and Ideology* 19/1, 11–32.

Yavuz, M. Hakan (2019) 'Understanding Turkish secularism in the 21th century: a contextual roadmap', *Southeast European and Black Sea Studies* 19/1, 1–24.

Yavuz, M. Hakan (2020). *Nostalgia for the Empire: The Politics of Neo-Ottomanism*. New York: Oxford University Press.

Yavuz, M. Hakan (2021) *Erdoğan: The Making of an Autocrat*. Edinburgh: Edinburgh University Press.

Yavuz, M. Hakan (2023) 'A torn country: Erdoğan's Turkey and the elections of 2023', *Middle East Policy* 30/3, 81–94. doi:10.1111/mepo.12705.

Yavuz, M. Hakan and Nihat Ali Özcan (2007) 'Crisis in Turkey: the conflict of political languages', *Middle East Policy* 14/3, 118–35.

Yavuz, Hilmi (2006) *Büyü'sün, Yaz! Toplu Şiirler 1969–2005*. İstanbul: Yapı Kredi Yayınları.

Yaycıoğlu, Ali (2018) 'Guarding traditions and laws – disciplining bodies and souls: tradition, science, and religion in the age of Ottoman reform', *Modern Asian Studies* 52/5, 1542–603.

Yeğenoğlu, Metin and Simten Coşar (2014) 'AKP ve Toplumsal Cinsiyet Meselesi: Neoliberalizm ve Patriyarka Arasında Mekik Dokumak', in Simten Coşar and Gamze Yücesan-Özdemir (eds), *İktidarın Şiddeti: AKPli Yıllar, Neoliberalizm ve İslamcı Politikalar*. İstanbul: Metis.

Yıldırım, Ali (1997) *Darağacında Kan Sesleri: Bir Cellatın Anıları*. Ankara: Doruk Yayımcılık.

Yıldırım, Mine (2015) *The Collective Dimension of Freedom of Religion or Belief in International Law: The Application of Findings to the Case of Turkey*. Abo: Abo Akademi University Press.

Yıldırım, Mine (2016) 'Grand Chamber judgment in İzzettin Doğan and Others v. Turkey: more than a typical religious discrimination case', *Strasbourg Observers*. Available at: https://strasbourgobservers.com/2016/07/18/grand-chamber-judgment-in-izzettin-dogan-and-others-v-turkey-more-than-a-typical-religious-discrimination-case/.

Yıldırım, Oktay (ed.) (2019) *(Gizli) Diyanet'in Tarikatlar Raporu*. İstanbul: Kaynak Yayınları.

Yıldız, Ahmet (2001) *Ne Mutlu Türküm Diyebilene*. İstanbul: İletişim.

Yıldız, Gültekin (2009) *Neferin Adı Yok: Zorunlu Askerliğe Geçiş Sürecinde Osmanlı Devlet'nde Siyaset, Ordu ve Toplum (1826–1839)*. İstanbul: Kitabevi.

Yılmaz, Hakan (1997) 'Democratization from above in response to the international context: Turkey, 1945–1950', *New Perspectives on Turkey* 17, 1–37.

Yılmaz, İhsan (2005) 'State, law, civil society and Islam in contemporary Turkey', *The Muslim World* 95/3, 385–411.

Yılmaz, İhsan and İsmail Albayrak (2022) *Populist and pro-violence state religion: the Diyanet's construction of Erdoğanist Islam in Turkey*. Singapore: Palgrave Macmillan.

Yılmaz, İhsan and Nicholas Morieson (2023) 'Civilizational populism in domestic and foreign policy: the case of Turkey', *Religions* 14/631, 1–19.

Yılmaz, İhsan and Erdoan Shipoli (2021) 'Use of past collective traumas, fear and conspiracy theories for securitization of the opposition and authoritarianisation: the Turkish case', *Democratization* 29/2, 320–36.

Yılmaz, İhsan, Greg Barton and James Barry (2017) 'The decline and resurgence of Turkish Islamism: the story of Tayyip Erdoğan's AKP', *Journal of Citizenship and Globalisation Studies* 1/1: 48–62.

Yılmaz, Zafer (2017) 'The AKP and the spirit of the "new" Turkey: imagined victim, reactionary mood and resentful sovereign', *Turkish Studies* 18/3, 482–513.

Yılmaz, Zafer (2018) *Yeni Türkiye'nin Ruhu: Hınç, Tahakküm, Muhtaçlaştırma*. İstanbul: İletişim.

Yılmaz, Zafer (2019) 'The genesis of the "Exceptional" Republic: the permanency of the political crisis and the constitution of legal emergency power in Turkey', *British Journal of Middle Eastern Studies* 46/5, 714–34. Available at: https://doi.org/10.1080/13530194.2019.1634393.

Yılmaz, Zafer (2020) 'Erdoğan's presidential regime and strategic legalism: Turkish democracy in the twilight zone', *Southeast European and Black Sea Studies* 20/2, 265–87.

Yılmaz, Zehra (2015) *Dişil Dindarlık: İslamcı Kadın Hareketinin Dönüşümü*. İstanbul: İletişim.

Yurdakul, İlhami (2008) *Osmanlı İlmiye Merkez Teşkilatı'nda Reform (1826–1876)*. İstanbul: İletişim.

Zaim, Sabahattin (2008) *1926–2007 Bir Ömrün Hikayesi*. İstanbul: İşaret Yayınları.

Zihnioğlu, Yaprak (2003) *Kadınsız İnkılap: Nezihe Muhiddin, Kadınlar halk fırkası, Kadın Birliği*. İstanbul: İletişim.

Zilfi, Madeline C. (1997) *Women in the Ottoman Empire: Middle Eastern Women in the Early Modern Era*. Leiden: Brill.

Zürcher, Erik Jan (1991) *Political Opposition in the Early Turkish Republic: The Progressive Republican Party 1924–1925*. Leiden: Brill.

Zürcher, Erik-Jan (2016) *Jihad and Islam in World War I: Studies on the Ottoman Jihad on the Centenary of Snouck Hurgronje's 'Holy War Made in Germany'*. Leiden: Leiden University Press.

Zürcher, Erik J. ([1993] rev. edn 2017) *Turkey: A Modern History*. London: Bloomsbury Academic.

INDEX

12 March 1971, 16, 114, 117
12 September 1980, 116–17, 128, 141–2, 159, 174n, 181
28 February 1997, 155
15 July 2016, 10, 16, 185, 189, 198–9

Abdülaziz, 28, 30
Abdülaziz Bekkine, 128
Abdülhamid II, 30–2, 34, 37–9; *see also* Hamidian regime
Abdülmecid, 27–8, 51
Abdülmecid Efendi, 56
abortion, 171, 207
Abu-Manneh, Butrus, 23, 25, 27
Açık Radyo, viii, 152
Adalet Partisi (Justice Party/AP), 9, 105, 116, 118
Adalet ve Kalkınma Partisi (AKP), 2, 9–10, 14–16, 180–8, 190–3, 195–9, 201, 203, 205, 207–10, 219–26
Adıvar, Adnan, 58, 61
Adıvar, Halide Edip, 48, 61
Adıyaman, 37, 88, 114, 129

adil düzen (just order), 162
Adnan Hoca group, 215n
Adolphus Slade Pasha, 42n
Ahmed Cevdet Paşa, 29
Ahmed Ziyaüddin Gümüşhanevi, 36
Ahmet Rıza Bey, 31
Akbulut, Yıldırım, 159
Akçura, Yusuf, 31
Akdağ, Recep, 199
Akgün, Necati, 99
Akseki, Ahmet Hamdi, 68, 92, 93
Akşener, Meral, 195–6
Alevi, 7, 11–12, 15–16, 36–8, 68, 108, 123, 130–2, 168–70, 201–2, 204–5
Alican, Ekrem, 138n
Ali Suavi, 28
(Mehmed Emin) Âli Paşa, 28
Al Nabhani, 124
Alpdoğan, Abdullah, 79n
Alptekin, İsmail, 163
Altan, Çetin, 120
Altıkulaç, Tayyar, 108, 123, 147
Altındağ, Atıf, 65

Anavatan Partisi (Motherland Party/ ANAP), 145, 154, 158, 159, 161–2, 166, 196–7
Anatolian Tigers, 153
Anıtkabir (Atatürk's mausoleum), 135n
Arabesk music, 176n
Aren, Sadun, 164
Arendt, Hannah, 2
Arınç, Bülent, 167, 191
Armenian, 12, 26, 33, 37–9, 70–1, 96, 98, 171, 195, 205–6
Armenian Orthodox, 12
Asad, Talal, 3, 12
ASALA (Armenian Secret Army for the Liberation of Armenia), 171
Aslan, Yusuf, 115
Assyrian, 37–8, 195
Atak, Oğuz, 154
Atalay, Can, 225
Atatürk, Mustafa Kemal, 5, 48–52, 55–6, 58–65, 67, 69, 87–8, 93, 95–6, 99, 154–5, 173, 185
Atay, Falih Rıfkı, 88
Ateş, Süleyman, 108, 123
Ateşten Gömlek, 75n
Athinagoras, 94
Authoritarianism, 2, 31–2, 72, 184, 222
Ayasofya (Hagia Sophia), 58, 76n, 187
Aybar, Mehmet Ali, 119–20
Aydın, Koray, 196
Aydın, Necati, 206
Aydın, Şahin, 115
Aydınlar Ocağı, 8–9, 113
Ayna Şiirleri, 226
Ayşe, 134
Aytek, Nihat, 154
Ayverdi, Semiha, 200

Babacan, Ali, 196
Babacan, Hatice, 135
Bahçeli, Devlet, 162, 194, 195
Bahçelievler massacre, 115
Baha'i, 12, 206
Baha Said, 37, 47
Balan, Hüseyin, 123, 139
Baltacıoğlu, İsmail Hakkı, 55
Bardakçı, Ulaş, 115
Bardakoğlu, Ali, 188
Barış Partisi (Peace Party), 169
Bartholomeos I (Dimitrios Arhondonis), 171
Batı Çalışma Grubu (Western Working Group), 156–7
Bayar, Celal, 83, 86
Bayındır, Abdülaziz, 164
Baykal, Deniz, 160, 193–4
Bediüzzaman Said-i Nursi, 90–2, 165
Berk, Bekir, 125
Berkman, Hasan Tahsin, 123
Bektaşi order, 26
Bele, Refet, 58
Berberoğlu, Enis, 194
Bezmiâlem (Sultan), 27
Bilgiç, Saadettin, 138n
Bilgiç, Sait, 88
Bilmen, Ömer Nasuhi, 108
Bir, Çevik, 156
Birlik Partisi (Unity Party/BP), 123
Boran, Behice, 119–20
Boyner, Cem, 169
bozkurtlar (Grey Wolves), 121–2
Bozkurt, Mahmut Esat, 57
Bölükbaşı, Osman, 121, 138n
Börekçi, Mehmet Rifat / Börekçizade Mehmet Rıfat Efendi, 55

Bucak, Sedat, 179n
Buldan, Pervin, 195
Bulgarian (Orthodox) church, 39, 206
Bulut, Necdet, 115
Burç radio station, 166
Büyük Birlik Partisi (Great Unity Party/ BBP), 162, 167, 219
Büyük Doğu, 88
Byzantium, 4, 185

Caliphate, 4, 25, 35, 50, 53, 56, 59–60
Caliph-sultan, 3–4, 50
Calp, Necdet, 159
Canavaris, 133
Catholic, 12, 38–9, 206
Catholic Armenians, 26
Cebesoy, Ali Fuat, 58
Cedit group, 175n
Celalettin Arif Bey, 49
(Ahmet) Cemal Paşa, 32, 44n
Cemgil, Adnan, 119
Cemgil, Sinan, 114
Cemevi, 11–12, 170, 204–5
Cem Vakfı (Cem Foundation), 11, 169, 204
Cem Vakfı v. *Turkey*, 11
Cevahir, Hüseyin, 114
Chaldean (*Keldani*), 12, 38, 206
Christian / Christianity, 7–8, 13, 27, 37–9, 51, 57, 72, 92, 144, 195, 205–6, 221
Cindoruk, Hüsamettin, 175
civic religion, 63
'civil Fridays', 189
Communist Manifesto, 18n

Constitution
 of 1876 (*Kanun-i Esasi*), 30
 of 1909, 32, 36
 of 1921 (*Teşkilat-ı Esasiye Kanunu*), 50, 52
 of 1924 (*Teşkilat-ı Esasiye Kanunu*), 52
 of 1961, 106, 108, 119, 144, 145
 of 1982, 9, 16, 142–5, 165, 168, 183
Constitutional Court, 16, 106–8, 114, 120, 122, 142, 163, 169, 173, 182, 185, 194–6, 211, 220, 225
Copt/Coptic, 39
Coşan, Mahmud Esad, 166
Coşan, Nureddin, 198
Council of Higher Education (*Yüksek Öğretim Kurumu*/YÖK), 148, 173, 193
coup d'état of 1960, 15
coup d'état of 1980, 15, 128, 141, 165, 167
Cömert, Bedrettin, 115
Cumhuriyetçi Millet Partisi, 88, 138n
Cumhuriyet Halk Partisi (Republican People's Party/CHP), 51, 63–5, 68, 71, 82–6, 88, 92, 99–100, 112, 116–18, 122–3, 131–2, 158–61, 180, 183, 190, 193–4, 204–5, 210, 219

Çağlar, Behçet Kemal, 78n
Çağlayangil, İhsan Sabri, 175n
Çalık, Mustafa, 175n
Çandar, Cengiz, 175n
Çatlı, Abdullah, 171, 179n
Çakmak, Fevzi, 69, 85
Çayan, Mahir, 114–15

Çetin, Hikmet, 160
Çınar, Hüseyin, 139n
Çiller, Tansu, 149–50, 161

Dağoğlu, Türkan, 218
Dar-ul Zafaran, 39
Darwin, Charles, 154
Dar Zamanlar (*Ölmeye Yatmak*; *Bir Düğün Gecesi*; *Hayır*), 174n
Dava, 165
Davison, Andrew, 3
Davutoğlu, Ahmet, 188, 196
Demirağ, Nuri, 82
Demircioğlu, Vedat, 120
Demirel, Süleyman, 9, 112, 117–18, 123, 125, 138n, 142, 161, 165, 168, 188
Demirtaş, Selahattin, 195, 210, 225
Demokrasi Partisi (Democracy Party/DEP), 163
Demokrasi ve Atılım Partisi (Democracy and Progress Party/DEVA), 190, 196, 220
Demokrat Parti (Democrat Party/DP), 15, 83, 86, 98, 161, 190, 197
Demokrat Parti (Democrat Party/DP) 2007, 190, 197
Demokratik Barış Hareketi (Democratic Peace Movement/DBH), 169
Demokratik Sol Parti (Democratic Left Party/DSP), 160–2, 196
Denizolgun, Arif Ahmet, 200
Dersim, 37, 68, 79n
Dersim Massacre, 68
Derviş, Kemal, 181, 210n
Derviş Mehmed, 60
Devrimci İşçi Sendikaları Konfederasyonu (DİSK), 114

devrim şehitliği (shrine of revolution), 135n
Dıblan, Makbule, 99
Dilipak, Abdurrahman, 113
Dimitrios I, 171
Dinç, (Hoca) Raif, 50
Dinçerler, Vehbi, 154
Din Görevlileri Federasyonu (Religious Officers Federation), 126
Dink, Hrant, 206
Dini Islah Beyannamesi (Declaration on the Improvement of Religion), 62
Din İşleri Yüksek Kurulu (Supreme Board of Religious Affairs), 146
Diyanet (İşleri Reisliği/Başkanlığı: Presidency of Religious Affairs), 6, 7, 9–11, 14, 16, 20n, 53–5, 62–3, 65–6, 78n, 79n, 92–4, 108–9, 119, 123, 125–7, 144–7, 156, 168–9, 187–90, 204, 207, 213, 223–4
Diyanet Akademi (The Diyanet Academy), 190
Diyanet İşleri Türk İslam Birliği (the Diyanet Turkish-Islamic Union/DİTİB), 146
Doğan, Lütfi, 108
Doğan, Lütfi (Dr), 108
Doğan, Muhammed (Molla Muhemmed el-Kersi), 165
Doğanay, Ümit, 116
Doğru Yol Partisi (True Path Party/DYP), 154, 161, 179n, 196–7
Dinçer, Gönül, 140n
dönme, 21n, 71
Druze, 38
Dursun, Muhammed Sıddık Şeyhanzade, 165

Dündar, Can, 194
Dünya radio station, 166
Dürrizâde Abdullah Efendi, 49

Eastern church, 38
Ebedi Şef (Eternal Leader), 65
Ecevit, Bülent, 117–18, 160–1
Ecumenical, 38–9, 72, 94, 171, 216n
Efsun, 210n
Eliaçık, Recep İhsan, 197, 201
Elmalı, İbrahim, 108
Elrom, Efraim, 114
Emeksiz, Turan, 135n
Emilyanos, 133
Enver Paşa, 32, 45n
Erakalın, Avni, 119
Erbakan, Necmettin, 122–3, 129, 156, 162, 166–7, 196
Erbaş, Ali, 188, 212n
Erdem, Hasan Hüsnü, 108
Erdoğan, Recep Tayyip, 65, 162, 170, 178n, 183–9, 191–2, 195–9, 201, 205–7, 212n, 214n, 217n, 218, 220, 222–4, 226
Erenköy community, 128, 167, 215n
Ergenekon case, 9–10, 183, 207, 211n
Erim, Nihat, 117
Erol, Abdülbaki, 167
Erol, Abdülhakim, 129
Erol, Feyzettin, 167
Erol, Muhammed Raşit, 129, 167
Ersoy, Mehmet Akif, 33, 45n, 74n
European Convention on Human Rights, 11–12, 148, 202, 225
European Court of Human Rights (ECtHR), 11–12, 142, 148, 175n, 182, 202–5, 211n, 216n, 225

European Union, 16, 150, 268
evkaf /vakıf (religious foundations), 3, 26, 50, 53
Evkaf-ı Humayun Nezareti, 26
Evren, Kenan, 142–3, 173
Eylem Zengin v. *Turkey*, 203
Eygi, Mehmet Şevket, 111
ezan (call to prayer), 62–3, 86, 213n
Ezidi, 38, 206

Fazilet Partisi (Virtue Party/FP), 130, 162–3
Fener Patriarchate, 94
Fergan, Eşref Edip, 88
Fetva, 49–50, 190
Fezleke (1869), 42n
freedom from religion, 6, 107
(Keçecizade Mehmed) Fuad Paşa, 28
Fidan, Hakan, 10, 184
Fikir Kulübü (Opinion Club), 111
Fikir Klüpleri Federasyonu (Federation of Opinion Clubs), 111, 120
Furkan Vakfı, 197

Gagauz, 8
Gazeteciler Yazarlar Vakfı (Journalists and Writers Foundation), 165
Gazi, 75n
Gece, 219
gecekondu (shantytown), 110–11, 214n
Gelecek Partisi (Future Party), 190, 196, 220
Gerçeker, Tevfik, 108
Geske, Tilmann Ekkehart, 206
Gezi events, 14, 184
Gezmiş, Deniz, 114–15
golden generation, 125

Gökalp, Ziya, 22, 32, 62
Gökçek, Melih, 162, 218
Gökçen, Sabiha, 69
Görmez, Mehmet, 187–8
Grand National Assembly of Turkey/ TBMM, 116; *see also* Turkish Grand Assembly *and* Turkish Grand National Assembly
Greek, 12–13, 27, 38–9, 48, 50–1, 58, 70–2, 94–8, 133, 150, 171, 206
Greek Orthodox, 12, 38–9, 51, 70, 95–8, 171, 206
Greek Orthodox Patriarchate of Fener, 94
Gül, Abdullah, 167, 182–3, 191
Gül, Hayrünnisa, 211n
Gülcügil, Mustafa, 133
Gültekin, Sönmez, 135, 136
Gülek, Kasım, 117
Gülen, Fethullah, 10, 125, 157, 165–6, 198
Gülen Movement, 125, 157, 165–6, 184, 186, 197–9
Gülhane Hatt-ı Hümâyunu (Gülhane Rescript-1839), 23, 27, 28
Gümüşhanevi, Ahmed Ziyaüddin, 36
Gümüşpala, Ragıp, 118
Günaltay, Şemsettin, 84
Gündüz, İrfan, 128
Güreş, Doğan, 150
Gürkan, Aydın Güven, 159–60
Gürsel, Cemal, 90, 113, 116–17

Hac, 84
Hacı Hasan Efendi, 167
Hagopian, Hagop, 171
hahambaşı, 38
HAK-İŞ, 177n
Hakses, Ali Rıza, 108
Halâskar Gazi (Liberator and Warrior for Islam), 50, 185, 212n
Halkçı Parti (Populist Party/HP), 158–9
Halk Fırkası (People's Party), 51, 63–4, 81n; *see also Cumhuriyet Halk Partisi*: CHP
Halkın Demokrasi Partisi (People's Democracy Party/HADEP), 163
Halkın Emek Partisi (People's Labour Party/HEP), 163
Halkların Demokratik Partisi (Peoples' Democratic Party/HDP), 186, 190, 195, 210, 220
Halidi suborder, 25, 36
Halki Seminary (Heybeliada Theological School), 207
Halveti Şabanniye group, 215n
Hamidian regime, 30–1, 36
Hamidiye Hafif Süvari Alayları (Hamidiye Light Cavalry Regiments), 37
Hanefi *fıqh*/Hanefi school of law, 203, 216n, 29, 36, 81n
Hareket Ordusu, 32
Hasan and Eylem Zengin v. Turkey, 203
hate speech, 13, 206
Hayırlıoğlu, Eyüp Sabri, 93, 108
Hayri Efendi (Ürgüplü), 33
Harput, 37
Helsinki Yurttaşlar Derneği (Helsinki Citizens' Assembly Turkey/HYD), 151

Hizbullah, 149, 181, 223
Hizbu't-Tahrir, 124
Hutbe, 77n, 187, 208, 213n
Hüda-Par (*Hür Dava Partisi*: Free Cause Party), 222–3
Hüseyin Rauf, 58

IBDA-C, 181, 206, 210n
Independence War, 59–61
Islahat Fermanı (Imperial Rescript of Reforms, 1856), 28
Islamic Cultural Centres, 127
Islam Mecmuası, 33
Islamism, 8, 31, 36, 124, 173
Islamophobia, 31
Ismail Gaspıralı, 31
Istanbul Ekspres, 95
Istanbul Convention (Convention on Preventing and Combating Violence against Women and Domestic Violence), 209
ışık evler (light houses), 125–6
Işık group, 215n
Işınsu Okçu, Emine, 134

İkinci Grup (Second Group), 50
İlerici Kadınlar Derneği (Progressive Women's Association/İKD), 135
ilmiye, 34, 42n, 45n, 127
imam-hatip (imam and preacher) courses, 68, 85
imam-hatip (imam and preacher) schools, 156, 203
İmamoğlu, Ekrem, 194
İnan, Hüseyin, 115
İnönü, Erdal, 159–60

İnönü, İsmet, 65, 70, 78n, 83, 86, 100, 112, 116–18, 159
İnönü, Mevhibe, 100
İnsan Hakları Derneği (Human Rights Association/İHD), 150
İnsan Hakları ve Mazlumlar için Dayanışma Derneği (Association for Human Rights and Solidarity for the Oppressed/MAZLUM-DER), 151
İpekçi, Abdi, 115
Irtica, 87–8, 102n, 112, 155–7
İskenderpaşa circle/community, 36, 166, 198, 215n
İskilipli Atıf Hoca, 59
İslamoğlu, Mustafa, 164
İsmailağa community, 199, 215n
İstiklal Mahkemeleri (Independence Tribunals), 59
İstiklal Marşı (national anthem), 45n, 74n, 113
İttihad, 124
İttihat ve Terakki Cemiyeti (Committee of Union and Progress), 31
İzzettin Doğan and Others v. *Turkey*, 12, 204

Jacobite (*Yakubi*), 38–9
Jandarma İstihbarat Terörle Mücadele (Gendarmerie Intelligence Counter Terrorism/JİTEM), 149
Janissary, 15, 26
Jerusalem, 112, 124, 155
Jew, 13, 38–9, 71, 98, 206
Jewish community, 12, 26, 39, 70–1, 96, 98, 144, 170
Jeune Turcs, 31

Kabaklı, Ahmet, 9
Kaçar, Kemal, 127, 200
Kadınlar Halk Fırkası (Republican Women's Party), 81n
Kadın Birliği (Women's Union), 81n
Kadın Gazetesi, 134
Kadın Sesi, 134
Kadirbeyoğlu, Zeki, 64
Kadiri order, 31, 150, 215n
Kafesoğlu, İbrahim, 113
Kahramanmaraş pogrom, 132
Kalmaz, Ali İhsan, 135–6
kamet, 86
Kara, (Hafız) Mehmet, 63
Karabekir, Kazım, 58, 75n
Karafakioğlu, Bedri, 115
Karamollaoğlu, Temel, 169, 196
Kavaf, Aliye, 217n
Kavala, Osman, 184, 225
(Kavalalı) Mehmed Ali Paşa, 27
Kazancıyan, Karekin, 98
Keldani (Chaldean), 12, 38, 206
Kenanoğlu, Ali, 140n
(Kıbrıslı) Kamil Paşa, 32
Karacan, Ali Naci, 88
Karakimseli, Zeki, 64
Karakocan, 37
Karayalçın, Murat, 160
Kavakçı, Merve, 174
Kaya, Şükrü, 6
Keçecizade Mehmed Fuad Paşa, 28
Kemalist, 3, 6, 8, 39, 54, 60, 63, 65, 86–7, 99–100, 106, 121, 123, 185, 187, 191, 226
Kıbrıs Türktür Cemiyeti (Cyprus is Turkish Society/Turkish Cypriot Association), 95–6

Kılıçdaroğlu, Kemal, 194, 205, 220
Kılıçkıran, Ruhi, 81, 111–12
Kırkıncı, Mehmet, 165
Kırkıncılar group, 165, 215n
Kısakürek, Necip Fazıl, 88, 137n, 210n
Kızılbaş, 36–8, 130
Kobani case, 225
Kocadağ, Hüseyin, 179n
Koraltan, Refik, 83
Koran(ic) courses, 7, 34, 56, 62–3, 93, 125–7, 136, 144, 156, 164, 166, 187, 189, 199
Korutürk, Fahri, 117
Kotku, Mehmed Zahid, 36, 128, 166
Köprülü, Fuat, 19n, 83
Köy Enstitüleri (Village Institutes), 66
Kubbealtı Foundation, 200
Kubilay, Mustafa Fehmi, 60
Kurd/Kurdish, 8, 16, 35–8, 48, 59, 68, 90, 125, 147, 149–51, 163–5, 172, 181, 184–6, 189, 193, 195, 198, 205, 220, 223
Kuriş, Alihan, 200
Kuriş, Konca, 30n
Kurtlar Sofrası, 82, 102n
Kurtuluş movement, 140n
Kuru, Ahmet T., 3, 235
Kutan, Recai, 163, 196
Kutlu Doğum – the Blessed Birth of the Prophet Muhammed, 190
Kutlular, Mehmet, 165
Kuytul, Alparslan, 201
Küçük Ağa, 61
Kürkçü, Ertuğrul, 115

laic, 3–4, 6, 15, 19n, 56, 67, 222
laicism, 1, 4–6, 67

laicist, 4–5, 15, 66
laicité, 1, 3–5, 19n
laiklik, 5–6, 9, 54, 63–4, 83–5, 88, 92, 102n, 106–8, 112, 119, 122, 144–5, 154–5, 183
Latin Catholic, 12
Laws
  Ceza Kanunname-i Hümayun (Criminal Code of 1840), 28
  Land Code (1858), 24
  Law on goods abandoned by the Armenians (*Emval-i Metruke/Tasfiye kanunları*), 70
  Law on High Treason (*Hıyanet-i Vataniye Kanunu*) 29 April 1920, 52
  Köy Kanunu (Village Law) 18 March 1924, 51
  Law on the Annulment of the Ministry of *Şeriat* and Religious Foundations and the Ministry of the General Staff (Law 429) 3 March 1924, 3, 53
  Law on the Unification of Education (Law 430) (*Tevhid-i Tedrisat Kanunu*) 3 March 1924, 3, 53, 55–6
  Law on the Annulment of the Caliphate and the Exile of the Ottoman Dynasty from the Frontiers of the Turkish Republic (Law 431) 3 March 1924, 4, 53, 56
  Law on the Annulment of the Religious Courts and Modification of the Judgement of the Organization of Judiciary (8 March 1924), 52
  Law on the Annulment of the Religious Courts and Modification of the Judgement of the Organization of Judiciary 8 April 1924, 4, 56
  Takrir-i Sükun Kanunu (Law on the Maintenance of Order) 4 March 1925, 59
  Hat Law (*Şapka İhdası Hakkında Kanun*) 25 November 1925, 59
  Law Banning Religious Shrines (*Tekke ve Zaviyelerle Türbelerin Seddine ve Türbedarlıklar ile Birtakım Unvanların Men ve İlgasına Dair Kanun*) 30 November 1925, 57
  Civil Code (*Türk Kanun-ı Medenisi/Medeni Kanun*) (1926), 30, 57, 172
  Law Adopting the Numerals Used Internationally (*Beynelmilel Erkamın Kabulü Hakkında Kanun*) 20 May 1928, 58
  Law on the Deed Registration of Real Estate Property Allocated to Immigrants, Non-Migrants, Muhacir and Others in Accordance with the Laws of the Republic of Turkey (*Mübadil, Gayrimübadil, Muhacir ve Saireye Kanunlarına Tevfikan Tevzi veya Adiyen Tahsis Olunan Gayrimenkul Emvalin Tapuya Raptına Dair Kanun*) 28 May 1928, 70
  Law on Revenue Recording of *Emval-i Metrûke* Accounts to the Budget (*Emval-î Metrûke Hesab-ı Cariyelerinin Bütçeye İrat Kaydına Dair Kanun*) 28 May 1928, 70

Laws (*cont.*)
    Law Adopting the Latin alphabet
        (*Türk Harflerinin Kabul ve Tatbiki
        Hakkında Kanun*) 1 November
        1928, 58
    Land Distribution Law 1950, 84
    Law on Crimes Committed Against
        Atatürk 24 July 1951, 87
    Law to Protect Freedom of
        Conscience and Assembly 23 July
        1953, 87
    *Kırşehir Vilayetinin Kaldırılmasına
        ve Nevşehir Kazasında Nevşehir
        Adıyla Yeniden bir Vilayet
        Kurulmasına dair Kanun* 1954, 88
    Law No. 633 on the Establishment
        and Duties of the Diyanet (1965),
        108
    Law Regarding the Dress Code
        for Personnel Working in Public
        Institutions and Organization
        (16 July 1982), 172
    Law on Population Planning
        (14 April 1983), 171
    Changes on the Law on the Diyanet
        dated 1 July 2010, 126, 187
    Personal Data Protection Law 2016,
        202
Leyla Şahin v. *Turkey* case, 182, 211n
LGBTI+, 195, 209–10, 223

Madımak massacre, 169
Manga, Kadir, 114
Mansur Yalçın and Others v. *Turkey*, 12
March 31 Incident, 32
Maronite, 206
Mahmud II, 15, 23, 25–7, 35, 42n
Manisa trials, 174n
Mansur Yalçın and others v. *Turkey*, 203
Mecelle-i Ahkam-ı Adliyye (Mecelle),
    28–30
Meclis-i Meşayih, 35
Medresetü'z Zahra, 90
Medtesetü'l Kuzat (madrasah of kadıs),
    45
Med-Zehra group, 165
Mehmed Reşad V, 33, 38
Mekkizade Mustafa Asım Efendi, 27
Mele, 189
Melen, Ferit, 117
Menderes, Adnan, 83, 86–9, 91, 95–7,
    105, 109
Menteşe, Halil, 32, 44n
Melkite Catholic, 39
Menzil community, 129, 167, 199
Mert, Hamdi, 168
Meşihat-ı İslamiye, 34–5
Meşveret group, 52, 165
Metadoxy, 19n
Mevlana Halid, 35; *see also* Ziyaeddin
    Halid *and* Şeyh Halid
Mevlid, 78n
Mızraklı, Selçuk, 195
Military Medical College, 31
Millet, 20n, 38–9, 47n, 52
Millet Partisi (Nation Party), 85
Milli Birlik Komitesi (National Unity
    Committee), 90, 109, 116, 118
Milli Görüş, 129–30, 162, 167, 191,
    196
Milli Güvenlik Kurulu (National
    Security Board), 142
Milli Güvenlik Konseyi (National
    Security Council), 143, 155

Milli İstihbarat Teşkilatı (MIT/ National Intelligence Organization/MİT), 10, 96
Milli Kalkınma Partisi (National Development Party), 82
Milli Nizam Partisi (National Order Party / MNP), 9, 122
Milli Selamet Partisi (National Salvation Party /MSP), 105, 117, 122
Milli Şef (National Leader), 65
Milli Tesanüd Cephesi (National Solidarity Front), 88
Milli Türk Talebe Birliği (National Union of Turkish Students), 124
milliyetçi, 20n
Milliyetçi Çalışma Partisi (Nationalist Labour Party/MÇP), 161–2
Milliyetçi Demokrasi Partisi (Nationalist Democracy Party/ MDP), 158
Milliyetçi Hareket Partisi (Nationalist Movement Party /MHP), 9, 121, 129, 132, 158, 161–2, 172, 187, 190, 194–6, 219–20
Milliyetçi Türk Kadınları Derneği (Nationalist Turkish Women's Association), 134
Milönü Mosque, 132
Ministry of Family and Social Services, 190, 208
Mirzabeyoğlu, Salih, 181
missionary, 38, 173
(Ahmet Şefik) Mithat Paşa, 30
modernity, 1–3, 5, 15, 125, 174, 198
Mondros armistice, 44n
Mor Çatı (Purple Roof Women's Shelter) Foundation, 172, 208

Muallem Asakir-i Mansure-i Muhammediye (Trained Victorious Muhammadan Soldiers), 26
Mudanya armistice, 51
Muhafaza-i Mukaddesat Cemiyeti (Association for the Preservation of Sacred Institutions), 50
multi-party regime, 2, 8, 14–15, 82–3, 86, 99, 109
Murad V, 30
Muslim Brotherhood, 124
Mustafa Fevzi Efendi, 128
Mustafa Reşid Paşa, 23, 27
Mustazaf-Der, 222–3
Müdafa-i Hukuk Cemiyetleri (Defence of National Rights Societies), 48
Müstakil Sanayici ve İş Adamları Derneği (Independent Industrialists and Businessmen's Association/MÜSİAD), 153
My Share in the Turkish Ordeal, 61

Naci, Fethi, 119
Nakşibendi order, 10, 25–7, 31, 35–6, 59, 92, 126, 128–9, 152, 200, 222–3
Nakşibendi-Halidi order, 46n, 223
Nakşibendi-Müceddidiyye / Nakşibendi-Mücahidi order, 25, 27, 41n, 126, 128
Namık Kemal, 28
Nationalist Front, 9, 117, 125
nationalism, 2, 6–8, 20n, 27, 33, 36–7, 54, 64, 113, 124, 155, 222–3
nation state, 2–4, 8, 36, 73, 99, 125, 188
(Selanikli) Dr Nazım, 32

Neo-Ottomanism, 175n, 213n
Nestorian Christian, 38
Neve Şalom Synagogue, 170–1
'New Turkey', 8, 10, 14, 186, 192, 214n
Nezihe Muhiddin, 73
Nizam-ı Cedit, 41n
Nizamiye courts, 28–9
non-Muslim minorities, 8, 12, 80n, 96, 98
Nubihar, 165
Nurculuk, 90, 92, 102n, 103n, 125
Nutuk (the Speech), 60, 77n

Oğan, Sinan, 195, 220
Okan, Gaffar, 223
Oksay, Kâzım, 145
Okur, (Hafız) Yaşar, 62
Okuyan, Mehmet, 164
Okuyucular group, 165
Okyar, Fethi, 77n
Orbay, Rauf, 58, 60
Orthodox, 12–13, 25, 37–9, 51, 70, 72, 94–8, 171, 205–6, 223
Osman Selahaddin Dede, 35
Ottoman Freedom Society, 31
Ottomanism, 31

Öcalan, Abdullah, 149–50, 181
Ödül, Şevket, 64
Öktem, İmran, 112
Özal, Turgut, 142, 149, 152, 158–9, 162, 164–6, 192
Özdağ, Ümit, 195
Özdoğan, Alparslan, 114
Özey, Ersan, 135n, 136
Özgökçe Ertan, Bedia, 195

Özgürlük ve Demokrasi Partisi (Freedom and Solidarity Party/ÖDP), 163–4
Özkan, Ercümend, 124
Özpulat, Nedim, 135n

Pamukçu, Mehmed Feyzi, 124
Pan-Islam / Pan-Islamic, 30–1, 33, 36
Papa Eftim, 72
Papandreou, 133
Pars, Muhittin Baha, 68
Partiya Karkeren Kurdistane (The Kurdistan Workers' Party/PKK), 149, 156, 223
patriarchate, 39, 72, 94, 98, 133
patriarchy, 40, 99
Peker, Recep, 68
People's Liberation Front of Turkey (THKP-C), 114
Phanariote, 42n
Pir Sultan Abdal Kültür Derneği (Pir Sultan Abdal Culture Association), 168–9, 216n
pogrom of September 6/7 (1955), 13, 97–8
Polatkan, Hasan, 109
population exchange, 8, 51
privatisation religion, 19n
Protestant, 38, 206
Presidency of Alevi-Bektaşi Culture and Cemevi, 12, 205

Rabitat'-ül-Alem'ul-Islam (Muslim World League), 147
Ramazanoğlu, Mahmut Sami, 128, 167
Refah Partisi (Welfare Party/RP), 130, 155, 157, 162
religious authority, 3–4

religious education, 7, 11–12, 50, 55, 63, 67–8, 84–5, 106–7, 144, 146–7, 150, 190, 199, 203, 222
Rıfai, Kenan, 200–1
Rıfai order, 31, 200
Risale-i Nur, 91, 165, 197
Roman Catholic, 38, 47n, 206
Ronî Mîna Evînê-Tarî Mîna Mirinê, 141
Rum, 13, 47n, 51, 70, 72, 133
Russian Orthodox Church, 94

Saadet Partisi (Felicity Party/Saadet), 130, 190, 196, 219
Saatleri Ayarlama Enstitüsü, 1
(Prince) Sabahaddin, 31
Safa, Peyami, 99
Sağduyu Partisi (Common Sense Party), 199
Sakallı Nurettin Paşa, 64
sacralisation of the state, 1
sacralisation of the political realm, 2
Sahnenin Dışındakiler, 45n
Sait Halim Paşa, 32
Salkım Hanımın Taneleri, 80n
Samanyolu, 166
Sancar, Mithat, 195
Sargut, Cemalnur, 200
Saturday Mothers', 225
Sayar, Edibe, 100
Sazak, Emin, 64
Shah İsmail I, 36
Sebilürreşad, 33, 88, 93
secular, 2–4, 8, 18, 25, 29, 53, 55, 87, 107, 122, 136n, 154–5, 173, 182, 186, 190–2, 195, 205, 209, 226
secularism, 1–2, 4, 6, 14, 17, 63, 106–7, 121, 186, 209, 226

secularity, 2–3, 18n
sela, 213n
Seyyid Hamza-er Rıfai, 200
Selek, Cemal Hakkı, 119
Selim III, 35, 41n
Serbest Cumhuriyet Fırkası (Liberal Republican Party), 59–60, 82
Sévres Treaty, 33, 51
Sezer, Ahmet Necdet, 142, 182
Sırat-ı Müstakim, 31, 93
Sinan Işık v. Turkey, 11, 203
Sodom ve Gomorra, 45n
Softa, 30
Sokak, 152
Sosyal Demokrat Halkçı Parti (Social Democratic Populist Party / SHP), 154, 159–60, 163
Sosyal Demokrasi Partisi (Social Democracy Party / SODEP), 159–60
Soyer, Tunç, 215n
Stalin, 65, 94
state feminism, 73
State Ministry for Women's Issues and Women's Status, 208
state security courts (*Devlet Güvenlik Mahkemesi*/DGM), 148, 166
Struggle for Independence, 48, 55, 74n
Sublime Porte, 28, 39, 42n
Sufism, 35, 92, 102n
Sultan Hamid Düşerken, 44n
Sunalp, Turgut, 158
Sunay, Cevdet, 117, 122
Sunni, 2–3, 5, 7, 9–11, 25, 36–7, 51, 92, 108, 119, 122, 129–30, 144, 168, 203–5, 222–3
Surp Haç Tibrevank Seminary, 98
Susurluk incident, 171

Süleymancılık, 126–7
Süleyman Efendi community, 123, 126–7, 146, 166, 200
Süryani (Syrian), 38–9, 206
Swiss Civil Code, 30
Syrian Catholic, 39
Syriac Orthodox, 12
Syriac Chaldean, 12

Şakir, Bahaettin, 32
Şemdian family of Nehri, 36
Şener, Abdüllatif, 167
Şeriat/sharia, 3, 27, 29, 32, 35, 47n, 52–3, 60, 113, 155
Şer'iyye ve Evkaf Vekaleti (Ministry of Religious Affairs and Pious Foundations), 50, 74n
Şeyh Halid, 35–6; *see also* Ziyaeddin Halid *and* Mevlana Halid
Şeyh Said, 59, 91
şeyhülislam, 4, 26–7, 29, 32–4, 38, 49
(İbrahim) Şinasi, 28

Tahşiyeci group, 165
(Mehmet) Talat Paşa, 32, 44n
Talu, Naim, 117
Tandoğan, Nevzat, 66
Tanilli, Servet, 115
Tanrıöver, Hamdullah Suphi, 55, 68
Tanzimat, 15, 27–9, 34, 39, 80n
tarikat, 6, 10, 35–6, 92, 124, 222
tekke, 4, 35–6, 57, 127
Terakkiperver Cumhuriyet Fırkası (Progressive Republican Party), 58, 82
Teşkilat-ı Mahsusa, 33
Thracian incidents, 71

Ticani, 102n
Timisi, Mustafa, 123
Timuçin, Aliye, 100
Tlabar, Nazlı, 100
Tola, Tahsin, 88
Tonguç, İsmail Hakkı, 66
Topbaş, Musa, 167
Topbaş, Osman Nuri, 167
Topuz, Mahmut, 154
Treaty of Lausanne, 12, 70, 133
Truman Doctrine, 65
Tunahan, Süleyman Hilmi, 126–7, 200
Turkish Association of University Women, 134
Turkish Grand Assembly (Türkiye Büyük Millet Meclisi/TBMM), 50, 52, 72, 86, 93, 119–20, 134, 160, 174, 194, 195; *see also* Grand National Assembly of Turkey/TBMM
Turkish Grand National Assembly/TBMM, 49; *see also* Grand National Assembly of Turkey/TBMM
Turkish-Islamic synthesis, 8, 16, 113, 162, 166
Turkish Orthodox Church, 72
Turkish Radio and Television (Türkiye Radyo ve Televizyonu/TRT), 154
Turkish Teachers' Union (TÖB-DER), 112, 131
Turkish Women's Union (*Türk Kadınlar Birliği*), 73, 100, 134
Turkishness, 8, 12–13, 55, 95, 162
Turkism, 20n, 31, 121–2
Türk (newspaper), 31
Türk, Ahmet, 195

Türkeş, Alparslan, 121, 162
Türk Ev Kadınları Derneği (Turkish Housewives' Association), 134
Türkiye Güvenlik Köy Korucuları (Security Village Guards of Turkey), 177n
Türk Halk Kurtuluş Ordusu (People's Liberation Army of Turkey / THKO), 114
Türkiye Birlik Partisi (Union Party of Turkey/TBP), 123
Türkiye Devrimci Gençlik Federasyonu / Dev-Genç, 120
Türkiye Diyanet Vakfı (Turkish Diyanet Foundation/TDV), 109
Türkiye İnsan Hakları Vakfı (Human Rights Foundation of Turkey/ TİHV), 151
Türkiye İşçi Partisi (The Workers' Party of Turkey/TİP), 118, 220
Türk Kadınlar Birliği (Turkish Women's Union), 73, 100, 134
Türk Kültürü, 113
Türk Kültürü Araştırma Enstitüsü (Turkish Culture Research Institute), 113
Türkiye Milli Talebe Federasyonu (National Students Federation of Turkey), 95
Türk Yurdu, 38
Tütengil, Cahit Orhan, 116

ulema, 26–7, 29, 34–6
ulusalcı, 8, 20n
Ulusoy, Ali Naki, 139
Ulusoy, Kazım, 139
Ulusoy, Yusuf, 139
Ulusu, Bülent, 143, 147
Uniate Church, 38
United Nations Convention Against Torture and Other Cruel, Inhuman or Degrading Treatment or Punishment, 142
Uras, Ufuk, 164
US Sixth Fleet, 111
Ustaoğlu, Hasan Fehmi, 87
Ustaosmanoğlu, Mahmut, 129, 199

Üç İstanbul, 45n
Üç Tarz-ı Siyaset (Three Types of Politics), 31
Ülkücü, 130, 134, 161, 165, 196
Ülkücü Gençlik Derneği (Nationalist Youth Association), 162
Ümmü Kenan Dergahı, 200

Vahdettin, Mehmed VI, 33, 51
Vaka-ı Hayriye (Fortunate Event/ Auspicious Occasion), 26
Vakıflar Genel Müdürlüğü (General Directorate of Foundations), 94
Vatan Cephesi (Homeland Front), 89
Velioğlu, Hüseyin, 177, 181
Veziroğlu, Ali Haydar, 169
Voltaire, 112

War of Independence, 13, 34, 45n, 74n, 75n, 101n, 212n; *see also* Independence War, Struggle for Independence
Wealth Tax, 13, 71–2, 80n, 221
Western Thrace, 51, 96
Wittgenstein, Ludwig, 3

Women and Political and Social Life, 135
Women, Family and Youth Centre (KAGEM), 189
Women's Problems Research and Application Centre, Istanbul University, 172
Women's Works Library and Information Centre, Istanbul, 172
Women and Socialism, 134
World War I, 33, 44n, 91
World War II, 65, 78n, 87, 142

Yahyalı group, 215n
Yakubi (Jacobite), 38–9
Yalçınkaya, Abdurrahman, 182–3
Yalman, Ahmet Emin, 87–8
Yaltkaya, Şerafettin, 66, 78n, 79n, 93
Yasincizade Abdülvahhâb Efendi, 26
Yassıada (trials), 97, 109
Yavaş, Mansur, 215n
Yazıcılar group, 165
Yazıcıoğlu, Muhsin, 162, 167
Yazıcıoğlu, Mustafa Sait, 147
Yeni Asya, 124–5
Yeni Asya group, 124–5, 165, 197
Yeni Demokrasi Hareketi (New Democracy Movement), 169
Yeni Refah Partisi (New Welfare Party), 219

Yeni Türkiye Partisi (New Turkey Party / YTP), 116
Yıldırım, İzzettin, 165, 177n
Yıldız, Bekir, 155
Yıldız, Taner, 199
Yılmaz, Mehmet Hüseyin, 222
Yılmaz, Mehmet Nuri, 147, 188
Yılmaz, Mesut, 157, 159
Yılmaz, Ziya, 115
Yorgun Savaşçı, 75n
Young Ottomans, 28
Young Turks, 31
Yücel, Hasan Ali, 66, 78n
Yüksekdağ, Figen, 195
Yüksel, Serdengeçti Osman, 138n
Yüksel, Uğur, 206

Zaim, Sabahattin, 80n
Zaman, 165–6
Zaviye, 4, 19n, 57, 76n
Zehra group, 165
Zehra Education and Culture Foundation, 177n
Zirve Publishing House, 206–7
Ziya Bey (*later* Paşa), 28
Ziyaeddin Halid, 35; *see also* Şeyh Halid *and* Mevlana Halid
Zoğrafyon High School, 98
Zorlu, Fatin Rüştü, 95, 109
Zorlutuna, Halide Nusret, 134

EU Authorised Representative:
Easy Access System Europe Mustamäe tee 50, 10621 Tallinn, Estonia
gpsr.requests@easproject.com

Printed and bound by CPI Group (UK) Ltd, Croydon, CR0 4YY
02/03/2026
02063692-0014